Years of Childhood

YEARS OF CHILDHOOD

Serge Aksakoff
1791–1859.

YEARS OF CHILDHOOD

BY

SERGE AKSAKOFF

TRANSLATED FROM THE RUSSIAN

BY

J. D. DUFF

FELLOW OF TRINITY COLLEGE, CAMBRIDGE

WITH PORTRAIT

LONDON

EDWARD ARNOLD

1916

TO
A. C. D.

TRANSLATOR'S PREFACE

SERGE AKSAKOFF, the author of this autobiography, was
born at Ufa, in the district of Orenburg, on September 20,
1791. His father held some office in the law-court of the
town, and his grandfather lived in the country as the
owner of large estates, to which Aksakoff ultimately
succeeded. The Russians were then only settlers in the
country, and the population consisted mainly of Tatars
and a number of Finnish tribes often mentioned in this
book.

Aksakoff's childhood is here described down to the
winter of 1799, when he went to school at Kazan.   From
school he proceeded to the university of the same city,
and left it in 1807, when many of his class-mates were
joining the Army to fight against Napoleon. He entered
the civil service in 1808 and served, with some intervals,
in various capacities until he finally retired in 1839. He
married in 1816; and his two sons, Constantine and Ivan,
both played a conspicuous part in the public life of Russia.
He remained during his whole life a passionate lover of the
country and of all country occupations and amusements.
He died at Moscow, after a long and painful illness, on
April 30, 1859.

Aksakoff was always keenly interested in literature
and wrote a number of books; but his reputation, which
stands very high in Russia, depends mainly upon two
volumes of Memoirs which he wrote at the end of his life.
The first of these he called *A Family History*, and the
second, which is here translated, *Years of Childhood*.
The first volume begins with the history of his grandfather,

and goes on with his own school and college days, so that
the right place of this second volume is in the middle of
the first. The later volume has been chosen for translation, because it seemed better fitted to introduce this
author to English readers. Though pseudonyms, *e.g.*
Bagroff for Aksakoff, are used, it should be understood
that the early recollections of Aksakoff himself are here
recorded.

Years of Childhood, published in 1858, was Aksakoff's
last book : he wrote it when he was almost blind, a prisoner
to his room, and suffering constant pain for which death was
the only cure; yet he never once alludes to the conditions
under which it was written. If his powers of observation
and memory are extraordinary, his power of self-control
is hardly less wonderful.

As to the merits of the work, it is difficult for a
translator to judge impartially, and I shall therefore quote
from the description given by Mr. Maurice Baring, who is
referring, of course, to both the volumes of Memoirs. He
says :

"The story is as vivid and interesting as that of any
novel, as that of the novels of Russian writers of genius,
and it has the additional advantage of being true. . . .
It is impossible to put down the narrative after beginning
it, and I have heard of children who read it like a fairy-tale.
. . . The pictures of nature, the portraits of the people, all
the good and all the bad of the good and the bad old
times pass before one with epic simplicity and the magic
of a fairy-tale. One is spellbound by the charm, the
dignity, the good-nature, the gentle, easy accent of the
speaker, in whom one feels convinced, not only that there
was nothing common or mean, but to whom nothing was
common or mean, who was a gentleman by character as
well as by lineage, one of God's as well as of Russia's
nobility." * Mr. Baring adds that no book in Russian so
richly deserves translation into English.

* *An Outline of Russian Literature*, pp. 156 foll.

This translation has been made from the eighth Russian edition published at Moscow in 1906. I believe, strange as it seems, that the work has never been translated into any language. The book, of which I had never heard before, was given to me in 1908 by my dear friend, Aleksandra Grigoryevna Pashkova. I read it, and at once thought that, if leisure came, I might try to lift the veil which hides a book so curious and delightful from English readers. Circumstances have now brought that leisure, and I have here made the attempt.

I hope before long to translate *A Family History*, which contains the sequel of the present narrative as well as the earlier history of the Aksakoff family.

J. D. D.

October 28, 1915.

AUTHOR'S PREFACE

I do not know myself whether it is possible to rely entirely upon all that my memory has preserved. If all that I remember really happened, then these recollections might be called recollections of infancy as well as of childhood. Of course, there is no regular sequence or connexion in such recollections; but many incidents do survive in my memory, as bright and clear as what happened yesterday. When I was three or four, I told some people that I remembered being weaned. They laughed at the details I gave, and declared that my mother or nurse had told me what I believed I had seen myself. I disputed this and tried to prove that I was right by quoting facts which could not have been told me, and could be known to three persons only—myself, my foster-mother, and my mother. Inquiry was made, and it often turned out that I was right and that no one could have told me what I knew. Still I had not seen all that I thought I had seen: the same inquiries often proved that I had been told of the facts and had not seen them.

Accordingly, of what I may call the pre-historic epoch of my childhood, I shall relate only those incidents of whose reality I can have no doubt.

CONTENTS

CHAPTER   PAGE

I. SCATTERED RECOLLECTIONS 1

II. CONSECUTIVE RECOLLECTIONS 9

III. THE JOURNEY TO PARASHINO 17

IV. PARASHINO 32

V. THE JOURNEY FROM PARASHINO TO BAGROVO . . . 43

VI. BAGROVO 50

VII WE STAY AT BAGROVO WITHOUT OUR PARENTS . . . 61

VIII. A WINTER AT UFA 75

IX. SERGÉYEVKA 96

X. OUR RETURN TO TOWN LIFE AT UFA . . . 118

XI. A JOURNEY IN WINTER TO BAGROVO 126

XII. BAGROVO IN WINTER 130

XIII UFA 149

XIV WE ARRIVE AT BAGROVO TO LIVE THERE . . . 167

XV. CHOORASSOVO 190

XVI. BAGROVO AFTER CHOORASSOVO . . . 213

XVII MY FIRST SPRING IN THE COUNTRY . . 219

XVIII A SUMMER VISIT TO CHOORASSOVO 261

XIX A JOURNEY IN AUTUMN TO BAGROVO . . . 286

XX LIFE AT BAGROVO AFTER MY GRANDMOTHER'S DEATH . 296

APPENDIX. THE SCARLET FLOWER . . 317

YEARS OF CHILDHOOD

CHAPTER I

THE very first objects that survive on the old picture of the distant past—a picture much faded in many places by time and the lapse of sixty years—objects and images which my memory still retains, are my foster-mother, my little sister, and my mother ; at that time they had no distinct meaning for me, and were only images without names. My foster-mother comes before me at first as a kind of mysterious, almost invisible being. I remember myself lying at night either in my crib or in my mother's arms, and merely crying ; with tears and cries I repeated the same word again and again, calling somebody ; and somebody appeared in the darkness of the dimly-lighted room, took me in her arms, laid me to her breast, and my troubles were over. Later, I remember that nobody came in answer to my cries and appeals, but that my mother pressed me to her heart, sang over and over the same lullaby, and carried me up and down the room till I fell asleep. My foster-mother, who loved me passionately, comes up again sometimes in my recollections, either looking at me from behind other people by stealth and at a distance, or kissing my hands and face, and crying over me. She was a peasant's wife and lived thirty *versts* * away; she used to start from her village on foot on Saturday evening and reach Ufa on Sunday morning ; when she had had her sight of me and rested, she started off again on foot to her village of Kasimofka, to be in time to work for her master. I

* Twenty miles a *verst* is two-thirds of a mile

B

remember she once brought with her—perhaps she got a lift on that occasion—my foster-sister, a healthy, red-cheeked little girl.

My little sister I loved at first more than all my toys, more than my mother ; and this love took the form of a constant desire to see her, and a feeling of pity for her : I always fancied that she was cold or hungry and in want of food, and I wished constantly to give her my food and dress her in my clothes ; of course, I was not allowed to do this, and that made me cry.

The constant presence of my mother is part of every recollection I have. Her image makes an inseparable part of my own existence, and therefore it is not prominent in the scattered pictures of my earliest childhood, although invariably a part of them.

Next follows a long interval, that is, a dark spot or faded place on my picture of the past ; and, when my recollection begins again, I am very ill, and not at the beginning of the illness which lasted more than eighteen months, nor at the end of it when I was on the way to recovery : the precise point of recollection is a state of such weakness that my life was in danger every moment. Once in the early morning I woke, or became conscious, and could not recognise where I was. All was unfamiliar : the large, lofty room, the bare walls of fir planks, new and very thick, the strong smell of resin. The sun—a summer sun, apparently—was just rising ; and, as it shone through a window on my right above a thin canopy spread over me, was brightly reflected on the opposite wall. Near me was my mother sleeping uneasily, in her clothes and with no pillows. Even now I seem to see her black hair straying in disorder over her pale thin face. I had been brought the day before to the village of Zubofka, ten *versts* from Ufa. The journey and the sound sleep due to exercise had evidently given me strength, so that for some minutes I looked through the curtains with satisfaction and curiosity at the new objects around me. Not wise enough to let my poor mother sleep on, I touched her and said : " How bright the sun is ! What a good smell ! " My mother sprang up, frightened at first ; but, when she heard the strength of my voice and saw the freshness of my face, fear gave place to joy. How she caressed me and called me by fond names and wept for joy! Such things cannot be told in words. My canopy was removed; I asked for food. and food was given me with half a glass of the old Rhine-wine which was supposed to be of sovereign efficacy in restoring my health. The wine was poured out of an odd kind of bottle with a long thin neck and wide flat bottom; I have never seen bottles like them since. Then I begged successfully for little bits or drops of the fir resin which was everywhere on the walls and window-frames, melting and dropping and making little streams, cooling and drying as it went, and hanging in the air like little icicles, with a shape exactly like the common icicles of winter. I was very fond of the smell of resin which was sometimes used to fumigate our nursery. I smelt the sweet transparent blobs of resin, admired them, and played with them; they melted in my hands and made my long thin fingers sticky; then my mother washed and dried my hands, and I began to doze Visible objects became confused before me . I thought that we were driving, and that I refused to take some medicine which was offered me, and that the figure beside me was not my mother, but my nurse Agatha, or my foster-mother. . . . How I went to sleep, and what happened afterwards, I have quite forgotten.

I remember myself constantly in a carriage; and the carriage was not always in motion, nor had it always horses in it. I have a clear recollection of sitting, dressed very warmly, in my mother's or my nurse's arms, while the carriage we sat in was standing in the cart-shed or some-times drawn out into the yard; I am wailing and saying, "Soup, soup," again and again in a feeble voice; of the soup I got only a little at a time, in spite of the morbid hunger which at times tormented me and took the place of utter aversion to food. I have been told that in a carriage I cried less and was in general much quieter. I believe that the doctors made mistakes at first in their treatment of my illness; they went on dosing me till my digestive organs were completely enfeebled, and I nearly died. Perhaps the excessive anxiety of a mother's love and the constant change of remedies, were the cause of the desperate condition in which I found myself.

Sometimes I lay unconscious, in a sort of middle state between sleep and fainting, my pulse almost stopped, my breathing so weak that a mirror was placed to my lips to ascertain if I was alive; yet I remember much that was done to me at that time and said by those around me, who supposed that I could no longer see or hear, nor understand that I was dying. The doctors and all around me had long ago sentenced me to death, the doctors judging from infallible symptoms, and the rest from infallible signs; but the falsity of both was very convincingly shown in my case. My mother's sufferings it is impossible to describe; but her passionate presence of mind and her hope to save her child never left her. More than once I heard Mme. Cheprunoff, her distant relation and devoted friend, say to her: "Sofya Nikolayevna, my darling, cease to torment your child; have not the doctors and the priest told you that he is not for this life? Submit to God's will; place the child under the *icons*,* light a candle, and suffer his innocent soul to depart in peace out of his body. You are only hindering and troubling it without doing any good." But such speeches my mother always met with anger: she replied that, while there was a single spark of life in me, she would not cease to do all she could to save me. Once again she bathed my lifeless body in some invigorating fluid, or poured Rhine-wine or chicken-soup into my mouth, or rubbed my back and chest for whole hours with her bare hands; and, if this was of no avail, she inflated my lungs with her own breath—and I, after a deep sigh, would begin to breathe more strongly and wake up, as it were, to life; I became conscious and began to take food and speak, and even to get better for a time. This happened more than once. I could even amuse myself with my toys which were placed on a little table near me; of course I was lying in my crib all the time, for I could scarcely move a finger. But my chief satisfaction was when my little sister was brought to me and I was allowed to kiss her and stroke her head; and then her nurse sat opposite me holding her,

* Sacred images kept in a case hanging on the wall of a room

while I looked long at the child and pointed to one or another of my toys and asked that they should be given to my sister.

When my mother noticed that movement seemed to do me good, she drove with me constantly either to the estates of her brothers near Ufa, or to those of our friends. Once we took a long journey, I do not know where ; my father was with us. On the way, rather early in the morning, I felt so ill and grew so weak that it was necessary to stop , I was taken out of the carriage and bedding was spread for me in the high grass of a forest ride, under the shade of the trees ; and there I was laid almost lifeless. I saw and understood all that went on around me. I heard how my father in tears tried to console my mother's despair, how fervently she prayed, raising her hands to heaven. I heard all and saw all clearly, but I could not say a single word, or even move—when suddenly I woke, as it were, and felt better and stronger than usual. The forest, the shade, the flowers, the fragrant air, pleased me so much that I begged not to be moved ; and we actually stayed there till evening. The horses were unharnessed and put to graze near me ; and I enjoyed that A spring was found somewhere near, and I heard the talk about this ; a fire was kindled and tea was drunk, while I was given my horrible camomile to drink in Rhine-wine. Then dinner was prepared and eaten, after which all rested ; even my mother slept long. I did not sleep, but I felt an unaccustomed vigour and a kind of internal satisfaction and peace ; or rather, without understanding my own feelings, I was happy. Rather late in the evening, in spite of my prayers and tears, I was placed in the carriage and taken a short distance to a Tatar village on our road, where we spent the night. Next morning, I still felt fresher and better than my wont. When we returned to the town, my mother saw that I had gained a little strength ; she reflected that for a week past I had not taken the usual mixtures and powders ; so, after prayer to God, she determined to give up the doctors of the town, and took in hand to treat me herself according to Buchan's *Domestic Medicine.** I became hourly better,

* William Buchan, a native of Roxburghshire and educated at Edinburgh, published his *Domestic Medicine* in 1769. It was soon translated into

and within a few months I was almost well. But all the time between our picnic in the forest ride and my actual recovery is an almost complete blank in my memory. One event, however, I remember clearly enough, which happened, as I am assured, in the very middle of my recovery.

When I began to recover, my feelings of pity for all suffering became morbid and excessive. The first object of this feeling was my little sister: I could not bear to see her tears nor hear her cry without beginning at once to cry myself; she too was unwell at that time. At first my mother had the child taken to another room; but, when I noticed this, my excitement and distress (as I was afterwards told) were such that the child was hastily brought back. Recovery was slow, and it was long before I could walk: I lay whole days in my crib with my sister beside me, amusing her with different toys or by showing her pictures. Our toys were of the simplest: small smooth bricks or pieces of wood, for which we had names of our own. Out of these I made dungeons of a kind, and my companion took delight in knocking them to pieces with a movement of her little arm. Later I began to creep about and to sit at the window which opened directly on the garden. Birds of all kinds, even sparrows, were a great attraction and pleasure to me. My mother, who spent with me all the time she could spare from social duties and household cares, at once got me a cage and a pair of tame pigeons, which passed their nights under my crib. I have been told that my enchantment with my pets was so great and expressed in such a manner, that it was impossible not to be affected by the sight of my joy. Once I was sitting at the window (from that moment my clear remembrance of things dates), when I heard a strange pitiful cry in the garden; my mother heard it too; and, when I began to beg that some one should be sent to see who was crying—" surely some one is hurt "—she despatched a maid who after a few minutes brought us in her joined hands a tiny puppy, still blind. Trembling all over, tottering on

Russian, as well as other languages, and the Empress Catherine sent a gold medal to the author, he died in 1805 Readers of *Little Dorrit* will remember that Mrs Tickit's favourite volume was Buchan's *Domestic Medicine* its crooked legs, and poking its head in all directions, it whined pitifully. I was so sorry for the puppy that I took him and wrapped him up in my frock. My mother had warm milk brought in a saucer and, after many trials, taught him to lap by pushing his blind face into the milk. From that time, for whole hours, the puppy and I were inseparable; to feed him several times a day was my chief amusement. He was called "Soorka," and grew to be a smallish beast of the watch-dog kind. He lived sixteen years with us, not in the house, naturally, but in the court, and always kept a special attachment for me and my mother.

My recovery was considered to be a miracle: this even the doctors admitted. My mother attributed it, in the first place, to the infinite mercy of God, and next, to Buchan's *Domestic Medicine.* Buchan was called my preserver, and my mother taught me in infancy to pray to God for his soul's rest in my morning and evening prayer. Later, she got from somewhere an engraved portrait of Buchan; and four French verses, printed beneath the portrait, were translated by some one into Russian, written out fair on paper, and gummed on the top of the French verses. But this, I regret, to say, has long been lost beyond recall.

I attribute my recovery (apart from the first cause mentioned above, without which nothing could have been done) to my mother's sleepless care, unwearying protection, and infinite watchfulness, and also to travel, by which I mean movement and air. Here is a specimen of her watchful care: though she was constantly in need of money and had to look twice at a shilling, she regularly got me old Rhine-wine from Kazan, 500 *versts* away, through an old friend of her father—Dr. Reislein was his name. I think; the price of the wine was then excessively high, and I drank it several times a day, though little at a time. Again, the town of Ufa did not then provide the white loaves called French bread; so once a week, *i.e.* by each post, the post-rider, who was liberally rewarded, brought us three white loaves, also from Kazan. These facts are merely instances of her general system. My mother would not allow the flickering flame of life in me to be quenched · the moment it began to sink, she fed it with the magnetic infusion of her own life and her own breath. Whether she had read of this in some book or heard of it from a doctor, I do not know. The marvellous effect of travel upon health is beyond all doubt. I know many people who have recovered health in this way when they were given up by their doctors. I believe also that the twelve hours during which I lay on the grass in the woodland ride, gave the first impulse in the right direction to my enfeebled frame. More than once I have heard my mother say that from that very time there began a trifling change for the better.

CHAPTER II

CONSECUTIVE RECOLLECTIONS

AFTER my recovery I begin to remember myself as a child, not sturdy and mischievous, as I afterwards became, but gentle, quiet, full of pity for suffering, a great coward, and at that time reading constantly, though slowly, a child's book with pictures, called *The Mirror of Virtue*. How I learnt to read and when, who taught me, and by what system—I have no idea; the art of writing was acquired much later, and the process was very long and slow. We lived then in the city of Ufa, the capital of the Government, and occupied the large wooden house of my mother's family, which my father had bought, as I learnt later, at auction for 300 roubles. The outside boards of our house were not painted; rains had darkened it, and the great pile had a very mournful appearance. The house stood on a slope, so that the windows towards the garden were very near the ground, but the dining-room windows on the opposite side of the house, which looked on to the street, were raised seven feet above the soil. More than twenty-five steps led up to the front door; and from it nearly the whole breadth of the river Byélaya* could be seen. The two nurseries in which I and my sister lived, were painted light blue over the plaster; they were near my mother's bed-room, and looked out into the garden; and the raspberries planted below grew so tall that the canes peeped in at us through the panes, which was a great comfort to me and my inseparable companion, my little sister. The garden, though fairly large, was not pretty : here and there currant-bushes grew and gooseberries and barberries and a score of stunted apple-trees; there were round flower-beds with marigolds, crocuses, and asters, but not one large tree and

* *I.e.* the White River.

no shade. Still even this garden gave pleasure to us, especially to my little sister, who knew nothing of hills, fields, and forests ; but my travels had extended (so I was told) to 500 *versts*, and, in spite of my feeble health, the greatness and beauty of God's world had made a secret impression on my childish heart, which lived on, without my knowing it, in my imagination : our poor town garden could not satisfy me, and I often described to my sister different wonders which such an old traveller as I had witnessed ; and she listened with curiosity, fixing her pretty eyes full of rapt attention on me, while their expression clearly said, " Brother, I don't understand a word." Nor was that surprising, as the narrator was just five years old, and the audience three.

I have said before that I was timid and even cowardly. Perhaps long and severe illness had weakened my nerves and refined them to an excess of sensibility ; perhaps nature had not given me courage. My first feelings of terror were due to my nurse's stories. Her chief business was with my sister, but she had to keep an eye on me too. Though strictly forbidden by my mother even to talk to me, she managed from time to time to communicate to me some information about bogies, and brownies, and ghosts. I began to fear the dark at night, and dark rooms even by day. Our house contained a very large parlour, from which two doors led into a pair of smaller rooms, both rather dark, because their windows looked out into a long entrance-hall which served as a passage. One of these rooms was used as a pantry ; but the other was closed ; it had been used as a study by my grandfather in his lifetime, and all his things were collected there—a writing-table, an arm-chair, a book-case, and so on. Nurse told me that my grandfather was sometimes seen there, sitting at the table and putting papers in order. I was so terrified of this room that I always shut my eyes in passing it. Once I was walking along the entrance-hall, when I forgot and looked in at the study window. The nurse's gossip came back to me, and I thought I saw an old man in a white dressing-gown sitting at the table. I screamed out and fainted away. My mother was out of the house. When she

1eturned and I told her of all that had happened, and of
what I had heard fiom the nurse, she was very angry : she
ordered the study to be opened, foreed me to go with her
though I shook with fear, and showed me that there was
no one there, only some linen hanging on the back of the
chair. She made every effort to convince me that all sueh
tales were nonsense and mere inventions of ignorance and
stupidity. She drove the nurse from her and would not
allow her to enter our nursery for some days, till necessity
compelled her to summon back the same woman and put
her in charge of us again. Of course, she was strictly forbidden to talk such nonsense, and even foreed to swear that
she would never speak to us of popular superstitions. But
this did not cuie me of my fears. Nuise was a strange
old woman. She was very devoted to us ; and my sister
and I both loved her dearly. When banished to the
servants' quarters and forbidden even to enter the house,
she managed to creep to our room at night and kissed us
in our sleep, and eried over us. This I saw myself, as I
was once awakened by her earesses. She tended us very
zealously ; but her ignorance and obstinacy weie so
confirmed that she did not understand my mother's requirements, and secretly set them at defiance. A year later
she was finally sent off to the country. I mourned her
long : I could not understand why " mamma " was so
often angry with " kind nana," and I remained convinced
that my mother simply disliked her.

Every day I read my one book, *The Mirror of Virtue*,
aloud to my little sister. without an inkling of the fact
that she was too young to undeistand anything except
the pleasure of looking at the pictures. This child's book
I knew then by heart from end to end ; but now, out of
a full hundred stories, only two remain in my memory,
and two pictuies, though there was nothing to distinguish
these from the others. They were " The Grateful Lion "
and " The Boy Diessing Himself." I remember even the
expression on the faces of the lion and the boy ! At last
The Mirror of Virtue ceased to absorb my attention and
satisfy my childish curiosity—I wanted to read other books,
but found it impossible to get them : those which my

father and mother read sometimes, I was not allowed to read. I made an attempt on Buchan's *Domestic Medicine,* but for some reason my mother considered this reading unsuitable to my age; she selected, however, some passages which she marked with parentheses and let me read. And this was really interesting reading; for it contained descriptions of all the herbs and salts and roots which are only alluded to in the body of the work. At a much more advanced age I read these descriptions over again, and always with satisfaction, because the whole subject is set forth and translated into Russian very sensibly and well.

The kindness of fortune soon sent me a new and un-expected pleasure, which produced a very strong impression on me and greatly extended the circle of my ideas. Opposite to our house, in a house of his own, lived M. Anitchkoff, a rich old bachelor, who had the reputation of a very clever and even learned man. This belief was confirmed by the fact that he had been sent as representative of Orenburg to serve on the famous Commission, which Catherine II. brought together to revise the existing laws. Anitchkoff was very proud—so I was told—of this distinction, and often talked with confidence of what he had said and done, though he admitted himself that the Commission had been a failure. He was not popular, but he was respected; and his sharp tongue and unbending temper were even feared. To my parents he was well disposed, and even lent them money at times, though no one else dared to borrow of him. Somehow he had heard from my parents that I was an intelligent boy with a great love of reading, but with nothing to read. The old Commissioner, being more enlightened than his neighbours, was the natural patron of all seekers after knowledge. Next day he sent his servant to fetch me; but my father took me there himself. Anitchkoff made full inquiries: What had I read? how far did I understand what I read? what did I remember? Much pleased with the answers, he ordered a bundle of books to be brought, and presented them to me. Oh, joy! It was *Reading for Children, to benefit the Heart and Head,* by N. I. Novikoff, published gratuitously together with a

Moscow newspaper. I was so delighted that I threw myself, almost weeping, into the old man's arms, and then sprang up in my excitement and ran home, leaving my father to converse with Anitchkoff. I remember, however, the friendly and approving laugh of my host, which rang in my ears and gradually died away as I got further off. Fearing that some one might rob me of my treasure, I ran straight through the hall into the nursery, lay down on my bed, drew the curtains, opened the first volume, and at once forgot all my surroundings. When my father returned and laughingly told my mother what had happened in our friend's house, she was much alarmed, as she did not know of my return. I was looked for and found lying on my bed, book in hand. My mother told me afterwards that I behaved just as if I were insane : I could not speak or understand what was said to me, and refused to come to dinner. It was necessary to take the book from me in spite of my bitter tears. The threat that I should never see my books again, forced me to dry my tears and get up and even eat my dinner. Dinner done, I clutched my book again and read till evening. My mother naturally put an end to such excessive reading : she locked away the books and let me have one at a time at regular hours fixed by her. There were twelve of the little books, which were odd volumes out of the twenty of which *Reading for Children* is composed. I read my books with passionate interest, and, for all my mother's prudent care, had finished them all in a little more than a month. The result was a complete change in my childish ideas, and the revelation of a new world. In the " Account of Thunder " I learnt the nature of lightning, the atmosphere, the clouds ; the formation of rain and the origin of snow were explained to me. Many natural phenomena, which I had looked at with interest but without understanding them, now got sense and meaning for me, and became even more interesting. Ants, bees, and especially butterflies with their changes from eggs to caterpillars, from caterpillars to chrysalises, and finally from chrysalises to lovely butterflies—these mastered my attention and interest. I felt an intense desire to observe all these wonders with my own eyes. Less impression was

produced by the articles whose main object was to convey
a moral; but how I laughed at "An Amusing Method of
Catching Monkeys," and the fable of "The Old Wolf,"
which every shepherd made fly before him! How enchanted I was with "The Goldfish"!

For some time past I had noticed that my mother was
not well. Without taking to her bed, she grew pale and
thin, and lost strength daily. The ill-health was of long
standing, but I did not see it at first, and did not understand the cause to which it was due. It was only later
that I learnt this from the talk of those around me: my
mother's illness was due to the bodily exhaustion and
mental suffering which she had gone through at the time
of my illness. The constant fear of losing the child she
passionately loved, and the effort to save his life, had strung
her nerves, and had lent her unnatural strength and a
kind of factitious energy. But, when the danger was past,
all her energies began to flag, and her strength failed her.
She had pain in the breast and side; and then fever set in.
The same doctors, who had treated me with so little
success and whom she had given up, took in hand to treat
her. Once I heard her say to my father that she was in
the early stages of consumption. How far this was true,
I do not know; for the patient was said by all to be very
despondent about herself; and I do not know whether
my father and the doctors were speaking the truth or
not, when they assured her she was mistaken. I dimly
understood already that "consumption" was some terrible
disease. My heart grew cold with fear; and the thought
that my mother's illness was due to me, was a constant
torture. Then came grief and tears on my part; but my
mother found means to shake my belief and quiet me. Nor
was this difficult, because she could do with me exactly what
she wished

Not feeling complete confidence in the skill of the
doctors at Ufa, my mother decided to travel to Orenburg
to consult a Dr. Deobolt, who practised there, and was
famous over all the country for his marvellous cures of
desperate cases She told me this herself with a cheerful
face, and assured me that she would come back well.

I believed her absolutely : my fears vanished, my heart grew light, and I began to press my mother to start at once. But money was needed for the journey ; and besides there were two little children : how were they to be disposed of ? who was to look after them ? Constant discussion on these points went on in my hearing between my father and mother. At last I learnt that the matter was arranged. Money was provided by my benefactor in the matter of the books ; while it was decided that the children, *i.e.* my sister and I, should be taken to Bagrovo,* and left there with their grandparents. I was much pleased when I learnt that we should travel all the way in our own carriage, and have our meals out of doors. Of the way I treasured a dim but very pleasant recollection ; my father was very fond of it, and his stories of it and, still more, of Bagrovo, promised me a host of new and unknown pleasures, and inflamed my childish imagination. I was anxious, too, to see my grandfather and grand-mother. Though I had seen them already, I could not remember it : I was only eight months old at my first visit to Bagrovo ; but my mother often told me that my grandfather had liked having us, and had long ago asked us back, and was even angry that for four years we had not been there once. This was due to my long illness and slow recovery, and then to my mother's bad health. My father, indeed, had travelled to Bagrovo the year before, but only for a very short stay. It was my habit—a habit inherent in my nature—to share my impressions with others ; so I talked about all my pleasant hopes and dreams to my little sister, and tried to explain them first to her, and then to all the household. Our packing began. I was first in the field, and packed up my books, that is, *Reading for Children* and *The Mirror of Virtue,* though I had not even glanced at the latter for a long time ; nor did I forget my bricks, which my sister was to play with as well as I. Two volumes of *Reading for Children* which I had read through thrice already, I left out for the journey. Then off I ran with beaming face to tell my mother that I was ready to start, and only sorry to leave Soorka behind.

* A pseudonym for Aksakovo, which still belongs to the family.

My mother was sitting in an armchair, with a sad look on her face; though tired out by the packing, she refused to leave her place and went on giving directions. She smiled at what I said, but gave me a peculiar look which frightened me, though I could not understand its meaning Again my heart grew cold, and I was ready to burst out crying ; but her caresses quieted me and gave me courage. She told me to go to the nursery and there to read my book and amuse my sister : she added that, as she was too busy to be with us now, she trusted me with the care of the child. I obeyed and went slowly back. Some feeling of grief had suddenly poisoned my merriment, and even the thought that I was put in charge of my sister, which at another time would have been very agreeable and flattering to me, could not comfort me now. Our preparations for departure went on some days longer, till at last all was ready.

CHAPTER III

On a hot summer morning at the end of July my sister and I were wakened earlier than usual and had tea at our little table ; then the carriage came round to the front steps and, after a prayer to God, we all went to take our seats. Arrangements had been made for my mother to lie down ; beside her sat my father, and opposite him nurse with my sister ; I stood at the carriage window, held by my father, and sat from time to time wherever I could find a little room. The descent to the river Byélaya was so steep that it was necessary to put wedges under two of the wheels. My father and I with nurse and my sister walked down the hill.

And here there began a series of impressions which were all new to me. I had crossed the river more than once already ; but I was then so ill and so young that neither my eyes nor my mind were impressed by the novelty ; now, however, I was struck by the rapid flow and width of the stream, its sloping sandy bank, and the green border of wood on the opposite side. Our carriage and covered cart were placed upon the raft ; then for ourselves came a large boat which we had to enter along two planks laid between the bank and the gunwale of the boat. The ferrymen, in their striped shirts, wading up to the knee in the stream, gave a hand to my mother as she crossed, and to nurse carrying my sister ; then one of them, a tall sunburnt fellow, caught me in his arms and carried me straight to the boat, while my father walked beside me along the plank, smiling and encouraging me ; for I, in the cowardice which still dominated me, was much alarmed by such an unexpected way of travelling. Four rowers sat down by the

c

oars; the man who had carried me across grasped the
rudder; and we pushed out from the side with a pole.
Then all the five ferrymen crossed themselves, and the
steersman said in a loud voice, " Call God to our aid " : off
flew the boat across the stream, slipping over the eddying
current which ran fast close to the bank. I was so much
struck with this strange sight that I became quite dumb,
and answered not a word to my parents' questions. All
laughed and said that fear had robbed me of my tongue ;
but that was not quite just. I was overcome, not so much
by fear as by the novelty of the surroundings and by the
noble spectacle, whose beauty I felt though, of course, I
could not explain it. When we got near the steep bank
on the other side, and were poling our way through shallow
water to the landing-place, I was quite myself again, and
in as good spirits as ever I was in my life. Clean white
sand, with banks of many-coloured pebbles, spread wide
before us. One of the rowers sprang into the water, towed
the boat by the painter to the landing-place, and made the
bow fast to a post ; another did the same with the stern,
and we all landed with no alarms. How many new objects
I saw, how many new words I heard ! My tongue was
at once untied, and I began to ask all sorts of questions
of the ferrymen. I cannot forget the kindness of these
good people, nor how simple and sensible were their
answers to all my questions, and how great their gratitude
to my father when he gave them something for their trouble.
We had a rug and pillows on the boat with us ; and these
we spread out on the dry sand, at a little distance from the
water, because my mother was afraid of damp, and she
lay down on them, while my father took me off to pick up
pebbles. To me these were an entire novelty, and I was
enchanted when my father found me some of the pretty
smooth stones, shining with different colours, and some
with very pleasing and diverting shapes. In fact, as I
became convinced at a later time, there is no place with
such a variety of pebbles as the river Byélaya. We picked
up some fossils too, which were long treasured in our
household, and might be called rarities : they were—a
large piece of bees' wax, and a rather large flake or lump

of fish's roe, completely petrified. It took long to bring across our carriage and covered-cart with nine horses, so that I had time to collect a whole heap of what seemed to me marvellous pebbles ; great was my grief when my father would not let me take them with me. He chose out a mere dozen or so and pronounced the rest to be rubbish ! When I tried to prove the contrary, I was not listened to, and with great regret I had to leave behind the heap I had gathered. We took our seats in the carriage and started again on our journey. The open air seemed to have a good effect on my mother's spirits, and I eagerly began to tell of the treasures with which my pockets were crammed, and to exhibit them. My little sister was much pleased with the pebbles, and I made her a present of some of them. We had a number of boxes with us in the carriage, and my mother emptied one of these and put it at my disposal ; with a great effort I managed to pack my treasures in it.

At first our road went through the border of wood that fringed the river ; huge oaks, elms, and poplars impressed me by their size, and I kept calling out, " Oh, what a big tree ! what is it called ? " My father satisfied my curiosity. The road being sandy, our horses went at a walk, and our servants were able to pick leaves and branches for me, which they handed into the carriage, and which I looked at with much pleasure, noting their peculiar differences. The day was very hot : when we had driven fifteen *versts*, we stopped to bait the horses, our special object being that my mother might not suffer too much fatigue from the crossing and the journey. Our first meal was eaten, not in the open air, but in a Russian * village, of which I remember very little ; but, to make up, my father promised me that we should camp next day by the river Dyoma, where he wished to show me a kind of fishing of which I knew nothing, except from his accounts. While we rested in the shed of a peasant's farmyard, my father occupied himself in preparing fishing tackle for himself and

* The Russians wore only settlers in the district of Orenburg ; the natives were either Tatars, or belonged to one of the Finnish tribes— Choovashes, Bashkirs, Mordvinians, and Meshtchers

for me, and to me this process was another new delight.
Our fishing lines were made of hairs pulled out of the horses'
tails; I was allowed to hold the hairs together while my
father plaited them into a fine line. We were helped by
Yephrem Yevséyeff, a good-natured servant who was
devoted to me. His method was different : working on his
knee, he made stout lines for big fish. Sinkers and hooks,
provided beforehand, were then firmly fixed to the lines ;
and all these appliances, seen by me for the first time, were
first wound round pieces of wood, next wrapped up in paper,
and then packed away for safety in my box. With what
attention and curiosity I surveyed these novelties, how
quickly I understood their purpose, how easily and surely
I learnt their names !

We were to spend the night in a Tatar village; but
the evening was so fine that my mother expressed a desire
to remain out of doors ; so, just by the outskirts of the
village, we swerved a little to the side and pitched our camp
on the steep bank of a little stream. This was unexpected
by us all. My father had supposed that my mother would
fear the damp night air ; but the place was unusually dry :
there were no marshes and not even trees near, for we were
at the point where the Bashkir steppe begins ; even the
dampness of the night air was not perceptible. Here was
a fresh sight for me. The horses were taken out ; and, as
it was impossible for them to graze on the open field, the
grass of the steppe being sunburnt and withered, we sent
to the village for fresh hay and oats and provisions of all
kinds. Our servants set to work to kindle a fire : one
brought dry wood from the village, cut it into logs, and
planed off shavings and sharpened brands to put under the
fire ; another dragged to the spot a whole heap of brush-
wood from the river ; while a third (the cook, Makéi, to be
precise) produced flint and steel, struck a spark on a large
piece of tinder, wrapped the tinder up in dry flax (which we
carried with us for such occasions), took it in his hand and
began to wave it vigorously, backwards and forwards, up
and down, and went on till the flax flared up. Then with
the shavings and brands they set fire to the pile of wood
that stood ready ; and the flame began to blaze. Next

the travelling *samovar* * was put on ; the rug was spread
out and pillows placed on it ; my mother lay on them and
prepared to pour out tea ; she was feeling more energetic.
I asked leave to light a small fire near wheie we were
sitting, and, when I was allowed, began, beside myself
with joy, to work at it with the assistance of Yephrem, who
on the journey had suddenly turned into my personal
servant. Words cannot convey the pleasure I got from
the kindling of this fire : I ran constantly from the big
pile to the small one, carrying shavings and sticks and dry
grass, to keep the flame bright, till I got so hot that my
mother had to make me sit down beside her   We had tea
and then chicken broth, which was boiled for us by our
cook.   It was then settled that my mother and the children
should pass the night in the carriage, and my father in the
covered cart.   My mother soon lay down and put my sister
beside her ; the child had long been asleep in her nurse's
arms.   But I had no wish to sleep : I sat up with my father,
talking of our halt next day, to which I looked forward with
joyful impatience ; but, in the middle of our talk, we both
for some reason became thoughtful and sat for a long time
without saying a word.   The sky glittered with stars ;
the fragrance of the drying grasses of the steppe filled the
air ; the streamlet babbled in the hollow beneath ; the
blazing fire threw a strong light on our servants, as they sat
round a kettle and supped their smoking porridge, laughing
and talking merrily ; the horses too, as they munched their
oats, reflected the fire-light on one side.   " Time for you to
go to bed, Seryozha," † said my father, after a long silence.
He kissed me and made the sign of the Cross on me, and
then put me in the carriage, taking care not to wake my
mother.   It was long before I went to sleep.   I had seen
and learnt so much that day that my childish fancy continued to conjure up a confused picture of all the scenes
and objects that had passed before me.   And then the
events of to-morrow, by the marvellous Dyoma !   At last
I was overcome by drowsiness and went to sleep in a kind
of blissful intoxication.

We made such an early start next morning that it was

hardly light when my father came to join us in the carriage
It was difficult for him to find a place, because the sleeping
children took up so much room.   In a kind of dream, I
saw him sit down, and felt the carriage start and move at a
foot-pace through the village, and heard the barking of dogs
which followed us for some time ; then I went sound asleep,
and, when I woke, we were half-way over the forty miles of
uninhabited steppe which we had to cut across.   When I
opened my eyes, the others had long been awake ; even my
sister, seated on my father's lap, was looking out of the
open window and babbling merrily.   My mother said she
felt better :   she was tired of lying down and wanted to
get up.   We stopped, and all got out, to alter the arrangements for the night into those suitable for the day.   All
round us was the steppe, whose treeless undulating expanse
stretched far away ;   in the dim distance scattered trees
were visible and a patch of dark blue further off .   " That,"
said my father, " is the course of the Dyoma, and the
blue is the steep wooded bank."   The steppe was not so
delightful and fresh as it is in spring or at the very beginning
of summer—that aspect my father had often described, and
I saw it myself later—for now the grass in the hollows had
been mown and piled into haycocks, while in other places
it was burnt brown by the summer sun , and the wild oats,
not yet fully shot, nor having changed from blue-green to a
whitish colour, spread in waves over the vast expanse.
The steppe was very still :   my father explained to me that
all the birds had stopped singing, and were now hiding with
their young ones in low-lying places where the grass grew
tallest and thickest.   We got into the carriage again, where
nurse, who again took my sister on her lap, took her seat
with us.   My mother joined cheerfully in our talk, and I
chattered without ceasing of yesterday's adventures.   She
reminded me of my books, and I confessed that I had
forgotten all about them.   I got out one volume of *Reading
for Children*, and began to read ; but I was so distracted
by other things that for the first time I could not fix my
attention on my book :   though I read out in a loud voice,
" ' Canaries !   pretty canaries,' cried the peasant under
Masha's window " . . ., I was thinking of something else,

and chiefly of the Dyoma flowing over there in the distance. My parents could not help laughing at my divided attention; but I felt rather uncomfortable and vexed with myself. At last, when I had finished the story of the " Canary that died of Hunger " without the distress that I used to feel, I asked leave to shut my book and began to look out of the window, following attentively the blue distance, which seemed to come closer to us, as if to cut across our path. The road began to wind upwards; Trophim, the coachman, shook the reins, and called out cheerily, " Gee up, my beauties ! Dyoma's close " ; and our good horses set off at a fast trot. Already we could see the green valley through which the river flowed with its thick green border of wood. My father looked out of the window : " Look, Scryozha," he said ; " do you see that strip of green running straight to the river, with sharp white points sticking up here and there ? Those are the felt covers of the waggons in which the Bashkirs pass the summer—the Bashkir caravans. If it were not so far, I would take you to see them ; well, we'll manage it some day " I looked eagerly and saw far off the summer quarters of the Bashkirs, with their flocks and droves of horses grazing round them. Though I had often heard of this from my father, it was the first time I had seen it myself. And now at last the river came in sight, and a number of islands, and the long bend of the channel in which the river formerly ran. The descent into the wide green valley was steep and winding : it was necessary to wedge the wheels and drive down carefully ; the delay tantalised my impatience, and I ran from one window to the other, making as much bustle as if I could hasten the approach of the longed-for halt. I was told to sit down and be quiet, and had reluctantly to obey. But at last we reached the river bank, just by the ferry ; the carriage turned and stopped under the shade of a gigantic poplar ; the doors were opened, and I sprang out first, in such haste that I forgot the fishing-tackle in my box. My father smiled at my haste and reminded me of the tackle. I begged to go and fish at once ; but he told me not to be in a hurry—to wait till he had given directions for my mother's comfort and for the feeding of the horses : " Meanwhile, you can walk about with Yephrem and take a look at the ferry ; and get some bait, both of you ! " I caught Yephrem's hand, and we walked to the ferry. The Dyoma lay before me—not a broad river, nor very rapid, but the sight of its smooth still water brimming to the level of its banks was of wonderful beauty. Fish, large and small, were constantly jumping. My heart beat hard, and I trembled at every splash, whenever a pike in pursuit of the small fry sprang above the surface of the water. On each bank there was a stout pole driven into the ground, to which a dripping rope, as thick as a finger, was fastened ; along the rope ran a raft, made like the wooden floor of a room, and supported on two huge wooden beams. I soon noticed that one man could drive the raft with ease across from bank to bank. The two ferrymen were Bashkirs, and wore Bashkir caps, conical and made of felt ; they talked broken Russian. Yephrem, otherwise Yevséitch (that was my name for him), holding my hand tight, walked with me on to the raft, and asked one of the Bashkirs to take us across. He very readily cast the raft loose from the landing-place, raised his brawny arms, turned to face the opposite bank, and then, standing firm on his feet, began to draw the rope towards him with both hands The raft parted from the bank and began to float across the stream ; in a few minutes we were on the far bank, and Yevséitch, still holding my hand, walked along the side in search of good places for fishing—he was a very keen fisherman— and then took me back across the river in just the same way. Next he began to talk to the ferrymen, who lived in a hut of wattles situated on the bank, and asked where we could get worms for fishing : he spoke in broken Russian, hoping they would understand him better, and mixed words of Tatar with it. One of the Bashkirs quickly guessed what was needed, and led us to a small shed, where two horses were standing out of the sun ; here we found abundance of the worms we wanted. On coming near the carriage, I saw that all preparations had been made : my mother was lying down in the shade of a leafy poplar, the canteen was open, and the *samovar* was beginning to hiss. Provisions for our meal had been bought over-night in the Tatar village; even oats were not forgotten, and fresh new-mown hay for the horses was bought from the Bashkirs. We were in the middle of noble trees; and the great variety—there were fruit trees and other kinds—was strikingly picturesque and beautiful. Wild cherries, as large as forest trees, were covered already with their dark fruit; clusters of service-berries were turning red; bushes of ripe black-currants filled the air with their fragrance; the pliant clinging stems of the bramble, covered with large blackberries still green, wound round everything they touched; of raspberries, too, there was abundance. My father made me look at this profusion which he much admired; but I confess that my mind was so full of fishing that the richness and beauty of the scene around were but dimly felt by me. As soon as we had finished tea, I began to beg my father to show me how to fish. At last we started, accompanied by Yevséitch. He had already shaped some tree-branches into rods; we made floats out of the thick green reeds, tied on our lines, and began to fish from the raft, relying on the information of the Bashkirs. Yevséitch had prepared for me a very light rod with a thin line and small hook; he now put on a piece of soft bread, dropped the line, and put the rod in my right hand while my father held me fast by my left. The same instant the float turned and sank in the water, Yevséitch called out, " Pull, pull ! " and with a great effort I pulled out a fair-sized perch ! I trembled all over like a fever-patient, and was quite beside myself with joy. I caught my prey in both hands, and ran to show it to my mother, Yevséitch going with me. My mother was unwilling to believe that I could have caught the fish myself; but, choking and stammering with excitement, I assured her that I had really pulled out that splendid fish with my own hands; and Yevséitch, to whom I appealed, confirmed my statement. My mother had no liking for fishing; she rather disliked it, and I was much hurt by her cool reception of my joyful tidings; but, worse still, when she saw me so excited, she said I would make myself ill, and must not leave her till I had calmed down. She made

me sit down by her, and sent Yevséitch with a message to
my father, that she would send me when I had rested and
become calmer. To me this was an unexpected blow ;
the tears literally gushed from my eyes, but my mother
had the firmness to keep me till I was quite quieted. After
a little my father came himself to fetch me. My mother
was not pleased : she said she had never supposed, when
she let me go, that I would fish myself. But my father
persuaded her to allow me, for this once, to catch a few
more fish, and my mother, after some time, consented.
How grateful I was to him ! I believe that the disappointment would have made me ill, if I had not been allowed to
go. My little sister begged to go with me, and, as our
fishing was only fifty yards off, she was allowed to go with
nurse to watch our sport. When we got there, my father
showed me some big perch and trout which he had caught
in my absence ; the other fish were not taking then,
because, as Yevséitch explained to me, it was too late in the
day, and too hot. I caught a few more perch, and each
gave me nearly as much delight as my first. As I had leave
only for a short time, we soon returned. My father told
Makéi, the cook, to boil and fry some large trout, and to
give all the rest of the fish to the servants. for them to make
fish stew of.

I went quite mad over fishing ! I could think and speak
of nothing else. My mother was vexed, and said she would
forbid it, as such excitement might lead to illness. My
father assured her that the second time would be different
and that my excitement would pass off ; I was convinced
that it never would, and listened in terrible suspense to the
decision of my fate. The baited hook, the quivering and
diving float, the bending rod, the fish flapping on the line—
the mere recollection of these things drove me wild with
excitement. For the rest of our halt I was unhappy, not
daring to speak about fish even to my father or sister ; and
indeed all seemed put out by something, and in this frame
of mind we resumed our journey. On the way my mother
tried to explain to me why it was wrong to abandon one-
self so passionately to any amusement, how risky it was
and even dangerous on the score of health ; she said that

even a clever boy might turn stupid, if he forgot everything
else for the sake of a mere sport ; I, for instance, instead of
looking contentedly out of the window, or reading my book,
or talking to my parents, was sitting there as silent as if I
had been drowned.   All this she said tenderly and affectionately, and I felt dimly the truth of her words : I quieted
down a bit and began to read my book aloud.   Towards
evening rain fell, and the road became muddy and heavy ;
poking my head out of the window, I could see the mud
sticking to the wheels and then peeling off in great slabs.
To me this was interesting and amusing, but our horses
found it troublesome and began to go slow.   At last,
Trophim, our coachman, bent down to the front window
and said that the state of the road would prevent us from
reaching Parashino in daylight ; we should be very late,
and wear out the horses ; would it not be best to spend
the night in a Choovash village,* close to which we had to
pass?   This plan had already been mentioned by my father ;
in the forenoon we had covered forty *versts*, which left
forty-five for the afternoon ; this was too much, and he
fell in with Trophim's suggestion.   My mother had no
desire to spend the night among the Choovashes, to whose
unclean habits she objected ; but there was no help for it,
and the order was given to turn off to the village; we were
fifteen *versts* short of Parashino.   A few minutes later we
left the road and entered the settlement.   It had no streets.
The houses were built on no plan ; each householder had
settled down where he liked ; and each dwelling had a
separate approach.   The sun had already gone down in a
cloudy sky, the rain went on falling, and darkness set in
early ; we were met by a fearful barking of dogs, of which
the Choovashes keep even more than the Tatars.   This
barking (which went on steadily all night) now mingled
with the shrill squeaky voices of the women, the jingling
of their copper and silver ornaments, and the loud voices
of our servants, as they abused the householders for hiding
themselves in order to escape the trouble of putting up
lodgers   For a long time our ears were pierced with this
concert.   At last, in spite of all concealments, the head-man

* See note to p 19

was found, or rather his wife, who was discharging her husband's duties in his absence. She billeted us on a rich villager, who owned several houses, so that it was possible to clear one out entirely for our use. It was damp, sitting in the carriage; so we went at once to the cabin which was already lit by the light of a torch. Here again was a feast of novelty for my eyes. The first thing that struck me was the dress of the Choovash women—a white shift with red embroidery and a black piece stuck on behind, while the head and breast were covered with silver coins, ranging from large to very small, which went jingle-jangle at every movement they made. Other wonders followed— the roomy cabin, blackened with smoke and covered with shiny soot from the ceiling right down to the broad wooden settles along the walls, the stove without a chimney, and lastly the burning torch that took the place of a candle: this was stuck into an iron socket, and the socket rested on a wooden stand, so that the light could be shifted from place to place. There was no dirt in the cabin, only a smell of smoke which was not unpleasant. We made very comfortable beds of the broad settles. My father tried to prove to my mother that she was wrong in her dislike of Choovash villages: nowhere else, he said, were there such roomy cabins and such wide settles, and they were far cleaner than Russian cottages; my mother replied that the people themselves were dirty and disgusting, which my father did not deny, only asserting that they were very good-natured and very honest. The brazier attracted my attention, above all: the burning torch which was fixed in it required renewing constantly, and some of the torches burnt, if I may say so, very capriciously. The flame at times burnt bright, then nearly went out, and then blazed up again; the burnt and charred stump sometimes bent out to the side, sometimes fell with a crackling noise and broke; sometimes a torch suddenly began to hiss and send out a puff of grey smoke, like a jet of water from a fountain, to the right or left. My father explained that this jet was not smoke but steam produced by the dampness in the wood. I was much taken up by all this, and was vexed when a candle was brought in from the carriage and the torch put out. We all spent a very good night, under our canopies, without which we never travelled anywhere. The rain passed off during the night, and the morning was fine; but we did not start very early, because my father wished to have a whole day at Parashino, which was fifteen *versts* away. Hearing the name often, I asked what Parashino was, and was told it was a large prosperous village, the property of my father's aunt, Praskovya Ivanovna Kurolyessova; my father was commissioned to inspect the management of the estate and report to the owner, whether all there was in good order. Eight miles from the village, we came to fields on the estate, covered with a tall thick crop of rye; the rye was ripe, and the reaping had begun. The fields stretched so far that there seemed to be no end to them. My father said that this year's harvest was splendid and he had never seen such crops. The labourers, men and women, who were working stripped to their shirts, recognised our servants and my father; they stuck their sickles into corn-stooks and hastened to the carriage. My father gave the order to stop. Sweat poured off the brown faces of the reapers, but the faces were merry; a score of them came round our carriage, and all were pleased. One who was older than the rest—an overseer, as I learnt afterwards—began the talk: " Good health to you, *batyushka* * Alexyéi Stepanitch; it is long since we saw you; *matushka* † Praskovya Ivanovna wrote to us that you were coming; we thought long for you." My father, without leaving the carriage, gave a kindly greeting to all and said, " Well, here I am, and I have brought my wife and children with me." My mother looked out of the window and said: " Good health to you, my friends." All bowed to her, and the same peasant spoke again: " Good health to you, Sofya Nikolayevna; you are welcome. Is that your little boy? "—he went on, pointing to me. " Yes," answered my father: " that is my son, Seryozha; the little girl is asleep." I was held up to the window, and all bowed to me as well and called me Serghéi Alexyéitch, a name that was quite new to me: " We are glad to see you

* Father   † Mother   Both words are affectionate diminutives.

all, *batyushka* Alexyéi Stepanitch," said the same man. Their pleasure was no pretence : one could see it in every face and hear it in every voice.   I was puzzled by a feeling of emotion I did not understand : I felt affection for these kind people who loved all of us so much.   My father went on talking, asking many questions which I could not understand, but I heard them answer : " We get on not so badly, glory be to God !   But we don't know how we can keep pace with the crops, because many of the people are down with illness."   When my father asked why they were working for their owner on a holiday—it was the first of August and therefore a feast of the Church—they replied that such were the orders of the bailiff, Mironitch ; they used not to work on that feast, but had done so for the last four years ; the older men and the women with children had gone to the village the night before, but all would return after the church service ; only the young people were now present, about a hundred sickles, in the charge of the overseer.   My parents then took farewell of the reapers, both men and women.   To their salutes I replied with a profusion of bows, though the carriage was already moving ; I thrust my head out of the window and cried out, " Goodbye ! good-bye ! "   My parents smiled when they saw me ; and then, much excited, I began to ask questions : " How do these people know our names ?   Why are they so glad to see us ?   What do they love us for ?   What does ' working for their owner ' mean ?   Who is Mironitch ? " and so on.   My father found it difficult to answer all my questions, but he got help from my mother.   They told me that half the peasants at Parashino had been born serfs of the Bagroff * family, and knew very well that some day they would again belong to us.   They knew my father because he often went to Parashino with his aunt, and loved him because he had never done them any harm ; and for his sake they loved my mother and me ; and that was how they knew our names.   Mironitch was the bailiff ; and that word I understood perfectly ; but ' working for their owner ' was a little more than I could understand at my age.

* A pseudonym for Aksákoff

On this occasion, as on many others, when I failed to understand some of the answers to my questions, I was not content with uncertainty, but invented explanations of my own. This is a common custom with children ; and so it often happened to me later to call a thing by its right name without perceiving the obvious connection between the thing and the name. Life will, no doubt, explain all such things ; and it is sometimes amusing to discover one's mistakes, but at other times very mortifying.

After the rye came fields of spring wheat which were beginning to ripen. My father, as he looked at them, often said sadly : " It will be impossible this year to clear the fields before the bad weather comes : the rye was late, and now the wheat is early. But what crops ! I never saw anything like them in my life." I noticed that my mother was quite unmoved by my father's lamentations. But I, without understanding why, shared his regret that there would not be time enough to reap the fields.

CHAPTER IV

PARASHINO

OUR road now sloped upward, leaving the table-land on which we had been travelling ; and at last we saw beneath us the prosperous village of Parashino, with a stone church, and a fair-sized pond in a hollow. The proprietor's stack-yard stood up like a town made of corn-ricks ; and we could see that even the peasants had in their yards many sheaves of last year's corn. My father was delighted to see such abundance and said : "It warms one's heart to see such good husbandry." I shared his pleasure but noticed that my mother took no interest in what he said. At last we entered the village, just when the priest, wearing all his vestments and carrying the Cross above his head, preceded by the deacon with censer, banners, and *icons*, and accompanied by a large crowd, came in procession out of the church to perform the ceremony of blessing the water. The singers' voices were drowned by the ringing of bells and only at intervals made their way to my ears. We stopped the carriage at once, got out, and joined the crowd. My mother held my hand : my sister, in her nurse's arms, gazed with unusual interest at a sight new to her ; while I, though I had seen something of the kind before at Ufa, was charmed to see it again.

After the ceremony, we all kissed the Cross and were sprinkled with holy water. The priest congratulated us on our safe arrival ; and we walked to the Great House which was only across the street from the church. A crowd of people came round us, and they were just as pleased to see us as the reapers had been ; several old men pushed their way to the front, and bowed, and gave us a very friendly greeting ; the first of these was a man past

his youth, short and broad-shouldered, with hair turning
grey and such odd eyes that I was quite terrified when they
rested on me. The crowd accompanied us to the steps of
the house, and then dispersed ; but the man with the
terrible eyes ran up the steps, opened the door, and invited
us to enter : " Welcome, *batyushka* Alexyéi Stepanitch !
welcome, *matushka* Sofya Nikolayevna ! " When we went
in, it seemed as if all had been prepared for our visit ; but
I learnt later that our aunt's chief agent and man of business always stayed there on his occasional rounds—
Mihailushka my parents called him, but every one else gave
him the respectful title of Mihaila Maximitch—and therefore the house was always prepared for visitors From
what my father said, I guessed at once that the short man
with the terrible eyes was that very Mironitch about whom
I had been asking questions on the journey. My father
asked him questions about the farming of the land and then
sent him off, saying he would be summoned when wanted,
and bidding him send some of the older men, whose names
he mentioned, to the house to see him. Young as I was, I
noticed that Mironitch did not approve of this order.
His " Yes, Sir," seems to sound in my ears at this moment
and clearly meant, " What you are doing is quite wrong."
When he had gone, a conversation took place between my
parents, which puzzled me exceedingly. First, my mother
said that Mironitch was certainly a scoundrel. " He looks
like it," said my father, smiling ; " and queer stories about
him have come to my ears before now ; but then he is a
relation and favourite of Mihailushka, whom my aunt
relies upon entirely. The old men whom I told him to
send here are our own people ; they know I won't give them
away, and will tell me the whole truth. But Mironitch
did not like it." My father added that after dinner he
would drive round the fields, to look at the work going on
there. He invited my mother to go with him ; but she
gave a decided refusal, and said she had no wish to see it.
" If you like, you can take the boy with you," she added
I was charmed, and begged to go ; and my father readily
agreed. " All right," he said : " after tea Seryozha and
I will have a look at the horses, and then we'll drive to the

D

water-springs and the mill." Of course I was delighted at
this extension of the plan, of which my mother approved.
So after tea we started for the stable, which was behind
the house, across a grass-grown yard. The head-groom,
Grigori, was waiting for us at the stable door with other
stable-men ; I fell in love with him at first sight, and he
was very friendly with me. But before we had time to
enter the stable, that horrid Mironitch turned up, and stuck
close to my father all the rest of the day. The stable was
a long building with a wide entrance ; two passages ran
to right and left, and in separate compartments along these
there were horses standing, mostly big full-grown animals,
though some were young and small. I heard for the first
time that these compartments were called " stalls." On
the wall just opposite the door hung an image of St.
Nicholas the Miracle-worker, Grigori told me. When my
father had looked at both sides of the stable and praised
its cleanliness, he went out again into the yard and ordered
some horses to be brought out. Grigori did this himself
with the help of another groom. The animals, being
highly fed and little worked, neighed and reared, while
both grooms, lifted off the ground, hung on to the horses'
necks and gripped the halters with their right hand. I was
frightened and kept close to my father ; but, when some
of the splendid beasts were made to gallop and jump at the
end of a long rope, and the grooms who held the rope,
though they stooped and pressed their feet hard on the
ground, could scarcely control them—then I was full of
admiration. Mironitch was constantly interfering, and I
was vexed when he spoke to the head-groom as Grishka,*
though my father called him Grigori. My father asked the
groom, where the horses in the fields were grazing. His
question was answered by Mironitch, who added : " If it
is your pleasure, Alexyéi Stepanitch, to examine the wheat
and rye and the ground for autumn wheat (we shall have
service in the church to-morrow and then begin the sowing),
would it not be a good thing to have the droves of horses
moved there ? It would save you distance." " Very
well," said my father.

* A diminutive and less respectful form of Grigóri

Leaving the stables, we started for the water-springs. Running water, and especially water from a spring, was always a pleasant sight to my father; and to me even the water running down the streets was a joy, so that I was naturally delighted by the splendid springs of Parashino, of which there were more than twenty. Some were very strong and spouted from the centre of a hill, others flowed busily at the foot of it, and some were on the slopes. These last were enclosed in wooden frames, which were roofed over and held wide troughs of linden-wood, where the water was so transparent that the troughs seemed empty; in each trough the water brimmed over the edge and trickled down the sides like beads of glass. I watched the peasant women coming with their pitchers. They pulled out the wooden pin at the end of the trough and placed a pitcher on the large stone flags. The water gushed out in an arch, because the bottom of the trough was raised high above the ground. In one minute the first pitcher was filled, and then a second. All these springs, and many others which were left to nature, flowed into the same pond over beds of small pebbles, among which my father and I found many shaped like sugar-loaves; they were rather long and perfectly rounded, and were known as " Devil's Fingers." Having never seen them before, I took a great fancy to them and stuffed my pockets with them. As my father was quite unable to explain their name, I teased him for a long time with questions · " What is the Devil like ? Why does he have such hard fingers ? "

Before I had got over these impressions, so new and delightful, I passed to another scene which, if less delightful, was not less interesting. This was the mill, to which my father next took me; a mill was a thing I had no conception of. There was the pond, fed by the springs and fairly deep; then the mill-dam, a broad artificial dyke, which bounded the pool and kept in the water; and lastly the mill standing on the centre of the dyke, and containing a single pair of mill-stones. The mill worked properly only at high water : the difficulty was not, as my father explained to me, that there was little water in the pond but that the water trickled everywhere through the dyke.

To me this crazy old mill seemed a miracle of human skill. First I saw the stream of water pouring through a pipe right down on the wheel; then the wheel, turning rather slowly, green with damp and covered with drops of bubbling water; the sound of the water mixed with another sound, of creaking and groaning. My father then showed me the wooden box or hopper, broad at the top and narrow below (I noticed this later), into which the grain is dropped. Next we went down below, where I saw the mill-stone revolving and the hopper shaking above it as it poured the grain under the stone. Round went the stone with its wooden rim, crushing the corn and converting it to flour, which poured down a wooden shoot. Looking aside I saw another wheel called the "dry wheel," which revolved much faster than the other and caught hold of a small wheel with what looked like fingers, and turned the stone fixed to the small wheel. The mill was filled with flour dust, and shook all over so violently that it seemed to jump off the ground. The sight of these marvels kept me long in a state of astonishment, though I remembered that I had seen something of the kind among my toys. We stood a long time in the mill, and saw there a bent and decrepit old man, whose business it was to pound all the chaff for the proprietor's horses; he was grey-headed and looked ill, and was white all over with flour dust. I began to ask him questions; but, when I noticed that he was constantly choking and coughing, I felt sorry for him and addressed my remaining questions to my father. The hateful Mironitch was constantly interfering here too, though I was unwilling to listen to him. When we left the mill, I noticed that our clothes were white too, though not so white as the old man's. I begged of my father at once that the sick old man might be put to bed and given tea to drink. My father smiled; but turning to Mironitch, he said: "The miller's man is very old and feeble; he has a terrible cough which the dust of the mill will do no good to; he ought not to be brought here but to be relieved altogether from work, even from light work." "As you please to order, Alexyéi Stepanitch," replied Mironitch; "but won't others feel injured? If we relieve him, we must relieve others.

There are plenty of skulkers of that sort. Who will be
left to do the light work?" "Oh," said my father, "all old
men are not weak; we ought to look after the veterans and
let them rest; they have done a good stroke in their time.
You will soon get old yourself; then you will be a 'skulker'
and want to rest." Mironitch answered: "I obey, Sir; your
order shall be carried out. But we ought not to show
kindness to that man: his grandson is a disorderly fellow
and nearly strangled me the other day" My father answered in an angry tone which I had never heard from him
before: "What! punish that wretched old man for his
grandson's fault? No, no! punish the guilty." Mironitch
hastily struck in· "Do not trouble yourself, Alexyéi
Stepanitch; your order shall be carried out." I was
beginning, I don't know why, to feel an internal trembling.
Meanwhile the old man, seeing us stop, had moved slowly
towards us; hearing what was said, he stopped also; he
was shaking all over, and he bowed to us repeatedly.
When we got to the top of the hill, I looked round: and
there was the old man still standing there and bowing low.
When we got home, I forgot all about the springs and the
mill, and began to tell my mother about the poor old man.
She heard my story with warm indignation: she wished to
send for Mironitch and reprove him on the spot, to dismiss
him from his office and report his conduct to his mistress,
Praskovya Ivanovna; and my father found it hard to
restrain her from such precipitate steps. There followed
a long discussion and even dispute. Much of it I did not
understand, much I forgot, and all I remember is my father
saying: "Don't interfere in other people's business, or you
will spoil everything and cause the ruin of all that family.
At present Mironitch won't lay a finger on them; he will be
afraid in any case of my reporting him to his mistress.
But if it comes to turning out Mironitch, Mihailushka will
support him Then I may say a long good-bye to Parashino
and, as likely as not, my aunt will be angry as well." My
mother yielded, but only after a struggle. Meantime,
what a confusion of ideas went on in my small head!
"Why is the old man made to suffer? Why is Mironitch
so unkind? What is the power of Mihailushka and his

mistress ? Why did my father not allow my mother to
turn off Mironitch on the spot ? If my father, as it seems,
has power to discharge him, why does he not do it ? He
is good natured, of course, and never gets angry. Is that
the reason ? " Such were the questions with which my
young brain buzzed ; and I answered them all by deciding
that Mihailushka and his mistress were unkind people,
whom my father was afraid of.

My " Devil's Fingers " I gave up to my sister, who
had found it very dull without me. We placed the new
acquisition with our former treasures—the wooden bricks
and the pebbles from the river Byélaya. I eagerly described to my sister all that I had seen ; it was a regular
custom to let her know all that befell me in her absence.
But by this time I began to notice that she did not always
understand ; so I borrowed words from nurse and tried
to speak in language which a little child could understand.

After dinner my father and I started for the cornfields
in a long low car. The objectionable Mironitch took his
seat beside us. It was the first time in my life I had driven
in a car of this kind, and I much enjoyed it : seated on a
white mat folded in four, I was rocked just as if I was in
a cradle hung on a supple bough. In the road over the
steppe the cart sank so low in the ruts that the tall grasses
and flowers whipped my legs and arms, much to my amusement ; I was able even to pick flowers. But I noticed that
for grown-up people the position was uncomfortable :
they could not dangle their legs but were forced to stretch
them out and keep them up, in order not to strike the
ground ; but the grass only touched my shoes as I sat on
the car. Between the cornfields, we drove along broad
strips of untilled land, where cherry-trees and wild peach-
trees were growing ; the cherries were hardly red and the
peaches quite green. I asked my father to stop, and picked
myself a whole handful of wild cherries, as small as large
peas and quite hard, and filled one pocket with wild
peaches. I wished to fill the other pocket with berries and
take them back to my mother ; but my father said that my
mother would not even look at such " trash " ; the berries
would be crushed in my pocket and spoil my clothes,

and I must throw them away. But I was loath to part
with them so soon, and kept them for a long time in my
hand. At last I was obliged to drop them, but I don't know
how or when I did so.

Wherever the rye was not "laid" (as it is called), it
stood high enough to hide us, carriage and horses and all.
This was another new and pleasant experience for me. For a
long time we drove along the strips between the fields ; then
we began to hear voices and an odd noise some distance
off. The nearer we drove, the louder the sounds became,
till at last we could catch the flash of sickles through the
standing rye and could see ears of cut rye lifted up by
some invisible hand ; a minute more, and we saw the bending backs and shoulders of the reapers, about twenty men
and women. When we came out upon the field, the talk
ceased, but the rasping sound of the sickles on the straw
grew louder till it filled the whole field with a sound new to
me. We stopped our car, got out, and walked close to the
reapers. " God speed the work ! " said my father ; he spoke
pleasantly, and at once all stopped working, turned their
faces to us, and bowed low ; some of the older men exchanged greetings with my father and me. Their sunburnt
faces showed that they were pleased ; though some were
panting and others had fingers or toes on their bare feet
bandaged with dirty bits of rag, yet all were cheery. My
father asked how many they were, and whether the work
was hard. " Pretty hard," they replied ; " it must be,
with such a crop ; but the evening will put us right."
" Very well," said he ; " go on, and God speed the work ! "
In a moment the sickles were flashing again, and the hand-
fuls of rye passing over the heads of the reapers, while
the rasping of the stiff hard straw was heard over the field,
louder than ever. I stood fascinated. Suddenly, I was
attracted by a child's cry, and then noticed that here and
there cradles were hanging under three sticks tied at the top
and stuck in the ground. A young woman thrust her sickle
into a sheaf she had bound, and went without hurrying
to one of the cradles. She took the crying baby up in
her arms and, sitting down at once by a stook made of
five sheaves, kissed her child and caressed it and gave it

the breast. The child soon stopped crying and went to sleep; the mother laid it in the cradle, took her sickle, and began reaping with re-doubled efforts, in order to catch up her companions. While my father was talking to Mironitch, I could survey the surrounding scene at leisure. An intense feeling of sympathy for people who had to work so hard in the burning sun came over me; and I have never since been present in a harvest-field without recalling that first impression.

From this field we drove to another, then to a third, and so on. At first we got down to visit the reapers; but later we only stopped the car, and my father called to them, " God speed the work ! " The scene was the same everywhere—the same kind pleased faces and the same simple words, " Thank you kindly, *batyushka* Alexyéi Stepanitch." Even to stop everywhere was impossible for want of time. We went also to the fields where spring wheat was beginning to ripen. My father and Mironitch spoke anxiously of the difficulty in getting hands enough to do the work. " It's a real plague, Alexyéi Stepanitch," said the bailiff : " the rye ripened late and the wheat early ; on the top of that come the late oats, and now it is time to be sowing. God sent us enough rain yesterday to soak the furrows ; and I mean to send all the men to-morrow to begin sowing the wet land. Half the rye is still standing ; and the women alone won't make much of a job of it. Would you allow me, *batyushka*, to get some extra work out of the people ? " My father replied that the peasants had their own reaping also to do ; it was hard to rob them of a day at such a busy season ; it would be better to invite our neighbours to help. The bailiff was saying at some length that our neighbours lived far off and were not accustomed to help, when we drove up to some fields of peas and poppies. These attracted my attention ; and my father told Mironitch to break off a few poppy-heads—they were still green—and to uproot an armful of the unripe pea-haulms ; all of this he put at my disposal and even allowed me to eat one half-grown pod, of which the small flat peas tasted very good to me. At another time, this would have interested me much more ; but just then my mind was full of the rye-field and the reapers; so I did not care much for my dozen poppy-heads and armful of unripe pea-haulms, whose slender stalks I was holding in my hands. On our return, we visited the land for autumn sowing, and my father pointed out that it was pretty thickly covered with weeds and thistles. But Mironitch defended himself: the fields, he said, were too distant to drive the flocks there to graze them down, and all that green stuff would soon be cut down by the harrow and would never grow again. For all this, my father was still rather dissatisfied: he said that the ploughing was too shallow in places, and the furrows too far apart, which accounted for the quantity of weeds. The sun was now sinking, and we had hardly time to look at the two droves of horses, the property of the landowner, which had been driven on purpose near to where we were. One contained a number of young horses of all sizes, and the brood-mares with foals at foot; the foals did something to divert my thoughts from the harvest-scene: I liked to see them start and bound and then nuzzle against their mothers' flanks. The other drove could not even be approached without caution · my father made his inspection on foot with the herdsmen, and did not take me. These, I was told, were wild and dangerous animals which attacked strangers. It was getting dark when we reached home. My mother was becoming anxious and sorry she had let me go. Indeed, I was over-tired, and fell asleep without even waiting for tea.

Next morning, as no one called me, I slept till pretty late and awoke to find a great to-do going on and much coming and going. A number of peasants had come to see my father, with various requests which Mironitch did not dare, as he said, or more probably did not wish, to grant. This I learnt later from conversations between my parents. My father, however, would assume no authority: in each case he answered that he had been deputed by his aunt only to inspect the property and to report fully to her, but not to interfere with the bailiff's arrangements. Still, when he and Mironitch were alone, I myself heard him say: "You might do so-and-so for one man, and so-and-so for another." The bailiff's regular reply was: "I obey;

your orders shall be carried out," although my father
repeated several times, "I give no orders, brother; I only
suggest, in case you yourself think good to act so. And I
will report to my aunt that I gave you no orders; so don't
you make me responsible." My mother had even more
visitors than my father: the women came to her, some
with petitions about the payments due from them, others
complaining of divers illnesses. My mother would not
even listen to the petitioners; but to the sick she gave
advice and even medicines from the chest she carried about
with her. On the previous evening, when I was asleep,
my father had interviewed the old men for whose attendance
he had given orders. It was clear that they had said
nothing very bad about Mironitch; for my father was
much more friendly with him than on the previous day, and
even praised his zeal. The priest and his wife, when they
came to say good-bye to us, spoke favourably of Mironitch.
One thing the priest said was this: "The bailiff is a man
under authority and obeys his orders"; then he smiled
and added: "God only is without sin; the only misfortune is that Mironitch has so many relations in the village
and is so kind to them" I was much puzzled, thinking that
the more relations he had, and the kinder he was to them,
so much the better. Our packing took a long time, I do
not know why; it was about noon when we drove off,
accompanied to the end of the village by Mironitch, a few
old men, and a whole troop of the village children. We
were to drive forty-five *versts* and to spend the night by the
river Ik, of which my father said that it was as fine a stream
as the Dyoma and full of fish. So happy hopes began to
stir again in my breast.

CHAPTER V

WHAT an astonishing thing travel is ! What an invincible power it has to calm and to heal ! It detaches you suddenly from the familiar sphere—whether you like or dislike it, makes no difference—from the steady course of varied activity which constantly distracts your attention with a multitude of objects; it concentrates your thoughts and feelings upon the narrow world of a travelling carriage ; it directs your attention first to yourself, then to memories of the past, and finally to dreams and hopes for the future ; and all this takes place clearly and quietly, with no hurry or confusion. This was just what happened to me then. At first my head swarmed with a confused mass of new objects, figures, and ideas—the Dyoma, our night in the Choovash village, the springs, the mill, the feeble old man working there, the field of rye and the reapers. Then each object grew separate and clear ; but dark mysterious points presented themselves, like stains upon my mental pictures, and I had recourse to my parents, begging them to clear these up and explain them to me. But all their explanations seemed to me unsatisfactory, probably because they talked to me as to a young child, not noticing that my questions were much beyond my years. At last I started the most recent of all my puzzles : why did they talk of Mironitch at first as a bad man and then speak to him at parting as if he were good ? They tried to explain. There were few quite good people in the world, they said ; the old men, whom my father had long known, were honest and truthful, and their account of Mironitch was to the following effect. He showed sense and energy in his office, and attended to the interests both of his mistress and the

peasants. It was true, he favoured his own relations and
the rich peasants who were in Mihaila Maximitch's good
books. But that was a matter of course : blood was thicker
than water, and the chief agent must be treated with
respect   He drank at times, but was always sober when
work had to be done, and never used his fists without
cause ; he had not robbed his mistress nor the peasants
of a single *kopec*, but made much money out of birch-resin
and leather, because he was honoured by * the rich peasants
of Parashino, who traded in the resin burnt in the Bashkir
forests and bought skins of big and small animals from the
Bashkirs ; though these peasants were not much pleased
with Mironitch, they made large gains and were rich   In
conclusion, the old men begged that Mironitch might not
be disturbed, declaring that any change would be for the
worse. I was much taken aback by this explanation,
which needed to be explained still further at great length.
Worldly wisdom is incomprehensible to a child : compromise has no place in his innocent mind ; and I could not
reconcile myself to the idea that Mironitch might use his
fists without ceasing to be a good man. At last, my
questions proved a nuisance, and I was told either to read
my book or play with my sister. I did not care to read :
I began to sort my pebbles and Devil's Fingers, showing
them to my sister, giving them names, and telling stories
about them.

Our journey was again very long more than forty *versts*
About ten *versts* from Parashino we drove through a newly
settled Russian village, after which for thirty *versts* there
was no habitation of any kind, and the road ran over level
ground with trees here and there and fine woods in the
distance ; soon low hills presented themselves, and then,
on the right, a continuous chain of high rocky hills, in some
places covered with wood and in others quite bare.   As we
went down the slope leading to the river Ik, we had to pass
a village of Choovashes and Tatars, called Ik Karmala,
because it lies on the slopes of the Karmalka, a small stream
which runs into the Ik two *versts* from the village   We
stopped outside the village, meaning to send there to buy

* *I e.* got money from

oats and provisions, for our servants to bring to the bank
of the Ik where we had settled to spend the night. The
sun was still high ; it was as hot as midsummer. Suddenly
my mother suggested that it might be better to camp at
Karmala, where the air was so dry, while it would inevitably
be damp by the river at night. To me this was a death-
stroke. Nor was my father pleased, but he answered.
" As you like, my dear." My mother put her head out of
the carriage-window and glanced at the scattered huts of the
Choovashes ; then she pointed to one of the yards, which
stood apart from the rest and enclosed a little hill, and said,
" There is where I should like to stop " There were no
obstacles. The owner, who was a rich Choovash, was very
ready to let us camp there, because we did not ask for the
use of his dwelling. We drove quietly into the big yard,
which was still green, and established the carriage, at my
mother's wish, on the very top of the hillock. There was
a pretty view from there : we could see all the picturesque
surroundings of the Karmalka and the green woods of the
Ik, as it flowed in the valley below. But I had no inclination for picturesque views   To fish in a river as good
as the Dyoma, and fish in the evening when, according to
my father, fish took best—all these dreams had dispersed
like smoke, and I stood like one sentenced to some severe
punishment. Suddenly my father's voice rescued me from
despair. " Seryozha," said he, " I will ask the man here
for a horse and car ; and he shall drive you and me to the
Ik. There we will fish. At sunset I shall send you back
with Yephrem ; I shall stay till dark myself. Ask leave
of your mother," he added, looking with a smile into
my mother's eyes. I did not say a word, but one glance
at my face told her all. She felt it impossible to deprive
me of this pleasure ; but she was vexed and said to my
father : " I wonder you are not ashamed to tempt the
child. He will get just as excited again as he was on the
Dyoma." But now I got back the use of my tongue, and
eagerly assured her that I would be perfectly calm. Much
dissatisfied, she said : " You may go, but mind you are
back before sunset." The permission given so unwillingly
was like a douche of cold water to me. I tried to say that

I did not wish to go ; but my tongue would not obey me. In a few minutes all was ready—horse, fishing-tackle, and bait : and off we set for the river. In later years I found that the Ik was just as good for sport as the Dyoma, but I was not then in a state to be charmed by it. When I thought, that my mother had let me go unwillingly, that she was displeased and anxious about me, and that I was bound to return in a short time, I was impervious to all impressions of natural beauty and even to the charms of fishing which I already felt so strongly. And yet the spot to which we drove was really enchanting. A quarter of a mile above us, the river divided into two streams which flowed on quite close to one another. Below the division the water was shallower, and both channels were spanned by bridges carried over high posts ; in one channel the water was still and deep, in the other shallower and faster. The growth of wood on the banks was as wonderful as on the Dyoma ; both streams flowed to where it was thickest, and disappeared in a dense tangle of bushes and trees. To this point the Ik had flowed along a wide open valley ; but now, in the distance, hills began to advance on both banks, some wooded, others bare and stony, and seemed ready to take the river under their domination

My father chose a place to fish from, and he and Yevséitch soon set to work. A line, with a worm this time, and not bread, for bait, was given me, and I caught a small perch at once. The bait was renewed and the line thrown in, and I was given the rod to hold ; but I felt so unhappy that I laid it down and begged my father to send me back to my mother. He was surprised : it was still early, he said, and the sun would not set for another hour ; but I went on asking to go, and at last began to cry. My father had a great dislike to tears and was even alarmed by them ; so he told Yevséitch to take me home and then return as soon as possible, that they might enjoy the evening fishing together. My early re-appearance surprised and even alarmed my mother. " What is the matter ? " she called out ; " are you not well ? " I answered that I was perfectly well but did not want to fish. In my unsteady voice and tearful eyes she read at once all that was going

on within me ; she took me in her arms, and we both began
to cry.   She wished to send me back to the river, but I
eagerly begged her not to do so ; for my desire to stay
with her was quite sincere ; and she felt it would be as
unkind to send me now as it would have been to keep me
before.   Yevséitch ran back to join my father, while I
stayed with my mother and sister.   Suddenly my heart
became so light that I thought I had never felt such happiness before.   After many tender words and caresses, my
mother told me to play about the yard with my sister ;
but first she took care that all the owner's dogs were tied
and shut up.   Walking all round the hillock on which our
carriage was standing, we made a discovery so wonderful
that I ran back breathless with a joyful shout to tell my
mother of it.   It was this : a spring emerged from the back
of the hillock, half-way down ;   the owner had placed a
trough beneath it, and, as all the buildings in the court
were beneath the level of the spring, he had carried the
water first to his summer kitchen, then to a large tank for
washing clothes, and finally to the byres where his horses
and cattle were shut up at night.   I was enchanted by all
this and eagerly described it all to my mother.   She smiled
and praised the contrivance of the owner, which the
distance of the river made especially convenient.   To complete my satisfaction, she allowed me to make a little bonfire near the carriage, our yard being quite like open field.
The sun set in majesty behind the dark hills of the Ik.
We drank tea, and later had our supper by the light of my
bonfire.   My father had not yet returned ; and sometimes
the thought flashed through my mind : " What is hap-
pening on the banks of the Ik ? how are the fish biting ? "
But these thoughts never clouded my bright happy feeling
What an evening it was !   How wonderful the sunset
glow, as it gradually faded away and all the landscape
slowly grew dark !   Soon a white cloud of mist concealed
the trees along the river ;   and my mother said : " How
damp it is over there, Seryozha ; a good thing that we are
not camping there "   Still my father did not return, and
she was inclined to send to fetch him ; but we had hardly
lain down in the carriage, when he stepped up to the window

and said in a low voice, " Are you still awake ? " My mother scolded him for being so late. They had not caught much, but my father had landed a large bream. I was very anxious to see it; so Yevséitch brought a lighted pine-torch, and I gazed at the splendid fish without clambering out of the carriage. My father made the sign of the Cross over me, and then sat down to his supper. A few more words, a few caresses from my mother—and sound sleep came over me.

Having stopped early the day before, we made an unusually early start next morning. I was still half-asleep when I felt our carriage going down the hillock, and was quite awakened when my father got into the carriage beside us. I was excited by the thought that I should soon see the Ik again, and I remained awake till sunrise. When we drove up to the first bridge across the Ik, the first rays of sunlight were visible ; a smoke was rising from the trees and especially from the river. My father had shut the window, whispering to me that the damp was bad for my mother, and I dared not open it ; but I saw through the pane that all the trees and both bridges were soaking wet, as if after heavy rain. But how beautiful was the river ! A light steam rose from its waters as they flowed swiftly past, forming eddies here and there. The tall trees were half veiled in mist. But as soon as we got on higher ground, the mist vanished and the first sunlight shone into the carriage, lighting up the face of my sister who was sleeping opposite to me. A few minutes later we were all sound asleep. Thanks to our early start, we arrived early at our halting-place, which was Korovino, a large settlement of Mordvinians.* There was no suitable place there for us to dine out-of-doors, and my mother did not like to stop in the villages ; so we chose a place between the last house and the village barrier. The splendid bream, which arrived quite fresh in wet grass, was cooked for our dinner. My mother, who thought fish bad for her, would only just taste it when pressed by my father. I was given a little piece of the side and found it uncommonly good, as my father also maintained When the horses were fed,

* See note to p. 19

we set out about 2 p.m. on our last stage of 35 *versts* to
Bagrovo. We made haste, wishing to arrive early; for
at Korovino, where everybody knew my grandfather
and my father, we had heard that my grandfather was
unwell. On the way we twice crossed the river Nasyagai
over very bad bridges. The first bridge was so defective
that we had all to get out of the carriage; even the leaders
were unharnessed, and the two wheelers made a shift to
draw across our heavy carriage with its cargo of baggage.
There the Nasyagai was still small; but, when we crossed
it again ten *versts* further on, it was a fine river, very swift
and deep; yet it was hardly half the size of the Ik,
and the wood on its banks consisted of bushes only. The
sun was still high—two trees high, in the phrase of Yevséitch—when from the top of a steep hill we caught sight
of Bagrovo, lying in a valley between two large ponds half-
covered with bulrushes, and bordered on one side by high
woods of birch trees. I saw it all very well; for the steepness
of the hill made it necessary to wedge the wheels, and my
father and I walked down. My heart beat quick, I do not
know why. When my mother looked at Bagrovo out of
the carriage-window, I noticed that her eyes filled with
tears and that her expression was sad. I had guessed
before, from conversations between my parents, that she
disliked Bagrovo and was unwilling to go there; but I had
heard the words without understanding or even attending
to them, and only now realised that there were some
serious causes for my mother's distress. My father too
became depressed. I grew sad and took my place in the
carriage with a sinking heart. In a few minutes we drove
up to the steps of the house, which seemed to me melancholy
and even small in comparison with our own house at
Ufa.

E

CHAPTER VI

BAGROVO

My grandmother and aunt met us at the top of the steps. With cries and, as I thought, with tears they embraced and kissed my parents and then kissed my sister and me. Yet I felt at once that they showed less affection to us than the ladies who sometimes paid us visits at Ufa. My grandmother was an old woman and very stout; her dress and the handkerchief tied round her head were exactly like those of our nurse, Agatha, while my aunt had on just such a jacket and skirt as our maid Parasha.* I noticed at once that they were somehow quite different from my mother or our friends at Ufa. My father, followed by my mother, went in at once to see grandfather, leaving my sister and me alone in the parlour; my mother had just time to tell us to keep quiet, not to walk about through the house, and not to talk too loud. We were so dismayed by these injunctions after the want of warmth in our reception, that we felt afraid, and sat in silence on a settle. We were quite alone; for our nurse, Agatha, had gone out into the passage, where she was surrounded by the maids and the wives of the outdoor servants. Some time passed in this way; at last my mother returned and asked where nurse was. Agatha bounced out of the passage, vowing she had only left us that instant, though in fact we had never seen her since we entered the parlour, and had only heard the whispering in the passage. My mother took us both by the hand and led us into grandfather's bedroom. He was undressed and was lying in bed; there was a growth of white beard, nearly two inches long, on his face; and to

* A diminutive form of Praskóvya.

me he seemed very alarming. He stretched out a hand to
us and said, " How arc you, my little grandson and grand-
daughter ? " My mother whispered to us to kiss his hand.
" I can't see just now," he went on, blinking and placing
a hand over his eyes, " who Seryozha is like : when I saw
him before, he was too young to resemble anyone : but
Nadyézhda is like her mother, surely. To-morrow, God
willing, I will manage to get up. I'm sure the children are
hungry after their journey ; let them have something to
eat. Well, go now and make yourselves at home in the
new nest." We all went out and found the *samovar* waiting
in the drawing-room. Grandmother wished to give us
thick cream in our tea, and scones made with butter, and
we were willing enough ; but my mother asked for common
· white bread instead of the scones, and said we drank our
tea without milk and never got cream or any rich food.
" Well, well ! " said grandmother ; " you just tell us, my
dear, what your little ones eat and what they don't eat,
or else I shall not know what to give them. We arc plain
country people and don't know your town fashions." My
aunt chimed in, saying that her sister-in-law must make her
own arrangements and send for Stepan, the cook, and tell
him what should be dressed for the children. Though I
did not then understand what was behind this talk, I felt
at once something strange and unfriendly. My mother
answered very respectfully : there was no need for them to
trouble themselves about our food ; nothing but chicken-
broth would ever be needed ; she did not give me milk,
because my long illness had made her anxious ; and,
from my example, my sister had got into the way of
drinking tea without milk. Then grandmother asked my
mother to choose one of two rooms, the parlour or the
drawing-room, for our own use. My mother said she would
have preferred the drawing-room, but feared that the
proximity of such young children might disturb her sister-
in-law. My aunt replied that she would hear no noise, as
the wall between the rooms was thick and there was no door;
so we took possession of the drawing-room. We had with
us a double bedstead of iron, which unscrewed and came to
pieces. This was at once put together and set up by two of

our men-servants, while Parasha hung a very pretty curtain over it ; I am not sure of the material, but I believe it was muslin ; the bunches of flowers on it were so pretty that I found great pleasure, even when I was much older, in looking at them. When curtains of the same were hung over the windows, the room suddenly looked quite different, and my heart became much lighter. Our travelling trunks also were dragged into the drawing-room and covered with a rug   I did not forget my own little box which held the pebbles, or my books ; all these I set on a little table in one corner. Before supper, my parents went to grand-father's room and sat there some time. They wished to take us also to say good-night, but grandmother said that he must not be disturbed, and that it was time for children to go to bed. When we were left alone in the new nest, my sister and I began to chatter ; I say " alone," because nurse again left the room and began to talk in whispers with someone outside the door. I told my sister that I was unhappy at Bagrovo, that I was afraid of grandfather and wished to be travelling again in the carriage, and much more to the same effect ; but my sister hardly understood me, and, as she was nearly asleep, talked such nonsense that I laughed. When at last sleep overcame her, I called nurse, and she put the child to sleep in my mother's bed, where there was a little place prepared for me too ; for my father a bed was made on the sofa. I too lay down. At first I felt sad and then bored, till I fell asleep. I do not know how long I slept ; but, when I woke, I saw by the light of the lamp burning before the *icon*, that my father was lying on his sofa and my mother sitting beside him, crying.

For a long time my mother spoke in a low voice, sinking at times into a whisper, and I could not, though I strained my ears to listen, catch the connexion of all she said. Sleep fled from my eyes. I heard her say : " How can I leave them, and in whose care ? I shall die of grief, and no doctor will do me any good," and my father's reply : " Do take care of yourself, my dear ; you will certainly be ill to-morrow and unable to get up "—and these words, caught among many others by my straining ears, alarmed and terrified me. The thought of our staying alone at

Bagrovo without father and mother was not new to me, but I seemed never to have realised it till now ; and it suddenly came over me with such horror that for a time I was unable to hear and understand, and so lost much of the conversation which I might have heard. At last, at my father's urgent request, she consented to lie down. Before doing so, she prayed and made the sign of the Cross on both of us. I pretended to be asleep ; but I did not really go to sleep before she did.

My father's prophecy proved true : when I woke next morning, I saw him and Parasha busy at my mother's bedside ; she was very ill with a bilious attack and fever. When she had been ill before, she still went about ; but now she was too weak to rise. I had never yet seen her so ill, and fear and grief mastered me. I was old enough to understand that my tears would cause her pain and do her harm ; so I crept behind the high head of the bed, and cried quietly, wrapped up in the ample folds of the curtain My father saw me and held up a warning finger, pointing to my mother ; I nodded and shook my head, as a sign that I understood his meaning and would not cause her anxiety.

My father then went to see grandfather ; coming back he reported that he was better and wished to get up. In the parlour my aunt was pouring out tea. Nurse called to me to go there, but I refused to stir a step from my mother ; and my father, fearing that, if compelled, I would burst out crying, brought me tea himself and a roll made without butter, just like the rolls which used to be sent from Bagrovo to us at Ufa. My sister and I (and indeed all of us) were very fond of them : but now I could not swallow it and hid it under the large feather-bed on which my mother was lying, that I might not be forced to eat it. The parlour door was constantly opening, and I could hear my sister chattering gaily to her grandmother and aunt, and I was rather vexed with her. I heard her being taken to grandfather's room and felt sure my turn would come soon. My presentiment came true on the spot : my aunt hurried in and said that grandfather was asking for me. My father said in a loud voice, " Go to your

grandfather, Seryozha." My mother quietly called me
to her side ; she smoothed my hair and looked attentively
at my red eyes ; then she kissed my forehead and said in
my ear, " Be sensible, and friendly with your grandfather " ; and her eyes filled with tears. How much it
cost me to go ! My aunt led me off by the hand, while
my father stayed with my mother. My face must have
expressed much suffering and fear ; for my aunt stopped
in the servants' room to caress me and say, " Don't be
frightened, Seryozha ; grandfather won't bite you." I could
hardly restrain the tears that were ready to gush from my
eyes, and stepped timidly over the threshold of grandfather's room. He was sitting in a queer old armchair
covered with leather and decorated with copper bosses
along the edges. Strangely enough, the armchair and the
copper bosses were the first things I noticed : they attracted my attention and served to give me some courage.
He wore his dressing-gown, and my sister was on his knee.
As soon as he saw me, he put my sister down on the floor,
stretched out a hand, and said in a kind voice, " Come
here, Seryozha." I kissed his hand. " Why are your eyes
red ? You've not been crying ? Why, you want to cry
now ! I see you're frightened of your grandfather and don't
love him." " Mamma is ill," I said, mustering up all my
strength in order not to cry. At this point, my grandmother and aunt broke in, explaining that I was intensely
attached to my mother and would not stir a step from her,
and that she had trained me to this. They said much to
this effect, but grandfather seemed not to listen to them :
he watched my face attentively, but so good-naturedly that
my fears began to pass off. " Do you know who Seryozha
is like ? " he said at last in a loud, cheerful voice ; " he's the
picture of my uncle, Grigori Petrovitch ! " Next he took
me on his knee, stroked my hair, kissed me, and said,
" Don't cry, Seryozha ; mother won't die this time " ;
and he began to ask me questions, which went on for a long
time, about Ufa and what I did there, and our journey,
and so on. I plucked up courage and talked, especially
of my books and the journey, while he listened attentively
and smiled in a way that flattered me. At last he said :

" You do well to love your mother : she did not spare
herself, when she nursed you. Now go back to her, but
don't make a noise and disturb her ; and don't cry." I
answered that my mother would not see me at it ; for I hid
in the curtains when I wished to cry. Then I kissed his
hand, and ran back to her, leaving my sister in the room.
When my mother heard my quick steps, she was frightened ;
but the sight of my happy face comforted her. At once
I began to describe my interview with grandfather in the
minutest detail, and the leather armchair with the copper
bosses was not forgotten ; my father and even my mother
could not help smiling at my eager and particular account of
the armchair. " Glory to God," said my mother, " I see
that your grandfather was pleased with you. You must
love him ; he is so kind. " I do love him," I replied ;
" and, if you like, I will go back to his room at once."
My mother said this was not necessary, but asked my
father to go and sit there ; what she really wished was
to hear what the old man would say of her children.
Though I was satisfied, to all appearance, with grandfather's reception of me, yet he was not so pleased to see
me as I had expected from what I had been told ; and I
asked my mother the reason. She replied that grandfather
was not well just now and had other things to think of ;
which explained his bearing to us.

Together with Parasha I now began to be busy about
the sick-bed and nurse the patient, giving her some medicine
which she made up on Buchan's instructions, and a drink
made of cranberries. She had asked for lemons ; but the
servants said they had never even seen such a thing.
" How stupid I am ! " she said and then asked for cranberries. Parasha at once brought a whole slop-basin full
of them, adding : " They have plenty of cranberries here ·
a whole cart-load is brought every year from Old Bagrovo,
when the roads are first open in winter." Then my
mother asked for black bread and vinegar, to tie on her
head ; I liked it so much that I put little pieces in my own
mouth Next she wished to go to sleep and made me read
aloud ; I began at once upon *Reading for Children ;* and
she did really go to sleep and slept a whole hour. Through

the window I could see my sister playing in the garden
with her nurse, Agatha, among currant bushes and
barberries ; the bushes were old and larger than I ever
saw before or since. Birds with red-yellow tails kept
flying out of the bushes ; and once a striped cat sprang
out of one. I felt a strong inclination to join them.

My mother awoke and said she felt a little better. My
father then came in ; and I asked at once if I might play
in the garden with my sister. My mother gave me leave
but told me not to go near the river, which was my chief
object, as my father had often told me of his dear Boogoorooslan, and I wanted to have a close view of it. The garden,
I found, was not a real garden, even less so than those I had
seen at Ufa : it was more like an orchard or kitchen garden.
It consisted mainly of currant-bushes, laden with their
white, red, and black berries, and of apple-trees ; but,
most of these having been killed by the last winter, the
branches had been sawn off and new grafts inserted. Round
these were high banks of manure on which grew melons of
different kinds and gourds, and a vast quantity of rows of
cucumbers and vegetables of all sorts—peas, beans,
radishes, and carrots. Besides all this, in every vacant
space, sunflowers and fennel were grown ; and lastly, a
hollow, which was under water every spring, was green with
a huge multitude of cabbages. This mixture of things was
not pretty, but it pleased me then, and pleases me still,
certainly far more than walks of pollarded limes or beeches
or unhappy yews cut in the shape of pyramids, or spheres,
or chests of drawers. On the right side of the garden,
the swift and deep river flowed close to the house, and then
took a sudden bend to the left, and in this way actually
bounded the so-called garden on two sides.

I had barely time to go round and examine it, and to
talk to my sister, who with nurse's help told me how grandfather had kept her a long time and been very kind to her
and finally sent her to play in the garden—when Yevséitch
came running to call us to dinner. It was twelve o'clock, at
which hour we usually had lunch, dining at 3 ; but Yevséitch said that grandfather always dined at midday and
had already sat down at the table. We hastened back to

the house and entered the parlour. Grandfather gave
orders that we should be put directly opposite him at table ;
and as we had no high baby-chairs with us, a pile of cushions
was placed under each of us, and I laughed to see my sister
perched so high, though I was nearly as high myself. Then,
remembering I had not seen my mother when I came indoors, I began to ask if I might go now ; but my father
told me in a whisper to be quiet—I could go after dinner ;
I had never heard him speak so severely, and I held my
tongue. Grandfather wished to help us to different things
he was eating; but grandmother stopped him; she said that
Sofya Nikolayevna gave nothing of that kind to her children
and that broth had been made for them. He frowned and
said, '' Very well ; let their father give them what he thinks
fit." He himself and all his family were on " fast " diet ; *
it was the first day he had been out of bed, and yet he ate
cold fish-soup, fish, lobster, porridge with oil for milk,
and mushrooms. The smell of the colza oil forced itself
up my nose, and I said, " What a bad smell it has ! " My
father pulled my sleeve and again whispered that I must
not dare to speak like that ; but grandfather had caught
my remark and said, " Hullo, brother, how squeamish you
are ! "—at which my grandmother and aunt smiled but
my father blushed. After dinner grandfather went to
see my mother, who was lying in bed and ate nothing all
day. After sitting there a little, he went to lie down ;
and at last we four, parents and children, were left alone.
I now heard that grandfather had come to our room before
dinner, and was very sorry when he saw how ill my mother
was. He had advised her to start at once for Orenburg,
though before, as I knew from my parents' talk, he had called
this journey a caprice and a useless waste of money, as he
did not believe in doctors. My mother replied (so I was
told) that her present illness was a trifle, which would soon
pass off, and that she needed a little time to get fit for the
journey to Orenburg. Again the thought of separation
from my parents came over me. To remain a whole month
at Bagrovo, alone with my sister, seemed so terrible that
I did not know what to wish. I remembered how at Ufa

* See note to p 227

I had begged my mother to lose no time in going to see the doctor ; but the words I had overheard the night before— " I shall die of grief, and no doctor will do me any good "— shook my belief that she would come back cured from Orenburg. All this I explained to them as well as I could, accompanying my explanations with tears ; but it was not hard for my mother to make me believe whatever she wished, and to calm my fears. In spite of my dread of the separation, I soon had only one wish : that she should start as soon as possible for Orenburg where the doctor would be certain to cure her. I noticed that from this time my mother was on her guard, and never said, before me, anything likely to alarm me and make me anxious ; or, if she did, she spoke too low for me to hear. She made me read longer than usual, or play with my sister, or go for walks with Yevséitch ; she even sent me out with my father to see the mill and the island. I liked the mill-pond and the island well enough, but at any other time I would have liked them better ; later I had a perfect passion for them.

In a few days, my mother could get up ; the bilious attack and fever were over, but the whites of her eyes were yellow, and she was even thinner than before. I soon noticed that they were preparing in earnest for the move, and that my grandfather himself pressed them to start soon on their long journey. My mother once said to him, before me, that she did not like to burden her relations with the care of the children, and was afraid of causing him trouble, if one of us fell ill. He replied with some heat : " That is all nonsense The children are not strangers' children ; who should look after them, if not their own grandmother and aunt ? " My mother said that she did not trust our nurse ; she would put me in charge of Yevséitch, who was very good-tempered and conscientious, and he would go out walks with me. Grandfather answered, " Well, that's all right : Yephrem comes of a good stock ; or, if you like, I will give you my maid Aksinya to look after the children." She declined this gracious offer, on various pretexts . in fact, she knew that Aksinya was cross. Grandfather was rather hurt · " As you please," he said : " I and my Aksinya don't want to be a nuisance to anyone."

Also I heard my mother when with tears she begged and
prayed my grandmother and aunt to be kind to us and
watch over us, to give us no rich food, and not to dose
us, in case of illness, with their stock remedies ; for they
treated young and old alike, whatever their complaints, with
" Haarlem Drops " and " The Elixir of Life." My grandmother and aunt were not pleased, and indeed made no
concealment of it, to have us left upon their hands ; yet
they promised, in submission to grandfather's authority,
to keep a constant watch over us and to fulfil all my
mother's requests. In case of emergency, my mother
left some drugs, out of her own medicine-chest, with written
directions for their use, if either of us fell ill. These were
the charge of my aunt Tatyana, who was kinder than grandmother and could not but pity the tears of a sick mother
parting for the first time from her little children.

Till my mother's departure I was constantly uneasy
and divided in my mind. When I saw her pale and thin
and weak, I had only one wish, that she would go as soon
as possible to consult the doctor. But as soon as I was
alone, or with others of whom she was not one, I was overcome with grief at the approaching separation, and fear
of staying behind with relations who were less affectionate
than I wanted them to be, and either did not love us, or
loved us so little that my heart did not turn towards them ;
and my imagination, too active for my years, suddenly
put before me such terrible pictures that I threw aside my
occupation, either books or pebbles or walking in the
garden, and ran off to my mother, as if out of my mind
with grief and fear. Sometimes I was on the point of
springing into her arms and begging her not to go or to take
us with her ; but her suffering face always recalled me to
myself, and the wish that she would go to see the doctor
always conquered my fear and grief. I do not understand
now, why it was settled to leave us at Bagrovo. They
were going in the same carriage, and there was as much
room for us as there was before ; but my mother never had
this intention and told me, even at Ufa, that she could not
on any account take us and must travel to Orenburg alone
with my father ; her purpose never once wavered at

Bagrovo, and I was fully convinced that to change it was impossible.

The next week, in spite of my grief and painful anxiety, passed more quickly than usual for me; and at the end of it my father and mother went away. At parting I was unable to control myself · my sister and I wept and sobbed, and so did my mother When the carriage turned out of the court and vanished from my sight, I became quite wild, dashed down the steps, and ran in pursuit of it, crying, " Mamma ! Mamma ! come back ! " As this was unexpected, it was impossible to stop me at once : I had time to run across the court and reach the road. Yevséitch, behind whom a number of servants came running, was the first to come up with me ; he caught hold of me and carried me back, grasping my arms tightly. Grandfather and grandmother were standing on the top of the steps; my aunt, who had come down to meet us, tried to comfort and caress me. But I would not hear a word : I screamed and wept and tried to wrench myself from the strong arms of Yevséitch. He climbed the steps and set me on my feet before grandfather, who called out angrily, " Stop that yelling ! What are you crying about ? your mother will come back ; she won't stay for ever at Orenburg " His words quieted me. He went into the house and to his own room, and I heard grandmother say, as she followed him, " There, *batyushka*, you see for yourself what trouble we shall have. These children are very spoilt." My aunt led me by the hand to the drawing-room, which was our bedroom. My dear little sister, holding my other hand and herself crying quietly, kept saying, " Don't cry, brother, don't cry ! " When we entered the room and I saw the bed where we always slept with our mother, I threw myself upon it and began again to sob loudly. My aunt, Yevséitch and Agatha the nurse tried every means to calm me—my books, and bricks, and toys. Yevséitch tried to staunch my tears by talking of our journey, of the Dyoma, of fishing, and of fish. But it was all in vain : only when I was worn out with tears and sobbing, I did, I don't myself know how, at last fall asleep.

CHAPTER VII

My sister and I spent more than a month, in the absence of
our parents, as unwelcome guests at Bagrovo. Most of
the time we were shut up in our own room; for damp
weather soon set in and put a stop to our playing in the
garden. I will describe the course of this monotonous and
gloomy life. As soon as we woke, which we did regularly
at eight, nurse took us to see our grandparents, who, after
good mornings were said, spoke a few words, or sometimes
did not speak at all, and then sent us back to our own room.
About twelve we went to dinner in the parlour; though
there was a door leading straight to the parlour from our
room, it was locked, and even curtained over; and we
went along the passage from which at that time a door led
into the drawing-room. At dinner we were always seated
at the bottom of the table, opposite to grandfather, and
always on high cushions. Sometimes he was in good
spirits and talked to us, especially to my sister whom he
used to call his little fawn; but at others he was in such a
bad temper that he spoke to nobody. As my grandmother
and aunt were silent too at such times, my sister and I,
feeling bored, would begin to whisper together; but
Yevséitch, who always stood behind my chair, at once
stopped me, whispering in my ear to be silent; and
Agatha treated my sister just the same. They told us
afterwards that we must not dare to speak, when the " old
master " (as they called grandfather) was in low spirits.
After dinner we went at once to our own room, where tea
was brought us at six. Supper was usually at eight, and
we were taken to the parlour and seated opposite grandfather, just as at dinner; immediately after supper we

said good-night and went to bed. On the first few days our aunt looked into our room and showed some sort of interest in us ; but she soon came less often, and at last never came at all. We saw her and the rest only at dinner and supper, and to say good-morning and good-night At first the maids in the house and the wives of the outdoor servants came to see us on various pretexts, and asked to kiss our hands, which we refused to let them do, being unfamiliar with the custom ; they asked some questions and went away ; and soon not one of them came near us. I think this was due to some order of my grandmother or my aunt. I myself heard the latter say that Sofya Nikolayevna did not wish her children to talk to the servants. Our nurse, too, Agatha, was in the habit of disappearing from the time of early tea till dinner, and again from dinner till tea in the evening. On the other hand, Yevséitch never left us the whole day, and even slept every night in the passage at our door. He told stories to amuse us, or shared in our games, or listened to my reading. The tie between me and my dear sister became stronger than ever, though she was still so young that I could not fully share with her my thoughts and feelings and wishes. For instance, she did not understand, what I understood perfectly, that we found little love in the household ; and for that reason she was bolder and merrier than I, and often began of herself to talk to her relations. Hence she was liked much better than I was, and especially by grand-father : he sometimes sent for her and kept her in his room for a long time. Though I was quite aware of this, I was not jealous : first, because I loved her ; secondly, because I had no friendly feeling to grandfather, and could not help being frightened in his presence. I ought to say that I had a special reason for fearing rather than loving him : I once saw him with my own eyes when he was stamping on the ground with rage ; and then from our room I heard terrible and pitiful cries, which puzzled me. But our nurse, Agatha, made haste to explain it all to me, though the worthy Yevséitch scolded her for telling a child what a child had no business to know.

And so by degrees we settled down to a life of our own

in our small corner, in the drawing-room which we occupied.
The first days after the departure of my parents I spent in
constant grief and tears ; but by degrees I grew composed,
took my bearings, and settled down.   Every day I gave
my little sister a reading-lesson ; this was a complete
failure, as she had not mastered even the alphabet at the
end of our stay at Bagrovo.   Every day I made her listen
while I read *Reading for Children*, taking all the stories
and articles in order, and leaving out none, though there
were many which I could not understand myself.   My
poor little listener often yawned and sometimes fell asleep
while I read, though she tried hard to keep her pretty eyes
fixed on my lips ; then I played games with her, building
towns and churches of our bricks, or houses, of which the
inhabitants were her dolls.   But her favourite game was
" Visitors."   We sat in opposite corners, and I took one or
two of her dolls and paid a visit with them to my sister,
which I did by walking across from one corner to the other.
She had a number of dolls, all of which she called her
daughters or nieces ; this gave rise to many conversations
and entertainments in complete imitation of grown-up
people.   I remember how I gave full play to my imagination and described many surprising adventures that had
befallen me, taking some hint or model from incidents
I had read in my books or overheard.   Thus, for example,
I described a burning house, and how I jumped down from
the window with two children—the children being two dolls
which I was holding in my arms ; another scene was an
attack by robbers, all of whom I put to flight ; my final
effort was a dragon, which lived in a cave in the garden,
with seven heads, which I intended to hack off.   I was
much flattered by the impression which these narratives
produced on my sister.   Sometimes I succeeded in frightening her : one night she slept badly and awoke crying ;
she said she had dreamt of robbers and dragons, and that
her fright was due to me.   Nurse threatened that she
would complain to grandfather ; so I reined in these fiery
flights of my youthful fancy.

During our parents' absence, three aunts, sisters of my
father, paid visits at Bagrovo.   The first, Alexandra, made

on me a very unpleasant impression, and so did her
husband, though he was very fond of us, often taking us
on his knee and constantly kissing us. This new aunt did
not like us at all: she was always making fun of us
as "cockneys" and "milksops," and, as far as I could
understand, she spoke very unkindly of my mother, and
expressed contempt for my father. Her husband's behaviour was at times eccentric and even alarming: he
made a great noise—stormed, and sang, and used language
which must have been very objectionable, because both
the aunts tried to shut his mouth with their hands, and
warned him that grandfather was coming. This made him
disappear at once, as he was in great awe of grandfather.
The second aunt who came to the house was Aksinya,
my godmother. She was a very good-natured woman,
and very kind to us, especially when she was alone with us ;
she even brought us presents, some raisins and prunes,
which she gave us in secret and told us to eat when no one
was looking. She scolded our nurse for the dirtiness of our
room and clothing, told her to change our frocks oftener, and
threatened to let Sofya Nikolayevna know the state in
which she had found us. We were delighted by her kind
way of speaking to us and became very fond of her. But
one thing troubled me—her telling us to keep secret the
dainties she had given us. My parents had always taught
me to do nothing underhand ; so I decided to put away
the raisins and prunes till my mother returned. The third
aunt, Elizabeth, who was called by everybody "The
General's lady," came for a short time ; she was a very
proud lady, and never spoke to us at all. She brought
with her two daughters, a little older than I, and left them
with her parents when she went off at the end of three days.
The presence of two cousins should naturally have cheered
us up and made our life pleasanter ; but it turned out quite
the other way, and our position, or mine at least, became
still worse   I saw very well that they were treated differ-
ently from us : they were loved and petted, and got many
good things to eat ; they even got more sugar in their tea
than we did, as I chanced to find out when I took one of
their cups by mistake. These girls, of course, were not at

all to blame : if they did not seek our company, they only
behaved as they were taught and told to do. I tried
reading to them, but they would not listen, and called me
a little preacher. They were at home in the house, known
and liked by all the servants about the place ; so they had
a very gay time, while no one ever looked at us. I often
heard through the door whispering and suppressed laughter
in the passage, and sometimes great noise and loud merriment : Yevséitch explained that the maids were playing
with the young ladies, and hiding behind the boxes in the
feather-beds and cushions with which both sides of the
broad passage were lined. He proposed that I should join
in, and I wished to, sometimes ; but I had not the necessary
boldness ; also, my mother, when she left, had forbidden
us to play games with the servants at Bagrovo or make
companions of them. In the course of those five weary
weeks Yevséitch became my guide, philosopher, and friend ;
and I became very fond of him. I even read to him sometimes from my favourite volumes . once it was " The Story
of the Unhappy Family who lived under the Snow." When
I had ended, he said : " I don't know, my little falcon "
(his regular name for me), " whether all that is written
there is true. But I will tell you something which really
happened. In this very village, last winter, Aréfy Nikitin,
a *moujik*,* drove his cart to the forest to get firewood.
It was only four *versts* to the wood the people have in
common ; but he took his time, and a snowstorm came
on. Neither he nor his horse was able for much. He
thought he had missed the way, and began to look for it.
The snow was deep, and he became exhausted and stuck
fast in a hollow, till the snow covered him. The horse
stood still ; it was perished with cold. After resting a
while, it went on at a walk and got home with the cart.
They were expecting Aréfy at home ; when they saw the
horse come back alone, they told the village-elder and
raised the alarm ; and a dozen *moujiks* went in search of
him. The terrible storm made it impossible to see a yard
before them. They went and searched and came back
without him. Next day, the whole village turned out

* Peasant.

F

but they found nothing either   On the third day, a
moujik was going along quite another road ; he was coming
from Kudrin, and had with him a sporting dog. The dog
smelt something not far from the road and began to scrape
away the snow with his paws. The man thought it was
some beast : he stopped his horse and walked close to see
what it was   He saw that the dog had dug a hole in the
snow, and that steam was coming out of the hole.   Then he
too set to work digging, and found a hollow place inside
just like a bear's hole, and saw a man lying there asleep,
with the snow melted all round him   He knew about
Aréfy, and made sure it was him.   At once he covered up
the opening with snow, jumped on his horse, and galloped
to the village.   The people collected in no time   They
hurried off with spades, dug out Aréfy, put him on a sledge,
covered him with a sheepskin, and carried him home.
When they got there, they rubbed him for a long time with
snow before taking him into the house ; he was stiff all
over, and kind of asleep from the cold and snow.   When he
woke, they carried him indoors, but he was still unconscious.
Next day he came to himself and asked for food.   He is
quite well now ; only he can't speak right since.   Well,
there's a real true story for you, my little falcon.   If you
wish, I will show him to you, next time he comes to our
back door."   I was much taken up with the story of Aréfy,
and Yevséitch pointed him out to me a few days later ;
he often came to beg of grandfather.   Every one spoke
of him as " silly " ; and in fact he was quite unable to
tell me his story—how he was buried in the snow and his
subsequent adventures.[1]

---

* It is remarkable that this poor fellow, who lived for three days under
the snow in a hard winter frost, was actually frozen to death twenty-five
years later, in a very slight frost in September after heavy rain   As before,
he had gone to the very same place for firewood , as before, he lost his
horse which got home alone , as before, he must have wandered about in
search of the path   Cold and fatigue evidently made him so weak, that
at last, when close to the village, he fell into a shallow ditch and had no
strength to climb out of it   Autumn nights are long , so it is impossible
to tell at what time he fell into the ditch   He was found at eight o'clock
next morning by the writer who was driving out to follow game ; he was
then dead and quite stiff.   (*Author's Note*)
    The case of Mrs Elizabeth Woodcock, who survived after being buried

I once asked my aunt for some books to read. It appeared that her library consisted of three volumes · a "Song Book," an *Interpreter of Dreams*, and a dramatic composition of the vaudeville kind. For some reason, she did not think fit to give me the "Song Book"; but the other two came into my possession and made a strong impression upon me. I learnt by heart the significance of different dreams, and for long I was fond of interpreting my own dreams and those of other people, and believed in the truth of these interpretations; nor was it till I reached the University that this superstition was entirely removed from my mind. The interpretations given in the book were utterly absurd : they had not even that feeble support of observed facts which one may hear among the common people I still remember some of them; and here are a few specimens · "To catch a fish means bad luck." "To drive in a cart portends death." "To dream that you are standing on a dung-heap is a sign of riches to come."

The play had two names : the first I forget, but the second was, "A Trifle for the Stage." Trifling indeed it was; but how I enjoyed it! In the first scene, a shepherdess or peasant girl, driving home a flock of geese, sang some verses which began and ended with a refrain :

> " Geese, geese, come home !
> Geese, cease to roam ! "

Two more verses of another song I remember :

> " Cornflower blue,
> How I love you ! "

That is all I remember ; I only know that it was the story of the love of a shepherdess for a shepherd, and that her grandmother refused her consent to their marriage and then relented. Thus began with me a strong inclination towards dramatic composition, which grew stronger every year.

for a week under snow at Impington near Cambridge, in February, 1799, is very like this. The details are given in Gunning's *Reminiscences of Cambridge*, vol. ii., p. 122. (*Translator's Note.*)

Grandfather received only one letter from Orenburg. It contained a little note from my mother to me, written in large letters, to make it easier for me to decipher. I was delighted by the note, and also much impressed by this new sensation : for the first time I was conscious of speech addressed to me by somebody who was hundreds of miles away. And who was that somebody? My mother, whom I loved so passionately, whom I was always thinking of and often grieving for. Nobody had ever before written me a single word ; and indeed, though I read print well, I could not make out writing.

It was now the fifth week of this lonely life, and my childish mind and heart began to suffer much under it. Not only my face but my whole appearance expressed a timid grief and my feeling that I was a kind of orphan. Whether I played with my sister, or read my books, or listened to Yevséitch's stories, I could not attend to anything. Often, I put aside *Reading for Children* and fell into a reverie, in which my fancy painted me pictures full of sadness and, later, of horror. I imagined that my mother was dying, was dead ; that my father was dead too, and that we would spend our lives at Bagrovo, beaten, and dressed in peasant's clothing, and banished to the kitchen (I had heard punishments of this kind spoken of) ; and that at last my sister and I would both die. These pictures of fancy became more definite every hour ; and I shed floods of tears as I sat at my book over some cheerful story. Then my sister would rush to kiss me and ask the reason of my tears ; sometimes I could not answer, and she too began to cry without knowing why. Nurse had begun to be more with us, now that the young master and mistress —so my parents were called in the house—were expected home ; but she and Yevséitch were at their wits' end. The consolations usually given in such circumstances failed entirely. When asked why we were crying, my answer was, "Mamma is certainly ill or dying" ; and my sister said, "I feel sad when brother cries." My aunt was told ; and she received just the same answers when she came to see us. She begged us not to cry, and assured us that our mother was well and was expected to return every day ;

but I was so convinced of the truth of my sad presentiments
that I refused altogether to believe my aunt, and obstinately
repeated the same answer again and again: "You are
saying all that to deceive me." She was vexed and went
away. Next day, when we went to say good morning to
grandfather, he said to me rather sternly: "I am told
that you are always whimpering; you are a cry-baby;
and the sight of you makes my little fawn cry too. Mind
I hear no more of your tears." I turned pale with fright
(I was told this afterwards); and I did not venture to cry
all that day, but I cried nearly all night. I became still
more frightened of grandfather. Imitating my aunt,
Yevséitch and nurse kept constantly repeating: "Your
mamma is well and will arrive very soon; she is driving
up to the village now, and we will go to meet them." At
first these last words had a strong effect on me, and made my
heart beat fast; but soon it was pain to hear them. Two
more days went by; my sorrow increased, and I became
quite unable to occupy myself in any way. My dear sister
never stirred a step from me: often she begged me to play
with her, or read aloud, or tell her a story. I did as she
asked, but with so little inclination or spirit that I often
stopped in the middle of our reading or game, and we looked
at one another in silent grief with eyes full of tears. On one
of these weary heavy days, one of the maids came running
into our room and called out loudly, "The young master
and mistress are arriving!" It may be strange; but I
did not believe this news at once and entirely. I was
accustomed, indeed, to hear words to the same effect from
Yevséitch and nurse; still it is strange that I was so
incredulous in my joy. But I thank God that it was so;
if I had been quite convinced, I believe I should have gone
mad or fallen ill. My sister began to dance and cry out,
"Mamma has come, Mamma has come!" Nurse, who
for once was alone with us, asked in an anxious voice,
"Do you really mean it?" "Yes, I do," said the maid;
'they are quite close, and Yephrem Yevséitch has run
to meet them'; and off she ran herself. Nurse quickly
put our frocks straight and brushed our hair, and led us
both by the hand to the servants' room. The house door

was wide open ; and my grandmother with my aunt and
two cousins was already standing in the hall. As the
rain was pouring in torrents, no one could go out upon the
steps. A carriage drove up, and I got a glimpse of a figure
at the window ; it was my mother—and from that moment
I remember no more. When I became conscious, my
mother was sitting on a sofa, and I was on her knee with
my head laid on her breast. Ah ! that was joy, that was
happiness !

As soon as I had quite recovered, I wished to talk and
ask questions ; but my mother got up and hastened to
grandfather ; frightened by my swoon, she had not gone
to his room and had not yet greeted him. In a few minutes
Yevséitch appeared, with instructions to take me to the
" old master." For once I went with perfect confidence :
my mother was there, and in her presence I feared no one.
Grandfather was sitting on the bed, with one of my parents
on each side of him , grandmother occupied grandfather's
armchair, and my aunt and cousins were also seated. I
had not seen my father, or rather, I did not remember
having seen him ; so in my joy I sprang straight into
his arms and began to embrace and kiss him. " So you
love your father too, and not your mother only," said
grandfather in a cheerful voice ; " I thought it was only
her you missed." " Well, Sofya Nikolayevna," he went
on, " your little boy is a terrible cry-baby : he made us
all sad and made my little fawn cry a great deal. I had
to shout at him a little, and that quieted him." My
mother replied that my long illness had made me inseparable
from her. My little sister was so bold that I looked at her
in astonishment : when I entered the room, she ran to
meet me with shouts of delight—" Mamma has come !
Papa has come ! ' —and then, still shouting, ran from her
mother to all the others in turn, and even clambered up on
grandfather's knee.

My parents arrived two hours before dinner. After
dinner all dispersed to lie down, as usual, and we were left
alone ; and I described in detail what had happened to us
in their absence. I did not understand the effect which
my story was bound to have on a devoted mother's heart,

nor that it was doubly painful to my father to hear it.
Even if I had understood, I should have told the real truth
all the same, having learnt perfect frankness from my
mother's training. Once or twice, my mother interrupted
my tale ; her eyes flashed, the colour came into her pale
face, and in a voice choking with emotion she spoke to
my father in language which I could not quite understand.
Each time he signed to her to stop, and tried to soothe her :
" For God's sake be careful, and spare Seryozha ; what
must he think ? " And each time my mother controlled
herself and made me go on with my story. When I had
ended, she sent my sister and me off to the parlour, telling
nurse that she wished to lie down, and we were to sit quiet
and not walk about. But I soon guessed that we were
got rid of, because my mother wished to speak to my father
with no one present. I even heard through the locked and
curtained door the sound of whispering, expressive and
distinct, and then a heated discussion carried on in a low
voice, sometimes raised for a few words. I only half
understood the situation , but I made out that my mother
was raging at our relations for their treatment of us, and
that my father was taking up the cudgels in their defence.
From all this I drew the conclusion that our further stay
would be short ; and I was not mistaken.

Next it came to my turn to ask my parents about their
experiences at Orenburg. From their accounts, and their
conversations with others, I learnt to my great joy that
Dr. Deobolt had found no sign of consumption in my
mother. But he did find other alarming symptoms, for
which he began to treat her. At first the treatment did her
much good, but later the separation from her children
was so distressing to her that the doctor had to let her go.
He had given her medicines to last through the winter ; and
in spring she was to drink *koumiss*,* for which purpose we
were to go to a pretty village where my father and Yevséitch
and I would fish. All this brought peace and joy to me ;
and, best of all, as others said and I could see for myself,
my mother grew better and stronger. My timidity quickly
passed off, and gloomy Bagrovo became a cheerful place.

* Mare's milk, fermented.

I thought—and perhaps it really was so—that every one there became kinder and more attentive to us, and cared more about us. In my childish mind I believed that they had all become fond of us. Even now, however, I think that, during that last week of our visit, grandfather did become fond of me, and that his change of feeling began from the moment when he saw with his own eyes my warm attachment to my father. He told me himself that he had taken me for a spoilt mother's darling, caring little for my father and still less for his relations, and despising every one at Bagrovo. This had clearly been suggested to him; and the old man was confirmed in these opinions by my bearing · I was not demonstrative and looked sad. and his presence was a cause of timidity and even terror. But now, when he was kind to me, when my grief and fear for my mother had ceased, when my heart was light and I showed affection to him—it was very natural that he began to love me. A few days worked a complete change in me : I became lively and even mischievous ; I ran constantly to grandfather to tell him whatever came into my head, and at once gave him the treat of hearing me read my favourite book. Grandfather accepted all this with cordiality : the gloomy old man seemed to have become kind and affectionate. I remember well his admiration of the affection between my sister and me. She would be sitting on his knee, listening to my chatter or reading ; suddenly, for no reason, she would jump down, run to me and kiss me, and then climb up on his knee again. When he asked, " What made you jump down, little fawn ? " she would answer, " I wanted to kiss brother." In a word, there grew up between grandfather and me such loving ties and such frank relations, that every one else had to respect them and dared not interfere with them. Our cousins, who were in high favour before, now had chairs by the stove. while we sat on grandfather's bed ; when they saw that he was taken up with us and paid no attention whatever to them, the " General's daughters " (as they were called) got tired of silence ; taking no interest in our conversations, they stole out of the room to the servants' hall, where they found it much more lively.

Though my mother said nothing to me, yet I found out from her conversations, not always quite pleasant, with my father, that she had had a heated interview with my grandmother and aunt, or, to put it plainly, had quarrelled with them. "Don't blame us," grandmother had answered; " we did not venture to go near your children. We mind our own business ; we are plain country people, and don't know your town ways." But my mother's anger fell chiefly on our nurse. Agatha shed tears when rebuked, and I felt very sorry for her ; but she went on telling lies all the time, solemnly swearing that she had never left us day or night, and appealing to Yevséitch and me as witnesses. When I asked, " Why do you say what is not true, Nana ? "—she answered that it was a sin and a shame for me to attack her, and burst out in floods of tears. I was dumbfounded; I even wondered whether I was really guilty of false witness against Agatha ; but then Yevséitch, who had caught her in the act when she was gadding all about the village, gave peace to the scruples of my childish conscience. After this scene my mother told my father that nothing in the world would induce her to keep Agatha as nurse : on our return to Ufa, she should be dismissed without fail.

Preparations for our journey were hastily begun. My father's leave of absence had come to an end, and it was now autumn. The day before our departure, my aunt Aksinya came over ; my sister and I were delighted to see our kind aunt, and made much of her. My mother, before grandfather and all the party, thanked her warmly for all her kindness and attention to her godson and the little girl, and assured her that she would never, while she lived, forget what her sister-in-law had done. Young as I was, I noticed that grandmother and my Aunt Tatyana were much alarmed by what my mother said. I learnt the reason later—they were afraid of grandfather. I also heard my father scold my mother : " A good thing," he said, " that my father did not hear how you thanked my sister Aksinya, and did not draw his conclusions from it; if he had, it might have ended in mischief. Surely you have had it out already with my mother and sister, and need not bring

his wrath upon them. You know, we are off to-morrow."
My mother sighed and said she had lost patience and
forgotten herself when she said it, and confessed that she
had acted heedlessly. But when my godmother came to
our room, my mother thanked her again with tears and
kissed her hands

At last our packing and preparations were complete.
Grandfather took a kind farewell of us, made the sign of
the Cross on us, and went so far as to say : " It's a pity it is
so late in the season ; else you should have stayed a week
longer. Things were not comfortable for you this time ;
I will have a separate room built for you and the children."
The others all said good-bye many times ; the kissing and
embracing went on for a long time. and tears were shed.
I was quite convinced that they were now much attached to
us, and was sorry for them, especially for grandfather.

On our way back to Ufa, we again visited Parashino,
but only for the night ; and our journey was far less agreeable   The weather was either damp or cold : it was impossible to camp out of doors, and the Choovash and Tatar
villages, where we halted for meals or for the night, were
not to our taste. With the Tatars we were better off,
because their huts were " white," i.e. furnished with
chimneys ; but our halts in the smoky Choovash huts
were beyond bearing. We started so early each morning,
that we had to stop to feed the horses at an hour when the
fires were still burning in their stoves ; though the door
was kept open we were obliged to lie down on the settles,
to escape suffocation from the smoke. My mother was
much afraid that we would catch cold ; and we generally
had a warm coverlet over us as we lay. My mother's eyes
were affected by the smoke ; and it was a whole month
before they got better. We drove for five days and
arrived at Ufa on the sixth.

CHAPTER VIII

A WINTER AT UFA

AFTER such a long, tiresome, and fatiguing journey, I was much pleased with our spacious house at Ufa and its large high rooms, with the company of my dog Soorka who was delighted to see me again, and with freedom to run about and play and make a noise where I liked. We found in the house unexpected guests, whom my mother was very glad to see : these were her two brothers, Serghéi Nikolaitch and Alexander Nikolaitch, officers in some dragoon regiment, who were on furlough for several months. I fell in love at first sight with both my uncles : both were young and handsome, kind and merry, especially Alexander, who laughed and jested from morning till night, and kept us all amused. Having been educated at Moscow in a boarding-school connected with the University, they liked reading and could repeat poetry To me this was an entire novelty : till then I had no notion what poetry was, or how it should be read. Besides all this, my Uncle Serghéi was very fond of drawing, and drew and painted well ; he had with him a paint-box and brushes, an enchanting sight in itself to me. I liked to look at pictures, and the art of making them seemed to me something magical and preternatural; hence my Uncle Serghéi was a superior being in my eyes.

The last week at Bagrovo had done much to remove the painful impression made on me by our life there ; and also the long journey had prepared me for the life which awaited us at Ufa ; but still I felt an indescribable happiness, which soon passed into calm confidence, when I saw what love was shown to me by my uncles and the intimate friends of my parents, and how much kindness by all their acquaint-ances. This feeling had such an effect on me that I

suddenly " developed," as people said : that is, I became
bolder, sturdier, livelier. All saw the change and said that
I had grown in wisdom and stature. I must confess that I
also became more vain and selfish, as a result of these
compliments.

My uncles were put up in a room by themselves, with
one door opening into the parlour and another which led
through a passage-room into a large carpenter's shop.
In the lifetime of my maternal grandfather, this had been
his office ; but now Michéi, the husband of our nurse,
Agatha, a very passionate and rude man, lived and worked
there at his trade as a carpenter. I hardly knew of his
existence before; but my uncles liked to go to the workshop
sometimes, to tease Michéi. He got angry, abused them,
chased them, and sometimes struck them with his wooden
mallet ; while they were much amused and laughed
heartily at his vehemence. I was amused too, never
suspecting that I should have to suffer much myself from
amusement of this kind.

My mother's health was obviously better ; and I
noticed that we had many more visitors than we used to
have. I may, however, have been mistaken ; for I was
still a child the year before, and not quite restored to
health, so that I took less notice of what went on in the
house. I knew little of most of our visitors ; only those
who came almost daily and were devoted to all our family,
were well known to me then and are not forgotten now.
I will give a list of them : old Mme. Myortvavo and her two
sons, Dmitri and Stepan ; the Chichagoffs ; the Knyazhevitches, who had two boys about my age ; Mme.
Voyetskaya, who had a special attraction for me because
she was called Sofya Nikolayevna like my mother, and
her sister Mlle. Pekaiskaya. Among officers, our most
frequent visitors were General Mansuroff with his wife and
two daughters ; General Count Langeron, and Colonel L. N.
Engelhardt ; Adjutant Volkoff and another officer, Christo-
phovitch, were friends of my uncles, and came to the house
almost daily. So did Dr. Avenarius, a very old friend of
the family. We made friends with the Knyazhevitch and
Mansuroff children and often played with them. The two

boys were active and vigorous. Brought up hardily by their parents, they knew nothing of colds, and ate what they liked, while I, on the contrary, never dared to eat anything outside my regular diet without leave from my mother, and was not allowed to go out in damp weather. It must be remembered that I had lain in a critical condition for eighteen months; it was not surprising that I should be watched and coddled; but my little sister had no reason to be confined to the same strict diet and abstinence from fresh air.

Sometimes there was a dinner-party; and then—my word! what pains my mother took together with our cook, Makéi, who understood his business very badly. There was one dish of almond pastry, or almond cake, which she always made herself; and to watch the process of its production was one of my chief delights. Under my attentive eyes, she soaked the almonds in boiling water, cleaned off the skins when they loosened, and chose out the very cleanest and whitest almonds; then she had them pounded, if a cake was to be made of almond paste; if not, she cut them up herself with scissors, and kneaded the cut pieces into the white of eggs beaten up with sugar, and made wonderful shapes out of them, little wreaths or crowns, or flower-heads, or stars. This was laid on an iron plate dredged over with flour, and then placed in the kitchen stove, from which it came forth just before the dinner, quite ready and baked to a turn. At a sign from me, my mother would run out of the drawing-room and put on a long white apron over her pretty evening dress; then she would carefully remove the wonderful pastry from the iron plate with a knife, and pour raspberry vinegar over each of the little figures; finally she placed it on a large dish, and went back to her guests. As I sat at table, I was always impatient for the appearance of the almond pastry, partly because I had a sweet tooth, but more because I anticipated with such pleasure the compliments paid to the pretty dainty by our guests, when they took up one little figure after another, and declared that for almond pastry no house could compare with Sofya Nikolayevna's. In my triumph I could not sit quiet on my high chair : I could not help whispering to my neighbour at the table, " Mamma made it all herself ! "

I remember that our parties were gayer then than they ever were during the rest of our life at Ufa ; and yet I knew that the want of money was felt every day, and that we were poorer and lived less comfortably than our friends. Of the officers who came to the house, my favourite at first was Leo Engelhardt ; his bulk and stature made him seem a hero among the rest, and he was handsome as well. I was a great favourite with him, and often sat on his knee, fascinated by his big voice and stories of war, and looking with awe at the two crosses which hung on his breast, especially the little gold cross with rounded points and this inscription, " The Taking of Otchakoff, December 6, 1788." I said that he was my favourite *at first*, because I afterwards came to fear him. He frightened me by saying one day, " Would you like to join the Army, Seryozha ? " " No," said I, and he went on : " You ought to be ashamed of yourself ; as a noble, you are bound to serve your country with the sword. not the pen Would you like to be a grenadier ? I'll bring you a grenadier's cap and dirk." I was terrified, and ran away from him. He took a fancy to continue the joke, and said to me next day, when he saw me keeping away from him, " O you little coward, if you are afraid to enter the service, I will take you by force." After that I never went near the Colonel, unless I was specially told to by my mother, and then I cried. I was confirmed in this fear by a boy who often came to the house, known as " one-eyed Andrusha," the son of a kind woman who was devoted to our family. He was older than I, and I believed him. Later I thought that he spoke thus on purpose to frighten me.

Next to reading, I took most delight in watching my Uncle Serghéi while he drew. Less fond of society than my other uncle, his younger brother, who was generally called a flirt, he often painted small pictures for me and also fairly large pictures for himself. I found it hard to wait till he sat down at the table in his room, on which I had placed beforehand a glass of water and a clean china plate. Some time before the appointed hour, I kept close to my uncle and tried to catch his eye ; if that failed, I pulled his sleeve, saying in the most beseeching voice, " Uncle, let us go and paint." At last he sat down at the table, rubbed his colours on the plate, and dipped his brush in the water : from that moment my eyes were riveted on his hand, and I welcomed with exclamations of joy every new leaf added to a tree, or beak to a bird, or any feature to a human countenance. Seeing my enthusiasm, my uncle took a fancy to teach me the art. With much pains he prepared models for me, circles and semi-circles, large and small, shaded and unshaded, placed in squares traced beforehand ; and, later, eyes, eyebrows and so on. As soon as he sat down to paint himself, he made me draw at another table. But at first the lessons were a failure, because I was constantly jumping up to watch him at work ; and, when he ordered me to sit still, I gazed at him with staring eyes or climbed on my chair, hoping to get at least a glimpse. Seeing that this would be useless, he made me draw at different hours. He was not mistaken : in a short time I was, for my age, brilliantly successful. He was delighted and prophesied that I would do great things as an artist. But not all prophecies are verified ; and, when I grew up, I could not draw those very circles which I had drawn as a child.

In the book department, my library, which consisted of *The Mirror of Virtue* and the twelve parts of *Reading for Children*, was doubled by the acquisition of two new books— *The Child's Library*, of Shishkoff, and *The History of the Younger Cyrus and the Return of the Ten Thousand Greeks*, by Xenophon. These books too were the gift of my old friend, M. Anitchkoff ; and he also gave me a thick manuscript volume, of which I cannot now give even the title. I only remember that it contained a number of plans and drawings very carefully made and coloured. I did not understand it at all, but I much enjoyed turning over the leaves with my sister and explaining to her the meaning and purpose of each illustration. But I had to invent every word, as I had not the least idea what the book was about. How amused I should be now to hear the nonsense I talked then ! *The Child's Library*, composed by Herr

Campe, and translated from the German by A. S. Shishkoff, and especially the songs for children which I soon learnt by heart, enchanted me. That was little wonder; but it is surprising that Xenophon pleased me just as much and became my favourite reading in the years that followed. Even now I recollect this book, as if it had never left my table; its appearance even is so deeply engraved in my memory that I seem to see it before me, with the ink-stains on many of its pages, the thumb-marks, and the dogs' ears on some of its leaves. The battle of Cyrus against his brother Artaxerxes, his death in the battle, the return of the Ten Thousand Greeks under the hostile observation of a great Persian army, the Greek phalanx, the Dorian dances, the constant skirmishes with barbarians, and at last the sea, their means of return to Greece, the sea which the brave soldiers beheld with such rapture, exclaiming " Thalatta, thalatta ! "—all this became so familiar to me that even now I remember it all with perfect clearness.

Such was the calm and happy current of my life during the first few months. I cannot remember exactly when it began to get rough : the change came gradually. My two uncles and their friend, Volkoff, began to find pleasure in teasing me. Beginning with military service, they told me that an *ukase* * had been published, requiring the eldest son of every noble to serve in the Army. When I replied that this was a mere invention of theirs, the rogues wrote out an *ukase* in large letters and attached a seal of some kind to it; and this device was too much for me. My belief was due mainly to " one-eyed Andrusha," who now came daily to the house and was probably in league with the officers. This silly jest, which went on some time, cost me no little emotion and mortification and many tears. The worst was that I, being naturally hot-tempered, resented their ridicule and began to say rude things, of which I had been incapable before. The laughter caused by my language encouraged me to carry my abuse to such lengths that I was scolded and told to apologise. But, in my childishness, I thought myself entirely in the right and refused to apologise; so that I was made to stand in the

* Imperial edict

corner and reduced at last to the necessity of asking pardon.
My mother did, indeed, explain to me that it was all a
joke, and that I ought not to get angry but to reply with a
jest ; but here lay the trouble, that a child cannot clearly
distinguish the boundary between jest and earnest. Sometimes, for a long time I disbelieved what my persecutors
said, and answered them with laughter , but then suddenly
I began somehow to believe them ; and all at once I was
hurt by their ridicule, lost control of myself in my rage, and
paid my enemies back, as well as I knew how, with violent
abuse. Volkoff caught it from me more than the others ;
but the scene always ended in my discomfiture. When they
tired of teasing me about the Army—custom had made me
less irritable on that point—they found out another means
of working on an equally sensitive chord in my heart.
One day, my uncle unexpectedly informed me, with a
serious air of mystery, that Volkoff wished to marry my
sister and carry her off with him to a campaign.   I
believed him, and though quite puzzled, understood this
much, that it was intended to separate my sister and me
and to turn her into a kind of soldier.   I had never liked
Volkoff, and now rage and hatred, such hatred as a child
can feel, filled my heart against him.   To keep up the
joke, Volkoff told me next day with an important air,
that my father and mother had agreed to give him my
sister's hand, and begged for my consent as well.   This
led to many sad consequences.   Furious with anger. I
abused Volkoff, and threatened to shoot him if he laid
a finger on my sister.

Just at this time, the same gentleman had an absurd
and unpleasant adventure, which looked like a punishment
for his love of teasing.   In my folly, I was delighted at it,
and said, " You see, God has punished him for wanting
to carry off my sister."   The adventure was as follows.
There was a ball at the Governor's house, on the occasion
of some festival.   Volkoff, with his hair powdered, and in
evening dress with silk stockings and pumps, drove to our
house, intending to go with my uncles to the ball.   While
they were dressing, Volkoff, for want of occupation, went
into the carpenter's shop and began to tease Michéi as

G

usual, and hinder him at his work. Michéi was more out of
temper than usual ; at first, he kept to abuse, but soon he
lost all patience and hit Volkoff such a shrewd blow with
his mallet, that a huge bump rose on his forehead in one
moment, and one eye was closed up. To go to the ball
was out of the question. My uncles laughed heartily, but
Volkoff wept with pain and vexation at missing the ball on
which he had set his heart. Of course, the affair became
generally known, and the sight of Volkoff raised a laugh ;
he was forced to keep the house for some days, and did not
even visit us. For a whole month I was safe from his
hateful teasing.

Earlier than this, I had heard casually that my father
was buying some land among the Bashkirs ; and now this
purchase was legally completed. Over 19,000 acres of
excellent land on the river Byélaya, thirty versts from Ufa,
with a number of islands of which one was about three
versts in length, were bought for a trifling sum. My
father's description was enthusiastic and detailed ; he
told me of the great quantity of birds and fish in the district,
the berries of all sorts, the islands, the grand woods that
grew there. His descriptions charmed me and excited my
imagination so strongly that even in my sleep I talked of
this new and beautiful land. In addition, in the legal
documents it was called " the Sergéyef estate," and the
village, which was to be built there the following spring, was
already called Sergéyevka, after me This pleased me.
The feeling of property, of the exclusive possession of anything, though it may puzzle a child, has power to interest
him, and gives him a peculiar satisfaction (it was so with
me at least) ; and therefore, though I was not a grasping
boy, I set great store by the fact that Sergéyevka was mine,
and never spoke of it without adding this possessive pro-
noun. My mother was to go there in spring to drink
koumiss, according to Deobolt's prescription. I counted
the days and hours in anticipation of this happy event,
and never tired of speaking about Sergéyevka to all our
visitors, my parents, and my sister with her new nurse,
Parasha.

I forgot to say that Agatha had been sent away long

ago. My mother took as her own maid instead of Parasha a hump-backed woman, whose name was Katerina, though she was always called "The Princess," apparently as a joke, for there was no reason for it. She was a Kalmuck woman, who had been bought at some time by my maternal grandfather, and received her freedom after his death. My mother, out of charity, had let her live in the maids' room and given her food and clothing; but now that she had set her own maid to mind my sister, she tried " the Princess " in Parasha's place. But it soon proved quite impossible to get on with the Kalmuck woman : she was a true Asiatic, cunning, servile, bad tempered, and capricious, so that my mother soon grew tired of her and sent her back to the maids' room. We were forbidden to speak to her; and indeed conversation with her might have been bad for children. All her superiors, old and young she was in the habit of flattering to their faces, and was profuse in her servility ; but behind their backs, her language was very different. She was constantly carrying tales against all our servants to my parents ; but with the servants she abused my parents, and nearly made mischief between my mother and Parasha. She even tried in passing to sow discord between my sister and me. I never concealed from my mother anything I heard, or indeed a single thought of my own ; so, of course, I made her my confidante in this case, and she made haste to remove this dangerous creature from proximity to us. The hunchback, however, lived on in our house under the name of "the Princess" to an advanced age.

When the bump produced by Michéi's mallet on Volkoff's forehead had been forgotten, he and my uncles began again to torment and tease me ; and this time my dear Sergéyevka served as a very effectual means for their object. First Volkoff urged me to give him Sergéyevka ; next he proposed to buy it of my father. Of course, I got angry and said various foolish things. Then they repeated their former device, again with complete success : they composed and wrote out, not an *ukase* this time, but a contract of marriage, which stated that my parents, with my consent as the reputed owner of Sergéyevka, gave it as my sister's dowry to P. N. Volkoff to be his property for ever. The document was signed by my father and mother, of course with forged signatures; but, as I could not write, my Uncle Serghéi, had signed it for me! I, poor child, was utterly dumbfounded. I did not believe in the consent of my parents, and I knew my own dissent only too well; but at the same time I fully believed that this document, which my uncle called a title-deed, robbed me at once of my sister and of my estate. Apart from my bitter grief at such appalling losses, I was irritated and wounded in my inmost heart by such an impudent fraud. My fury went beyond all bounds and darkened my judgment. I poured out on my uncle all the abusive words I knew: I called him a cheat, a pettifogging swindler, and a thief; and as for Volkoff, the chief culprit and criminal, I intended to shoot him without mercy, whenever I could get a gun, or hunt him down with Soorka (the house dog, as my readers may remember); but, not to postpone my revenge, I ran like a madman out of the room, rushed into the workshop, caught up a mallet, ran back with it to the drawing-room, and, when I got close to Volkoff, hurled it straight at his face. Such are the lengths to which foolish joking can drive a good-natured and peaceable child! Luckily, the blow was trifling; but I was dealt with severely. A punishment, of which I knew nothing previously but by hearsay, was put in practice for my benefit. I was dressed in garments of some coarse grey stuff, shut up in a quite empty room, and made to stand in a corner, under the eye of Yephrem Yevséitch. How my dear little sister cried and sobbed, when she witnessed the tragedy! It took place in the morning; all the time till dinner I raged and wept; in vain Yevséitch tried to convince me that it was wrong to fly into such a passion, abuse my uncle, and fight with Volkoff; in vain he said that it was all a joke, that little girls don't get married, and that it was impossible to take Sergéyevka from us against our will. He urged me to confess and ask pardon, but in vain: I turned a deaf ear to his advice. At last I stopped crying, but I hardened my heart and declared I was not guilty: if they did it on purpose to deceive me, that made no difference; they ought

to be punished for it by degradation to the ranks and be
sent to the front ; it was *their* duty to ask *my* forgiveness.
My mother, who suffered more than I, came constantly to
the door, to hear what I was saying, and to look at me
through the key-hole ; but she had the firmness to stay outside till dinner-time. Then at last she came and stayed
alone with me, using every effort to convince me of my
fault. For a long time she went on ; her words now
tender and affectionate, now severe and monitory, but
always carrying conviction, and her tears over my
obstinacy, at last shook my resolution : I confessed my
fault towards her and even towards my uncle, whom I
loved very much, especially for the painting ; but I refused
absolutely to admit any fault against Volkoff , I was ready
to beg pardon of all except him. My mother was unwilling
to accept any compromise : she hardened her heart and
said that I should have no dinner and stay in the corner
until I was conscious of my guilt and sincerely asked pardon
of Volkoff; then she went away to dinner, at which visitors
were expected. I only learnt later what I had no idea of
then—the suffering which this firmness inflicted on her
loving heart. But her darling's moral good, sometimes
perhaps mistakenly conceived, always counted for more
with her than her own suffering, which was at that time
dangerous to her health. Yevséitch was told to sit in the
next room, and I was left alone. At once my imagination
set to work. I imagined myself a hero and a martyr, such
as I had read or heard of, suffering for truth and justice.
Already I could see my hour of triumph : open flew the
door ; in came my father and mother, my uncles and the
visitors ; they praised my fortitude, acknowledged themselves in the wrong, and said they had only wished to put
me to the proof; I was dressed in new clothes and taken
in to dinner. Alas ! the door remained shut, nobody
came in, and the only sound came from Yevséitch, who
was beginning to snore in the next room ; my bright
visions vanished like smoke, and I began to feel weariness,
hunger, and headache. But again my imagination became
busy : I fancied myself banished from home for my
obstinacy and wandering through the streets at night ; no

one would give me shelter ; I was attacked by fierce mad dogs (a great terror of mine) ; they were just going to bite me, when Volkoff appeared, saved my life, and took me back to my parents ; I forgave Volkoff, and my generosity gave me some satisfaction. A host of similar pictures swarmed through my brain ; and in all I played the chief part, I was the hero, in his hour of triumph or of final ruin. The word " hero " was unknown to me then ; but the meaning of it, so seducing to a child, was clearly present in all my fancies. At last I was worn out by emotion and tears and long standing. I might, of course, have sat down on the floor, as there was no one in the room ; but I had been told to stand in the corner, and, weary as I was, nothing would have induced me to sit down. Two hours after dinner, our kind friend, Dr. Avenarius, came to see me. He too urged me to apologise to Volkoff ; but I would not. He offered me a plate of soup ; but I refused. I said : " I will eat it if mamma tells me to ; but I don't want food myself." Avenarius was soon followed by my mother ; I saw that she was much distressed. She told me to eat, and I did what I was told submissively, though I had no fancy for food. She asked me : " Don't you feel you have done wrong to Volkoff ? don't you repent of your fault and wish to apologise to him ? " I replied that I was innocent as regards Volkoff, but I was ready to beg his pardon, if she told me to   " You are obstinate," she said ; " when you think better of it, send Yevséitch for me ; then I will forgive you." Yevséitch brought in a candle and placed it on the window-sill. My mother told him to stay with me, to sit by the door, and not to speak ; then she went out. Very soon after taking food, I felt unwell : my head ached severely, and I was hot. Drowsiness began to master me ; my knees gradually began to bend ; at last weariness conquered me, my legs somehow slipped from under me, I sat down in the corner and fell fast asleep. I was told afterwards that Yevséitch was drowsy too, and that my father found us both asleep, when he came to our room. When I woke, the doctor was feeling my pulse and head ; I was very feverish, even delirious, and he ordered that I should be taken to the nursery and put to bed. When I woke, or rather, became conscious, quite late next day, I was still weak and feverish and took some time to understand the position of affairs; but at last I understood that excitement and weariness had brought on an illness. All were alarmed by my condition, and my mother was in despair. And now my dreams came true, though not for the reasons I had imagined. All felt that they were to blame : my Uncle Serghéi sat by my bed and shed tears ; Volkoff stood outside the door, on the verge of tears, too, and not venturing to come in, for fear of exciting the patient ; my father looked sadly in my face, and my mother—one look at her face showed clearly enough what sort of a night *she* had passed ! Then the doctor came in and cleared the room, giving orders that I was to be kept perfectly quiet for the present. It took me some time to get well. Two days later, I was out of bed and sitting at a table, playing some game with my sister, who could not express her joy at my recovery. Suddenly I felt a strong desire to see my persecutors, to beg their forgiveness, and to make it up with them in such a way that no one should feel anger against me. At once I called my mother from her bedroom and told her my wish. She embraced me, with tears of joy (so she told me) because of my goodness. Volkoff was with my uncles at the time, and all three came together to my room. They kissed me and promised never to tease me again. My mother smiled and said very decidedly : " Even if you do take it into your heads, I will never allow it again. I was the chief sinner, and I have been the chief sufferer. It is a lesson which I will never forget."

When I had quite recovered my health, I was soon as cheerful and playful as ever. I soon forgot the sorrowful affair ; but I could not forget that I had been called " illiterate," and that for this reason my uncle had signed for me the document, the so-called contract or settlement. At the time I denied the imputation ; but now I wished to remedy this defect and begged my parents to teach me writing. My Uncle Serghéi offered to satisfy my desire. At first my teacher made me draw pot-hooks and hangers, which did not please me at all, because I wished to begin

at once with letters , but my uncle asserted that I should
never write a good hand unless I learnt the art according
to the rules, and that I must go through the preliminary
training and then set to work at copies. Resistance was
useless, and I had to obey; but meantime I learnt by
myself to write the whole alphabet, drawing each letter
from printed books. The process of learning to write was
long ; my uncles' leave came to an end, and they returned
to their regiment, with a firm resolve, however, to leave the
Army before long, as they found life at Ufa so agreeable.
My Uncle Serghéi, who was an excellent writer himself,
at his departure urged my father, who was anxious that I
should write a good hand, to get for me a teacher from the
local school. This man's name was Matvyéi Vassílitch
(his surname I never heard) ; he was a quiet and good-
natured man. He wrote copies in a hand as good as print,
and engaged to teach me on the same lines as my uncle.
An endless prospect of pot-hooks and hangers bored me
and made me idle ; so, in order that I might be more
ready to take trouble, Andrusha was set down to learn with
me. He had begun long before me at the local school
under the same teacher. This plan worked to some
extent : I was ashamed that Andrusha should beat me in
writing, and, as his performance was not at all remarkable,
I tried to catch him up, and actually did so very quickly.
Each lesson lasted two hours ; and, at the end of it, it was
the custom of our teacher to write on our copy-books one
of the following words : " middling," " not bad," " satisfactory," " good," " excellent." I soon noticed that
Matvyéi Vassílitch was unfair ; for, if Andrusha and I
both wrote badly, he gave me " not bad," and him
" middling " ; but, if we both wrote satisfactorily, then
I had " very good " or " excellent," while Andrusha had
only " good " ; and on the somewhat rare occasions when
my companion wrote better than I, we got identically the
same mark Observing this, I asked myself why our kind
master acted thus. No doubt he likes me better, I reflected,
probably because I have two sound eyes, while poor
Andrusha has one goggle-eye that looks like a white
button. I was soon confirmed in my belief by noticing

for the first time that Matvyéi Vassílitch showed more
liking for me than for my companion. All my observations
and inferences I repeated at once to my parents. They
exchanged glances and smiled but said nothing to me.
But soon there came a change in the verdicts upon our
work : exactly the same words made their appearance
in both copy-books—" not bad," or " satisfactory," or
" good." Then I understood that my father had probably
given a hint to our teacher. But Matvyéi Vassílitch continued to the end to treat me more kindly than Andrusha.

Even now I cannot understand what causes induced
my mother to send me once with Andrusha to the local
school. Probably, some one advised her to do so, and the
most likely person was M. Knyazhévitch ; and yet, if I
remember aright, his children did not attend the school.
However intelligent my mother was, still, owing to her
defective education, the notion of sending her son to such a
school could never have entered her head. It was a wild
notion then ; now things are changed ; and such a thought
might be intelligible in the case of any one, and might
serve to explain such a step. Be that as it may, once and
only once, on a day memorable to me, Andrusha and I
were conveyed in a sleigh, under the supervision of
Yevséitch, to the local school, which was held in a smallish
wooden house at the opposite end of the town. Yevséitch
handed us over personally to Matvyéi Vassílitch, who took
my hand and led me into a large ill-kept room, with much
noise and loud voices coming from it, which stopped the
instant we appeared. The room was furnished with rows
of desks, and benches of a kind new to me ; before the
front desk there stood a large square black-board, fastened
upon supports of some kind, and a boy stood by the board
with a pointed chalk in one hand and a dirty rag in the
other. Half the benches were occupied by boys of various
ages ; on the desks before them lay note-books, lesson-
books, and slates. Some of the scholars were very big and
tall, some very small ; many of them were in shirt sleeves,
many were dressed like beggars. Matvyéi Vassílitch led
me to the front desk, where he told the scholars to make
room for me at the end of the bench. He sat down himself

on a chair with a smallish table before it, not far from the
black-board. All this was quite new to me, and I looked
on with eager curiosity. Andrusha had disappeared from
my view upon entering the schoolroom. Suddenly
Matvyéi Vassilitch spoke in a tone quite unfamiliar to me :
in an angry voice and in a kind of sing-song, he said .
" Don't you know ? Then kneel down." At once the boy
beside the black-board placed the chalk and the dirty rag
very quietly on the desk, and knelt down behind the
board, where three boys whom I had not at first noticed
were kneeling already. They were all very cheerful
and began to scuffle and fight, whenever the master turned
his back to them. It was a lesson in arithmetic. The
teacher went on calling up the boys from a list, one after
the other. Thus he checked their attendance at the same
time ; and it turned out that half the scholars were absent.
The master marked the absentees on his list, occasionally
adding, " Three times absent, four times absent ! That
means a flogging ! " I grew stiff with fear. The boys who
were called up advanced to the board. where they had to
write the required figures with the chalk and count them
by some rule from right to left, repeating, " Units, tens,
hundreds." Many made mistakes in the counting, and it
seemed to me complicated and difficult, though I had
taught myself long before to write figures. Some of the
scholars showed knowledge and were praised by the master :
but even his praise was accompanied by words of abuse.
most of which were unknown to me. Sometimes a particularly choice phrase excited a general laugh, which
burst out in a moment and was hushed as quickly. When
he had gone through all the names on his list and tested
their relative knowledge of the subject, the master set
another arithmetic lesson for next day, about the places of
figures and the effect of a cipher. I did not understand it,
partly from ignorance of the matter, and partly because I
was sitting there more dead than alive, amazed by all that
I had seen. When he had set the lesson, Matvyéi Vassilitch
called in the school-keepers. Three of them came in,
armed with bundles of birch rods, and set to work to flog
the boys who were kneeling down. To me this scene was

terrible and disgusting : as soon as it began, I shut my
eyes and stuffed my fingers into my ears. My first instinct
was to run away, but I was shaking all over and dared
not move. The cries of the victims and the brutal comments of the master made their way to my hearing, in
spite of my stopped ears. At last they died away ; I
opened my eyes and found a lively noisy scene going on
around me. All the boys were collecting their belongings
and running out of the class-room, and the victims, running
with them, were just as merry and mischievous as the rest.
Then Matvyéi Vassilitch came up to me with the same
friendly air as usual, took my hand, and in the old quiet
voice asked me to present his humble respects to my father
and mother. Leading me out of the deserted room, he
handed me over to Yevséitch, who quickly wrapped me up
in a *shooba*,* and placed me in the sleigh. Andrusha was
sitting there already : " Well," he said, looking in my face,
" did you like the school ? " Getting no reply he added,
"Not frightened, were you ? It's like that every day."
When we got home, I terrified my mother, first by my
speechless excitement and tears, and then by my furious
denunciations of Matvyéi Vassilitch and his criminal proceedings. If my mother had had any idea of the ordinary
methods in vogue at a national school, nothing would have
induced her to expose me to such a violent shock. To calm
and console me was utterly impossible at first : for the
moment even my mother's power over me had no effect.
At last, when I had described in the minutest detail all
I had seen and heard, when I had vented my displeasure in
the strongest expressions known to me from books and
conversations, and when I had condemned Matvyéi Vassilitch to all the punishments I had ever heard of—then,
and not till then, I calmed down and became able to listen
intelligently to my mother's sensible comments. She
went on a long time, and, in order to quiet me, was obliged
to touch on much which was new to me and hardly within
the scope of my intelligence at that age. It was hard for
me, with a child's mind and feelings, to reconcile myself
to such ideas as these : that the sight I had witnessed was

* Fur coat

not downright wickedness, like highway robbery, for which
Matvyéi Vassilitch deserved to suffer the death of a criminal,
that such actions were not only permitted but required of
him in the performance of his duty ; that even the parents
of his victims were grateful to him for his severity, and his
victims themselves would be grateful hereafter ; and
finally that Matvyéi Vassilitch, though he raged like a wild
beast and flogged his scholars, might yet remain a quiet,
honest, and kind man. I was still too young for an impression so heartrending, a lesson so terrible. It clouded
the clearness and calmness of my young mind. It was
long before I could get peace of mind ; and to Matvyéi
Vassilitch I took such an unconquerable aversion, that
within a month it became necessary to stop his visits. I
continued my writing lessons alone, or sometimes with
Andrusha   As there was no other teacher in the town,
my parents undertook the duty themselves ; their chief
care was that my writing should resemble the copies as
closely as possible.   As my mother for some reason did
not altogether approve of the companionship of Andrusha,
his visits became rarer.   So for society of my own age,
apart from the Knyazhevitch and Mansuroff children
who sometimes paid us visits and often took part in our
games and amusements, I was confined to the company of
my dear little sister, who grew more intelligent every day,
and thus more capable of sharing all my hobbies, impressions, and amusements.

My mother's health had improved but was not quite
satisfactory ; and, in order that we might take advantage
of the summer at Sergéyevka, preparations were now made
for our move. Some huts and outhouses were bought
there ; and during Lent these were removed and erected
on a different spot chosen by my father, who went there on
purpose. In spite of my earnest entreaties, my mother
would not let me go with him. Sergéyevka filled my
thoughts to the exclusion of everything else ; and my
father's descriptions every day added fire to my imagination. The journey to Bagrovo and all the beauties of
nature I had seen then, were not forgotten, but only
covered up to some extent by the novelty of other

impressions, by life at Bagrovo and life at Ufa ; but, when
spring came on, my warm love of nature awoke . I longed
so to see the green fields and forests, the waters and mountains, to scamper over the fields with Soorka, to throw my
line into the rivers, that the present lost all its interest for
me, and I woke up and went to sleep every day thinking
of Sergéyevka. Holy Week went by, unnoticed by me.
I was too young of course to understand its deeper meaning ;
but I paid little attention even to what is intelligible to
children—the happy faces and holiday clothes, the ringing
of bells, the constant arrival of visitors, the coloured Easter
eggs, and so on Our parish church stood high, and the
snow round it had long been melting. My great satisfaction was to watch the turbid and noisy course of the
spring floods as they ran past the high steps of our house ;
a still greater pleasure, but one seldom permitted me, was
to take a little stick and clear out the rivulets of spring
water. From our steps we could see the river Byélaya,
and I waited impatiently for the ice to melt. Whenever
I asked my father or Yevséitch when we should start for
Sergéyevka, their regular answer was, " Oh, when the
river comes down." And, at last, that longed-for day and
hour arrived. Yevséitch hurried to my nursery, looked
in, and said in an excited happy voice, " The river is
moving ! " My mother gave leave, and in a moment I
was warmly wrapped up and standing at the top of the
steps. There I eagerly followed the movement, between
solid banks, of a huge strip of ice, blue and dark and, in
some places, yellow. The ice-track across the stream had
already floated some distance down ; and an unlucky
black cow was running. like a mad creature, from side to
side of the track. The women and girls beside me greeted
with cries of pity each unsuccessful movement of the
distracted creature , the sound of its lowing came to my
ears, and I felt very sorry for it. The river made a sudden
bend behind a steep cliff, which soon concealed from us
the track and the black cow rushing about on it. Suddenly
two dogs were seen on the ice ; but their frantic springs
excited laughter rather than pity from the bystanders, as
all were convinced that the dogs would not be drowned, but

would make their way to the side by jumping or swimming. Glad to believe this, I forgot about the poor cow
and joined in the laughter. The dogs soon justified the
general expectation by getting across to the bank. Still the
ice kept coming down and down, in a hard, thick, unbroken
mass. Yevséitch, fearing the high cold wind, said to me :
" Let us go back into the house, my little falcon , it will
take time for the river to break up, and you will be frozen.
Better let me tell you, when the ice begins to crack." Very
unwillingly I obeyed ; but my mother was much pleased
and praised both Yevséitch and me. Not less than an
hour passed before Yevséitch came and announced that the
ice was breaking. Getting my mother's leave for a short
absence, I was wrapped up still more warmly and went out.
There I saw another new and strange scene. The ice was
cracking and breaking up into separate blocks, between
which the water splashed ; the blocks pursued one another ;
a big and strong one would submerge a weaker, or, if it
met with stubborn resistance, would rear up one edge into
the air and float far in that position ; sometimes both
blocks were smashed into little pieces and sank with a
crackling noise in the water. A dull noise, sometimes like
the sound of grinding or distant groaning, came clearly
to our ears. After admiring for some time this majestic
and even awful sight, I went back to my mother and eagerly
described what I had seen. My father came home from the
law-court, and I began with fresh eagerness and at greater
length to describe to him the melting of the river ; I saw
that he took more pleasure than my mother in the description. From that day the river became the constant
object of my observation. It began to overflow its banks
and inundate the meadow-land on one side. Every day
the picture was different, till at last the flood stretched
more than eight *versts* and became indistinguishable from
the clouds. To the left a sheet of water, clean and smooth
as glass, stretched further than the eye could see ; and
directly opposite our house, it was dotted either with the
tops of trees or with tall oaks, elms, and poplars half-
submerged, whose height one had never before quite
realised ; these looked like little floating islands. It was

long before the fields were clear of water ; and this delay
tantalised my impatience In vain my mother assured me
that she would not travel to Sergéyevka till the grass grew ;
I continued to believe that the river was the obstacle, and
that we should not start till it had returned within its
banks.   At last we began to have warm, even hot, weather ;
the river went back to its mean level, resting in its sandy
bed ; the fields had long been green, and the woods by the
river were green too—but we were still at Ufa. My
father declared that it was difficult to drive over places
inundated with spring floods, that the mud was terrible,
and that the road in the valleys was either washed
away or covered deep with slime ; but all such obstacles
seemed to me quite unworthy of attention. The wish to
hasten our departure became with me a morbid concen-
tration of all my thoughts and feelings upon one object.   I
was difficult to manage ; for nothing could occupy or
interest me   This might have been foreseen ; and
practical steps should have been taken to govern this
excitability of mine, this tendency to get entirely absorbed
in one idea, and to rush into extremes. In later years, I
have heard my mother regret that she paid too little
attention to this feature in my character, which proved a
serious hindrance in life and the cause of many mistakes.

I thought we should never start, when suddenly—Oh,
happy day !—my mother told me that we were to go
to-morrow !   I was half frantic with joy. My sister shared
my joy, but I think her feeling was mainly caused by mine.
I slept little that night.   I was quite ready before any one
was astir.   But at last the household awoke ; there was a
noise of running to and fro and of packing. The horses
were put in, the carriage brought round ; and at last, at
ten in the morning, we drove downhill to the ferry over the
river. As an addition to all my joy, Soorka was with us.

CHAPTER IX

SERGÉYEVKA is one of the red-letter periods in my earliest recollections of childhood. My feeling for nature was now stronger than at the time of our journey to Bagrovo, though far less so than it became some years later. My feeling at Sergéyevka was a quiet happiness, with none of the emotion that is almost pain. All the time I spent there that year seems to me like a happy holiday.

Just as we did the year before, we crossed the Byélaya in the ferry. I found just the same sand and pebbles on the far bank, but I took little notice of them now : the picture of Sergéyevka rose before me, *my* Sergéyevka, with its lake and woods and the river Byélaya. I waited with impatience, while our carriage and cart were crossing ; I looked on with impatience, while the horses were got ashore and put into the shafts ; and the loose white sand, along which we had to crawl for more than a *verst*, I found very tiresome. But at last we emerged from it into the wood by the river, green and flowering and fragrant. From every side came the cheerful singing of birds ; but all other notes were drowned by the whistles and calls and cadences of the nightingales. Whole swarms of bees and wasps hung buzzing round the trees in flower. Ah ! how delightful it was ! Traces of the recent inundation were everywhere to be seen : withered twigs and straw, coated with slime and mud already dried up by the sun, hung in tufts on the green bushes ; the trunks of great trees were thickly plastered high above their roots with slime and sand ; and the sand, now dry, sparkled in the sunlight. "Do you see, Seryozha, how high the flood came ? " said my father ; " that elm is almost covered with the stuff washed along ;

nearly all of it must have been submerged." My father
gave me many such explanations, which I handed on to
my sister, although she was sitting beside us and heard
my father as well as I did. Before long the truth of his
apprehensions was repeatedly confirmed: even now in
many places the road was damaged or washed away by
the spring floods; and in some hollows there was such a
slough that our strong horses had difficulty in dragging
the carriage through it. At last we got on to firm ground;
the horses set off at a brisk trot, and at 3 o'clock we reached
the village of Sergéyevka, as we already called it. As we
approached, we again came upon low ground, dotted with
bushes and trees here and there, and broken up by a
number of lakes, some of fair size and all already green with
rushes. Here the Byélaya, flowing about a *verst* distant
from Sergéyevka, covered the low ground with each spring
flood. Next we mounted a steepish hill, on whose level
surface we found a group of peasants' huts, new and old;
on the left, the long strip of the lake of Kishki and the
high bank on its far side were visible; immediately
opposite us lay a large and scattered Tatar village. To the
right were the green water meadows, which we had just
cut across; the pools of water sparkled like glass. We
turned a little to the right and came to our " manor-house,"
which was surrounded by a fresh green paling. The house
consisted of two peasants' huts, one new and the other old,
connected by a passage; near them was the hut for the
servants, still unroofed; while the rest of the enclosure
was occupied by a long shed thatched with straw, to serve
as a coach-house and stables. There were no steps up to
our door, but two large stones had been deposited there,
one on the top of the other. The new hut had no door,
and no window frames, though the openings for them had
been cut. My mother was not altogether pleased, and said
so to my father; but I found everything much more to my
taste than our town house at Ufa. My father declared
that the window frames would come next day: as the
weights were not ready yet, the frames would be fixed on
from outside; for a door, he advised her to make shift
with a rug. Then the unpacking and arrangement began:

H

chairs, beds, and tables had come before us. We soon sat
down to dinner. Our meal had been cooked beforehand on
a gridiron, in a hole dug near our paling, and tasted to us
very good; in this hole it was intended to make a clay oven
for our cooking in hot weather. My mother's fears were
calmed . she grew cheerful, and let me go with my father
to the lake, on which all my thoughts and wishes were
fixed. Yevséitch went with us and carried the fishing-
tackle which we had ready. My mother looked at us and
said laughing : " You forgot the doors and windows, but
you remembered the hooks and lines." I was so happy
that I could not feel my feet under me ; instead of walking
I ran and jumped, so that it was necessary to hold my hands.
And there it was at last, my noble lake, which I had so long
desired to see ; and noble it really was. The lake of
Kiishki was three *versts* in length and full of bays and capes ;
in breadth it was very uneven, varying from 150 yards to
half a *verst*. The far side was formed by a wooded height,
which sloped gently down to the water. On the left. the
lake ended suddenly in a narrow channel, by means of
which the Byélaya poured into it during the spring floods.
The other end of the lake, hidden by a bend of the shore,
was close to the large village already mentioned, called
Kiishki after the lake. The Russians naturally called both,
and also the new Russian village Sergéyevka, by the name of
Kishki * ; and the name suited the lake very well, because
it was long and crooked. The pure transparent water,
the sandy bottom, the leafy woods mirrored on the surface,
the green grass on the banks—all made such a delightful
picture that my father and Yevséitch were charmed as
well as I. Our side was especially picturesque, covered
with young grass and field-flowers ; there being no houses
there, it was free from all pollution. A score of oak trees,
of uncommon height and breadth, grew on the bank.
When we got to the waterside, we saw a wooden jetty projecting over the water. and a boat moored to it ; these were
fresh delights for me. Both were new : my father had
arranged about them beforehand, because the water was
so shallow, that it would have been impossible to fish

* *I.e.* kidneys.

without the jetty ; it turned out very handy also for washing clothes. The boat was intended for fishing with a net. Behind the jetty stood an enormous oak, whose trunk would have required several men to surround it with their arms ; and near it was the tallish stump of another oak, far thicker than the surviving tree. For curiosity, we all three climbed on to this mighty stump, and took up only a little corner of it. My father said that twenty men could have sat on it. He made me look at the axe-marks on the stump and on the tree, and told me that the Bashkirs, the real owners of the land, made marks of this kind on great oaks every hundred years. Many of their old men had assured him of this custom. On this stump there were only two marks, but five on the living tree; as the stump was much thicker and therefore much older, it was evident that the remaining marks were on the severed part of the trunk. My father added that he had seen an oak very much thicker, which had twelve marks and was therefore 1200 years old. I don't know how far the tales of the Bashkirs were true ; but my father believed them, and to me then they seemed gospel truth.

The lake swarmed with large fish of every kind. In flood-time the fish came in from the river; and, when the water began to fall, the native inhabitants blocked the channel of communication which was neither broad nor deep, so that all the fish were imprisoned in the lake till next spring. Large pike were constantly jumping out of the water in pursuit of the small fry which rushed wildly before them. In places near the grass banks, there was a ripple caused by shoals of fish crowding towards the shallows and even jumping out on the bank ; I was told that these were dropping their spawn. The commonest fish in the lake were perch and especially bream. We shook our lines free and began to fish. My father took the largest rod with a strong line, baited it with an uncommonly fat worm, and cast as far as he could ; he wanted to catch something big. Yevséitch and I had smaller tackle and small brandlings for bait. Our sport began instantly : fair-sized perch and pollen, a fish I had not seen before, took constantly. I got so excited—mad, Yevséitch called it—that I trembled in every limb and was hardly conscious of what I did. Every moment, a fish was landed and the line thrown in again; and my shouts, and Yevséitch's attempts to instruct me and restrain my transports, caused such a din that my father said, "It's impossible to get anything worth taking here beside you." He got into the boat with his big rod, and rowed to some distance, where he anchored himself with a stone and a rope, and began to fish. The fish were so numerous and so easily caught, that my excitement began to cool down; and so did my attendant's, who, to tell the truth, had been quite as excited himself. He began to consider how we could catch bigger fish. "We must go deeper, my little falcon," said he; "I'll put more worms on the hooks, and throw in a third line baited with bread." Of course I agreed at once. We raised our floats, so that they no longer stood but lay on the water; we put on larger worms, and Yevséitch fixed nearly a dozen on his own hook; then he baited the third line with a piece of bread-crumb the size of a hazel-nut At once the fish stopped taking, and complete still-ness began to reign around us. Then, as if on purpose to confirm what my father had said, a big fish of some kind took his bait; he played it a long time, while Yevséitch and I, standing on the jetty, took a lively interest in his proceedings. Suddenly he called out, "Broken away!" and pulled up his loose line; the hook, however, was all right. "I didn't give it time to swallow the bait," he complained; again he baited his hook and again threw in his line. Yevséitch was much distressed. "Dear, dear," he said, "no other fish will take now; the first getting away is a sure sign of bad luck." I had not seen the fish, because my father had not raised it to the surface; nor had I felt its weight, as I was not holding the rod; and I did not understand that it was possible to judge the size of a fish by the bending of the rod. Hence I did not take the loss so much to heart, and said that perhaps the fish was a small one. For some time we sat in perfect silence, without getting a single bite. I got tired of it, and asked Yevséitch to alter my tackle to what it was at first He did so, and at once my float turned up and the fish began to take.

But Yevséitch made no change in his own tackle, and his
floats lay quietly on the surface. I had now caught more
than twenty fish, two of which I could not pull out without
Yevséitch's help. To tell the truth, he had quite enough
to do, in taking each fish off my hook, throwing it into a
bucket of water, and baiting the hook again. This left him
no time to attend to his own lines ; and so he did not notice
at once that one of the rods had vanished from the jetty,
a fish having carried it fifty yards away. Suddenly
Yevséitch gave such a yell, that I was frightened and
Soorka who was with us began to bark. Yevséitch began
to beg and beseech my father to catch the floating rod ;
and my father hastened to fulfill the request : he pulled
up the stone by which he was anchored, and, using the oar
as a paddle, quickly caught up the rod and pulled out a
very large perch, which, without unhooking it, he placed
in the boat and brought over to us on the jetty In this
incident I took a much more lively interest ; the anxiety
of Yevséitch and his cries for help had excited me; I jumped
for joy, when we carried the perch to the bank, unhooked it,
and placed it in the bucket. Apparently the fish were
frightened by the noise and motion of the boat as it came
near ; for they stopped biting, and we sat a long time,
waiting in vain for more victims. Only towards evening,
when the sun was near setting, my father caught a large
bream, but kept it in the boat, for fear of frightening the
fish near him : he held up his prize with both arms, that we
might see it from where we were. The pollen were beginning to take with me again, when my father suddenly
noticed that a mist was beginning to rise off the lake, and
told Yevséitch to take me home. I was very unwilling to
go ; but I had had such a delightful day's fishing already
that I did not venture to ask leave to stay. With both
hands helping Yevséitch to carry the bucket full of water
and fish, though he did not need my help at all and was
rather hindered by it, I went gaily back to my expectant
mother. While I was fishing—either pulling out a fish,
or watching the motion of the float, or momentarily expecting a bite—I felt only the excitement of fear and hope
and the avidity of the sportsman ; real satisfaction and

complete happiness only came now, when I recalled all the
details with delight and told them over to Yevséitch, who
as a partaker of the sport, knew them as well as I did, and
yet, like a true sportsman, found equal pleasure in the
repetition and recollection of every incident. As we went,
we both spoke at the top of our voices and interrupted one
another ; sometimes we even stopped and set our bucket
down, in order to complete some exciting reminiscence—
how the float bobbed and was dragged under, how some
fish resisted or broke away ; then we caught up the bucket
again and hastened on. My mother was sitting on the stone
steps or, to speak more accurately, on the two stones which
took the place of steps as an approach to our unfinished
abode. she heard us coming some way off, and was surprised that we were so long in appearing. " What were
you and Yevséitch arguing about so loudly ? " she asked,
when we got close. Again I began to describe our doings,
and Yevséitch joined in. Though I had noticed more than
once before that my mother did not care to listen to my
eager descriptions of fishing, at that moment I entirely
forgot it. To confirm our story, Yevséitch and I kept pulling
out of the bucket first one fish and then another ; then, as
this proved troublesome, we shook out all our catch on the
ground ; but alas ! our fish produced no impression whatever upon my mother. When my story came to an end,
I noticed that a small fire was burning in front of my mother
with the smoke of its few sticks blowing straight in front of
her. When I asked the reason, she replied that she did
not know what to do, for the midges ; and at the same
instant she looked at my face and cried out, " Just look
what they've done to you ! Your face is all swollen and
bleeding." In fact, I was so bitten by the midges that my
face and neck and hands were all swollen ; and yet, in
my passion for the sport, I had never noticed it. Never
in my whole life and in no place have I found such multitudes of midges ; and they were reinforced by another kind
of gnat which I find even more intolerable, because it
makes its way into the mouth and nose and eyes. The
abundance of trees and of stagnant water accounted for
the number of insects. At last the midges actually routed

us, and my mother and I retreated to our own room. Having no door or windows, it offered no protection; but we sat down on the bed under an open-work canopy; and though it was stuffy sitting under it, yet we had peace. A canopy is the only specific against the attacks of midges and mosquitoes. It was dark before my father returned; he had caught two more large bream, and said that the fish had gone on taking, and, but for his fear of alarming us, he would have stayed all night in the boat. "Oh, when shall I be grown up," thought I, "and spend whole nights with Soorka fishing on the bank of river or lake?" The boat, I confess, rather alarmed me.

I slept sound under the same canopy as my sister, and we rose early next morning, active and cheerful. My mother was pleased to see that the wounds, inflicted on me the day before by the wicked midges, had left hardly any trace: my face, neck, and hands had been rubbed with some stuff at night, and now the swelling had gone down, and the redness and heat were less. My sister had not been much bitten, because she lay down early under our canopy.

The practical arrangement of our half-nomad life now began; and the chief thing to arrange was the special preparation of the *koumiss* and the regular use of it. For this purpose, it was necessary to have an interview with a Bashkir chief, Mavlyoot Iséitch—he was addressed thus, but spoken of as Mavlyootka—who was one of the landowners who had sold Sergéyevka to us. He lived either in the village of Kiishki or very near it; for, when my father sent to arrange an interview, the messenger returned very soon with the answer that Mavlyootka would come at once. And in fact we had hardly drunk our tea when a surprising figure, huge and shapeless, appeared on horseback at our gate. The figure rode up to the paling, dismounted easily, hitched his horse to the hedge, and rolled into our enclosure. We were sitting on our steps; my father walked to meet our guest, held out his hand, and said, "*Salaam malikum,** Mavlyoot Iséitch." I gazed openmouthed. Before me stood a man of vast height and

* For the Arabic *salamun 'alaikum,* "Peace be on thee!"

bulk—I heard afterwards that he stood over seven feet high
and weighed more than thirty stone—he wore a Cossack
tunic and very baggy plush trousers ; on the very top of
his huge head was stuck a Tatar skull-cap, embroidered
with gold but much stained. He had no neck at all, there
being no transition between the head and the vast shoulders.
When I saw his great sword trailing on the ground, I could
not help being afraid ; I thought at once, that the cunning
Tissaphernes, commander of the Persian army which fought
against the Younger Cyrus, must have been like that.   I
whispered this surmise of mine to my sister, and then to
my mother. When my mother laughed heartily, my fears
vanished. Mavlyootka sat down with some difficulty on
a seat which was brought out for him ; tea was offered him,
and he drank cup after cup. The business of preparing
the *koumiss* for my mother, about which she enquired
herself, was very simply and conveniently arranged. One of
Mavlyootka's seven wives was appointed on the spot to
discharge this duty : she was to come to us daily, bringing
a mare with her, to milk the right quantity from the mare,
and to ferment the milk in our pans, under my mother's
eyes. My mother was most particular in insisting on
perfect cleanliness in the preparation of the *koumiss*.
The payment was settled, and something was paid in
advance to Mavlyootka, which, as I noticed, pleased him
very much. I could not help laughing when I heard my
mother trying to speak broken Russian like Mavlyootka
in talking to him   Then followed a conversation between
my father and the chief, which attracted all my attention ;
from it I learned that the land bought by my father was
claimed by other Bashkirs than those who had sold it to
us ; that it was necessary to turn the people of two villages
off this land ; that, when a government survey was made,
there would be many disputes ; and that we ought to
get our own surveyor at once. " The surveyor will settle
it all," said Mavlyootka in his squeaky voice and in the
queerest Russian ; " white boundary-marks * are needed ;
I'll come myself for the survey." Then Mavlyoot Iséitch
departed : he unhitched his horse, of which he said, among

* See p 154

other things, that it was the only horse he had which could carry him ; next he put on his conical woollen cap, got into the saddle with singular agility, cracked his fearsome whip, and rode off home. I had good reason to mark this conversation between the Bashkir chief and my father. When alone with my mother, he looked anxious and unhappy while discussing the matter ; and I discovered that my mother had never approved of the purchase, because the land so acquired could not become our property without much delay and annoyance. It was already occupied by the people of two villages ; and, though their tenure was only that of settlers, it was very difficult to transfer them to other land belonging to the Crown. But what she disliked most was the disagreement between the Bashkirs who had sold it : each of them claimed to be the real owner and called all the rest impostors. The account I give here was due to later knowledge ; at the time I could not understand the real facts : I only feared that people would quarrel and fight and possibly come to blows over the land. I had a presentiment that *my* Sergéyevka would not long be mine ; and I was not mistaken.

Our half-nomad existence got more and more settled every day. The window-frames were brought and, for want of the weights, nailed on firmly enough from outside ; but there were no doors, and we continued to use carpets instead, which seemed to me just as good. A large new white covered-cart was placed in the yard ; the side-curtains of felt could be raised, and then the cart with its framework looked like an immense umbrella with a round hole at the top. To keep down the number of flies in our rooms, we generally had dinner there and raised one side of the cart, the side which was in the shade. The making of the *koumiss* was managed very well, and my mother got to dislike it less ; but I felt an invincible aversion to it, or at least assured myself and others of this, though my mother was very anxious that I should drink it, as I was very thin and all thought it would make me fatter ; but I was refractory. My sister too could not endure it ; to her it was positively injurious. To confess the truth, I think that I might have got accustomed to it; but I was afraid of losing the best time for fishing, if I drank *koumiss* and took the morning walks which were an essential part of the treatment. The passion for fishing steadily grew stronger; merely from fear that my mother would forbid me to sit by the lake with my rod, I forced myself to work at reading, writing, and the first two rules of arithmetic, under my father's teaching. I became rather artful at concealing my thoughts, and often started long discussions with my mother, while all the time my one thought was how soonest to escape with my line to the jetty, and when every moment of delay was a sore trial. The fish were taking wonderfully: there were no bad days, or only to this extent that sometimes we got few large fish. My little sister sometimes went with her Parasha to fish, but found no pleasure in it and was soon driven home by the midges.

At last we began to have visitors. Once there was a fishing party; General Mansuroff, the kindest of men and devoted to all forms of sport, was there with his wife; so was Ivan Bulgakoff, with his wife too. A great expedition to drag the lake was planned; the net was got, I think, from the Bashkirs, and also some boats. Two of the largest boats were lashed together and covered with planks laid across and nailed down so as to form a little raft, with a place for the ladies to sit on. In the stillness of a wonderful moonlight night, we all except my mother set out for the water. I sat with the ladies on the raft. Quickly and cautiously the net was brought up and let down into the water, so as to surround a long reach of the lake where the bank was shaped like a prolonged semi-circle. Countless shoals of bream came to the shallow water there at night. As soon as the sides of the net had been drawn close to the bank, the multitude of imprisoned fish began to be evident; from the raft we watched the centre of the net, where such a commotion was soon visible that our ladies, and I with them, uttered cries of excitement; many large fish, chiefly pike, leaped over the top of the net or dashed into the narrow space between the sides and the bank. The fishermen, who had been silent till now while dragging the net or drifting in boats beside it, now began to shout and slap

the water with the net-ropes, in order to force the fish back
into the centre of the net. We got the raft ashore quickly,
to watch the process of drawing out the catch For a
wonder, I did not share the general excitement and so was
able to watch attentively the whole lively and animated
scene. Mansuroff and my father were more excited than
anyone else. My father, who acted only as manager, was
constantly calling out : " Keep the edges even ! Get the
bottom ropes closer together ! See that the centre does
not get out of place!" Mansuroff went beyond mere words.
He waded knee-deep in the water, caught hold of the bottom
ropes of the net, and dragged them along, pressing them at
the same time against the shallow bottom ; for this purpose
he had to bend double and walk backwards. His wife
(a sister of Bulgakoff) and Bulgakoff's wife, in spite of their
excitement over the fishing, laughed heartily at the
ridiculous figure he thus presented. At last, whole heaps of
dripping meshes, forming the sides or wings of the net, were
brought out and thrown down, and the centre appeared,
not long and narrow as when empty, but broad and round,
owing to the multitude of fish it contained. It soon
became difficult to draw the net along the shallows ; and
the risk of breaking the centre made it necessary to stop.
Then the upper ropes were held up high, to prevent the
fish from leaping over ; and men with buckets and pails
dashed into the water and caught hold of the fish which
were forcing their way into the sack-like centre and filling
it to bursting. The men filled whatever they carried with
fish, rushed to the bank, shook out their victims on the
ground, and dashed back for more. When the weight of
the draught was thus lightened, the whole party caught
hold of the top and bottom ropes with a will, and with a
loud shout drew the centre out on to the bank. We caught
so much more than we expected, that we had to send for
a cart. Most of the fish were gold and silver bream, which
sparkled bright in the moonlight ; but there were also
pretty large tench and dace and perch , the pike had all
managed to scramble out, thanks to their cunning, said the
fishermen. What a scene it was of bustle and excitement
and noise ! The ladies too were keenly interested. Many

a time I heard Yevséitch call out, " That's something like
a bream ! As big as a shutter ! " *   But it seems that I
was born an angler ; for even then I kept saying to Yevséitch, " If only we could land a bream like that with the
rod ! "   I even felt depressed by the netting of so many
big fish, which might have taken our bait ; I felt sad to
see the lake emptied in such a way, and said to Yevséitch
that we should never have such good sport again ; but he
comforted me by declaring that we should do just as well
as ever—the lake was large and the stock of fish enormous ;
and our jetty was a long way from the place where the net
had been drawn.   " You shall see for yourself to-morrow,
my little falcon," said he ; and I was quite reassured and
able to take a more lively interest in what was going on.
By degrees order was restored : the cart was filled with
large fish, and the rest were carried in buckets and pails.
All the company walked merrily home behind the loaded
cart ; and merriest of all was General Mansuroff, though
he was covered with mud and wet nearly to the waist.

My mother was sitting out of doors, with the
samovar and tea-things before her, and a fire burning to
keep off the midges.   Loud and lively voices told her of
our exploits ; but she was astonished at our excitement,
refused to understand it, and made fun of us, especially
of the fat wet General, who positively refused to change
his clothes.   She first made sure that my feet and clothes
were dry ; then she gave me tea and put me to bed under the
same canopy as my sister who had long been asleep.   When
she went back to our guests, I went blissfully to sleep under
the canopy, thinking of the recent sport, hearing, through
the rug which served as a door, the sound of loud laughter
and merry talk, and dreaming of next morning, when
Yevséitch and I would be sitting on the jetty with our rods.
Next day I woke earlier than usual and saw that my mother
was up already : she was about to drink her *koumiss* and
take her walk in our enclosure and along the road leading
to Ufa.   My father was up too, but our guests were still
asleep.   The ladies occupied the only spare room, next
our own and divided only by a partition ; the men lay in

* See p 268 these "shutters" must have round edges

the garret, on a thick bed of hay covered over with skins and sheets. I dressed quickly and ran to my mother, to say good-morning and to ask leave to fish. She gave it without the least demurring, and I, leaving tea untasted, hastened with Yevséitch to the lake. Yevséitch had spoken the truth! Never had the fish taken so well as that morning. "There, you see, my little falcon," said Yevséitch; "there are more fish than ever. That net last night frightened them, and they have all come here." Whether this inference was true or not, the fish took splendidly. Strangely enough, my passion for the sport was soon cooled by the thought that we could never dispose of all the fish, when what we were taking now was added to all that had been caught the night before. As time went on, I felt this more and more strongly, and my enthusiasm grew cooler and cooler. I imparted my doubts to Yevséitch; and he said it was all right, and that all the fish would be dried or smoked that very day. Though this explanation consoled me a little, yet I returned home much earlier than usual.

Our guests stayed two more days with us. Mansuroff could not rest content without sport of some kind, and in the evening of the same day he went out with my father and Theodore, Parasha's husband, to snare quails with a net and a reed-pipe. Though I was very anxious to watch them, my mother would not let me go. Theodore brought me back a live quail, which I put in a cage plaited by Yevséitch out of green twigs. Next day Mansuroff went out shooting, again accompanied by my father, and took with him two setters which he had brought to the house. The sportsmen brought back some ducks and ten couple of snipe, all of which I surveyed with close attention. I did not venture even to ask leave to accompany the shooters: though I could see no reason why I should not take the field myself with Soorka, still it was certainly out of the question for me to tramp behind the sportsmen over hillocks, bogs, and reed-beds. To make up for this, our guests both came with me every evening to the lake to fish; but, for want of skill, they caught little, and were so fiercely attacked by midges, especially at sunset, that they often dropped their lines and ran home; and I had to go with them, though very unwillingly, as the midges had ceased to have terrors for me.

At last our guests departed, having made my parents promise to come in the course of a few days to Almantayevo, an estate belonging to Bulgakoff, about twenty *versts* from Sergéyevka ; Mansuroff, with his wife and children, would also be there. I was glad when our guests went away, and not much pleased by the prospect of this visit ; but my sister was delighted at the thought of seeing her little friends and acquaintances of Ufa : the Mansuroff girls were her friends, the others only acquaintances.

Throughout my childhood and for some years later, this peculiarity was noticed in me, that I did not make friends with other children and found their presence tiresome, even when it did not interfere with my outdoor occupations, to which even as a child I was passionately devoted. This peculiarity got me credit for unsociability, shyness, and timidity : people said that I was *afraid* of strangers. Such accusations I always resented ; and they certainly served to increase my discomfort in society. This peculiarity was not natural to me—in later years I was very sociable and outspoken to a fault—but was probably due to my long illness, which brought with it separation and solitude ; and such a life forces even a little child back upon himself and confines him to an inner world of his own, which it is difficult to share with those who are not in the secret. It was due still more to my habit of constant reading. My knowledge was beyond my years, and I was not satisfied with the society of children of my own age : yet for older people I was myself too young.

My mother's health was now evidently better. In addition to her daily walks every morning and every evening she often went for a drive in the country, especially on cloudy days, taking my father and sister and me with her on a long country car a vehicle with which I had already become acquainted at Parashino. She found these drives tiresome but believed that they did her good ; indeed, they had been prescribed by the doctors as part of her treatment. To my father too the drives were wearisome, but I disliked them most of all, because they interfered with my fishing and sometimes robbed me of the best part of the day. My mother seldom let me go to the lake with my father or Yevséitch before she came back from her morning drive; and it was just the same in the evening; yet almost every day I found time to fish.

In the middle of June the weather became very hot and put a new obstacle in the way of my amusement. For my mother was afraid of the effects of the midsummer sun. One day she noticed that my neck was red and covered with small pimples, as if it had been blistered; this was, no doubt, due to the sun; and she gave orders that I was always to be indoors by 10 o'clock in the morning. How I prayed to God for cloudy days! For on such days I was allowed to fish on till dinner, and the fish also took more greedily. That was real bliss—to sit at peace on the jetty with Yevséitch, to bait my line and cast it, to keep an eye on the floats, without being disturbed by the thought that it was time to go home. From time to time I glanced at Sooika, who was always sitting on the bank or lying asleep in the sun. On the other hand, in reading, writing, and arithmetic I made very slow progress, and my childish games with my sister began to lose interest and pleasure for me.

A week later, we went to the Bulgakoffs at Almantayevo. The place did not please me at all, as might have been expected from my unwillingness to go there; but indeed there was little to please anyone in that flat country, where the house stood, with no garden or shade, baking in the sun on a bare bank. There was, indeed, a river, the Oorshak, which flowed not far from the house, a rather strong stream and very full of fish; and on it, below the village, was a large mill with a wide pond; but even the river had no charm for me—first, because the water was hidden by the reeds which grew all over it, and secondly, because it was so bitter as to be unfit for drinking and distasteful even to animals. Yet the bitterness of the water had no bad effect on the fish which was abundant there: it was pronounced by all who tasted it to be excellent. To fish near the house was impossible, owing to the thick growth of reeds on the sloping banks; at the mill, it was the custom to fish only from the dam close by the sluice, and especially in a deep hole excavated by the water under the sluice. Our whole party once drove there, but, of course at midday, that is, at the worst time ; and we caught very little But the miller assured us that in the early morning before sunrise in spring and autumn very large fish were taken there, and the best in the hole under the sluice.

Our host, Ivan Bulgakoff, was a great lover of horses and hounds, and a good rider. All the household, including the ladies and children, could ride. I was a special favourite with our host, and he insisted that I should ride too. Being ashamed to say that I was afraid, I consented. My belief was, that my mother would not allow me ; but, as if to spite me, she said that she was very glad I should ride, if I was not afraid. My vanity was pricked by what she said : I plucked up courage and said that I was not afraid. All the company came out on the steps to watch ; a pony was brought round, I was placed in the saddle, and the reins were put in my hands. While Yevséitch continued to lead my horse, I mastered my fear ; but, as soon as he let go the bridle, I lost my head entirely and dropped the reins ; and the pony, for want of a guiding hand, trotted off towards the stable. Fear now got the better of vanity, and I began to scream. I lost my balance and would inevitably have fallen off, but for a groom who ran to meet me and stopped the steady old animal. The laughter of all on the steps hurt my childish vanity : utterly crushed, as soon as I was taken off the horse, I rushed through the back-door to our room I wept inconsolably for a long time, and could not look anyone in the face the whole day. This incident is especially memorable to me, because it was the first time in my life that I was conscious of anger against my parents. "Why do they join in the laugh at me ? " I asked ; " can they not see how hurt and ashamed I am ? Why does my sister not laugh ? She is sorry for me and even cries." At the time I only recognised with sorrow my own cowardice, and my peace was long troubled by the thought. Luckily we left the house next day : my mother had wished to stay another day, but the *koumiss,* of which we brought a whole cask with

us in ice, had curdled so that she could not drink it. Oh
with what joy I returned to my dear Sergéyevka !

Sergéyevka pleased me more than ever, though, to tell
the truth, the only good points about it were the lake and
the old oaks. Again the current of our life flowed on in
peace and happiness. and I began by degrees to forget the
sad mishap with the pony, which had brought my cowardice
to light and covered me, as I thought then, with perpetual
shame. My parents never spoke of it, and of course my
sister did not. But my faithful attendant, Yevséitch,
would not have his mouth stopped, and he reproached me
often. " Fie, fie, my little falcon," he would say ; " what
were you frightened of ? The pony was quiet enough ;
yet you must scream. It wasn't the horse you were afraid
of, but the strange people ; I always said that you were
afraid of strangers. But what sort of soldier will you turn
out ? You like to read about war and tell stories about
it ; to hear you, you would march alone against a whole
regiment." These simple words. spoken with no unkind
intention, seemed to me the most cutting of rebukes. I
tried to prove to Yevséitch, that this was quite different,
that in battle I would feel no fear, and that I would have
marched with the Greeks against all the barbarians. But
I made two unspoken vows : first, never to speak to
Yevséitch of the campaign of the Younger Cyrus, which I
was fond of describing to him ; and secondly, to master my
fear and learn to ride. With this object, I began to worry
my parents, and was vexed when they only answered,
" Oh, you are too young to ride yet." Meanwhile Yevséitch
continued to reproach me ; and I was so hurt, that I
sometimes got angry with him and sometimes cried when
I was alone. I made up my mind to ask him to drop
the subject ; and my good-natured Yevséitch ceased at
last to speak of it. I calmed down and began to forget
it myself. But, when the Bulgakoffs with their children
came to visit us, I felt a sudden stab at the heart I
thought that they would begin to laugh, as soon as they
saw me ; and, though this did not happen at our first
meeting, yet I was so confused by the constant expectation of their mockery, that I was always blushing

I

for no reason. But, thank God, all had forgotten my shame except myself. Our guests stayed several days. In the absence of Mansuroff, that kindest and most amiable of men, our amusements did not catch on, though we dragged the lake (by day, and therefore, of course, with less success), and went out shooting one day, and angled all together on the lake. All, however, were merry except me. I saw off our guests, young and old, with secret joy, though the young people were very kind and good-natured.

When he was seeing our guests off, my father took a fancy to draw a net through a famous reach for fish on the river Byélaya, which flowed half a *verst* from our house. He was very anxious to catch sturgeon, and even said to me, " Just fancy, Seryozha, if we found a salmon or a royal sturgeon in the net ! " I declared that we were certain to do so. We drove off after dinner, with a whole train of waggons holding the net, two boats, and all our men-servants. The Byélaya is not broad there, above the point where the Oorshak and the considerable stream of Ufa fall into it ; but I liked it better than below the town : there was less sand, and the river-bed was more compact, and the banks much more picturesque. My father took his gun, and, sure enough, we met a whole covey of partridges on the way ; he fired and killed two. This first discharge of a gun at game, in my presence and very near me, produced a strong impression on me—not fear, but a kind of pleasant excitement. When I saw the shot partridge, and especially when I was carried away by the example of others and rushed in pursuit of the other wounded bird, I felt an eager delight which was new to me. What had become of my former tenderness of heart ? These pretty birds, flutter-ing and bleeding, aroused no sympathy in me.

We had hardly time to lower the net before a whole crowd of Meshtchers * came hurrying to the place, shouting loudly and arguing that we had no right to fish in the Byélaya. as its waters were already let to fishermen. As my father did not wish to quarrel with near neighbours, he ordered the net to be taken out, and we had to set off home empty-handed. Our servants were so dissatisfied

* See note to p 19.

and so unwilling to give way, that my father's orders were not instantly obeyed; and, but for his presence, they would certainly have come to blows I too was much vexed, in spite of a vague feeling that our disturbers were in the right; and the two dead partridges, which I held in my hands, were my only consolation.

The wild strawberries had long been ripe; and we were allowed to eat as many as we liked. My mother was very fond of these berries herself, but was forbidden by the doctors to eat them during her cure. Instead of her former aimless expeditions, she now began to drive into the country, especially the fallow lands, for berries. This amusement, which was an entire novelty to me, gave me much pleasure at first. I soon grew tired of it, but all our household, both men and women, devoted themselves with enthusiasm to this occupation. Every soul in the house went out to pick strawberries: the only exception was Makéi, our cook; and even he got leave after dinner, and always returned in the evening with a large basket of splendid berries. Pails and baskets of all sorts and sizes were used to hold them: each picker suited himself. As a rule, my mother soon tired of picking; then she got into the car, made for the road, and drove about there for an hour or more, after which she came back to us. At first she took my father with her; but after a few days I begged to go, and after that she always took me in the car with her. My sister and I had pretty little baskets of birch bark, with lids and a pattern carved on them. My dear little sister was not a good picker: I mean that she could not distinguish ripe strawberries from unripe. I often heard her nurse Parasha, who was always very kind and good-natured, saying, as she shook out the child's basket, "Well, I declare, green ones again!"—and then she filled the little basket out of her own big one. But I claimed that I was a skilful picker, and that my strawberries were finer than Yevséitch's; which was certainly not the case. To support my claim, I always revealed that my sister had not picked for herself, and said I had seen Parasha giving up her own berries to her. On our return home, the fruit afforded a new occupation. All the berries were emptied out into a large clean trough of linden-wood : then the largest were picked out for jam, the next in size for eating, and the next for bottling : the rest were used to make either Russian or Tatar pastry : for the former, which was thick, the fruit was mixed with honey or sugar and passed through a strainer ; the latter was thin as a wafer, and, having all the seeds of the berries in it, was rather sour to taste. These operations interested me at first almost more than picking, but at last I got tired of them. I liked best to watch my mother making jam in bright copper pans over a gridiron with a fire beneath, perhaps because the sugary scum taken off the boiling pan was mostly given to my sister and me. We usually sat beside her on the ground with our legs tucked away beneath us, waiting with impatience till the mixture of fruit and sugar should begin to swell and bubble and form a whitish skin over the pan.

My father went out sometimes to catch quails with nets and reed-pipes. My mother would not give me leave to go, though I often asked for it. When I had stopped asking, she quite unexpectedly gave me leave for once to go with my father and Theodore to watch this sport. I was delighted by it. When the quails came running at the low note of the pipe, and got close to the net spread out on the grass, and when we three sprang up and a startled quail, as it rose, got into the net, I was much excited. But I wanted to take a more prominent part, in fact, to decoy the birds myself. I had learnt already to blow the pipe from Theodore, who was considered a capital hand at it ; and I at once fancied that I was equally skilful. My father and Theodore could not resist my entreaties, and my wish was granted. But experience showed that I had no skill at all : when I piped, the quails were so far from coming to the net that they did not even answer my calls. I was much hurt and did not ask leave another time to go with the sportsmen.

The time for drinking *koumiss* as a medicine was now coming to an end. As the grass had reached maturity and was beginning to wither in some places, the mares' milk was losing its healing virtue ; and we returned to Ufa at the end of July. The *koumiss* and country life had done much for my mother. Sorrowfully I left Sergéyevka, and said good-bye to its splendid lake and the jetty where I used to fish and which I knew so well, and the very look of which lives to this day in my grateful recollection ; I said good-bye to the magnificent oaks, under whose shade I often sat, and which I always looked at with admiration. I said farewell—and it proved a long farewell.

CHAPTER X

Our two months on our country estate—or more accurately in our half-built little house by the lake—with pure air, and freedom, and fishing, for which I had such a passion as only a child can feel, were so different from our town life, that Ufa was repulsive to me. I came back brown as a berry, and all our acquaintances declared that I was a perfect little savage. Our garden offered me no attractions · I would not look at it, even when my dear little sister was running about there quite happily. In vain she called me to run and play with her, or to admire the flowers with which the beds were filled as usual. I even got angry with my little companion, and pointed out to her that, after Sergéyevka with its oaks and lake and fields, our garden with its stunted apple-trees was a disgusting sight. Occasionally I went out, only to stroke and caress Soorka and play with him : life at Sergéyevka had brought us so close together that the mere sight of the dog was pleasant to me, because it reminded me of my blissful life in the country Meanwhile, because my sunburn did not pass off, my mother began to give me some treatment for it ; I was much vexed, and submitted very reluctantly. I could not go back at once to my former occupations and amusements : I considered that I had grown out of them. Writing I found a nuisance, because my success with it was small, in the absence of a teacher ; and I did not feel inclined for reading, as I had long ago read all my books more than once, and had learned much of them by heart. For about a week. I was listless and idle ; then I began to write, under compulsion, and to read my old books, which soon gave me pleasure M Anitchkoff continued to inform himself of what I was doing. He invited me again to visit him, put me through a second examination, and was so much pleased with the result, that he gave me a pile of books which Yevséitch could hardly carry ; it was quite a small library in itself. The books included *The Library of Antiquity*, the *Rossiad* of Cheraskoff, and a complete collection of the works of Sumarokoff in twelve volumes. After a glance at *The Library*, I left it undisturbed ; but the other two books I read with eager rapture. One of my uncles was fond of reciting poetry ; I was infected by his example and tried to imitate him. My parents evidently were pleased with my recitation ; for they made me display my powers before our visitors, who were much fewer than in the preceding winter : my uncles were with their regiment, and some of our most intimate friends had left the place. My mother was in better health than before and less taken up by society ; thus she had more leisure, and I was with her more. My chief pleasure was to read the *Rossiad* aloud to her, while she explained words or phrases which I could not understand. I read with such eager sympathy, and my fancy reproduced the faces of my favourite heroes, Mstilavsky, Prince Koorbsky, and Paletsky, in such lively colours, that I seemed to see them and counted them as old friends. I drew pictures of them. filled in the details of their lives, and eagerly described their appearance ; I narrated in detail what they did before battle and after battle, and how the Tsar took counsel with them and thanked them for their brave deeds, and so on. My mother laughed to hear me ; but my father was surprised, and said one day, " Where do you get all that from ? You must not turn out a little liar." " Never mind," said my mother ; " it won't last." Nevertheless, she would not let me describe to our visitors the domestic life of my three favourites. What a master-piece I thought the description of Prince Mstilavsky !—

" This hero in the fight was neither rash nor bold ,
Tough as the flint was he , and, as the flint seems cold
But flashes into flame when rubbed against the steel,
So, when opposed, the Prince flashed fire from head to heel "

Gidromir and Astalon were my personal enemies, and I was grieved to the heart that Gidromir was not killed in the single combat with Palctsky. I was delighted, too, when the Cossack horsemen,

> " With swords that flashed like sunbeams in their hands,
> And daggers pressed between their teeth, rushed down
> And drove our warriors o'er the field in flight.
> Even as a flock of swans hides from the hail,
> So o'er the hills our soldiers fled their swords ;
> And soon the enemy had stormed our camp,
> Had not our champions forth to meet them fared,
> That princely pair, and stopped the bloody fray."

The last two verses I pronounced with pride and joy ; and I must confess that I still feel satisfaction in pronouncing them. and find in them something strong and stirring. I did not omit to display my powers as a reciter of the *Rossiad* to my patron, M. Anitchkoff ; he heard me to the end, and then praised me and promised to give me the works of Lomonossoff.

All was quiet and peaceful in the town and in our household, when suddenly an event took place, which, not by its own importance but by the universal impression it produced on others, forced me to share in the general excitement. One fine autumn day—it was either Sunday or some festival—we had been at mass in our parish church, dedicated to the Assumption of the Virgin, and were returning home. We had just mounted the high steps outside our house, when suddenly we noticed some commotion and loud talking among the people returning from church. Next, along the street at full gallop came a Cossack orderly : to all whom he passed, he cried out, " Go back to the church, to take the oath of allegiance to the new Emperor ! " At the church he drew bridle. The people had been scattering ; now they stopped, formed groups, and walked back. Their numbers grew and grew, till they reached the church in a dense crowd. Even before one of the hurrying crowd had told us the news that the Empress * was dead, the cathedral bells broke into a peal,

---

* The Empress Catherine died in September, 1796, when Aksakoff was just five years old

the bells of ten other churches chimed in, and the sound
spread all over the town.   My parents were much affected :
my father even shed tears ; my mother, with tears in her
eyes, crossed herself and said, " The kingdom of heaven
be hers ! "   I was much impressed, without knowing why.
All the household joined us on the steps, with dismay and
grief depicted on every face ; the people walking along the
street were weeping.   A clerk came from the law-court,
out of breath with haste, and told my father he was to go
to the cathedral, to take the oath.   My father hastily
put on his uniform and left us.   I went with my mother
to her bedroom and my sister came too, quite aware that
something had happened   My mother prayed for a time ;
then she sat down in an armchair and gave herself up to
sorrowful thought, while we two sat on a stool opposite
to her and looked at her with silent attention.   At last
she took notice of us and began to talk to us, to me
especially ; for my sister was still too young to understand
her and soon went off to the nursery and Parasha.   Suiting
her words to my age, my mother explained, that the Empress
Katerina Alexyéevna was wise and good, and during her
long reign had tried to improve the condition and education
of all her people ; that she knew how to choose good men
and brave generals ; and that, during her reign, our neighbours had not hurt us, and our soldiers had won victories
and gained glory.   Of all this I had some inkling already,
but I understood it better now, and I felt very sorry for
the death of the Empress.   " Who will be our Empress
now ? " I asked.   " We shall have an Emperor now, her
son, Pavel Petrovitch."   " And will he be as wise and
good ? "   " That is as God pleases ; but we shall pray that
he may be," she replied.   I said, " God will surely wish
Pavel Petrovitch to be wise and good."   To this she made
no reply, but told me to go to the nursery and read or play
with my sister.   I begged her to explain what was meant
by " the oath of allegiance," and, when she had done so,
expressed a firm intention to take the oath myself   " The
oath is not administered to children," said she ; " go and
join your sister."   I felt hurt.   My father soon came back,
and was followed by some of our friends.   They were all

hot against V., our military governor or commander of
the troops—I am not sure which,—for his open display
of joy at the death of the Empress; he had ordered the
bells to be rung all day, and had invited all the town to
a ball and suppe1 at his house in the evening   I felt sure
at once that Governor V. could not be a good man.   I
now heard that he had personal reasons for rejoicing : he
was a favourite of the new Emperor and hoped to rise high
under his 1eign.   This inci eased my displeasui e with him :
what business had he to be glad, when every one else was
sorry ?   At first my mother said it was impossible to attend
the Governor's ball, and others agi eed with her ; but then
they turned round and all said that it was impossible to
stay away.   My mother did not oppose them, but said that
she would stay at home.   My father went, but soon
retui ned, saying that it was more like a funeral than a
ball : only four people there were enjoying themselves,
the Governor, his two *aides-de-camp*, and the old Commissioner Anitchkoff, my kind book-giver, who could not
forgive the late Empress for dismissing the Imperial Commission which she had summoned to investigate the laws.
" High time," said the old gentleman, " for a masculine
hand to grasp the sceptre of government."

This was a day which brought me new and sti ange
ideas, and forced unfamiliar feelings upon me.   When I
lay down in my crib at night, and the cui tains of my
canopy were drawn, and all grew still around me, my
fancy brought before me a striking scene—the dead
Empress, of more than human statui e, lying under a great
black canopy in a church hung with black (I had overheard talk of this kind) ; and the new Emperor, another
gigantic figure, kneeling beside her and weeping, while
behind him all the people were sobbing aloud, assembled
in such numbers that they would have stretched from Ufa
to Zubofka, *i e.* ten *veists*   Next morning I told my
waking dream to my sister and Parasha, as if I had seen it
all myself or read a description of it

For a long time, people went on talking about the death
of the Empiess   at first, indeed, the gossip grew every
hour.   The talk went on in my mother's bedroom, in the

drawing-room, and even in our nursery, where Annushka, Yevséitch's wife, and the hunchbacked " Princess " looked in from time to time from their own quarters. In the bedroom and drawing-room, the common theme was the changes in the government which must inevitably come about ; and it was said that the Emperor would remove all his mother's favourites, whom he could not endure for their bad treatment of him. I often heard a phrase, which was then a complete mystery to me : " The sun is shining now on the Gátchina * people." In our nursery the talk was different : in fact, only rumours found their way there from kitchen and pantry, where the favourite topic was the sudden death of the Empress, with the addition of horrible details which frightened me exceedingly. I ran to my parents for explanations, and was only calmed by their strong and positive assurance, that all these rumours were utter nonsense and mere gossip Back I ran to the nursery, where I tried hard to convince Parasha and her visitors of the folly of their stories. But I failed utterly : they only replied that I was too young to understand I was much hurt and very angry I learnt later that Parasha and the rest had strict orders for the future to tell me nothing of idle stories that were current among the people.

News of changes was expected every day , but Ufa was so remote that information took long to get there from the capitals.† The Governor soon left ; and it was whispered that he had been secretly summoned by the Emperor.

Severe winter weather soon set in, and we were permanently confined to our nurseries, where we occupied only one of the two rooms. With more time on my hands, I naturally gave more to reading, writing copies, and arithmetic which I disliked and found difficult ; fewer visitors came ; and it was impossible to take walks A day came when I had to fall back on *The Library of Antiquity.*

Once, in the middle of some conversation, I caught some words about " illness " and my " grandfather " ;

* Gátchina was the place where the future Emperor Paul used to drill his regiment

† Russia has two capitals, Petrograd and Moscow.

but I do not think any one was alarmed by his condition,
and I had nearly forgotten it. But one day, when we
were all sitting at dinner, my father received a letter
brought by special messenger from Bagrovo. He unsealed
it and began to read ; then he burst into tears and handed
it to my mother. She read it and was much affected,
but not to tears. We hurried through our dinner, and I
noticed that my parents ate nothing. After dinner they
went to their room, sent us away, and had a long conversation ; when we were allowed to come back, my father
was getting ready to drive somewhere, and my mother
said to me, looking vexed as well as grieved : " Seryozha,
we are all going to Bagrovo ; your grandfather is dying."
I heard her with sadness and bewilderment. I knew
already that every one must die ; and death, which I
understood in my own way, seemed to me an evil spirit
and a horrible thing, of which I was afraid even to think.
I was sorry for grandfather ; but I was resolved not to
see him die, nor to be listening in the next room, when he
should begin to cry and call out, at the moment of death.
I was dismayed by another thought, that it would surely
make my mother ill. " How can we," I thought, " travel
in winter ? My sister and I are still little, and we shall be
frozen." Thoughts of this kind took a firm hold on me ;
and I sat in silence, anxious and distressed to the bottom
of my heart, and giving myself up to the dismal pictures
of my excited imagination, which got more and more beyond
my control. Apart from my fear that grandfather would
die in my presence, Bagrovo itself was not attractive to
me. I had not forgotten the sadness of our stay there in
the absence of our parents ; and I had no wish to go there,
especially in winter. Now my father returned ; he came
hastily into the bedroom, and said, with a cheerful air that
surprised me greatly, " Thank God ! I have got everything. Anitchkoff will give us a sledge, and the Misailoffs
a covered-cart. So now, my dear, get ready at once.
To-morrow I shall get leave of absence, and we will start
the same day, using post-horses " My mother was not
pleased ; but she answered sadly, " All my things will
be ready, but your leave of absence may be a difficulty "

Our preparations began the same evening : clothes were packed and food was cooked for the journey ; I was allowed to take a few books with me. I told all my doubts and fears to my mother, some of them she could not dispel, but she laughed at my fear of being frozen, and said that we should find it even hot in the sledge.

By dinner-time next day our preparations were really complete, and everything put into the sledge and the cart ; nothing kept us but my father's leave of absence. He received this at 3 o'clock. We had to drive some stages along the Kazan high-road. Post-horses were therefore brought round, and the same evening we began our journey.

CHAPTER XI

OUR journey lasted almost forty-eight hours, and remains in my memory as a most wearisome and unpleasant episode. As soon as we left the house to take our seats, I was horrified by the low leathern sledge with its little door which made entrance difficult. In this confined space, my sister and I, with Parasha and Annushka, had to find room. I begged to go in the cart with my mother; but the frost was terrible, and I was sternly told to get into the sledge. My mother could not travel in a shut carriage in winter, without feeling sick and faint; even in the cart she sat in a fashion peculiar to herself, quite exposed to the air on all sides. It soon got warm in the sledge, and it became necessary to undo the wrap which I wore over my *shooba* and fur-cap. We went at a gallop along the smooth track, and I had my first experience of the pleasure of quick driving. Each of the doors had a small square window which was tightly shut. I managed to creep to a window and enjoyed the view from it: the moon shone bright; stout guide-posts and sometimes trees flashed past. But, alas! my enjoyment was soon over: first a mist came over the window-panes; then the frost worked patterns on them; and soon they were shrouded with a thick layer of impenetrable rime. I thought of the gloomy future before us—the dismal house at Bagrovo surrounded by snow-wreaths, and my grandfather at the point of death. My sister had long been asleep, before kindly slumber visited me. When I woke next morning, I thought it was still early; there was daylight in our sledge, or rather twilight, as the windows were coated more thickly than ever. The others seemed to have been awake some

time, and my sister was eating something ; she crept close
to me and kissed me.   It was really hot in the sledge
My car was soon caught by the loud creaking of the runners,
and I felt that we were hardly moving.   The reason of
this I now heard · after driving two and a half stages we
had turned off the highway and were now going along a
cross-road, having exchanged our three post-horses harnessed abreast for horses of the district driven in single
file.   This increased my gloom, and my kind sister could
not cheer me up.   She knew my tastes and at once asked
me to read to her out of a book which lay in a wallet at
the side of the sledge ; but I was so sad that I would not
even read.   We crawled on till we reached a Tatar village
where we had to change horses ; our coachman, Stepan,
had ridden on ahead to get them ready.   We entered a
peasant's hut which had been prepared to receive us,
intending to drink tea and breakfast there.   My mother
looked quite ill and upset : she had had no sleep all night,
and felt giddy and sick ; and her sufferings added to my
distress and misery.   The Tatar hut had a chimney, and
a wide wooden frame to sleep on ; a heap of rather dirty
feather-beds rose from the frame almost to the ceiling,
covered at one end with a rug, while the rest of the frame
was hidden under a white mat.   My mother spread out
her travelling cloak on the mat and placed her own pillows
at the head of it ; then she lay down and soon fell asleep,
having told us to drink tea without her.   For a whole hour
she slept, while my father and sister and I, talking in
whispers and careful to make no noise, drank our tea and
ate some roast meat warmed up in the stove.   My mother
woke refreshed, and we resumed our journey.   In the
evening the same scene was repeated, with a difference :
we stopped to change horses and got out as before, but our
new shelter was not a clean Tatar hut but a regular pig-stye
inhabited by Mordvinians and an assortment of live stock.
I think that I never in my life came across anything more
disgusting than this hut, with its filth and evil smell ; to
crown all, the wooden settles were so narrow that my
mother, though quite worn out by the journey, could not
lie down, till my father made it possible for her to do so

by propping a seat against one of them   Although we were warmly shod, we sat with our legs up on a settle because there was such an appalling smell from the floor. We were told that the frost had become much harder : whenever the door opened, the cold air rushed in and filled the whole hut in a moment with clouds of what looked like white steam. We had another meal of heated-up soup and pies, and started again. As one door of our sledge had been carelessly left open, it was a long time before it was warmed up again by our presence and breath.

I cannot describe the distress and anxiety which I suffered then. I had a presentiment and a conviction that some misfortune would befall us, that we should either fall sick or be frozen, like the sparrows and jackdaws which, according to Parasha, fell dead in mid-flight. But all my apprehensions were much more on my mother's account than on our own : our sledge had warmed up again, but she had no cover from the cold in her vehicle. My gloomy presentiments robbed me of sleep. Suddenly we stopped, and in a few minutes I became so uneasy that I awoke Parasha and implored her to knock on the door, so that some one might come and tell us the reason of the stoppage. Parasha was generally a good-tempered girl ; but she was vexed at being wakened, and said rather roughly : " It's no good knocking now : no one will come. There are plenty of reasons for stopping " She would certainly have had pity on me, if she had known what torture my ignorance was causing me. Thank God, the sledge soon moved on. In the morning, when we stopped again for tea, I learnt that my fears were not entirely unfounded : a Choovash, who was riding as postilion in front of the sledge, had been nearly frozen. Being thinly clad, he was so affected by the cold that he fell off his horse unconscious. The other men rubbed him with snow and succeeded in bringing him alive to the next village. I first felt then —and I have never lost it—an intense aversion to travelling in winter over country roads, drawn by relays of country horses. Everything about it is really horrible : your harness is made of rope ; your horses are not up to the work and poorly fed, never getting a feed of oats ; and your driver has not enough clothing to bear a stage of even ten *versts* in a hard frost. Our route was quite different (though I did not know it at the time) from that which we took on my last visit to Bagrovo, when there was a road over the steppe, which winter had entirely obliterated. In winter, owing to the long distance, we did not attempt a direct line, but followed the paths which ran from one village to another.

In the morning, when I climbed out of our prison into the kindly daylight, I felt a little braver and quieter; my mother, also, had got accustomed to travelling and felt stronger; and the frost was less severe The short winter day was soon over; and the darkness, which came on sooner in the sledge than elsewhere, again filled my timid heart with fears and sad forebodings. And these, unfortunately, were again realised. I say " unfortunately," because I have had ever since that time a rooted belief in presentiments, and throughout life have suffered more from them than from real misfortunes, although my presentiments hardly ever came true. As we got near Bagrovo that evening, our sledge drove over a stump and upset. I was half-asleep and cut my forehead against the round copper head of a nail, on which a wallet was hanging; I was also nearly smothered, as Parasha and my sister and a number of pillows fell on my face, and it was some time before the sledge could be turned on its right side. When we were set free, I did not notice the cut on my head; my one feeling was joy that I had not been smothered. But, much to my vexation, the two maids and even my sister, who did not understand that I might have been smothered to death, laughed both at my fear and at my joy. Thank God, my mother did not know that we had been upset.

K

CHAPTER XII

BAGROVO IN WINTER

AT last we heard dogs barking, and pale flickering fires
began to twinkle in peasants' cottages as we passed; their
feeble light found its way through the sledge windows
which were now less thickly blinded with snow. We
guessed that we had reached Bagrovo, or else the other
village which lay on our final stage of twelve *versts* We
stopped at the first house, and my father sent, as I afterwards
heard, to inquire about grandfather; the reply was that
he was still living. We drove very slowly, and our horses
had bells. We were expected, and the people at Bagrovo
made sure that we were in the carriage; therefore, in
spite of the late hour and the cold, we were met at the
front door by my grandmother and my Aunt Tatyana. Both
were weeping and sobbing. We went in quietly. My
aunt undertook to attend to my sister and me, while my
parents went to see grandfather, who was near death but
quite conscious and impatient to see his son and daughter-
in-law and their children. As before, the drawing-room
was given up to us; for the separate room, which grandfather had promised us, was not furnished yet, though it
was built and the roof was on. The house was quite full:
all my aunts with their husbands had assembled. Mme.
Yerlykin and her two daughters were living in my aunt
Tatyana's room; her husband and Ivan Karatayeff slept
somewhere in the workshop; and the other three aunts
were put up in my grandmother's room which was next to
the sick-room. In the parlour it was bitterly cold, and
not warm in the drawing-room. With some trouble a
bed was found for my mother; my sister and I slept on
the sofa; and a feather-bed was laid on the floor for my

father. The *samovar* was brought, and we were having
tea when my mother returned ; her face was quite damp
from the heat and closeness of grandfather's room which
was like a Turkish bath. She felt it cold and at once set
to work to raise the temperature of the room : the door
into the parlour was closed and curtained over, and mats
were spread over the floor. The room, which had two
stoves, soon warmed up, and remained quite warm during
the whole time of our stay.

Meantime my brain was in a perfect whirl of confused
impressions and recollections, fears and forebodings ;
and, on the top of all these, I had in reality a bad headache
caused by the blow I had suffered. My mother soon
noticed that I was not well and that one of my eyes was
swollen ; and we were obliged to tell her of our mishap ;
some fomentation was applied, and the eye bandaged.
But my mother was suffering more than I, from the sleeplessness, fatigue, and sickness, which she had endured
throughout our journey. She fell, rather than lay down,
on her bed, utterly exhausted ; we also were, of course,
put to bed at once. My father spent the whole night beside
grandfather, whose death was expected at any moment.
My mother was soon asleep ; but I lay awake for hours.
Every minute I expected that grandfather would begin
to die ; and, as I firmly believed that death was neces-
sarily attended by agonising pain and suffering, I was
constantly listening and wondering when grandfather
would begin to cry out and scream. I was much troubled,
too, about my mother ; my head ached, and my eye was
closing up ; I felt feverish and on the verge of delirium,
and thought I was going to be ill. But the healing power
of sleep did not fail in this instance. I woke before it was
light, and looked at my mother : I was glad to see that
she was asleep. The pain in my head and eye had passed
off ; but the eye was swollen and quite closed, and the
bruise had turned blue. My father's bed had not been
slept in ; it was clear that he had not come in at all. Then
I began to look round the room : everything was just as
it had been the year before ; the only difference was in the
window-panes, on which the hard frost had wrought its

wonderful patterns. Having nothing to do, I gave full play to my fancy ; more precisely, I began to compare our present condition with what was likely to befall us in future. All my notions were, of course, those of a child. I thought that, when grandfather died, grandmother, being old and grey-haired, would probably die too ; in which case we would take my aunt Tatyana back to Ufa with us, and she would live in the nursery we did not use. But if grandmother did not die, we would take her too, and the house at Bagrovo would be transported to Sergéyevka and placed right on the lake ; and we should spend the summer there, and fish, and my aunt would fish too. But these dreams vanished entirely at the thought of grandfather's death, which all were convinced would happen soon. I knew that he wished to see us ; and I must confess that the thought of this inevitable meeting filled me with indescribable horror. My chief fear was, that grandfather would begin to say good-bye to me and would die with his arms round me ; his arms would stiffen, so that I could not be released from their grasp ; and it would be necessary to bury me in the earth with him. Such a fear was probably due to stories I had heard of dead people and their stiffened limbs , but it was strangely at variance with the sensible ideas I had on many subjects. The terror of this thought seemed to paralyse my heart ; my breathing stopped ; a cold sweat burst out on my forehead ; I could not lie still, but started up and sat across the sofa ; I even tried to wake my sister ; and, if I did not cry out, it was probably because I had lost the power of utterance. At this moment my mother awoke and ex-claimed when she saw my face : the bandage had fallen off, and she was alarmed by the black and blue bruise over my eye. My imaginary fears vanished before my mother's real alarm : I ran to her bed, and assured her that I was perfectly well and in no pain. She was reassured, and told me that the bruise would soon disappear. Sleep had given her strength ; she got up hastily and dressed and went to grandfather's room. It was now light, and my sister awoke ; at first she was frightened by the appear-ance of my eye, but was comforted when a bandage was put on. She was not in the least afraid of grandfather; but she was very sorry for him, and actually wished to go and see him. Her courage and affection for grandfather made me ashamed and gave me some courage. Soon my mother came back. She said that grandfather was sinking, but he was still conscious and wished to see us and give us his blessing. In spite of all my efforts to control myself, I could not hide my fear, and even turned pale. My mother tried to encourage me: " How can you be afraid of grandfather," she said, " when he is hardly breathing and is at the point of death?" "That is just what I *am* afraid of," I thought; but I dared not say so. She led us into grandfather's room. He was lying on his bed, with his eyes shut; his face was pale and so changed that I would not have known him. Grandmother was sitting in an armchair at the head of the bed; my father was standing at the foot, with his eyes swollen and red with tears. He bent down to the old man's ear and said in a loud voice, "The children have come to say good-bye to you." Grandfather opened his eyes; without speaking a single word, with a trembling hand he signed us with the Cross, and touched our heads with his fingers; we kissed his thin wasted hand and began to cry. At this, all the people in the room began to weep and even to sob; and I noticed for the first time that all our aunts and uncles, with grandfather's personal servants and some old women besides, were standing round us. My fear had entirely vanished, and for the moment I was full of love and pity for my dying grandfather. The room was unbearably hot and close; and my mother took us back without delay to the drawing-room, where we both cried so, that it was long before they could stop us. In order to distract our thoughts, my mother invited our cousins to join us. They were much more composed than we; they were friendly to us, and we calmed down a good deal and began talking. We talked on till dinner, which took place as usual in the parlour; there were a number of dishes, and all the party except my mother—my father did not even appear at table—ate with appetite and talked with tolerable composure but in low tones. After dinner, our cousins joined

us in the drawing-room, and I began to chatter in quite a
lively style and to tell them whatever came into my head.
Unconsciously, I wanted to crush down by idle talking
the haunting thought of grandfather's death From time
to time my mother left us for the sick-chamber ; and she
allowed us to go to our cousins' room. To get there, we
had to go down a passage and through the maids' room,
which was packed full of women, young and old. I noticed
their dress with interest : some wore striped frocks, others
were in short jackets and skirts, and others had only shifts
and petticoats ; all were sitting at frames and spinning
flax. This was a novelty to me, and I watched the spinners
with curiosity, while with one hand they pulled at the tufts
of flax and with the other twirled their spindles and the
thread wound round them. All their motions were quick
and pretty ; and, as they were all silent, a peculiar sound,
which was new to me, was produced by the humming of
the spindles and the twitching at the tufts of flax. I was
still looking and listening attentively, when the sound of
crying came from grandfather's room ; I started, and in
one moment the maids' room was empty. Dropping
their spindles and leaving their frames, the women had all
rushed in a body to where their master was lying. I
believed that grandfather was dead ; and the horror of
the thought drove me mechanically to my cousins' room,
where I climbed on my aunt's bed and hid in a corner behind
the pillows. Parasha, too, leaving us alone, ran to see
what was going on in the room of the poor old master ;
this increased my fear ; but she soon came back and said
that he had rallied again after the " agony " had apparently
begun " All the same he will die to-night," she added
very coolly We stayed with our cousins two hours , but
my chattering was at an end, and I sat there speechless.
We were summoned to the parlour for tea ; my mother,
grandmother, and aunts all came, but one at a time and
not for long. My father did not come, and I was sad at
not seeing him for so long ; I was old enough to understand how much he suffered in watching his father die.
After tea, the cousins again visited us in the drawing-room ;
and again I could take no part in the conversation , after

two hours they went away to bed. How I envied them
for feeling no fear, and how I wished they would not go !
In their absence my fear grew much worse. My little sister
was sad about grandfather and spoke of him constantly :
" Grandfather will not eat ; they will bury him under the
snow ; poor grandfather ! " She cried ; but she was not
in the least frightened and soon went to sleep. Every
other feeling in me was crushed by fear, and I was sure
that I would lie awake all night. I implored Parasha not
to leave us, and she promised to stay till my mother came.
Our night-light burned dimly, and I begged her to light a
candle I soon noticed that she was drowsy, and began
to talk to her · I asked, " Why does not grandfather cry
out ? Surely it hurts him to die." She laughed and said :
" No ; when the hour of death comes, there is no pain ;
a dying man has ceased to feel anything. Your grandfather can recognise no one and cannot speak ; he wants
to say something, and his eyes stare, but he can only move
his lips." At once my fancy drew a new and still more
terrible picture of the dying man, which I could not banish
for a moment from my sight. I felt that infinite horror
which cannot be told to others, because the sufferer has
lost the power of speech. Silently I clutched Parasha's
hand and would not let go. The candle-wick required
trimming, but I would not let go her hand for a moment :
she had to take me with her, and then move the candle to
a table near me, so near that it was possible to trim it
with the snuffers without getting up. Again she began to
doze, but I woke her again and again, repeating in a piteous
voice, " Please don't go to sleep, dear Parasha ! " At last
my mother came ; she was surprised to find me awake,
and, when she heard the reason, took me across to her bed
and lay down, without undressing, beside me. Clasping
her with both arms, and comforted by her assurances that
grandfather would not die immediately, I soon went to sleep.
For some hours I slept quietly, but the waking was terrible.
When I opened my eyes, I saw that neither my mother
nor Parasha was in the room ; the candle was out, the
night-light had burnt low, and the fiery tongue of its
expiring wick had fallen into the tallow at the bottom of

the saucer, where it threw from time to time a flicker of light round the room, and threatened every moment to leave me in utter darkness. No words can express my terror. There was a burning pain at my heart, though at the same moment my whole body seemed turned to ice. I buried my head under the counterpane and felt the cold sweat breaking out on me. In vain I shut my eyes tight —grandfather stood before me, staring at me and twitching his lips, as Parasha had described him. The faint tapping of insects in the bare wood walls of the room pierced my ears, I believe I should have died of fright if there had been a sudden bang or crash at that moment. Suddenly I heard a distant sound of crying; at first, I thought it was imagination; but the crying soon gave place to loud shrieks of lamentation and woe. My powers of endurance were at an end : I threw off the coverlet and screamed at the top of my voice ; my sister woke and began to scream too. It is probable that our screams were unheard for a long time; for it was just then that grandfather really died, and all the household rushed to his bedside and wailed so loudly that it was impossible to hear our childish cries. I was losing consciousness and was on the verge of fainting or madness, when Parasha ran into the room. She had been sleeping soundly in the passage close by our door, till awakened by the cries of the household ; luckily, she heard my sister and me first, because we were nearer. She lit a candle at the dying night-light, took us both on her knees, and tried to quiet us. At last my mother came in, looking wretched and ill, she told us that grandfather died at 5 o'clock that morning, and that our father would come at once and lie down, as he had not slept for two nights. He did come soon, kissed us and made the sign of the Cross on us, and said, " Your grandfather is dead " ; then he began to weep bitterly, and we cried too. The noise of general lamentation in the house ceased. He lay down and instantly fell asleep. A candle burnt in a corner, with its light shaded in some way, and there was a glimmer of white in the windows, which made me suppose that dawn was near. The thought gave me courage, and I soon went to sleep, in bed with my mother and sister.

I overslept myself next morning, and, when I opened my eyes, the bright winter sunlight was peeping in at our windows. The sound of singing as in church first struck my ears; and then I heard weeping and sobbing. The event of last night revived in my memory, and it occurred to me at once that people were praying for grandfather's soul. There was no one in the room. "Parasha and my sister must have gone to the service," I thought, and set myself to wait patiently till some one came; I was not afraid to be alone by day, when the sun was shining. My sister soon came in with her eyes red, and Parasha with her. "You *have* overslept yourself," said Parasha, "it will soon be dinner-time"; and she began to dress me in haste. I was washing, when suddenly I heard some one chanting in a low monotonous voice, which seemed to come from the parlour. I asked Parasha what it was; she was pouring cold water over my head from the jug, as she answered, "They are chanting the Psalms for your grandfather." I had no idea of what she meant, and was composed enough till my sister said, "Let us go to the parlour, where grandfather is lying." This frightened me. I was still puzzled and asked, "But how did grandfather get into the parlour? Is he still alive?" "Alive, bless you!" said Parasha; "he has long been stiff and stark. His body has been washed, dressed in the *savan*,* brought into the parlour, and laid on the table. There has been a service for the dead, and the priest has gone. What you heard was old Yekim chanting the Psalms. Never mind what your sister says. I don't advise you to look at your grandfather; it would frighten you; one of his eyes is not closed." Every word she spoke overcame me with fresh horror; and the last detail affected me so, that I rushed with a cry out of the door, down the passage and through the maids' room, to the room occupied by my cousins; Parasha and my sister ran after me but could not induce me to return. Fear is ridiculous, I admit; and I don't blame Parasha for laughing, as she urged me to go back and even tried to carry me off by force, while I resisted with arms and legs; but the tortures that fear

* *I e.* shroud   the word is said to be derived from the Greek

applies to a child's heart are so terrible that it is a sin to laugh at them. Parasha went for my mother, who, as I learned afterwards, was busy with others attending to my grandmother, who had fainted after the service at which she had cried herself into hysterics. My Aunt Elizabeth came with my mother. I rushed into my mother's arms and begged her not to take me back to the drawing-room. She was not pleased and felt ashamed before my girl cousins that I, though a boy, was such a coward. She wished to use force; but that brought me to such a state that she was frightened herself. My aunt now took pity on me and offered to move with her daughters, who had no fear of dead people, to our room. At any other time, nothing would have induced my mother to accept such a favour; but now she agreed with eager gratitude. A stone seemed to roll off my heart, when it was settled that we should move to this corner room, quite away from the parlour. In it neither the voice of the chanter, nor the "keening" of the women could be heard. This loud wailing over the dead was regarded in those days as an essential duty. Not only my aunts, but all the older women of the household and the estate, took turns in the parlour, wailing and lamenting. "You are our father and protector," they cried; "we have none left to care for us, we are miserable orphans!" Our change of room was quickly carried through; I was not present, because we were called to dinner. The meal was at a large round table in grandmother's room. After my sister and I came in, my grandmother, aunts, and cousins, all with black kerchiefs tied over their heads and some with the same round their necks, sat down side by side in silence; both my uncles were there too The general aspect of the scene made me feel sad. They all kissed us and cried and repeated in a sing-song voice, "Your grandfather and protector has left you," and something else of the same kind which I forget The table was soon covered with a number of dishes; the waiting was done—I do not know why—entirely by women. My father was busy about something in the workshop, and we waited for him some time. At last my mother said to her mother-in-law, " Why

do you not sit down to dinner, mother ? Alexyéi Stepanitch
will be here directly." But grandmother replied that
"Alosha was now the rightful owner and master of the
house; so it was proper to wait for him." My mother
tried to answer her : "He is your son, and you will always
be the mistress in his house." But grandmother said,
with an impatient gesture, "No, no, daughter-in-law;
that is not according to our custom. Let the cobbler
stick to his last, and me to my place!" To all this I
listened with great attention and curiosity. Suddenly
the door opened, and my father came in. It was long since
I had seen him ; I had only had a glimpse of him during
the night; he looked thin and pale and sad. Instantly
all rose and went to meet him ; even grandmother, who was
very stout and could not walk without some one supporting
her, dragged herself towards him ; and all his four sisters
fell down at his feet and began to "keen." It was impossible to catch all they said, and part I now forget ; but I
remember the words, "You are our father now; be kind
to us poor orphans!" My father with tears lifted them
all up and embraced them ; when his mother advanced
towards him, he bowed to the ground before her, kissed
her hands, and vowed that he would always submit to her
authority, and that no changes would be made by him.
When this was over, they all turned to my mother ; they
did not bow to the ground again before her, but they
called her the real mistress of the house, and begged her
not to deprive them of her grace and favour. I saw that
my mother heartily disliked this scene ; for she knew that
these women did not love her and were willing to spite her
in any way. She replied coldly, that she would never
assume any authority, but would continue to show respect
and affection to them all. Then they sat down to table
and began to eat so heartily—my mother did not—that
I watched them with astonishment. My Aunt Tatyana
helped fish-soup out of a large tureen, and, as she put bits
of roe and liver on the plates, she begged all to do justice
to them : "How poor father loved the roe and the liver!"
she repeated ; and I actually saw the tears fall from her
eyes into her plate. And just so the others shed tears and

ate soup with wonderful relish. Dinner over, all went to
lie down, and slept till tea. As I went through the maids'
room to our new quarters, I glanced timidly into the passage
which led straight to the parlour. From the parlour came
the sound of that monotonous wearisome chanting. My
parents also lay down, while my sister and I talked in
whispers. My courage had returned in daylight, and I
was even able to admire the bright sunbeams. I liked
our new room exceedingly : for one thing, in it I was far
from the dead body ; and also it was a corner room, and
one side looked out on the river Boogoorooslan, which
never froze, because of its rapid current and the number of
springs it contained. Just opposite the windows, it made
a sharp bend. The view of the rapid river in the snowy
landscape, the summer kitchen on an island and the high
bridge leading there, the other island with its tall graceful
trees covered with rime, and in the distance the mountain
with its jutting cliffs—this picture had a pleasing and
calming effect on me. For the first time, I felt that nature
even in winter may have a beauty of its own.

My composure lasted till dark ; but with the dying
rays of the setting sun, I began, without being aware of
it, to lose courage. At tea-time, I was afraid to go to
grandmother's room, because in the maids' room I had to
pass close to the dreaded passage. My mother told me
sternly to go, and I found power to obey ; but, as I ran
through the maids' room, I put my fingers in my ears and
turned my face away from the passage. After tea in
grandmother's room, they began to talk of grandfather's
death, and of the provisions of his will, and also of his
funeral, which was to take place in two days. My mother,
who saw that I was made uneasy by these topics, soon
took my sister and me away to our corner room, and invited
our cousins to come there ; they sat and talked with us
some time. When they left and bed-time had come,
fear again mastered me and was so clearly visible on my
face, that my mother understood what I should suffer in
the night if I were alone. My heart swelled with fervent
gratitude, when she said, " Seryozha, you shall sleep with
me to-night." That was all that I could wish ; and I

should certainly have asked it, and it would have been
granted ; but how difficult and how humbling would have
been the request ! I could not have brought myself to
it on the spot ; an hour, two hours, of torment would have
passed, before I came to that point Blessings on those
who have mercy on a child's timid heart, and spare him
the humbling confession of his cowardice ! The night
passed peacefully. Awake before dawn, I overheard
much interesting conversation between my parents. I
learnt that my father intended to retire from his profession,
and come and live at Bagrovo—very unpleasant news to
me ; for my experience of Bagrovo had twice proved
unfortunate, and it had no attraction for me. Sergéyevka,
where I had spent such a happy summer, was the object
of all my hopes and plans. I also learnt another piece of
news, that I should soon have a new little brother or sister.

The next day proved a repetition of its predecessor .
by day I was fairly cool and courageous, but at night-
fall my fears began again. My chief anxiety was caused
by the doubt, whether my mother would let me sleep with
her. I waited anxiously for the time when our beds would
be laid ; and great was my joy, when I saw my own pillows
placed on her bed I heard something new : grandfather
was to be buried the next day at the village of Nyeklyoodovo
This was contrary to his wishes ; for he had always
felt a dislike to the place. Why this was done, I do not
understand to this day ; but I remember that some grave
reasons for it were given. I must confess my fervent wish
that poor grandfather should be taken away as soon as
possible ; I felt that I should not enjoy true peace of mind
till then. Many people throughout life have a fear of dead
bodies ; I had, and never saw one till I was twenty. It is
hard to define this fear. Probably the grown-up man
fears the effect on his own mind : he knows that the sight
will disturb him and haunt his imagination. But I, at
that age, had a positive fear : I was convinced that, whenever I looked at grandfather, he would come alive again
for a moment and clutch hold of me !

The sad and solemn day came round. All the household rose early, and a constant running to and fro began,

accompanied by the slamming of doors. Earlier than usual, we went to grandmother's room for our tea, and found her and all our aunts already dressed for going out ; by the front steps stood a number of sledges, with horses harnessed in single file.   The court and the road were full of people : the peasants on his own estate were there with their wives, the old and the young ; and people from the villages round had come also, to say farewell to my grandfather, whom they all respected and loved like a father.   When all was ready, there was a general move to look for the last time on the dead.   Then the "keening" cry rose in the parlour and filled all the house with noise   I was much moved, but I felt no fear now—only a dim conception of the importance of what was going on, pity for poor grandfather, and sorrow that I should never see him more. Every door in the house was opened wide, and the cold was terrible.   My mother told Parasha not to take my sister, who was crying in her eagerness to go through the cold to say farewell to grandfather.   So we three were left alone in grandmother's warm room.   Suddenly, there was a dull sound in the parlour, and the tread of many feet ; and the sound of weeping and "keening" kept pace with the feet past our door.   Soon after, I saw a wooden coffin going down the front steps ; it seemed to be supported on men's heads.   Then the dense crowd parted ; and I could see that the coffin was carried by my father and two uncles and an old man who himself was supported by others.   My grandmother, too, was led along at first, but soon put into a sledge, while my aunts and my mother walked behind.   Many of those who were standing in the court bowed to the ground   The crowd moved slowly forwards into the road, stretched out all along it, and at last disappeared from my sight.   Standing on a chair and looking out of the window, I wept and wept, filled with a real feeling of love and tenderness for my grandfather whom all loved so warmly.   For one moment, I even wished to see him once more and kiss his thin wasted hand.

We sat in sad silence in grandmother's room.   The noise and movement in the house had given place to a deathly stillness.   But suddenly a sledge drove up to the

steps ; and my mother and our two cousins got out. I
believed that every one had gone to Nyeklyoodovo, twenty
versts away ; and I cried out for joy to see them. Their
arrival was soon followed by crowds of peasants returning
from the procession. My mother had followed the body
to the end of the village, where the coffin was laid on a
sledge, and all who were going on to the grave took their
places in other sledges. We went back to our corner
room. My mother, very weary and very sad for the death
of one whom she loved dearly, remained almost all day
lying down, and left us to ourselves. Our cousins spent
the day with us, and we had much friendly talk. It is
true, they did most of the talking, and from them I learnt
much that was new to me and even much that I had
thought impossible. For instance, I discovered that they
had little love for their parents : they feared them, and
constantly told lies to deceive them. I tried to reprove
them for this conduct ; I wished to show that they were
wrong and to teach them how good children ought to
behave. For this purpose, I drew upon my reading and
still more upon my own experience ; but my cousins did
not understand me, or laughed at me, or declared that their
papa and mamma were quite unlike mine.

Late in the evening my father returned. My grandmother was staying the night at Nyeklyoodovo with some
nieces ; and so were my aunts ; but my father had come
straight home from the graveside, declining all invitations
even to enter their house. He had eaten nothing all day
and was terribly tired, as he had walked a long way
behind grandfather's coffin. I slept that night in the same
crib as my sister. Fear came on me again in the evening,
but I concealed it. My mother would have let me sleep
with her ; but it interfered with her rest, and also she was
asleep before I went to bed. For long I lay awake ; a
coffin swaying up and down, with something lying inside
it, and slowly moving forwards on the shoulders of a crowd
of people—this picture would not leave me and banished
sleep to a distance. At last, after many efforts, thank God !
I fell asleep and slept till late

Grandmother, with my aunts and uncles, came back in

time for dinner next day. The whole house was scoured
the day before, and the stoves were kept hot, so that it
was warm everywhere except in the parlour, from which
every one was excluded for nine days. The chanting of the
Psalms went on day and night in the room where grandfather lived and in which he died   All our meals were
eaten in grandmother's room, which was the largest in
the house after the parlour ; and it was used generally as
a sitting-room also. For some days, my mother was not
herself again : she preferred to sit with us in our sunny
corner room ; it was colder than the rest of the house, but
my mother chose to remain there till our departure for
Ufa, which was to take place in nine days' time

Young as I was, I noticed that all my aunts, and especially the unmarried one, often kissed and embraced my
father, and said that he was now their only protector and
guardian. To my mother, too, they were very demonstrative   My Aunt Tatyana often came to our room, " that
her dear sister-in-law might not find it lonesome," and
invited her to discuss different household matters. But
my mother always replied, " that she had no intention of
interfering with their family and domestic concerns, that
her consent was not needed, and that all depended on
mother," meaning her mother-in-law   My father attended
certain family councils, and then reported to my mother,
that his late father had given verbal instructions to grandmother, before our arrival, to this effect   each daughter
(except Aksinya, my good-natured godmother) was to
have one family of serfs belonging to the house ; and for
Tatyana, land was to be bought from the Bashkirs, and
twenty-five peasants, whose names were specified, were
to be transferred to settle there ; also, he left among
his daughters a quantity of grain and personal property
of all kinds. " All my father said to me was this :
' Be kind to Tanyusha,* and let her have the same that
I gave to her sisters on their marriage ' , but I regard
his instructions to my mother as sacred, and shall carry
them out." My mother gave her approval to this resolve.
When my father signified his full intention to carry out

* Diminutive form of Tatyana

grandfather's wishes, all thanked him with low bows, and Tatyana bowed right down to the ground. She came, too, on purpose to embrace my mother and thank her; but my mother declined all thanks, saying that she had nothing to do with these arrangements.

From time to time, I noticed Parasha whispering to my mother, who sometimes listened but usually sent her about her business. But this same Parasha, when she was dressing me one day, said, "There you sit and do nothing, and they're robbing you all the time." Not understanding this, I asked her to explain. "Just see," she said, "how many peasants, and serfs, and gear of all kinds your father has given away among his sisters. And why? Your grandfather never said they were to have it. They asked him, right enough; but he replied, ' Be content with what your brother Alosha gives you.' Nikanorka heard all this with his own ears, and everybody in the house knows it." The whole matter was rather puzzling to me, and her words left no impression on my mind; but, following my regular custom, I told my mother about it. She was so angry with Parasha, that I was frightened to hear her speak so loud and so fiercely. Parasha cried and begged to be forgiven; she fell at my mother's feet, crossed herself, and took God to witness that it should never happen again. "The first time anything of the kind does happen," said my mother, "I shall pack you off to Old Bagrovo, to herd cattle." How sorry I was for poor Parasha! How piteously she looked at me and implored me to intercede for her! I did so with eagerness, and felt guilty for having brought such woe upon her. My mother forgave her, but nevertheless banished from our room a girl whom she liked and who was devoted to her. Parasha was never to appear, unless she was summoned; and I was strictly forbidden to pay heed to the talk of servants. The whole story, I was told, was made up by the servants in the house. At the time, of course, it never entered my head to doubt my mother's account of the matter; I was much older before I understood my mother's anger with Parasha, and her wish that I should remain ignorant of the sad truth which she herself knew too well. Then I understood

L

also why my mother blamed the innocent servants at Bagrovo, and I realised that on this occasion the servants had behaved better than some of their superiors.

My grandmother and aunt were now so kind to my sister and me, that I was convinced we were general favourites, and soon opened out to all and especially to grandmother. Before long, I proposed that all the party should hear me recite from the *Rossiad* and the tragedies of Sumarokoff. I was listened to with attention ; and my audience praised me and said that I was a clever boy and a good scholar.

In a few days my fears vanished entirely. I went all about the house, sometimes accompanied by Yevséitch. Once, when he was not with me, I even peeped into grandfather's room. It was empty : everything had been removed except his wooden settle and bedstead with cord sacking, which still stood in one corner ; in the centre of the bed was a slender board covered with felt, and on this the chanter, who was off duty, slept. There were two of them, Yekim Miséitch, who was old and decrepit, and Vassili, who was quite young and had red hair. The chanting went on day and night, and they took turns at it. The first time I entered this dismal room, Miséitch was chanting in a slow nasal voice ; even with spectacles he found it difficult to make out the print of the Psalter. A high stand in one corner was covered with a white cloth and supported a large *icon* with a yellow wax candle burning before it. At times Miséitch crossed himself, and at times he bowed. For some time I stood still, feeling moved and sorrowful. Suddenly, I felt a wish to chant the Psalms myself for grandfather ; I had learnt at Ufa to read the service-books. I asked Miséitch if I might, and he agreed. First, he made me say a prayer ; then I stood up on grandfather's low settle which was placed for me, and began to chant. At first, excitement seemed to choke me : I could hear my heart beat, and my clear childish voice shook ; but I soon got over this and felt an indescribable satisfaction. I had gone on for some time, when I was interrupted by the voice of Yevséitch, who had come in behind me and stood listening. "I think that's enough, my little falcon," said he ; "but you're a fine reader."

I looked round : Miséitch was leaning against the window,
asleep. When we awakened him, he thanked me and went
on with his chanting. I said a prayer before the *icon*,
looked at red-haired Vassili sleeping on grandfather's bed,
thought of all that was past, and sadly left the room.

And now the ninth day came, and with it the com-
memoration-service for grandfather. The evening before,
the whole party, including my two cousins, drove to
Nyeklyoodovo to spend the night. Only my parents
were left ; and they started early on the ninth day, to be
in time for the mass. My sister and I were alone in the
house ; but Yevséitch would not part with me, and I
proposed to go again to grandfather's room and chant the
Psalms. We found Miséitch reading and red-haired Vassili
sleeping, as before. At starting, I felt some emotion, but
my voice was steady now, and my secret satisfaction was
even greater than the first time. Yevséitch listened long
and patiently ; at last he said : " I think that's enough,
my little falcon ; I'm sure your little legs are tired." Once
more Miséitch was asleep, leaning against the window ;
once more I said a prayer, and prostrated myself on the
ground ; once more I looked sadly at grandfather's bed—
and we left the room. That was my last sight of the room
in that condition. As we went out, Yevséitch said to me .
" That was just right, my little falcon : while the rest were
praying over your grandpapa's grave at Nyeklyoodovo,
you were reading the Psalms for him in his own room."
I had a feeling of extreme satisfaction mixed with a kind
of pride.

The whole party returned from Nyeklyoodovo for
dinner, about which my aunts had been busy before they
left, as I noticed ; they brought with them my grandmother's nieces with their elder children. Before their
arrival, dinner was laid on the large table in the parlour.
My mother was very tired and upset, and my father's eyes
were red with tears ; but all the rest seemed to me fairly
cheerful. The moment they arrived, they sat down to
dinner. There were many dishes, and all so rich that my
mother hardly allowed us to eat anything. At the end of
dinner, piles of pancakes made their appearance ; and the

diners, who had been cheerful and talked loudly up till then, ate them with tears and even sobs. My mother ate nothing and was very sad ; I never took my eyes off her When she came to our room after dinner, I heard her say to Parasha, who had now been taken back into favour . " I could eat nothing, sitting at the very table on which his body was laid." I was so impressed by these words, that I myself felt a disgust for what I had eaten ; I actually turned sick. In the evening the visitors left, because there was no room for them in the house.

Next day, we made our preparations and packed ; and early on the third day we started. Our good-byes took a long time : many tears were shed, and there was much kissing and embracing. Grandmother said more than once : " For God's sake, Alosha, be quick and resign your post, and come to live in the country. How can I manage men's business ? I am a widow and an old woman. I am no use, and Tanyusha is young ; and we don't understand things. Your late father kept everything together ; but now no one will obey Tanyusha and me. We shall be left alone, now that everybody is going away. We are only women, and how can we get on ? " My father promised to comply with her wishes.

CHAPTER XIII

UFA

I MUST confess that I was not sorry to leave Bagrovo. Twice over I had stayed there, and each time I had been unhappy. The first time was in a rainy autumn; and the separation from my parents and the unmistakable indifference of our relations (though I should except my grandfather) had been hard to bear. The second time I went, it was a cruel winter, and grandfather died, and I was tortured by fear in a way which I did not soon forget. Thus, I had no reason to love Bagrovo. Our journey back to Ufa was much shorter and pleasanter: the frost was less severe, the sledge windows were not entirely veiled by snow, and the sledge itself did not upset.

At Ufa all our friends were very glad to see us again. The circle of our acquaintance, and especially of the children we knew, had grown much smaller: my godfather, M. Myortvavo, who, though he never made much of me, never teased me, had left some time before for Petersburg; the Knyazhevitches and their children had settled in Kazan; and the Mansuroffs also with all their family had gone to live somewhere else.

I had gained many new ideas and feelings, and I set to work to read my books over again. I understood much of their contents better than before, and even found there much that had entirely escaped me; hence the books themselves seemed to me in a sense new. More than a year had gone by since my unsuccessful attempt to teach my sister to read; my want of success was a real distress to me, and I started again on this important task; but my pains were still unrewarded. My sister could learn three or four of her letters in a morning and keep them in her memory till evening, for I always examined her at bedtime; but next morning her mind was an absolute blank. I could now write copies quite well; arithmetic I had long given up. I had hopes that we should go again to Sergéyevka in spring; but my mother told me this was not to be; for, in the first place, she was in good health, thank God; and, in the second, she would perhaps give me a new little sister or brother at the end of May. I was much interested and pleased by this prospect, but I parted with sorrow from my hope of spending the summer at Sergéyevka. My love of nature was growing strong; my love of fishing was also a powerful motive; and the approach of spring worked powerfully on a boy who was easily carried away and was later to be a passionate fisherman.

As soon as we returned to Ufa, I began to notice that discussions, and even heated discussions, were going on between my parents. The fact was, that my father wished to carry out exactly the promise he had given to his mother —to resign his post at once and move to the country, so as to save her from all the cares of management and assure the peace of her old age. He thought it essential for him to move to the country and manage the estate, even in case my grandmother would have agreed to live with us in the town—a plan which she would not hear of "Without the master's eye," he said, "everything will get out of order, and in a few years both Old and New Bagrovo will be changed beyond recognition." My father spoke much and long to this effect, always keeping his temper; but my mother replied with warmth to all his good reasons, that she disliked life in the country and especially at Bagrovo, where she was never well; that she was not liked by his relations; and that she would meet with constant annoyances there. There was another strong reason for moving to the country, in the shape of a letter from Praskovya Ivanovna Kurolyessova. When she heard of the death of my grandfather, whom she always called her second father and chief benefactor, she wrote to my father thus.

"It is absurd for you to go on living in a small way at Ufa, employed in some court or other and earning a pittance of 300 roubles. It will be far better for you to take up the management of your own estates ; and you can lend a hand as well to an old woman like me in managing mine. You can easily do so ; for Old Bagrovo is only fifty *versts* from Choorassovo, where I live all the year round."

At the end of the letter she said, that she ought long ago to have made the acquaintance of my mother, and hoped to see her now, and also the children who were to be her heirs. This letter my father read several times to my mother, and pointed out that it was impossible to refuse, unless they wished to displease his aunt and put an end to his expectations. To this my mother had no reply to make. I had settled before this in my own mind, that Praskovya Ivanovna was a masterful personage who expected to be obeyed, somewhat like the late Empress ; and now this notion was confirmed. The disputes, however, went on, and my father would not give way : one concession only my mother was able to secure—that he should not resign his post at once, but should postpone this step till she had recovered from her approaching illness, *i.e.* till summer. This approaching illness, it was explained to me, was connected with the coming of the expected brother or sister. After more than one rough draft, a letter was written to Praskovya Ivanovna ; and I too was made to write, on ruled paper, and say that I loved my grand-aunt and wished to see her. I did not really wish to see her, and I could not love her, because I did not know her. I knew that I was writing what was untrue, and untruthfulness was always severely judged in our house ; so I frankly asked, why I was made to write what was not true. My mother replied that I would certainly love this lady when I knew her, and that I ought to love her now, because she loved us and meant to be very kind to us ; my further questions and expostulations were not listened to.

Rumours of different kinds came constantly to the town from Petersburg, and caused general dismay and alarm. Exactly what they were, I could never find out, because they were never spoken of openly, and the regular answer to my questions was, that I was still a child and had no

business to know about such matters. I felt hurt; and one
answer in particular enraged me : " People who know too
much. soon grow old." But one fact could not be concealed. The Tsar ordered that all who were in the public
service should wear coats of a peculiar cut, with buttons
bearing the imperial arms—such a coat was called an
" Ober-rock "—and all their wives had to wear on public
occasions a kind of jacket over their dresses, the jacket
being embroidered in the same way as the men's uniform.
My mother was very skilful at dressmaking of every kind ;
and she set to work at once to make silver braiding which
looked very pretty on the light blue collar of a white
spencer or jacket. She wore this costume several times,
when going to church on festivals, or when calling on the
Governor's wife, and perhaps elsewhere. I always admired
her in it, and often escorted her to the door. Every one
called her a beauty ; and she was really more beautiful
than any one whom I knew.

Spring came on and brought with it sorrow rather than
joy to me. What did I care, if the torrents began to pour
down from the hills, if bare patches of earth were showing
in the garden and near the church, and if the river melted
once more and once more spread far and wide over the
fields ? I was not to see Sergéyevka with its splendid lake
and towering oaks : I was not to sit with Yevséitch on the
jetty and fish, nor to watch Soorka as he lay on the bank
and basked in the sun. Then I heard unexpectedly that
my father was going to Sergéyevka ; I fancy this was
settled some time before but concealed from me, to spare me
useless distress. Our land was to be surveyed, and a
surveyor was to go there for the purpose. The survey was
to be completed in a fortnight, as my father was bound to
return before the arrival of my new brother or sister. I
dared not ask to go with him. The roads were still impassable, and the river Byélaya in full flood . my father
had to take a boat for the first ten *versts*, and then make his
way, as best he could, to Sergéyevka on a peasant's cart.
My mother was very uneasy about him, and her uneasiness
spread to me. She also feared that he would be detained
by the survey ; and, to reassure her, he gave her his word,

that, if it were not over in a fortnight, he would drop everything and come back to us, leaving some one, perhaps
Theodore, Parasha's husband, to represent him on the
spot. At the parting, my mother could not refrain from
tears, and I simply howled. I was sorry to part with him
and afraid for him; and it was a bitter thought, that I
was not to see Sergéyevka or fish on the lake. Yevséitch
tried in vain to console me: he said that walking was
impossible in the mud, and fishing, in the flooded state of the
lake; but I felt some doubts, having noticed more than
once that, in order to set my mind at rest, people told me
what was not true. That fortnight was long in passing.
Though during our life in town I was not much with my
father, as he generally went to his office in the morning
and either dined out or had friends to dinner in the
evening, yet I felt listless and sad in his absence. He had
not time to explain properly to me what was meant by a
"survey"; so, to supplement my knowledge, I questioned
my mother and Yevséitch on the point; and, when I
learnt nothing new from them—they were quite ignorant
themselves—I invented an explanation of my own for
what seemed to me a solemn and important business
What the process looked like, I found out: I became
familiar with the posts, stakes, and chain, and the witnesses
in attendance. My fancy drew many pictures of it, in
which I wandered in thought with my father over the
fields and woods of Sergéyevka. It is odd that my
imaginary notions of surveying were a very fair approxima-
tion to the reality; I learnt this later by experience, and
my early belief in the solemnity and importance of surveying
always came back to me, as I rode or walked behind the
theodolite, which struck awe into the peasant who carried
it, while others dragged the chain and drove in stakes at
every twenty yards. Of the real object, i.e. to measure
the land and make a plan of it, I had, of course, no idea
then; and my ignorance was not confined to myself.

My father kept his word: he returned to Ufa in a
fortnight to the day. The return journey was much more
difficult the floods had begun to abate rapidly, leaving
bare earth in many places, so that he had to ride over the

ten *versts* which he had crossed in comfort in a boat a fortnight earlier. In the valleys and hollows there was still plenty of standing water, which sometimes came up to the horse's belly. When he arrived, he was splashed with mud from head to foot. We were all delighted to see him ; but he was not in good spirits. Many Bashkirs, and all the Russian settlers, *i.e.* the inhabitants of the two old villages, had disputed his claim ; and black posts had been erected round the land. (Black posts were used to indicate disputed land ; owners with an uncontested title might erect white posts.) When he had told all his adventures, my father added : " Well, Seryozha, it will be a long story before Sergéyevka is really yours ; I am sorry now we were in such a hurry to transfer peasants there." I was vexed, because the feeling of property was very pleasant to me ; and from that time I ceased to speak complacently, on every convenient occasion, of *my* Sergéyevka.

When the end of May approached, my sister and I were moved from the nursery to what we called the dining-room, though we never dined there. Parasha slept with us, and Yevséitch in the room between us and the workshop ; he had orders from my mother to be with me always. To be separated thus from my mother by the full length of our large house, seemed to me quite unnecessary, in spite of many assurances, that it was required by my mother's health, and that the life of the coming brother or sister depended upon it. It was not till later that I learnt the real cause of this separation.

It was at this time—on the first of June, I believe—that a violent thunderstorm took place and produced on me a strong impression of fear. It began about ten in the evening, when we were going to bed in the large room which had been the dining-room. Immediately opposite our windows the summer sun had gone down, and, though the western sky was still clear and threw a rosy light over the room, a black cloud was coming up, and from time to time discharged a dull rumble of thunder. I was standing beside my bed, saying my prayers, when suddenly there came a terrific crash of thunder which shook the whole house and deafened us. I threw myself on my bed and

got a severe blow on my leg. For a few moments I did
not realise where I was ; then I found myself sitting on
Yevséitch's knee, while the rain poured as if from a bucket
and the room was lit up by the glare from a fire. Yevséitch
explained that the cathedral belfry had been set on fire
by the lightning : that was where the glare came from.
My sister also had been frightened and was in her nurse's
arms. Suddenly the Kalmuck " Princess " came in with a
message, that the mistress wanted the children. We were
taken to the bedroom, where my mother was lying in bed ;
my father was attending to her, together with a certain
Alyona Maksimovna, whom everybody in the house
called " the midwife." I noticed that my mother was ill
as well as agitated ; she made us sit on her bed, and then
kissed and caressed us ; and I thought that she was
crying. When she saw my uneasiness, which my sister
was beginning to share, she said that the thunder and the
thought of our fright had alarmed her ; but she would
be quite well to-morrow. She gave us her blessing and
sent us off to bed. My father too gave us his blessing ; and
I noticed that he had all his clothes on, and was not preparing to go to bed ; from which I guessed that my mother
was ill. We went back to our own room. As the night
was warm, the windows were opened ; the deluge was over,
and a light rain was falling. Looking out of the window,
we could see three fires, which gave a tolerable light in
spite of the black clouds. Some officer rode up to our
window, and asked a question about my mother's health.
My sister soon grew sleepy, and Parasha put her to bed
and then went to sleep herself. I sat up for a long time
with Yevséitch, talking and looking out of the window.
My fear had passed off, and I began to ask him, what
lightning was, and why it burns, and what caused the noise
of thunder. His reply was : " The lightning is the fiery
arrow of the thunder : and whatever it strikes catches
fire." The sky became clear, the stars began to twinkle.
and the morning light was beginning to shine when at last
I fell asleep in my crib.

Next day my suspicion was confirmed : my mother
was really ill, and there was no further attempt to conceal

this from us. Our old friend, Avenarius, came to the house, and some other doctor as well. My sister and I saw our mother for a moment only; she kissed us and sent us away, saying that she wished to sleep. The green window-curtains were drawn and the room almost dark, so that I could not see her face clearly. My father looked pale and anxious. Grief oppressed my heart; I could not occupy myself in any way; I could only cry, and beg to go to my mother. My father must have been told of this; for he came to our room, and said that, if I wished mother to get well soon, I must stop crying and asking to go to her; I should pray to God and ask Him to be merciful to her; though my mother could not see me, yet her mother's heart knew of my tears, and this made her worse. I believed him; and, when I had prayed to God, I could keep back the tears, though I was not comforted. I tried to console my sister, who was sad too and cried more than once.

Next day, my mother was clearly worse; for we were not allowed to go to her, even to say good morning. The doctors came again and again to the house. The great image of Our Lady of Iberia was brought from the church, and a service was held in my mother's room. We were not allowed to attend it; but we saw the great image borne through the parlour and heard the chanting; and we knelt in prayer at the open door of our room. We were not even allowed into the garden that day, but were kept to the court yard—a large place and covered with grass like a meadow. We were told to run about, but we only walked quietly up and down. Soorka's advances met with no response from me, when he sprang up to my face, stood up on me, and licked my hands. Yevséitch and Parasha were sad and silent, or spoke to one another in whispers. Yevséitch had given up the attempt to cheer or comfort me: he only repeated, when he saw the tears constantly welling to my eyes, " Pray to God that your mamma may recover, my little falcon." When we returned from our sorrowful walk, I threw myself on my bed, drew the curtains close, hid my head under the pillow, and gave vent to the tears which I had repressed so long with an effort extraordinary for a child. This thought was in my mind too—that I was hidden and making no noise, so that my mother could not see or hear my grief. Yevséitch must have realised that it was impossible to stop such weeping as mine : he stood a long time near my crib and said nothing, though he knew that I was crying At last I could weep no more, and fell asleep. I slept fairly long and woke with a cry, as if in fear. My sister came running to me and said in a happy voice, " Mamma is better " ; and Parasha said the same Yevséitch was not there, but he soon came, and Parasha met him with the question, " Well, the mistress is better, is she not ? " " She is," he answered, but his voice shook. I noticed his voice, but still took some comfort. Our dinner-time was long past ; my sister had refused to eat in my absence, but now she was quite ready to sit down at table with me, and we took our dinner somehow. I asked Yevséitch to inquire about my mother ; he went, came back immediately, and said, " The mistress is asleep " ; a little later Parasha went and brought back the same report. A doubt began to creep into my heart ; I looked attentively at them both and said firmly, " What you are saying is not true." They did not reply at once, but glanced at one another, and looked disconcerted. Noticing this, I refused to listen to any further reassuring statements. While we were disputing over this, my father came in, and I guessed all from his face. " Come with me," he said in a low voice ; " your mother wishes to see you and give you her blessing." I burst into sobs, and my sister followed my example. " Now listen," he said ; " if your mother sees you crying, she will get worse , she may even die of it ; if you don't cry, it will do her good." The tears dried up in my eyes ; and my sister also stopped crying. After waiting a little, my father took our hands and led us to the bedroom. The room was so dark that I could only distinguish my mother's form but not her face. We went close to the bed and knelt down ; my mother blessed us with the *icon*, made the sign of the Cross over us, and kissed us ; then she made a hasty gesture, and we were removed at once. In the drawing-room we met a priest ; he blessed us too, and we went back to our room in a sort of stupefied state. I had

lost the power to think and even to understand : two things
went round and round in my head—the darkened room and
my mother's burning face   My state of mind could not
be called cold despair : the thought of my mother's death
never entered my head ; but I believe that my ideas had
become confused, and that this was the beginning of some
kind of insanity.   When bedtime came, Yevséitch undressed me and told me to say my prayer ; I did so, and at
the end, said aloud as usual, " God bless papa and mamma."
When I lay down, Yevséitch took a chair near me and began
to talk, but I did not listen.   I don't remember that I
slept, but Yevséitch declared afterwards that I went to
sleep and slept about an hour.   I only remember that
suddenly I heard joyful voices saying, " Glory to God !
Glory to God ! God has given you a little brother ; now
your mamma will soon be well."   It was Yevséitch and
Parasha, speaking to my sister ; and she, with a joyful
shout, ran to my bed, pulled aside the curtains, climbed up,
and threw her little arms round me.   All came back to me
at once ; I burst out sobbing wildly, and sobbed so long
that I damped the general joy and made them all uneasy.
My father was fetched.   When he came and heard my sobs,
he went up to me and called out, " What are you doing,
Seryozha ? You ought to rejoice, not to cry.   Glory to
God ! you have got a little brother, and mother will soon get
well."   He took me up and placed me on his knee, and
kissed and embraced me.   It was long ere my convulsive
sobs were quieted and I ceased to tremble and shake.
But by degrees calm was restored ; and the first thing I
saw was, that the room was bright with the morning light ;
and next I understood that my mother was alive and
would get well ! My heart was full of an inexpressible
happiness.

It was on the 4th of June that this happened ; and it
must have been very early, as the sun had not risen.   I
kept asking, why my sister had wakened, and why she had
heard the good news before me.   She declared that she was
not asleep when Parasha came running in ; but I was
unwilling to believe her.   I also insisted for a long time
that I had not been asleep ; but at last I was obliged to

admit that I was really asleep, when I was awakened by the loud voices of Parasha and Yevséitch and my sister's shout of joy. My father soon went away, and the two servants made haste to put us to bed. We did not go to sleep at once, but lay in our cribs, discussing what our little brother was like. At last, we were forbidden to talk, and sweet sleep came over us.

At a late hour we woke to happiness, and I asked at once to see my mother. I asked so persistently that Yevséitch went to tell my father ; but my father sent me a message that I must not think of it, and that I could not see her for some days. This grieved me. Then I asked to see the baby, and Parasha went down and got leave from Alyona Maksimovna for us to go quietly through the maids' room to our brother's nursery, which was divided from my mother's bedroom by another nursery which was generally occupied by my sister and me. Even outside the door we walked on tiptoe, which made Parasha laugh. In the little nursery a pretty cradle was hanging on a copper ring fixed in the ceiling. It had been a present from my maternal grandfather, when my eldest sister, who soon died, was born ; in it I and my second sister had been rocked. A chair was placed for me to climb on ; I pulled aside the green silk canopy and saw an infant in swaddling clothes sleeping there ; all I noticed was, that he had some black hair on his little head. My sister was held up, and gazed in her turn at the sleeping brother ; and we both approved of him. A foster-mother had been procured already, and was in the room, wearing her dress of office ; she kissed our hands. She had not yet taken the baby ; syrup of rhubarb was all he got at present. Alyona Maksimovna, seeing what good children we were, walking on tiptoe and talking in whispers, promised we should come every day to see the baby when she was going to wash him. Delighted by this prospect, we went cheerfully to play, first in the court and then in the garden Now I accepted with goodwill the advances of my favourite, Soorka ; and I believe that I ran and jumped and rolled on the ground more than he did. In the garden, I asked at once, why we had been kept out of it the day before. Parasha was often hasty, and she answered without thinking, " Oh, because your mother was crying out so yesterday, and in the garden you would have heard her." This news caused me such agitation and distress, that Parasha did not know how to put things to rights. She declared most solemnly, that it was all over now, that she had seen her mistress with her own eyes and spoken to her, and that she was not ill, only weak. She begged me to conceal her slip of the tongue from Yevséitch and every one else, declaring that she would be severely scolded for it ; and I promised to tell no one. I believed what Parasha said, and was relieved, and my heart grew light once more.

My happiness remained unclouded till the evening. Parasha's last words had made me understand more clearly the terrible nature of what had happened the day before ; but still I had no doubt that all was well over, and that my mother was nearly well. But in the evening, when the doctors came again and again, when the maids were constantly running from their room to the kitchen and hall, and above all, when I saw my father's sad face, on his coming to say good-night to us at bedtime—doubt and disquietude came upon me. In reply to my questions, my father had not courage to say that mother was well : he only said, " She is better ; God is merciful, and she will get well." And God was in truth merciful to us ; for, after a few days which I passed in anxiety and grief, I was relieved by the returning cheerfulness on my father's face, and by the assurances of Avenarius that my mother was really convalescent and I should see her quite well in a few days. Then, and not till then, I turned all my attention and interest and love on the new little brother. We went every day to see him in his bath ; but at first I looked on without interest ; for in thought I was living in my mother's room, beside her bed of suffering.

At last, after an interval of nearly a week, I did see my mother. She was pale and thin and still confined to bed ; the green curtains were drawn, and perhaps that was why her face seemed to me paler than ever. My father had instructed me beforehand : not only was I not to cry, but I was not to show too much joy, nor to be too demonstrative.

This perplexed me; for I did not then know how to hide warm feelings and moderate the expression of them. I must have seemed strange and unlike myself; for my mother said, " Seryozha, you're not a bit glad that your mother did not die ! " I broke down, and ran from the room. My father then explained the reason of my trouble. When I had had my cry out, I was called back to the room, and my mother tenderly embraced us both (but me especially), and said, " Don't be afraid; your love will not hurt me." I put my arms round her and cried on her breast : " If you had died," I whispered, " I would have died too." But my mother evidently felt that this interview was too exciting for her, for she said suddenly and hastily : " Go and see your little brother ; he is soon to be christened." We went straight to the nursery. The infant had just been washed, dressed in a fine new frock, and wrapped up in a new sheet and a pink velvet coverlet ; he was, as may be supposed, crying. I felt sorry for him ; but he soon grew quiet at the breast of his foster-mother. Seeing the preparations for the christening, and hearing it talked of, I asked an explanation of a ceremony which I had never heard of and never seen. When the explanation was given, I was determined to act as godfather to my brother. I was told that this was impossible : I was too young, and I had no godmother to stand at the font with me. But I easily got over the second difficulty, by saying that my sister would act as godmother. As I was obstinate, and likely to cry if disappointed, a trick was played upon me, which took me in at the time : my sister and I were placed beside the real godfather and godmother at the ceremony. The symbolical mysteries of the rite I could not understand ; but I watched with strained attention, surprise, and even alarm : I thought that the priest might cut my brother's head with the scissors ; and, when the infant was dipped in the water, I cried out with fear. By my importunity I won the privilege of holding my godson at the font—the nurse, as a matter of course. was holding him also—and I long retained the pleasing delusion that my brother was my godson ; I went so far as to sign him with the Cross, whenever we parted.

M

Within a few days, we were moved back from the dining-room to our old nursery. My mother's convalescence was slow : she hardly attended at all to household duties, and saw no one except the doctor, the Chichagoffs, and Mme. Cheprunoff. I was constantly with her and read various books to her aloud, some to amuse her, others to send her to sleep : for some reason, she slept but little at night. Amusing books were got from the library of M. Anitchkoff ; for the other object, we used my books for children, and also the *Rossiad* and Sumarokoff. Among the former sort, I remember in particular *The Life of the English Philosopher, Cleveland,** in fifteen volumes, I think, which I read with great satisfaction. Apart from reading, I very soon became accustomed to wait on my mother, and to give her her medicines at the regular hours with strict punctuality ; she did not often want her maid, and when she did, I summoned her. This was a satisfaction to my mother, because she did not care for the presence and society of servants, either men or women ; while I was happy and proud to think that I could be useful to my mother. While talking to me alone long at a time and often, she perceived, I think, that I could understand her better than she had supposed, and began to speak to me of matters on which she had been silent before. I noticed this, because sometimes the subject of our talk was beyond my age and powers of understanding. If, as sometimes happened, my questions showed that I was not following, she changed the subject at once, saying, " We will talk about this later." I disliked it especially, when she began to discuss a thing with me as if I was grown-up, and then suddenly changed her way of talking and adapted it to my tender age. My vanity always suffered from a sudden change of this kind ; and it was worst of all, that my mother thought it so easy to deceive me. Later, I began to play tricks : I asked no questions and pretended that I was never puzzled. For one thing, my mother told me how unwilling she was to go and live in the country. She had a number of reasons, the chief of which were as

* I cannot trace this person and think Aksakoff may have made some mistake.

follows : Bagrovo was damp and bad for her health ; she would certainly fall ill there, and it would be impossible to get medical assistance, as there was no doctor near ; she did not like her relations nor any of the neighbours, who were all ill-mannered and uneducated people, unable to converse on any subject ; life in the depths of the country, without the society of clever people, would be terrible, and we should grow stupid ourselves in consequence. " My one hope," she said, " is in the Chichagoffs ; luckily, they are moving to the country too and will be living within thirty *versts* of us. At least it will be possible to breathe freely in their society two or three times a year." I did not quite understand all this, but I believed my mother and shared her sad forebodings. She also disapproved of the proposed visit to Praskovya Ivanovna for a prolonged stay at Choorassovo ; she did not yet know that lady and supposed her to be like my father's other relations. The fact proved to be far otherwise. My dear little sister was very grieved to leave Ufa ; but I don't to this day know why she was.

As soon as my mother began to get better, my father sent in an application, asking leave to resign his post. At the same time, my two uncles came to us from their regiment ; both had retired from the army, the elder with the rank of major, the younger as a captain. This difference of rank caused general surprise : for both were enrolled in the Guards on the same day, transferred as captains to a line regiment on the same day, and retired from the army on the same day. I was very glad to see them, especially my Uncle Serghéi, whom I considered such a wonderful artist. I reminded him, how he used to tease me " when I was small," and added, with a feeling of my own importance, that it was no longer possible to play foolish jests on me. As a parting gift, my uncle painted me an incomparable picture on glass : it represented a marsh, a young sportsman with a gun, and a white setter with liver-coloured spots and close-cropped tail ; the dog had just found some game and was pointing at it, with one leg in the air. The picture was prophetic ; for I became a keen shot later. My uncle was very fond of the gun himself. Both uncles were much vexed that we were going to live in the country.

Without waiting for leave to resign, all preparations were made by my parents for the move to Bagrovo. Horses were brought from there, and a whole train of waggons, with belongings of various kinds, were sent off in advance. Good-byes were said to all our friends; and then, as the permission was still not forthcoming, it was resolved not to wait for it. The Governor granted my father leave of absence; and the permission was sure to be granted before that ran out. My uncles were left living in our house, with a commission to sell it.

We left Ufa on nearly the same date as we had left it two years before. But our travelling arrangements were different: my mother took with her our little brother and his foster-mother, while my sister and I with Parasha drove in a carriage without springs which constantly rattled and jingled, to our great amusement. We took the same way as before, and stopped at the same places—fishing on the Dyoma, stopping thirty-six hours at Parashino, and inspecting everything there. The impressions left on my mind by this second journey were as pleasant as ever, but not as fresh and new and overpowering; on the other hand, I understood them better, and felt them more deeply. Parashino was an exception: it made me feel sad and depressed. The harvest was a failure there that year: the rye was thin, and the wheat short and full of weeds. There seemed to be less work to do, and yet the harvesters found it more burdensome. One of them, a sullen-looking man, said to my father in a rough voice: "There's no pleasure in the work, Alexyéi Stepanitch. I don't like to see a field like this: it's all thistles and weeds. You walk and walk all day, and glean an ear now and again." My father answered, "We can't help it; it is God's will"; and the surly reaper replied with no trace of surliness in his voice, "We all know that, *batyushka.*"

It was some time before I understood the profound significance of these simple words; they calm all agitation and check all human murmurings, and under their beneficent power Orthodox Russia lives to this day. Clear and calm is the heart of that man, who can say them and hear them with conviction.

Most of the inhabitants of Parashino were in low spirits ; and the chief cause of this was a severe epidemic among their cattle, on the top of the bad harvest My father spoke long on the subject with Mironitch, who said, for one thing :

" If God has sent us a poor harvest, that does not matter so much ; we've plenty of last year's corn in the village ; and, if any one runs short, what else is the owner's granary there for ? But it does matter to a peasant with a family of small children, when God sends plague among the cattle. How can the children do well without milk, *batyushka* Alexyéı Stepanıtch ? Now there's the foreman, Archipoff, he had ten milk cows in his byre and not one hair of them is left ; and he has a lot of children. God is angry at our sins."

Parashino was a rich village, but it suffered often from cattle-plague. My father knew the real cause of this, and he said to Mironitch :

" You must look more strictly after the men who deal in leather. They buy for a song from the Bashkirs the hides of cattle that have died of plague ; and that accounts for the constant epidemics at Parashino."

Mironitch scratched his head and looked displeased as he answered, " You may be right, *batyushka ;* but in any case it is for our sins that God sends His punishments." My father did not forget to ask for the old man, whom he had seen working in the mill. He was now excused from all kinds of work, and died within the year. The old peasants from Bagrovo said this time of Mironitch, that his drinking bouts had become more frequent ; but they still declared that they did not wish any one else over them.

We drove out of Parashino at daybreak and made our halt by the Ik, that swift and deep and full river. We camped out at the last bridge on the most rapid branch of the stream. I had plenty of time to observe and admire the noble river, which is richly stored with fish. We halted more than four hours, and fished to our heart's content ; we caught some crabs too. That night we lay at Korovina, and about noon on the next day we saw Bagrovo from the hill. I was then in the carriage with my parents; there was plenty of room in it; and, when my mother was not lying down, I and my sister were admitted there in turns; but I confess that my turn came oftenest It was a fine hot day. My mother, sunk in the deepest gloom, sat in one corner of the carriage; my father was in the other, and he too seemed depressed, but I noticed that he could not refrain from a smile of satisfaction, as he looked down on the scene opening before our eyes— the reedy ponds, the green woods, the village, and the buildings of Bagrovo.

CHAPTER XIV

WE ARRIVE AT BAGROVO TO LIVE THERE

WHEN we drove up to the house, my grandmother, who had grown much older in six months, and my Aunt Tatyana, were already standing on the steps. Grandmother shed tears of sincere joy; she embraced my parents, crossed herself, and said : " Glory to God! the real owners of the place have come. I never thought I should live to see you. Tanyusha and I have counted the days and hours, and looked, till our eyes were tired, along the road from Ufa." We went straight to grandmother's room, the one which had been occupied by grandfather; her old room had been given to her daughter, and a door had been opened between the two rooms. When we arrived, the pair were having their dinner at a small table beside grandmother's bed ; they were waited on by women only, all the men having been sent out to field labour. Grandmother left her own dinner uneaten ; and the household bestirred itself in earnest to provide us with a meal. A bevy of maids hastened up and quickly laid the table in the parlour ; and very soon we all sat down to a fresh dinner. There proved to be a number of courses, as if we had been expected ; but all the dishes were so rich that my mother and sister and I rose almost hungry from table. Grandmother constantly spoke of grandfather with tears, and she ate a good deal ; after dinner she went as usual to lie down, while my parents arranged about their instalment in their new quarters. The " new room for the young mistress "—a name it always kept—was not yet completely furnished : two carpenters were at work in it, old Michéi and young Akim. For the time, we took the drawing-room and the

corner room, which had been my aunt's, for our occupation.
But the latter had lost all its charm, because the windows
and all the side that looked out on the river were blocked
by the addition of the "new room." This room was
separated from the corner room by a short passage which
opened on the garden ; but the door had not yet been made.
During the rearrangement of all the furniture we had brought
from Ufa, and until order was restored in the house,
Yevséitch took me out for walks, of course with my mother's
permission ; and we had time to inspect everything—the
river Boogoorooslan, rapid and full of deep pools, which
took a bend and flowed all along the garden ; the summer
kitchen, the island, the mill with its pond and dam. This
time I was so pleased with everything, that one minute was
enough to erase from my memory all the disagreeable impressions produced by my two former visits to Bagrovo.

My father was much occupied at first by starting on the
business of managing the estate. Grandmother insisted
on this ; and he himself looked on it as a duty which he
could not evade. But my mother, in spite of all requests,
positively refused to undertake the management of the
house, and, still more positively, to settle the payments due
from the labourers' wives and household servants, and the
spinning and weaving to be done by them. She declared
very firmly, that she would live there as a visitor and would
undertake nothing, except to give orders for dinner to our
town cook, Makéi, and this only on condition that grandmother should give orders for a dinner to suit her own taste,
to her country cook, Stepan. On this point there was much
discussion and debate. I noticed that my mother was in a
constant state of irritation, and spoke sharply, although
my grandmother and aunt spoke politely to her and even
timidly. I once said to her, "Mamma, you are displeased
about something : you are always angry." She answered :
"No, I am not angry, but I find my position painful. No
one here understands me. Your father will be occupied
from morning to night with estate business ; and you are
still too young to share my vexation." I could not in the
least understand what could be the cause of this vexation.

A number of changes were made in the house, before

the new room was finished. The door from the drawing-
room into the passage was closed up, and a new door opened
into the corner room; the door from grandmother's old
room into the pantry was also closed, and a new entrance
made to the maids' room. All these changes certainly
made for comfort and quiet; but, as they were all due to
my mother's contrivance, they were carried out with some
grumbling. For a fortnight, the noise of carpenters at
work never ceased in the house; there was not a quiet
corner; and, as the weather was fine, my sister and I
ran about from morning till night in the courtyard and
garden and in the birch wood, where jackdaws had already
settled and which was afterwards called "The Jackdaw
Wood." During this time I did no reading or writing; my
mother allowed me to go fishing every day with Yevséitch,
of whose zealous care she was by this time convinced.
Every day I grew fonder and fonder of fishing; and every
day I discovered new beauties in Bagrovo. In the deep
pools by the garden, and from the mill-dam, we caught perch
and roach, so large that often I could not pull them out
without Yevséitch's help. Between the summer kitchen
and the mill, where the stream divided and became shallow,
we caught gudgeons and sometimes other small fish as well.
The big fish, such as tench and others, had ceased taking at
that time of year; or rather—though I did not discover
this till much later—we did not know how to catch them.
In general, the art of angling was still in a most primitive
stage. I liked the island best of all. There it was possible
to catch both large and small fish: the old channel, where
the water was still deepish, was the place for the big ones;
and on the other side, where the stream ran shallow over a
clear bottom of sand and pebbles, the gudgeons took
splendidly. Merely to sit on the sloping green bank, with
no rod in my hand, in the shade of the birches and limes,
was so delightful, that even now I cannot recall that time
without emotion. The island was a favourite spot with my
aunt also · she was a great lover of angling, and often
sat there and fished with me.

At length, we ceased to hear the noise of axes and
planes, and the monotonous hissing of saws. All these

tools were objects of curiosity to me; and I liked to look
long and attentively at the lively activity of the carpenters,
whose work I hindered by my constant questions. The
room, which my grandfather had planned for my mother's
use, was now completely finished. A religious service was
held in it; the new walls were sprinkled by the priest with
holy water; and we moved into our fresh quarters. By
" we," I mean my parents and myself: my sister and baby
brother lived in the corner room. which had been my aunt's,
and was now turned into our nursery. My mother's room,
always called " the mistress's room " by the servants, was
even more cheerful than the old corner room, being nearer
the river. A spreading birch sapling, which grew on the
bank, nearly touched the wall of the room with its boughs.
I liked to look out of the window which faced the river;
I could see the distant point where the green valley of the
Boogoorooslan joined that of the Karmalka, and between
them the steep bare summit of the Chelyaef hill.

My father was in truth occupied with the business of
the estate from morning till evening. Every day he drove
to the fields; every day he walked to the stables and byres;
every day he visited the mill. An official of some kind
came from the town, read a formal document to the
assembled peasants, and inducted my father into possession
of the estate inherited by him from his father. All the
peasants and their wives were then entertained to spirits and
beer; they all bowed low before my father, embraced him,
and kissed his hands and face. Many of them, as they
spoke of my late grandfather, shed tears, crossed themselves,
and said, " The kingdom of heaven be his ! " I was my
father's only companion, and came in for a share of the
kissing and embracing. I felt proud to be the grandson of
my grandfather   I was no longer surprised at the affection
shown by the peasants to my father and me; I felt that it
could not be otherwise, because he was the son, and I the
grandson, of Stepan Mihailovitch. Nothing would induce my
mother to come out and greet the peasants and their wives:
to all persuasions of my father, grandmother, and aunt, she
persistently replied that the real mistress of the house and
land was " mother," meaning her mother-in-law. She

sent this message to the peasants ; but my father did not
give it : he said that their young mistress was not well
I thought that they were not pleased ; it is probable that
they all knew her to be quite well. I was vexed with my
mother for not coming out to see the kind people, and
ashamed to hear my father say what was not true. When
we returned to the house, I spoke of this to my mother
before them all, whereupon she reproved my father with
some heat for not telling the truth. He was vexed, and
said : " I was ashamed to say that you were unwilling to
be their mistress and unwilling to see them. What have
they done to offend you ? " There was another thing
which I thought odd and disagreeable · while my father
was being inducted into his estate, and while the peasants
were shouting their congratulations and good wishes—
" Health and long life to you, our father Alexyéi Stepanitch ! "—just then, my grandmother and aunt, who were
looking out of the open window, fell into one another's arms
with tears and loud cries of sorrow.

" What were grandmother and aunt crying about ? "
I asked, when I was alone with my mother. She reflected
and then answered : " They were thinking that they have
had full control here all their lives, and that now I, a mere
stranger, am the mistress ; that I might assume authority
to-morrow if I chose, though I don't choose at present ;
and that your grandfather is dead. That is what caused
their grief."

" But why, mamma, did you not go out to see our kind
people ? They are so fond of you."

" Because that would have made it worse for your
grandmother and aunt ; and besides I can't endure—but
you are too young to understand me." Nor could I induce
her by my persistent questions to say one word more. I
was long tortured by curiosity, as I puzzled over this
question : " What can it be that my mother cannot stand ?
Surely it cannot be our kind people, who said themselves
they they were so attached to us ? "

And now my aunts began to pay us visits. The first
to come was Aksinya ; I noticed no change at all in her :
she was just as good-natured and kind to us as before.

The next was Alexandra with her husband; and I saw at once that she was quite different. Not only had she become affectionate and respectful in manner; but she ran, as Parasha might have done, to do services for my mother; yet my mother showed no warmth towards her. The last aunt to arrive was Elizabeth with her daughters. The proud " General's lady " did not fawn upon my parents like Alexandra, but she too was changed: her manner, which had been cold and haughty, was now attentive and polite. Even my cousins were different Katerina, the younger of them, was naturally lively and gay; we had liked her best on our previous visit and wished to become close friends with her now. But the new politeness proved a barrier· she was so reserved and cold with us, that we were repelled and found it impossible to feel for her as for a near relation None of the aunts stayed long at Bagrovo.

At last the Chichagoffs came to us. My mother's sincere and keen pleasure in their visit communicated itself to me: I sprang into Mme. Chichagoff's arms and embraced her, as if she were my nearest and dearest. My face must have revealed my joy; for she looked at her husband and said with surprise, " See, my dear, how glad Seryozha is to welcome us! " For the first time in my life, M. Chichagoff took notice of me and patted me on the back; at Ufa, he had never spoken to me. After this, his feelings towards me grew warmer every year; and, as a schoolboy, I was quite a favourite with him. Mme. Chichagoff's mother, Mme. Myortvavo—for whom, as I was told, my late grandfather had great respect—had a reputation for exceptional tact and good sense. She occupied the rest of the party with her pleasant talk, while my mother carried off the Chichagoffs to her room, which was soon the scene of most lively and intimate conversation. Even I was told to go and join my sister in the nursery. This visit gave new life to my mother, whose spirits had been failing before. The visitors left after three days, having exacted a promise that we would come and stay a whole week with them.

Every year, it was the custom at Bagrovo to go hawking

after quails, which were a favourite delicacy, whether fresh
or salted, with all the household. This year as usual, two
hawks had been taken from the nest and reared in a coop.
Philip, my father's old falconer, had one of these birds ; and
Ivan Mazan, who had once waited on my grandfather, had
the other ; and, though he was sent to work at the harvest
every day till the time of our arrival, he refused to part
with his hawk and trained it at night When the season
for hawking began, the two men came home late every
evening with a goodly number of plump quails and landrails.
I was very anxious to see the hawking, but my mother
would not let me go, till at last my father went himself
and took me with him. I was delighted with it ; and, as
my father pleaded my cause and assured her that there was
no danger, my mother often let me go out with Yevséitch
Before long, I had a passion for hawking ; and on those
happy days, on which I got leave in the morning to sally
forth, I waited most impatiently for the appointed hour
At two in the afternoon, either Philip or Mazan, having had
a sleep after an early dinner, would appear, with a hungry
hawk on his wrist and his own dog on a lead—they both
had dogs which were given to chasing quails—and would
say, " It is time to be off, Sir." The horse had long been
standing between the shafts ; and off we set for the fields.
To watch the hawk in swift pursuit of his prey was only
one of my pleasures : everything about the sport was
delightful. First the dog—getting scent of a quail, and
showing his excitement by wagging his tail, snorting, and
pressing his nose against the ground, and then creeping
nearer and nearer to the bird, and getting more excited
every moment. Then the sportsman—holding the hawk
high on his right wrist, and tugging with his left hand at the
leash of the straining dog ; whistling to the dog and breaking into a run behind it in his own excitement. Suddenly
the dog stands petrified on the spot, with a sidelong thrust
of his body and his muzzle sticking out , the man calls out
sharply, " Hold up ! Hold up ' " and pushes the dog forward
with his knee. Then, from Heaven knows where, a quail
starts up under the dog's very nose and whirrs away.
Already the eager hawk is after it with her talons spread ;

up she comes with it, pounces on it, is borne forward some
distance, and then drops with her prey upon the grass or
stubble. These are sights which might please any one.
But I liked also to watch what followed, when the falconer
ran up to his hawk, trod the grass smooth all round, knelt
down, bent cautiously over his bird, smoothed her fluttering
wings, and carefully took the quail from her ; then he tore
off the head as a dainty for the hawk, before he started in
pursuit of fresh victims. I liked to watch the hawk fed,
when she shook off the feathers and down clinging to her
bloodstained beak, and cleaned her beak on the falconer's
sleeve ; at first she would greedily swallow large pieces of
meat, and even small bones, and gorge till her crop swelled
out to the size of a fist. My pleasure in these sights showed
that I was to be a keen sportsman. But alas ! in spite of
all my endeavours to please my mother and sister by
descriptions of this amusement, they both declared, it was
only painful and repulsive !

Though I had myself already noticed a great change
in grandmother, my attention was especially called to it
by a conversation between my parents, which I overheard
while reading my book.

"What a change there is in your mother since your
father's death !" my mother said. "She seems to me
even to have grown smaller ; nothing really interests her ;
she has lost hold of everything. She speaks constantly
of her loss ; she pays little heed even to her daughter.
When I say that Tatyana ought to be settled in life, and
that a husband should be found for her, she won't hear of
it . she only says, ' As God pleases, so it will be.' "

My father sighed and said, " Oh yes. mother is quite
changed ; I don't think she will live long."

I felt sorry for grandmother, and said, " We ought to
comfort grandmother and stop her from grieving." My
father was surprised by my sudden interposition ; he
smiled and said, " Yes, you and your sister should go and
see her oftener and try to cheer her up." Accordingly, we
began to go to her room several times a day. We usually
found her sitting on her bed, with a spinning-wheel before
her, and spinning goats' down, while a number of girls,

belonging to the house or estate, were squatting round her and cleaning the hairs out of the tufts of down. Each girl, when she had cleaned her tuft, handed it to the old lady, who held it up to the light and, if she found no hairs in it, laid it in a basket near her; but, if the tuft was not properly cleaned, she handed it back and scolded the girl for her carelessness. Grandmother's eyes were dull and leaden; often she grew drowsy over her work; sometimes she pushed the wheel suddenly away and said, " What is the use of spinning to me ? Time for me to go to Stepan Mihailovitch ! "—and then she would begin to weep. At first, my sister and I did not know how to make advances to her : we only sat there for a little and then went away. But we learnt from our aunt how to please her. In spite of her indifference to everything about her, she still kept her old liking for certain favourite dishes and dainties. Thus she was very fond of the berries of herb-paris, and of mushrooms fried in sour cream. Of the berries there were plenty in the kitchen-garden; our aunt went there with us and showed us the place; and the three of us picked a whole basinful and took them in to grandmother. She seemed pleased. " Splendid berries," she said; " so large and ripe," and ate them with enjoyment; she wished to give us some, but we said we dared not eat them without mother's leave. Next, our aunt showed us the place where the mushrooms grew. This was a hole or hollow in the centre of the courtyard, near my aunt's store-house; * there must have been some building there once, as it was the only place where these mushrooms grew. Grandmother called this place " the golden hollow "; and it was watered every day by Grusha, a deaf girl with a squint. Again helped by our aunt, we pulled out of the very ground a plateful of button-mushrooms and carried it in to grandmother. She was very much pleased, and ordered the cook to fry a whole panful for her. We had again to refuse her offer to treat us to mushrooms; she made an impatient gesture, and said, " Dear ! dear ! how odd you are ! " Having earned her favour in this way, we began to talk on different subjects to grandmother; and she was

* See p. 251.

getting more friendly and taking more notice of us, when
an unexpected incident occurred which cooled my feelings
so much, that for a long time I only said " Good morning "
and " Good-bye," when I paid her a visit. We were talking
cheerfully to her one day, when a red-haired village girl
handed her a tuft of down which had already been rejected
once ; grandmother held it up to the light, and, seeing that
there were hairs in it, with one hand caught the girl by the
scalp, while with the other she pulled out a whip from under
her pillows and began to lash the offender. I ran off   I
was reminded of the National School, and felt no further
wish to sit in grandmother's room, and watch her spinning
at her wheel and the girls picking hairs out of the goats'
down.

For a fortnight we had bad, or at least, damp weather,
and then the bright autumn season set in   There was
frost every night ; and, when I woke in the morning, I
saw all the ground, except where the sun was shining on it,
covered with white sparkling hoar-frost. " What a frost
there is on the ground!" Yevséitch used to say, as he handed
me my clothes to put on. And, in fact, the long and broad
strip shaded by the house lay there like a white table-
cloth, sharply distinguished from the damp dark soil
beyond it   The strip soon grew small and crooked, as the
rime disappeared at the first touch of the sun's rays,
which had a good deal of heat in them even at the end of
September. I liked to watch the sun routing the frost,
and was pleased when the objectionable patch of white had
entirely vanished.

I don't know why, but my father had never once taken
me to see the farm-work. The reason he gave was that
I should get weary, because he had to spend a long time
there. The reaping was long over ; most of the rye had
been carried already to the stackyard, the peas had been
threshed, and the poppy-heads shaken empty—and I had
seen nothing of it all ! At length, frost and sun had dried
the remaining sheaves, and all went to work with a will,
to finish the carrying, which was rather late that year.
From grandmother's room I could see the waggons laden
with sheaves slowly approaching our stackyard.   This

novelty excited my curiosity, and I begged to go with my father, who was just driving off to the fields. " Yes, you can come now," he said ; " I shall only make a round of the fields, and then stay at the stackyard, sending you home with Yevséitch." My mother gave her consent. As I had never once been in a cornfield since the time at Parashino, two years before, it was with great glee that I sat down beside my father in the cart. At starting, I suggested that it would not be a bad thing for him to take his gun, as he did sometimes ; and the gun went with us. My life in the town had, of course, given me no real notion of autumn in the country. Everything was new to me, and as delightful as it was surprising. We drove past a pond, where some remnants of ice were still visible on the sloping muddy banks ; a flock of ducks were swimming in the middle, and I asked my father to shoot one, but he pointed out that they were out of shot, and that no gun would carry so far. Then we went up a hill and came out upon the fields. The grass was withered and dark, and trailed on the ground ; the bare steep hillocks looked barer and steeper than ever ; the marmots' burrows seemed higher and more imposing, because the withered leaves had been blown off the wild-acacia bushes and no longer concealed the clay structures. But there were no marmots now : they had long been hiding in their holes, my father told me. And now we began to meet waggons laden with corn. The frames of these were short, with a post at each corner ; and the sheaves, very neatly packed in two rows between the posts, were kept in position by a weight on the top and firmly bound with ropes in front and behind. All this my father explained to me ; he said that a load of this kind would not be upset or disordered on our steep roads ; that a sensible horse, alone and unguided, would bring it home to the yard. In fact, the waggons were minded only by boys or girls ; each walked cheerfully beside his or her horse, and bowed low on meeting us. When we reached the cornfields, we saw some men working : they loaded the waggons with long forks, and then roped them, and sent them off in charge of the children. We greeted the labourers and said, " God speed the work ! "—and they

N

thanked us.   We asked if they had seen any black-cock, and
were told that any number of them had been sitting on the
stooks, but they had all flown   So the gun was not of any
use to us.   Most of the labourers, my father said, were
busy in the yard, where we should soon see them at work.
" But perhaps, Seryozha," said he, " you would like to see
the women threshing the buckwheat ? "   Of course I said
yes, and off we drove.   From some distance we heard a
dull sound like the tramp of many feet, but this was soon
drowned by the shrill noise of women's voices.   Yevséitch
was contemptuous :   " What a noise they make," he said,
" as if they were doing something useful !   Women, by
themselves, are like that."   The noise of voices grew
louder as we got near, and then suddenly stopped.
Yevséitch said scornfully, " Ah ! they've seen us, the
magpies ! "   In one of the fields a level space had been
cleared and swept for threshing ; on this a tall heap of
buckwheat straw was lying, and more than thirty flails
were plying up and down over the heap.   I had never seen
this operation before, and was fascinated by the grace and
dexterity of the regular rapid blows.   The flails flashed in
the air and fell nearly together, yet never got entangled,
though the women did not stand still, but now advanced
and now retreated.   Their skill seemed to me incredible.
Not to interrupt their work, my father did not greet them
till they reached the end of the row.   A foreman came up
to us and said: " They're going over it for the last time,
batyushka Alexyéi Stepanitch.   The straw was pretty clean
before ; but I told them to go over it once more.   Now
there won't be a grain left."   When they got to the end,
my father and I gave the usual greeting, " God speed the
work ! " and got the usual words of thanks from a chorus
of female voices.   On another threshing-floor two labourers
were winnowing a heap of the buckwheat grain : the breeze
carried away all the rubbish and the light meagre grains,
while the full and heavy grains fell, in a slanting rain, on
the ground , a third man cleared away all the refuse with a
broom.   It was not hot weather for working ; and, as the
people showed no signs of weariness, the threshing scene
did not produce on me the painful impression which I had

felt in the harvest-field at Parashino. On our way home, we went straight to the stackyard. I heard the foreman say in a low voice to Yevséitch, "Ask the bailiff what he means by not sending a cart for the buckwheat straw? Has he gone to sleep?" Several tall stacks of rye had been built already in the yard. When we arrived, they were just putting the top on one stack, and laying the foundation of another; the first was wheat, and the second spelt. Four men stood on each stack; the sheaves were raised to them on forks, or, when the stack grew high, tossed up neatly and quickly; still greater was the neatness and quickness with which the builders caught the sheaves in mid-air. Great was my admiration, and I became finally convinced that labouring men and women were much more ingenious and adroit than ladies and gentlemen, because they could do things which ladies and gentlemen could not. I felt a burning desire to learn to work like a labourer. But my father found something to criticise here: he pointed out to the bailiff that the sides of the wheat stacks were uneven and ill-built. The bailiff grinned as he answered:

"But those are rye stacks that you're looking at, *batyushka* Alexyéi Stepanitch; the wheat stacks will be quite different. Rye-straw is long, and wheat-straw short. That's why the sheaves trail so."

My father was rather put out, I thought. He stayed in the yard, intending to walk home himself, and sent Yevséitch and me back behind the horse. At home, I described to my mother all I had seen, my enthusiasm and excitement over my story were as great as usual; but I was mortified to notice—and it was not the first time—that she listened with indifference; and, as for my wish to learn field-labour, she called it childish nonsense. I was hurt and went off to my sister, who was surely bound to hear my story out. But I must confess that she too was not much interested. Parasha was worst of all. For, when I began to find fault with my sister for not attending and not being charmed by my descriptions, Parasha suddenly broke in: "There's nothing to listen to, and nothing wonderful in what you say. What need has your

sister to know how corn is threshed and stacks are built ? "
—and she burst out laughing. I was so angry, that I called
her a fool. She threatened that she would complain to
my mother ; but it was only a threat. When my father
came back, he and I talked and talked of field work. He
respected agriculture and spoke of it with affection ; and
it was pleasant to me to hear him speak and also to express
my own thoughts and feelings, childish as they were.

It was quite late in the autumn when we set off on our
visit to the Chichagoffs at Old Mertovtshina. My sister
and the baby were left with grandmother ; my father only
took us there and returned next day to his occupations at
Bagrovo. Knowing this beforehand, I feared I should find
the visit tiresome ; and, in case of emergency, I took with
me my books which I had read more than once already.
My fears were not realised. When my mother was shut
up with Mme. Chichagoff, old Mme. Myortvavo made me
sit beside her and talked to me for hours at a time. She
was a skilful questioner and even more skilful as a narrator,
so that I much enjoyed listening to her. She had seen much
and suffered much in the course of her life, and her stories
were more interesting than books. From her I got for the
first time the real history of Pugatchoff's revolt,* to
which I had only heard casual references before. The poor
lady and her family had suffered terribly at that awful
time : her husband had been murdered by the rebels. I
generally sat with her in the morning ; and after dinner
our host took me into his study. He was both an artist
and an architect : he had built a church for his mother-in-
law in the garden, near the house, and had painted all the
icons for it himself. He taught me what is meant by a
mathematical instrument, an easel, and oil-colours, and
showed me how to use the colours. Plan-drawing pleased
me most of all : M. Chichagoff was skilful at it, and the
compass and drawing-pen were for long favourite toys with
me. The possession of such treasures seemed to me the
height of happiness. To crown all, M. Chichagoff gave me

---

* Pugatchoff was a Cossack, who raised a serious rebellion in the East
of Russia , taken prisoner by Suvóroff, he was executed at Moscow in 1775
Pushkin's *Kapitanskaya Dotchka* contains an account of it.

The Arabian Nights to read. Scheherazade absolutely
fascinated me : I could not tear myself from the book, and
my kind host gave me two volumes—they were all he had—
of the magical tales At first, my mother feared that this
reading would be bad for me : she said to M. Chichagoff
that my imagination was excitable enough already, and
that *The Arabian Nights* would make me dream all day on
my feet. But he found means to convince my mother
that the book would do me no harm. Without understanding his arguments, I was convinced of their justice,
and delighted by my mother's consent. I don't think that
any book has ever aroused in me such sympathy and
interest. During our visit, I could only read the tales in
snatches ; yet I became entirely absorbed by them.
Now and again, I would run off to the bedroom which I
shared with my mother, and open the book, merely to read a
page—and I was lost in a world of dreams. Once my
mother noticed I was not in the room and came to look for
me ; she found me so absorbed in reading that I never
heard her coming into the room or going out. She then
brought our host back with her , and it was long before
I was aware of their presence : I had neither eyes nor ears
for anything ; it was only M. Chichagoff's laughter that
made me conscious of realities. My mother availed herself
of the situation ; here was proof positive of what she
feared. " You see for yourself," she said, " how apt he is
to get carried away, and why I think it bad for him to read
fairy tales ! " M. Chichagoff only laughed and said,
" That's all right ; it couldn't be otherwise ; I quite
approve." I was much alarmed . I did not believe that,
after such a flagrant instance of my propensity, my mother
would give way a second time ; but, thank God, it all
turned out satisfactorily. My mother let me keep the
books, but forbade me even to look at them during the
rest of our visit. For fear of worse consequences, I obeyed,
though reluctantly ; and during the last days of our stay
I paid even more attention to the stories of old Mme.
Myortvavo, and showed even more curiosity in my questions
addressed to my host. He had read everything and seen
everything ; his knowledge was universal, yet he was no

mere student ; and, besides all this, he was very cheerful and loved to talk. My admiration for his exceptional intelligence and parts grew greater every day.

There was another inhabitant of Mertovtshina who aroused in me curiosity mingled with fear. This was Ivan, a son of Mme. Myortvavo ; he was still young, but had been insane for some years. Nothing would induce his mother to put him in confinement : he lived in a separate part of the house, with a servant to look after him, walked about the fields and woods, and came whenever he chose, even at night, to the rooms occupied by his mother. I saw him two or three times every day, but always at a distance. At last, one day we were all sitting in the drawing-room, when he came in, unshaved, uncombed, and very oddly dressed. Muttering some words in Russian and French to himself, biting his nails, bowing repeatedly over his shoulder, he kissed his mother's hand, and then got out a card-table, which he placed in the middle of the room and opened ; next he fetched a pack of cards. His sister said in a low voice to my mother that to play cards by himself was his only amusement, and that he was a very good player ; to prove which, she asked her husband to play a game of piquet with her brother. M. Chichagoff at once agreed, remarking that he had often played with him but never won. I ventured close to the table and stood beside M. Chichagoff The madman played astonishingly fast ; often, without waiting for the scoring at the end, he made a mental calculation of the items and wrote down his gains or losses with chalk on the table ; I was told that he never made a mistake. He made strange grimaces all the time ; he laughed in a strange wild way, talked constantly, got up, bowed, and sat down again. He clearly supposed himself to be talking to some one ; but this did not prevent him from playing with great attention and success. After losing several kings, M. Chichagoff said, " No getting the better of you, brother," and, getting up, brought from his study a few copper coins which he handed over to Ivan. The winner was excessively pleased ; he then sat down beside his mother and talked to her for a long time , his voice rose and fell, was now sad and now happy, but he always

spoke with respect, and she listened with attention and
sympathy. He mumbled so that it was impossible to
understand a single word : but his mother always understood him, and her eyes rested on him with a singular
tenderness. At length she said .

" Well, my dear boy, I understand it all now. I will
think carefully over your plan and give you my advice.
Now go to your own rooms, and God bless you."

He obeyed her at once · kissing her hand respectfully he
left the room. We were all silent for some minutes ; the
old lady's eyes were full of tears. Then she crossed herself
and said in a low solemn voice :

" God's will be done ! But a mother can never become
accustomed to the sight of her son deprived of his reason.
My poor Ivan does not believe that the Empress is dead.
He fancies that he is in love with her and that his love is
returned, but that certain persons have slandered him ;
and therefore he intends to write a letter in French to the
late Empress."

This was a complete puzzle to me, but at least I could
understand the mother's love for her afflicted son, and
the son's respectful obedience to his mother, in spite of
his madness. The same day, on going to bed, I besieged
my mother with a host of questions, which it was no easy
task to answer in a way comprehensible to a child. My
chief anxiety was the possibility of going mad myself, and
for some days I kept a watch on my thoughts and worried
my mother with questions and doubts, whether I had not
got some symptoms of insanity. My father's arrival, and
our departure, fixed for the next day, drove the thoughts
of this possibility out of my head. We drove away, and
I could think of nothing but the meeting with my dear
sister ; I would read her *The Arabian Nights*, and tell her
about poor Ivan. On the way, my mother talked much
with my father of Mme. Myortvavo : she praised her and
said it was astonishing how that quiet old lady, who never
raised her voice, could command such respect from all the
household and such eagerness to carry out her wishes.

" Owing to their love and reverence for her," my mother
went on, " not one of the family or visitors or even of the

servants ever loses patience with her son or laughs at him, though he is often repulsive or ridiculous. Her power over him is such that, even in the fits of violence which he sometimes has, it is enough for her to appear on the scene and speak a few words—the raging madman becomes perfectly quiet."

All this was quite intelligible to me, child as I was, and was confirmed by my own feelings.

When we got back to Bagrovo, I lost no time in giving a detailed narrative of all that had happened at Mertovt-shina, first to my sister and then to my aunt. I had an unbounded and irresponsible desire to convey my impressions to other people with such precision and clearness, that their conception of the objects described should correspond exactly to my own; hence I began to mimic the mumbling voice and queer faces and bows of Ivan Myortvavo. I must have attained my object very completely; for I terrified my sister, and she ran from me, or shut her eyes and stuffed her ears, as soon as I began to imitate the madman. My aunt, on the contrary, laughed a great deal and said "What a rogue you are, Seryozha! It's Ivan Myortvavo to the life." This pleased me; and I repeated the performance before Yevséitch, Parasha, and others, making them laugh and praise my cleverness as a mimic.

On the first convenient opportunity I began to read *The Arabian Nights*; and for a long time the book dominated my fancy. I liked all the stories, and could not make up my mind which I preferred. They excited my youthful curiosity, astounded me by the surprising nature of the wonderful incidents, and stimulated my own tendency to invention. The genies, shut up in wells or earthen pots, the men turned into animals, the enchanted fish, the black dog which the lovely Zobeide flogs and then embraces with tears—how all these mysterious marvels impressed me as I read! With what avidity, with what insatiable interest I devoured these stories! Yet I knew all the time that they were mere inventions, descriptions of what never was and never can be in this world. What, then, is the secret of the spell they laid on me? I believe

it is to be found in that passion for the marvellous, which
is innate, more or less, in all children, and was less repressed by sober sense in my case than in most. While
reading the book I was carried away as usual by excitement
and enthusiasm ; but I was not content with reading it
myself : I began to repeat the contents to my sister and
aunt with such burning animation and what may be called
self-forgetfulness, that, without being aware of it, I filled
out the narratives of Scheherazade with many details of
my own invention ; I spoke of all I had read, exactly as if
I had been on the spot and seen it with my own eyes.
When I had excited the attention and curiosity of my
two hearers, I began, complying with their wishes, to
read the book to them aloud ; and then my own additions
were detected and pointed out by my aunt, whose objec-
tions were confirmed by my sister. Again and again my
aunt stopped me by saying—

"What you told us is not there. How's that ? You
must have made it up out of your own head. What a
story-teller you are ! It's impossible to believe you."

I was much taken aback by such an accusation, and
forced to reflect. I was a very honest boy at that age, and
could not endure lying ; but in this case I saw myself
that I had really put into Scheherazade's mouth a great
deal which she never said. I was surprised myself, not to
find in the book what I believed I had read there, and what
was firmly fixed in my head. I became more cautious, and
kept myself in hand, until I got excited ; when once
excited, I forgot all precautions, and my heated imagination
usurped absolute power.

The late autumn dragged slowly on, no longer damp and
rainy but dry, windy, and frosty. Without any snow, the
thermometer fell below zero , mud turned to stone, and
carts could drive over the ponds   In fact, it was real
winter, but without sledging, to which all looked forward
impatiently. I had long given up my walks and spent
most of my time with my mother in her new room ; there
my crib stood, and there my books, and pebbles, and fishing-
lines taken off the rods were deposited. My father had
no study and no room to himself. In one corner of the

parlour stood a writing-desk of alder wood, made in the
house by old Akim, our carpenter; and here my father
constantly sat and wrote. A blind old man might often
be seen standing in front of him. This was his clerk,
Pantelyéi Grigoritch—his surname, which was never used,
was Myakoff—well known for his management of lawsuits
and knowledge of law, though I was not aware of this till
I was older. He was a man of genius in his own line; but
how was it possible for such a development to take place
under the roof of my grandfather, who could hardly read
and write, and detested all law business? The explanation
was this. Mihail Maximitch Kurolyessoff, within a year
after his marriage to my grandfather's cousin, noticed
about the house at Bagrovo a fatherless and motherless
boy known as Pantyushka, and formed the opinion that
he was uncommonly sharp and intelligent. He offered to
take the lad to his own house and educate him, that he
might grow into a man of business, for my grandfather to
employ in all his dealings with the provincial law-courts.
My grandfather gave his consent. Pantyushka soon
became known as Pantelyéi, and showed such extraordinary parts, that Kurolyessoff, with my grandfather's
consent, sent him to Moscow for further education, to a
friend of his, a great jurist and a notorious taker of bribes.
In a few years, Pantelyéi was known as Pantelyéi Grigoritch,
and had a high reputation in his profession. In Moscow
he married a citizen's daughter, Natalya Sergéyevna, a
pretty girl with a good dowry, who, for love or from respect
for the ability of Pantelyéi Grigoritch, was not afraid to
marry a serf. In the very prime of life, when he had just
brought to a triumphant conclusion some case in the courts
conducted by another long-headed lawyer, utterly defeating
his old and wary antagonist, Pantelyéi was dining that
very day with his client, when, as he sat at table, he
suddenly lost his sight. The optic nerve was paralysed,
probably in consequence of persistent reading of manuscript, constant writing, and want of sleep; and no means
were successful in restoring his sight. For a year he was
under treatment in Moscow; then he moved to Bagrovo
with his wife and little daughter, Nastenka   Even when

blind he was constantly employed on legal business by
other people : agents brought him the papers and read
them aloud, and he dictated petitions to the Senate, and
was paid for his services a fee high for those days

This was the man whom I often saw standing in front
of my father, listening to documents and discussing any
proceedings which my father intended to take. His image
is before me now. He was a tall man, with good features
and long fair hair with a faint trace of grey in it ; he wore a
long pea-green coat with large copper buttons, blue striped
stockings with red clocks, and shoes with large silver
buckles ; and he leaned on a bamboo cane with a gilt knob
at the end. He was a remarkable example of that old
type of servant which is extinct now, and which is caught
with great success by Zagoskin in his novels. Nothing
would have induced Pantelyéi Grigoritch to sit down in my
presence, to say nothing of my father's ; and I could never
persuade him to give up the practice of kissing my hand.
His memory and his gift of language were surprising : he
knew by heart the text of all the laws and the exact date
of every imperial edict. He had always one or two pupils ;
they lived with him in the two rooms with a kitchen which
he had built on to our house at his own expense, and read
or wrote from morning to night under his eye, while he
usually sat curled up on the top of the stove, smoking a short
pipe. His hearing was so acute that he could distinguish
all his regular visitors, even me, by their step. I would
often have gone to hear his stories of Moscow, always
accompanied as they were by a present of sweets from his
wife or daughter, but the old man was unwilling to sit
down in my presence ; and this fact, combined with the
sweets of which my mother disapproved, restricted the
number of my visits to Pantelyéi Grigoritch.

At last, when both man and nature, as my mother said,
had long been waiting for it, snow fell in abundance ; and
we made hasty preparations for a long journey. Praskovya
Ivanovna insisted that my father should bring *all* his
family for her to see ; and her will counted as law. We
started, as soon as winter made travelling possible, at the
season when the track is as smooth as a table-cloth, and

one can still harness two or three horses abreast in a
sledge We took our own horses; I travelled with my
parents in one sledge, the two younger children with
Parasha and the foster-mother in another, made of matting
and covered. I will not describe our journey; with its
stoppages for food and sleep. it was just as wearisome and
uncomfortable as former journeys. I will only say that we
stayed a whole day in the large village of Vishenki, the
property of Praskovya Ivanovna. Just as at Parashino,
so here there were comfortable and warm quarters for the
agent on his visits; indeed they were even better here.
In the rooms once inhabited by the formidable owner of
the place, there were pictures in gilt frames on the walls.
To me they seemed marvels of art, especially one which
represented a warrior with a barred helmet, carrying a
spear and riding over a sandy desert. The people there
said, with a smile, that the late Mihail Maximitch—the
kingdom of heaven be his!—had been pleased to take all
the pictures from his neighbours' houses! Just as at
Parashino, my father inspected the estate, but would not
take me with him, because of the cold. This village was
famous for the prosperity of its inhabitants; and they
had a special fancy for thorough-bred horses which had
been introduced there by the late owner. Many of the old
men brought presents to the house—honey in the comb,
eggs, and live poultry. My father did not accept anything,
and my mother did not leave the house to meet the old men.
It was clear that the people looked on us as their future
masters, though they included no settlers from Bagrovo.

From Vishenki we went on to the village known as Old
Bagrovo, or Bagrovo near Simbirsk. We found there a
tumble-down house, in which my grandfather and grandmother once lived, and where my father and all my aunts
were born. I noticed that my father nearly shed tears,
when he went into the old rooms—family apartments
Yevséitch called them—and saw the effects of age and
decay. the sunk floors and sagging beams. These ruins
found no favour with my mother. "How could people
live," she asked, " in such a hovel, and where on earth were
they all stowed away?" And it was really difficult to

make out, how a whole family, including five daughters, could have found room in that house. Their requirements, in the way of comfort and convenience, cannot have been exacting. "Seryozha," said my father, "this is our ancestral estate, which was bestowed on our family by the Tsars; but now half of it is no longer ours." His last words produced on me a peculiar, unpleasant impression, which I could not make plain to myself. We got there in the morning, and by dinner-time the courtyard was full of peasants with their wives. For some reason unknown to me, my mother, in spite of the frost, consented for once to face this assembly, and took me out with her. We were greeted with cries of joy, tears, and reproaches: "What made you go and leave us, who were born your serfs?" they cried.

My mother, who did not like noisy greetings and demonstrations from dependants, was nevertheless overcome by the sincere feeling of our good peasants and shed tears; my father wept freely, and I began to yell! It turned out that there was nothing provided to enable us to treat the people; but my father promised to return in a week and make up for the omission. They answered that they wanted nothing; they only begged him to accept "bread and salt" * from them. It was impossible to refuse, though we had positively no room in which to dispose of their gifts. After dinner, my father managed to inspect his own small property and found, as he said, all in good order. We went early to bed, and started for Choorassovo next morning some hours before dawn; the distance that remained was fifty *versts*.

* This phrase stands for "hospitality" or, as here, for "presents" in general from inferiors

CHAPTER XV

CHOORASSOVO

WE fed our horses early in the village—formerly a town—
of Tagai and arrived before dark at the village of Choorassovo, which had some reputation in those days. As we
drove up to it, I saw that here was something different,
something unlike what I had seen hitherto. Two stone
churches with green cupolas—one small, the other large,
new, and still unconsecrated—the red roofs of the large
manor-house, of its outbuildings, and offices, and the
belfries on them—these were striking and surprising objects.
When we drove up to the front steps, which were roofed
over, a crowd of smartly dressed footmen hastened to meet
us, helped us to dismount, and conducted us to the hall.
There we heard that Praskovya Ivanovna had as usual
a number of visitors, and that the company had not long
finished dinner. My father and mother had scarcely had
time to remove their travelling wraps, when we heard a
loud clear voice in the parlour saying, "Oh, where are they ?
Bring them in here." The parlour-door was opened, we
went in, and I saw a tall woman with hair turning grey,
who quickly stretched out her hand to meet my mother,
and said, "At last ! I thought you would never come ! "
My mother, as she told me afterwards, received a welcome
so friendly and affectionate from our hostess, that in one
moment she fell in love with our " benefactress," and was
heartily glad that she could feel real affection as well as
gratitude. Tears of emotion came to my mother's eyes,
while Praskovya Ivanovna embraced and kissed her.
This lasted some time ; then, stroking and fondling her,
she took her to the window to see her better. My father,
wishing to greet his aunt, tried to kiss her hand, saying,

" How are you, aunt ? "—but she would not give him her
hand. " We are old acquaintance," she said in her downright way : " we have plenty of time to shake hands ;
for the present, let me have a good look at your wife." At
last she said, " Well, I believe we shall take to one another,"
and then, turning to my father, embraced him heartily
and whispered something in his ear. My sister and I had
long been standing in front of our new relation, with our
eyes fixed upon her, awaiting with some anxiety the time
when she should take notice of us. At last our turn came.
" Oh, these are our Bagroffs," she said in the same hearty
voice ; " I'm not very fond of kissing children. Well,
bring them to the light where I can see them " (it was
beginning to get dark by this time). My sister and I were
placed on chairs near the window ; and the baby was
carried there by his foster-mother. Praskovya Ivanovna
looked attentively at us ; then twitching her thick eyebrows,
she said : " What my late cousin Stepan Mihailovitch
wrote to me, was true : Seryozha is like Uncle Grigori
Petrovitch ; but the girl is like Cinderella, and the baby
a little Blackamoor.' She laughed heartily, took my
mother by the hand and led her to the drawing-room,
where a number of visitors were standing by the door ;
introductions and greetings followed. Though I was
inclined to resent these descriptions of my dear little sister
and baby brother, I could not help being impressed by the
magnificence of the parlour. The walls were painted in
bright colours with trees, fruit, and flowers which were
new to me ; there were strange birds too, and beasts,
and men. Two large crystal chandeliers, which hung
from the ceiling, seemed to me to be made of the diamonds
I had read of in *The Arabian Nights*. Golden snakes with
wings, fastened at intervals to the walls, held in their
mouths candlesticks with candles ; and crystal drops
hung from them. Round the walls were placed a number
of chairs, all covered with some red material. Before I
had time to study all these marvels with due attention,
Praskovya Ivanovna, accompanied by my mother and a
young girl, who had kind and intelligent eyes though her
nose was large and all her face scarred by small-pox,

returned from the drawing-room and said in her commanding voice—

"Alexandra, take Sofya Nikolayevna and her children to the rooms which I arranged they were to have, and settle them there."

The girl with the scarred face was Alexandra Kovrigina ; she was our cousin, and, having lost both father and mother in her infancy, had been brought up by Praskovya Ivanovna ; her present position was that of chief executrix of our hostess's orders. She was very cordial and pleasant, as she bestirred herself to instal us ; and she and my mother soon became friends. We were given a large sitting-room, with one door leading to the dining-room and another to a bedroom, which was also to be ours These were the two best rooms in the house ; but Praskovya Ivanovna had never occupied them since her husband's death ; favoured guests were sometimes put there, while ordinary visitors were put up in a wing of the house. We were told that the sitting-room looked much the same as in the lifetime of the late proprietor ; all spoke of him with awe. On one wall hung a picture in a gilt frame, representing a grey-haired old man fettered and in prison ; a young and beautiful woman—his daughter, according to Alexandra Kovrigina—was feeding him from her breast, while two monks looked in at the barred window and smiled. On the other two walls also there were pictures, but small ones ; one of these was a woman sewing, with eyes that seemed to be alive and directed towards any one who looked at her. In one corner stood a splendid mahogany writing-desk, inlaid in bronze, with a bronze rail and enamelled fittings to the locks. My mother decided to occupy the sitting-room ; and a large double bed, also of mahogany and with bronze ornaments, was moved there from the bedroom ; a sofa was fixed on as a bed for me, while the two children and the two nurses were established in the bedroom, which communicated directly with the maids' room—a convenient arrangement, my mother thought. When my mother had settled this arrangement, she left the execution of it to Alexandra, and dressed for supper before a great mirror reaching to the floor, such as

I had never seen in my life; then she went to the drawing-
room, and I was asleep when she came back after supper.
Theie was evidently mirth and noise at supper, for loud
voices and laughter were often audible to me through the
dining-room. Alexandra kindly stayed a long time with
us, and we took a great fancy to her. She looked sad, as
she asked me many minute questions about Bagrovo, my
grandmother, and my aunts. I was by no means loath to
gratify her; and before the evening ended she was well
posted, not only in our life at Ufa and Bagrovo, but also
in all my chief pursuits and amusements.

Awaking next morning, I saw the whole room lit up
with bright sunlight: the gilt picture-frames, the
chandeliers, the bronze on the desk and mirrors, were
absolutely ablaze. Looking round the walls, I was arrested
by the look of the woman sewing · she gazed fixedly at
me from her gilt frame, just as if she were alive. I shrank
from her gaze and turned away; but after a few minutes
when I stole a glance at her, behold ! she was looking
attentively at me just as before. Feeling uncomfortable
and even frightened, I hid my head under the coverlet
and lay still, until my mother got up and went off to the
bedroom, and Yevséitch came to put on my clothes. While
I was washing, I took a sidelong glance at the figure : she
was still looking at me and appeared to be smiling. I grew
still more uncomfortable and imparted my trouble to
Yevséitch. He made experiments from different parts of
the room, and remarked the same thing. He was surprised
at this peculiarity of the picture but ended by coolly
saying, " It is the way the artist painted her, that makes
her look straight at everybody "; and, though I was not
altogether satisfied by this explanation, yet I was comforted by the thought that the figure looked at Yevséitch
exactly as it did at me.

The visitors were not yet all out of bed ; and some who
had got up, drank tea in their rooms instead of coming
down for it. We heard from Parasha that our hostess
had long been up and dressed and was having tea in her
bedroom. My mother went and inquired of the con-
fidential lady's-maid, whether she could see her aunt.

" Yes," answered the voice of Praskovya Ivanovna. My mother went into the room and soon returned, looking very cheerful. " Your aunt wants to see you all immediately," she said. Off we went to the bedroom, where Praskovya Ivanovna gave us a welcome so simple and kind and pleasant, that I forgave her the nicknames of " Cinderella " and " Blackamoor," which she had bestowed on my sister and brother, and made friends with her once for all on the spot. She did not kiss any of us children : she looked at us a long time, stroked our heads, gave her hand to my sister and me to kiss, and said :

" I receive you thus in my bedroom, because it's the first time. I am no great lover of children, especially children in arms : I can't endure their screaming, and they are seldom sweet. Bring the children to me, when I send for them. Seryozha, of course, is older, and he may be shown to visitors. The children will have all their meals in their own rooms ; they will have the dining-room as well, to play and run about in. It's a mistake to mix up children and grown-up people. And now, my dear Sofya Nikolayevna, live in my house as if it were your own. State your wishes, give your orders—they shall be obeyed. When you want to see me, you are welcome here , if you don't want to see me, sit all day in your own room : I shan't be offended ; I can't endure tiresome people myself. I love you as if you were of my own blood, but I don't intend to put any constraint on myself on your account. All guests in this house are in that position. I don't make myself troublesome to any one, and I expect others not to make themselves troublesome to me."

With this explanation Praskovya Ivanovna, who was pouring out tea for herself, asked my father and mother to share it, and told us to go to our own rooms. I ventured to beg leave to look again at the painting on the parlour walls, and asked if we might call her " grandmother." * She laughed and said :

" Ah, you are a lover of pictures Then go with Yevséitch and have a look at the parlour and drawing-room, and the lounge where the paintings are best of all.

* This name may be given by Russian children to a grand-aunt

But don't touch anything, and don't call me grandmother, but merely ' Praskovya Ivanovna.' "

I do not know why she disliked that title ; anyhow, we never called her by it, as long as she lived. I was not slow to avail myself of her permission, and made off with Yevséitch to the parlour, which seemed to me even prettier than on the evening before, because I was freer and could look more carefully at the frescoes. It is quite certain that the artist was some domestic painter, not superior to the workmen who nowadays paint signs over barbers' shops ; but I was enchanted then by the Chinamen and Red Indians, the palms and beasts and birds, shining in all the colours of the rainbow. In the drawing-room, where we went next, I was not so much struck by the frescoes, of which there were few, as by the gilt picture-frames and rich furniture of the room, though it seemed to me at the same time rather dark and cheerless, probably owing to the muslin and silk window-curtains. What splendid sofas there were, how many armchairs, and all covered with dark blue silk ! A great chandelier hung from the middle of the ceiling, and large figures, carrying candle-sticks, stood on stone pedestals in the corners of the room. By the sofas at the sides of the rooms were columns deco-rated with bronze, and carved out of different woods ; and what wonderful birds, beasts, and even men were sculptured on them ! But I was especially attracted by the broad mirrors, reaching from the ceiling to the floor ; marble stands were fixed against them, supporting bronze candlesticks with crystal pendants. Compared to the houses I had seen and lived in, and especially to Bagrovo, the house at Choorassovo was bound to seem, and did seem, to me like a palace out of *The Arabian Nights*. The lounge, to which we went after the drawing-room, was just as luxuriously furnished ; I was past being surprised, but I liked this room best of all. There was a wide divan along the whole length of the inner wall, and sofas in corners, covered with some bright red material ; and they seemed to stand in green arbours made by the bushes painted on the walls. The lightly-curtained windows, and a glass door leading to the garden, let in plenty of light and gave a cheerful air to the room. Praskovya Ivanovna liked it too, and constantly sat or lay on this divan, when the company was smaller and consisted of intimate friends.

Together with Yevséitch, whose cries of astonishment were louder than mine, I surveyed and admired all the wonders and treasures—I thought so then—that adorned the house of Choorassovo. Then I hastened back to my room, eager to communicate my impressions to some one. But in the nursery I found Alexandra, talking to my sister and caressing my little brother. She told me that her " aunt " was deeply engaged in conversation with my parents, and had sent her away with the words, " Please be good enough to leave the room." As it seemed to me that Alexandra was hurt by this speech, I tried to console her : I hastened to inform her that Praskovya Ivanovna had turned all of us out of her room, and had forbidden me to call her " grandmother." Alexandra smiled sadly and said :

" She doesn't like to be called grandmother ; she told me to call her " aunt," and I have got accustomed to the name. I am the same relation to her that you are ; but I am only a destitute orphan, and you are her heirs "

I did not understand ; but there was a sadness in her tone which made me sad too, but not for long. Suddenly I thought of the pictures and splendid furniture in the house, and began excitedly to describe to my sister and the others the wonders I had seen. Alexandra smiled again and again ; at last she said in a low voice, " What a child you are ! " I was taken aback, and cooled down before the end of my description. Then she began to question me again about my grandmother and Bagrovo. I thought to myself, " Fancy speaking of Bagrovo, after Choorassovo ! " But clearly she was not of my opinion : she went on asking me questions about the smallest trifles. Then she told me her own story : how her parents had lived in poverty and want, till both died ; and how Stepan Mihailovitch, her grandfather and mine, took her to live at Bagrovo, till Praskovya Ivanovna came there and carried her off to Choorassovo, which had been her home for the last fifteen years. She was interrupted by the entrance of a tall stout woman, no longer young. Her face was unknown

to me; but she proceeded to kiss us. She was called
Darya Vassilyevna; her surname I never heard. Her
dress was somehow strange : her clothes were good, but
she had a handkerchief tied round her head, as peasant
women wear it. I heard afterwards that Praskovya
Ivanovna generally made her presents from her own
wardrobe, requiring her to wear the garments and not shut
them up in her box. I did not take a fancy to Darya
Vassilyevna at first sight, and I noticed that she was
unfriendly to Alexandra; but I was convinced later
that she too, though laughable, was a kind-hearted woman.
Praskovya Ivanovna had known her long, and favoured
her especially for her fine voice which she kept after her
youth was past. She began a chat, not with us but with
Parasha and the foster-mother. Alexandra was not
pleased. she whispered to me, " She has come to pump
the maids," and left the room. Being now free, I carried
off my sister to the bedroom where I slept with my parents,
and, forgetting Alexandra's disconcerting remark, I began
again my description of the drawing-room and lounge,
exaggerating as usual. My little sister was sorry that
she had not seen these rooms and the parlour, which she
had scarcely glanced at the day before. We began to
discuss, in our own fashion, all our new acquaintances.
My sister was so fond of me that she shared all my opinions ;
and she and I never differed about anything.

Meanwhile the house, which had been still and empty
during my inspection, began to get populous and lively.
Visitors appeared in the drawing-room and lounge; and
our hostess with my parents came out to meet them.
Alexandra also appeared to perform her duty of entertaining the visitors. On this occasion there were fifteen
of them, and I will give some of their names : Alexander
Karamzin and his wife ; Nikita Philosoffoff and his wife ;
M. Petin and his sister ; M. Bedrin, a landowner, whom
Praskovya Ivanovna scolded and made fun of to his face ;
M. Lyemivtseff and his wife ; and Pavel Minitsky and his
bride. The last two were known as the handsome couple,
and Praskovya Ivanovna was very fond of them ; both
were young and handsome and warmly attached to one

another. Before long, the Minitskys and my parents became friends. Living thirty *versts* from Choorassovo, they came once a week, and even oftener, to visit Praskovya Ivanovna. On that first day my father brought them to our rooms, where they made much of us and we took a great fancy to them Just before dinner, my mother came for us and took all three of us to the drawing-room. Praskovya Ivanovna showed us to her visitors, with this preface. "Here are my Bagroffs; I ask your kindness for them. How like Seryozha is to Uncle Grigori Petrovitch!" They all showed much attention to us, especially to my sister, and said she would be a beauty some day, which delighted me. On the score of my resemblance to some extinct ancestor, no one expressed any doubt, because none of them had ever seen him. I did not care very much for the visitors, except the Minitskys whom I knew already, and least of all for one young lady, some relation of my father's, who was constantly making faces and had a strange way of making her eyes start out; she was constantly scolded by Praskovya Ivanovna, but only laughed.

Just before dinner, we were sent off to "our wing," which became the regular name for our three rooms. Up till now, we had always dined with our parents, except when my mother was ill and during her visit to Orenburg; and even then we were not alone but had the company of our grandparents and aunt; and I did not at all like this separation and solitude at our dinner. Nor did I conceal this feeling from my mother; she understood it perfectly and shared it, but she said that we must do as we were told by Praskovya Ivanovna, who was very kind and fond of us. "Besides," she added, "I hope before long to arrange it somehow." She went out; and we two sat down sorrowfully in the big dining-room, where the end of a table, at which a dozen people could have sat, was covered for us. There were a number of footmen, and they began to run about and make a great noise; they not only talked and laughed loudly, but wrangled and pushed each other and nearly came to blows; and maids, apparently even more numerous, were constantly running to meet the men. From the dining-room a passage led

to the maids' room, so that the dining-room served as the
only means of communication in the house ; on its polished
wooden floor there was a regular track from the passage
to the men's room And now my sister and I saw and heard
things of which we had no comprehension before and which
we were, fortunately, unable to comprehend then.
Yevséitch and Parasha, who never stirred from our side,
were themselves surprised and even shocked by the impudent shamelessness and licence of these servants. I
heard Yevséitch whisper to Parasha : "What's this ?
Where have we got to ? A fine house it may be, but there
are fine doings in it ! It's highway robbery in broad daylight ! " Parasha's reply was to the same effect. Meanwhile, we had been completely forgotten. The remains of
the dishes, as they were brought out of the parlour, were
snapped up instantly and devoured by greedy maids and
men. Ivan, the butler, politely called "the cashier,"
had only one object in view : with due deference, he begged
them not to touch the dishes before they had been handed
round at table ! Yevséitch was at his wits' end. All his
demands and representations that "the children must
have something to eat," were entirely disregarded ; and
the "cashier," a quiet sober man, answered with a sigh :

"But what can I do, Yephrem Yevséitch ? You see
yourself, how they behave ! Every night when I go to
bed, I thank God that my head is still firm on my shoulders.
You must ask for a separate meal for the children."

Yevséitch was in despair that we should remain " without a bellyful " , there was no one to complain to : all
the ladies and gentlemen were at dinner. But my zealous
and warm-hearted attendant soon took decisive measures.
First of all, he removed us from the dining-room to the
sitting-room, shut the door, and told Parasha to lock it
on the inside. Then he hastened to the kitchen himself,
searched out some scullion who belonged to Bagrovo,
and told him to make soup for us and roast some meat in
the oven. Then he came straight back and waited for the
end of dinner, intending to send some one at once to
summon my mother, and to inform her of all that had
happened in the dining-room. But, as soon as we heard

the noise of chairs moving back from the table, Alexandra came in haste to our room. When she heard that we had not begun our dinner, she became very excited and indignant, and called the butler to explain. Being afraid of the servants, he lied shamelessly : he said that nothing came out from the dinner, so that there was nothing to give us. Though Alexandra, representing to a certain extent the mistress of the house, knew perfectly well that this was a mere falsehood—though she was well acquainted with these servants and had suffered much herself from them, still even she could not believe that anything like our recent experience was possible. She summoned the major-domo Nikolai and even Mihailushka, the chief agent, told them the whole story, and vowed that, if it ever happened again, she would inform her aunt. Nikolai replied that the servants were entirely out of hand, and that Praskovya Ivanovna had long been aware of this ; and Mihailushka, whom I looked at with great interest, clearly sided with the servants . he said with much dignity that it was the cooks' fault, that a meal would be served at once, and that he thought it unwise to trouble Praskovya Ivanovna with such trifles. They had hardly gone out when my mother came in. Alexandra, much excited, embraced her and asked her to forgive what had happened to the children. " If it comes to my aunt's ears," she added, " all her wrath will fall on me, though I am quite innocent." My mother reassured her very kindly, saying that it was a mere trifle, and that the children would have a meal later—she had heard already that food was being prepared on purpose for us : Praskovya Ivanovna should never hear of it. Thus comforted, Alexandra went away to join the visitors ; and I began to give my mother details of all I had seen and heard. She was so distressed by my story that she flushed all over and nearly cried. She thanked Yevséitch warmly for removing us from the dining-room, gave orders that we should always dine in the sitting-room, and laid strict injunctions upon him and Parasha, that they must let none of the house servants come near us. Then Yevséitch and Parasha went out, taking my sister with them.

When alone with my mother, I put my arms round her neck and at once asked her many questions about what I had seen and heard. She was much taken aback and found it difficult to answer me. I had long known very well, that there were good people and bad people, and I used the latter term to define all evil qualities and vices. I knew that there were masters who give orders and servants whose business it is to obey, and that I myself, when I grew up, would belong to the former class, and others would obey me; I knew that till then I must *ask*, for the fulfilment of any of my wants. But Praskovya Ivanovna I looked on as a supreme authority, whom all, even we ourselves, were bound to obey; it was, therefore, difficult to explain to me, why her servants refused, under her very eyes, one might say, to obey her orders. I remembered perfectly her saying to my mother, " Just give your orders, and all will be carried out." At first I thought that the men and women who devoured the dishes, were simply hungry and needed food; but I was told this was not so, which increased my disgust for them. Their coarse jokes and allusions were, of course, lost on me; and in their shameless behaviour I saw only roughness and rudeness, such as I had seen before among the boys of the National School; and my mother did not enlighten me on this point. I asked many questions about Alexandra, her position in the house, and her relation to our benefactress, Praskovya Ivanovna; but to these my mother gave no answer, and had recourse to the usual evasion, " You are still too young to understand about that." Meanwhile, the quiet butler and Yevséitch brought in our dinner and summoned my sister; we had a fine appetite by this time and enjoyed our food, all the more because my mother sat with us.

After our belated dinner, my mother went back to the visitors, and my sister and I set to work to arrange my personal possessions, which consisted mainly of my books, paper, ink-bottle, and ruler. But besides these I was the owner of a wonderful box, adorned with ivory carving and containing eight drawers full of my treasures—the fossils, Devil's Fingers, and other rare pebbles. One of the drawers contained my hooks and fishing-lines, sinkers and floats. All the eight drawers could be shut at once with a very cunning lock, the secret of which I revealed to no one except my sister. For this marvellous box, the very best and most conspicuous position was cleared : we placed it on the writing-desk and took the opportunity of examining, perhaps for the hundredth time, all my precious things. My father soon came in, and heard of our belated meal , he was very sorry for it but could not stay because he was playing piquet with our hostess. Tea was brought us immediately after our dinner ; tea over, my mother came and said she would not go back again to join the party : Praskovya Ivanovna herself had sent her off, seeing from her face that she was tired. Indeed, she seemed exhausted and went to bed immediately after our little supper. I was glad of the opportunity to be alone with her, and meant to question her on points that puzzled me, when Alexandra appeared unexpectedly. She was evidently attached to my mother ; for she often embraced her and spoke to her very affectionately. As they talked low, I could not hear all that passed ; but I made out clearly enough, that Alexandra was complaining of her sad lot, even with tears, though she explained that she did not blame her aunt but only her own unhappy fortune. I was sorry for her, yet I soon fell asleep, lulled by the low voice in which she spoke.

On waking next day, I heard a lively conversation going on between my parents. They had no reason to get up early and they had matter for conversation, as during the whole of the preceding day they had had not one spare minute to spend alone together. Giving no sign that I was awake, I listened with close attention. My mother spoke warmly of Praskovya Ivanovna, praising her plain good sense, her frank, cheerful, and direct nature, and her way of speaking, which if sometimes sharp and unceremonious, was always straightforward. While I was asleep the evening before, Alexandra had had time to communicate many particulars about her aunt ; but, in my mother's opinion, she misunderstood that character, when she saw in it nothing but caprice and eccentricity. My mother repeated what Alexandra had said ; it was to the following effect :—

Though every governor, on his appointment to the province, made a point of calling on her, Praskovya Ivanovna herself had no affection or respect for any one, and invited her guests either with an eye to her own amusement, or in order to treat them rudely to their faces. To save herself trouble, she paid no attention either to her own affairs or those of her peasants, leaving everything in the hands of her agent, Mihailushka, who was enriching himself at the expense of the peasants, and had utterly ruined the servants of the house by his indulgence, as could be seen from the way in which they had behaved to us, who were to inherit the property. She was very eccentric, detesting priests and monks and never giving a penny to a beggar, saying her prayers when she felt inclined, and, when she was not inclined, walking out of church in the middle of the service ; and, though she paid her parish clergy very highly, she would never admit one of them into her house, except a priest bearing a crucifix on the great festivals. Her chief amusement in summer was the garden, which she attended to like a paid labourer ; her winter pastimes were singing or listening to singing, reading, and playing cards. " Praskovya Ivanovna," she added, " has no affection and shows none for me, a poor orphan, and never gives me any money, though she allows me to order from the town or buy from travelling merchants whatever I choose. Respectable and disinterested people have often pressed her to settle some sum on me in her lifetime, with a view to my marriage ; but she would not hear of it, and said that the Bagroffs would never allow a kinswoman to starve, and that it was better for me never to marry at all than to be troubled with a husband, who would marry such a pock-marked goose for her money and then take his revenge by ill-treating me."

To this my mother added, that Praskovya Ivanovna, from her own experience, knew better than most what it was to be married to a fortune-hunter.

Overhearing all this, I felt very unsettled in my mind. If my mother had not begun by saying that Alexandra was mistaken in her opinion of her benefactress, I should have believed the niece's account, because she seemed to me so sensible and kind and honest.   I turned suddenly to my mother, and asked her, " Is it possible that Praskovya Ivanovna is so bad ? "   She started and said :

" If I had known you were awake, I would not have spoken of this before you.   You are quite mistaken in supposing that Alexandra is complaining of her aunt ; that is all nonsense, mere bad guessing and misunderstanding on your part.   I beg you will say nothing of this to your sister or Yevséitch or Parasha."

I floundered still deeper in confusion, and for long was completely puzzled by this question : Is Praskovya Ivanovna good, or is she only partly good ?   I confess that I had an involuntary leaning to the side of the niece.

Considering the matter now without prejudice, I am bound to say that Praskovya Ivanovna was by no means an ordinary woman, and that the existence of such a personality, at that time and in the sphere to which she belonged, is in itself surprising.   While still a child, she was married by her mother's relations to a dangerous ruffian : she actually underwent all the horrors we read of in old romances and French melodramas ; and then she lived twenty years after her husbands death.   Taking advantage of the independence secured to her by her wealth and the moral purity of her whole life, she was perfectly free and even wilful in the expression of all her thoughts and feelings.   Disregarding calculations of self-interest, and surrounded by general respect which she fully deserved, this woman, though quite uneducated, was free from many of those vices, weaknesses, and prejudices, which held undisputed sway over the society of those days.   She was just both in deed and word, strict with all alike and especially with herself ; she blamed herself severely even for slight departures from the moral principles which she recognised ; and, more than that, she did all she could to correct her mistakes   For want of education and enlightenment, it was impossible for her to rise above the level of her age ; and therefore she was blind to her obligations towards the 1200 serfs who were in her power. As she valued a quiet life above everything, she took no part in the management of her estates, declaring that she had no gift for it, and appointed Mihail Maximoff, a domestic servant of her own, to the post of chief agent. But she made no mistake about his character and did not trust him blindly as people supposed. She used to say :

" I know that Mihailushka is a rogue he does not forget to feather his own nest : he makes money out of peasants who have saved, and is making a purse for himself. I know that ; but I also know that he is a clever man and not ill-natured. I want my peasants to be well off, but I don't want to hear their quarrels and complaints I might get twice as much income as I do ; but the present state of things will last my time, and there will be something left for my heirs."

She was convinced that her peasants were prosperous and contented ; for she often made inquiries into their condition, sending trusty and devoted agents to the neighbouring estates to investigate. And it was true, as every one knew, that her peasants were well off ; but, owing to her system of management, the swarm of servants, in and about the house, were sunk beyond belief in idleness, insolence, and vice. If she happened to see any of the men-servants intoxicated, she ordered Mihailushka to pack off the culprit to the Army : " No good," she said, " letting that fellow loose among the peasants." If she noticed forward behaviour in a woman, again her orders were issued to Mihailushka : the offender was to be banished to some remote village to mind cattle, and afterwards to be married to a peasant. But these sentences, harsh and cruel as they were, were never pronounced except when the mistress herself detected the culprit under her very nose ; and, as this so very seldom happened, the result was an utter lack of discipline in the household. She saw nothing and knew nothing, and did not at all like to be told of anything of the kind.

She was pious without the least trace of bigotry : in the matter of fasting and other observances of the Church, she claimed complete freedom. She had built a large new church of stone, because the old church reminded her

of her husband who had built it ; and she wished to forget
him and never spoke of him. She liked magnificence and
display in the house of God ; she knew the church service
by heart, and sang in the choir, standing among her own
private singers. Sometimes she stayed away from church
for a long time, not attending even on the great festivals ;
at other times, she had frequent celebrations of the mass.
Sometimes, while praying devoutly, she would say that
she did not wish to pray any more, and would go out at
the beginning or middle of the mass : this was her chief
peculiarity and, more than anything else, surprised and
grieved her niece, Alexandra. Though she could hardly
write, she liked to read novels or listen to them ; and, as
she ordered a supply every year, she got together a tolerable
collection of books, which had, however, been started by
her husband. Religious books she read only on fast-days,
never at other times ; but this did not prevent her from
playing piquet, by way of relaxation on the evenings of
those days, with my father if he was there, or with
Alexandra. At such times she used to say, that it was
much less sinful to think about *pique* and *repique* than to
listen to empty gossip at the expense of her neighbours, or
give up her mind to idle thoughts. She did not always
observe Lent, but fasted two or three times a year when she
felt inclined, not confining herself to the strict diet, if she was
unwell. Monks and nuns were an abomination to her ; and
no black cowl or black hood ever ventured into her presence.

Though she was very reluctant to lend money, and
did not like to spend trifles in relieving beggars, yet, when
she heard of some respectable person overtaken by disaster,
she was generous in her aid.   But, as disasters seldom over-
take respectable persons, the occasions of her munificence
were rare ; and, in general, Praskovya Ivanovna was
not considered a kind woman. If the truth must be told,
of kindness in the ordinary sense of the word, and especially
of tenderness and sensibility, she had not much ; or one
might say with more truth, that these qualities were not
much developed in her ; and besides, she chose to hide
them rather than wear them on her sleeve. It is true that
she did not love many people ; for she loved no one whom

she did not respect. Out of all her large acquaintance, her favourites were the Minitskys, and after them came my mother. Lastly, it is also true, that her manner to her visitors was too unceremonious and sometimes even rude : she said "thou" to all alike, and showed no mercy in telling people to their faces of anything amiss which she had heard about them or had noticed herself. All felt, more or less consciously, that Praskovya Ivanovna took little interest in other people, and lived chiefly for herself, avoiding anxieties and enjoying her cheerful untroubled life. But this did not prevent a constant ebb and flow of crowds of visitors at her house, or a general expression of profound respect and devotion for her. There could be no interested motives in the case, because it was not easy to get anything out of her. The reason for the exceptional popularity of her house is therefore to be found in the qualities of the hostess : she was always inclined to talk, animated, gay, and fond of a laugh ; her guests had to tell news, or talk scandal, or draw the long bow, according to their talents ; and life at Choorassovo was comfortable, unconstrained, and amusing. Unfortunately, the complaints of Alexandra were not altogether unjust In her conduct to the two regular inmates of her household, Praskovya Ivanovna was inconsiderate and exacting ; they were no more than privileged maid-servants. Darya Vassilyevna, a stupid old woman, did not feel the humiliation of her position ; but the other was far from stupid and naturally kind ; and, as she did not fully understand the many good points of her benefactress and was unable to establish better relations between them, she suffered many mortifications ; and only the friendship of the Minitskys and my parents lightened the burden of her position.

I have described Praskovya Ivanovna, as I knew her myself in my early manhood, and as she long lived in the recollection of my parents and others who were intimately acquainted with her and understood her thoroughly.

Life at Choorassovo went like a clock : relays of visitors arrived and departed. Every day my mother rose in the good graces of Praskovya Ivanovna, and every day increased her friendship with Alexandra, and still more with

the Minitskys They were a really noble pair, especially
the husband, who combined with the artistic temperament
of a Little Russian, vigorous activity, stainless honour,
and strict principles. Passionately in love with his
beautiful wife—and she was no less devoted to her handsome husband—he worked with wonderful perseverance
to correct her early training and root out the seeds of
coquetry and vanity which had been planted in her fine
character while she was a child. My mother arranged
her day very well, thanks to the complete freedom which
Praskovya Ivanovna permitted and even encouraged in
her house. She always dined with us, a full hour before
the regular dinner. So she ate little at the later meal, and
at first the loud cheerful voice of our hostess was often heard
to say, " Sofya Nikolayevna, you are eating nothing " ;
but, when she learnt that her guest had already made half
a meal with the children, she laughed and ceased to press
her. When Praskovya Ivanovna sat down to cards, my
mother came to us ; but it was seldom possible to have her
to ourselves, even less so than in the morning ; for Alexandra
or the Minitskys, if not engaged, often came then to our
large room. The ladies lay down on the large double bed,
Minitsky sat on the sofa, and conversation began, which
often became so lively and intimate that my sister and I
were sent off to the dining-room or nursery. But my
mother did not approve of this change for us, because the
dining-room was a regular thoroughfare connecting the
maids' room with the men's ; and the maids often even
looked into the nursery. My sister and I went every day
to say good morning to our aunt, but we did not say good
night. Sometimes, when the party consisted of intimate
friends, I was summoned to the drawing-room or lounge
after dinner, and Praskovya Ivanovna was entertained
by my replies, at times rude and bold, to the questions
put to me, which were often puzzling and sometimes
absurd and unsuitable to my age. Sometimes she made me
recite from the *Rossiad* or the tragedies of Sumarokoff.
I felt that the company were amused, not interested, by
my performance ; I resented their attitude, and this was
why I sometimes answered questions with an impertinence

which was neither natural to me nor suitable to my
age. When we were alone, my mother scolded me for
this conduct ; but I answered that I was vexed when people
made fun of what I said, and talked to me only in order to
laugh at me. In general, my father was little with us.
he spent much of his time with the visitors and constantly
played cards with his aunt ; at other times he summoned
Mihailushka, who was one of the best pupils of our old
friend Pantelyéi Grigoritch, and pored over law-papers with
him. I discovered now that my father's conversations
at Bagrovo with our blind man of business were directed
to a practical object ; for he was bringing a law-suit against
the Bogdanoffs, with regard to an estate which had come
by inheritance to my grandmother, Arina Vassilyevna
Bagroff. For this purpose my father went to the town
of Lukoyanoff and entered a petition there. He was absent
much longer than he intended, and I was vexed to see that
my mother quarrelled with him more than once on that
ground after his return.

I forgot to say that my father went to Old Bagrovo and
gave an entertainment to our good peasants there. As a
matter of course, I asked for a minute description of this
event, and was pleased to hear how sorry they were for
the absence of my mother and the children.

I have said already, that there was a fairly good library
at Choorassovo. I lost no time in availing myself of this
treasure : authorised by Praskovya Ivanovna, I took out
books chosen by my mother, and read them with great
enjoyment. The first book that came into my hands was
Cadmus and Harmonia, by Cheraskoff, and *Polydorus,
Son of Cadmus and Harmonia*, by the same author. These
books were to my taste in those days ; for the florid style
and cadences of the poetical prose seemed to me perfection.
Next I read *Arphaxad, a Chaldean Tale*—the author's
name I forget—and *Numa, or the Palmy Days of Rome*,
by Cheraskoff, and many other books of the kind. I
glanced at some novels too, which were the favourite
reading of Alexandra ; they excited my sympathy and
interest ; but my mother would not allow me to read them,
and I only ran through a few pages by stealth. I confessed

P

what I had done to my mother, and she scolded me for it very mildly. In this fashion, I was able to glance at *Alcibiades*, and *Count Valmont, or The Error of Judgment*, and *The Memorable Life of Clarissa Harlowe.** It was long before I had a chance of reading these books through ; but scraps of them had made such a deep impression on my mind, that I never ceased to think of them and was not easy till I had read them. At Choorassovo I came at last upon *My Trifles* by Karamzin, and his collection of various pieces with the title, *The Muses*. These verses were quite unlike the poetry of Sumarokoff and Cheraskoff I was conscious of the difference ; but the matter of these verses did not satisfy me, in spite of my immaturity. The contents of all these new books, and the talk of the visitors, many of whom were complete strangers to me, gave me much food for thought ; and I had plenty of leisure time to think in. I tried to discuss everything with Yevséitch ; but he could not even understand what I meant, or what I wished to learn, or what my questions were about. Often and often he said to me : " How can you want to know that, my little falcon ? What reason or purpose can you have ? That's a thing even old men don't know, and you are a child still. God wills it so, and that's enough. Much better go and look at pictures."

This manner of life went on with little variation for more than two months ; and, in spite of the splendid house —as I then thought it—in spite of the frescoed walls which I liked better than the pictures and never ceased to admire ; in spite of the old and new songs which Praskovya Ivanovna sang often and sang very well in a chorus, and which I always heard with pleasure ; in spite of the quantity of new books which I eagerly devoured—this life became very wearisome to me. I was impatient to leave the stir of Choorassovo for the peace of Bagrovo and our poor house there ; I even missed my grandmother and aunt. But the chief cause of my boredom, as I clearly perceived even then, was this, that I spent so little time alone with my mother. It had been my regular custom to pour out without reserve all my thoughts and feelings into her loving

* Richardson published the first part of this book in 1749

ears, to try all my impressions by her wise judgment, to
listen to her animated talk and to find in it an inexpressible
pleasure. But at Choorassovo we were constantly hindered
by the Minitskys and still more by Alexandra; they even
distracted my mother's attention from me; and many
new questions and doubts and suppositions, constantly
suggested to me by the new people and new objects, remained unsolved and unexplained, neither approved nor
condemned by her authority. This was a cause of constant
uneasiness to me. My love for my sister grew steadily
warmer; her friendship was a great comfort to me, but,
as I was older and more developed than she was, it was
possible to communicate my thoughts to her but not to
ask her advice. There was probably another cause, which
I did not realise at the time, for the boredom I suffered:
this was the loss of perfect freedom. I was mostly confined to one room. I was not allowed to stay long in the
nursery with my baby brother, whom I was beginning to
be very fond of; he had pretty dark eyes, though Praskovya Ivanovna, Heaven knows why, had actually called
him a little Blackamoor! If I was ever allowed to go to
the dining-room, it was only for a few minutes, and the
presence of Yevséitch was indispensable. Praskovya
Ivanovna I did not understand: I took it on trust that
she was kind, but I never liked her treatment of us children.
She once ordered our baby to be whipped for crying loudly!
I am glad to say that my mother did not obey that order.

For all these reasons it is very natural that I was much
pleased when our departure began to be talked of. Praskovya Ivanovna had clearly become very fond of my
mother; for she put off our departure several times.

"What is there for you to do there in that hovel?"
she used to say; "your mother-in-law won't miss you,
let alone her daughters. I put no pressure on you; but
it is pleasanter to live where there's some society."

My mother did not contest her arguments; but my
father, with quiet persistence, let his aunt know that it
was impossible for us to stay longer: for three posts he
had had no letters from Bagrovo from his sister Tatyana;
his mother was in weak health and could not attend to

the management of affairs; since his father's death she was quite changed and very restless and unhappy. He added that the corn was being ground with very poor results, and that he would have nothing to live on. His aunt replied that this was all nonsense, and offered him not the smallest assistance from her purse. At last, our preparations were made and our hostess consented to let us go, having exacted a solemn promise from my parents, that they would return without fail at the end of summer and spend all autumn with her.

"Yes, my dear," she said to my mother, "you have never seen Choorassovo yet. The time to see it is summer, when all the trees are covered with fruit and all the springs —I have twenty of them—are spouting. Don't fail to come. If your husband can't come, come alone and bring the children, though I have no great fancy for children. Perhaps the best plan would be to leave the youngest, the little Blackamoor, with his grandmother; he can scream there as loud as he likes! If you don't come, I shall be angry."

My parents promised faithfully to come. Though I did not in the least expect it, Praskovya Ivanovna gave me several books; the actual volumes were *Cadmus and Harmonia, Polydorus, Son of Cadmus and Harmonia, Numa, or The Palmy Days of Rome, My Trifles,* and *The Muses.* This present went far to reconcile me with our hostess. We left on the day after my father's birthday, *i.e.* on February 22nd. On our return we took the same route, by Old Bagrovo and Vishenki. Without reckoning several days which we spent at these two places, we were travelling for more than eight days; the journey was the most wearisome and uncomfortable I had ever experienced; the snow was terrible, and there was a blizzard every day. Sometimes the track had entirely vanished, and in some places we had to have men walking in front to guide us. On the eighth day we reached Nyeklyoodovo and spent the night with the Kalpinskys, from whom we learnt that my grandmother and aunt were well. Early next day, when we had drunk our tea, we started again; and two hours later, I saw from the hill Bagrovo which I had now grown to love.

CHAPTER XVI

BAGROVO AFTER CHOORASSOVO

BAGROVO was a dismal place in winter, and was bound to seem still more dismal to my mother after Choorassovo. Lying in a hollow between hills, surrounded on three sides by bare leafless trees and on the fourth side by barren heights, and covered with snow-wreaths from which the thatched roofs of the peasants' huts peeped out—Bagrovo had a terribly depressing effect upon my mother. But my father and even I saw it again with pleasure : there he had spent his childhood and I was beginning to spend mine. In truth, when compared with the rich village of Choorassovo which was almost a town, Bagrovo looked like the winter quarters of some nomad tribe. At Choorassovo the peasants' houses, with their wooden roofs and large windows, stood high and looked cheerful ; the snow was so worn by traffic that it did not seem deep round the houses and in the street ; the court of the manor-house was kept swept, and sand was strewn over the road at the entrance. But at Bagrovo the snow was so deep round the peasants' cottages, that a passage had to be dug to each ; the court of our own house, owing to its extent, seemed even more desolate, and the wreaths seemed deeper, while over their tops ran separate tracks, like paths on a mountain, leading to the kitchen and servants' quarters. There was no sound nor sign of life. The buildings, buried in the snow, looked low and unlike their former selves. It surprises me more than I can say, that I did not feel this scene to be gloomy and sad.

Soorka and the other dogs met us in the court with cheerful barks of welcome ; two maids looked out to see whom the dogs were barking at, and then dashed back

to the maids' room. Next my aunt hurried out on the
steps. Glad as she was to see us, my grandmother was
still more so : from her eyes, which were cloudy and colourless and seemed to have no light in them, large tears rolled
down. She thanked my father and especially my mother,
kissed her hands, and said, " I did not expect you ; for
the letters told me that Praskovya Ivanovna had taken a
fancy to you, and I knew she would urge you to stay, and
she cannot be disregarded." I felt now the full value of
my father's good-natured firmness, which had proved too
much for his aunt, though she was to leave her immense
property to him and was accustomed to have all her wishes
complied with. My mother was much vexed to find quite
half the house unheated. From some strange motives
of economy, grandmother, not expecting us to return till
just before the snow melted, had not ordered our particular
part of the house to be heated. It could not be helped :
we were all put up in my aunt's room, and she moved to be
with her mother. In three days, all was put to rights, and
we settled down where we had been before.

Rich in the possession of new books and new ideas,
which grew clearer to me in the stillness of solitude and
unbroken freedom,—freedom, of which my life at
Choorassovo had taught me the true value—I constantly
talked on one subject or another with my mother, and was
pleased to discover that I had become older and wiser.
I knew this, because my mother and other people discussed
with me matters which earlier they had avoided. The
course of our life was regular and uniform. The frost
was still severe, and for long I was not allowed to take
walks, not even to run across to Pantelyéi Grigoritch and
his wife. But my father at once began to have interviews
with his blind man of business, and I listened with interest
to their conversation. My father described minutely his
journey to Lukoyanoff, his dealings with the district
judge, the petition he had entered, and the promise of the
judge that he would not fail to decide in our favour. But
Pantelyéi Grigoritch smiled at this, placed both hands on
the knob of his long walking-stick, and said :

" Better not trust the judge : he will favour the land-

owner on the spot ; we shan't manage it without an appeal
to the Senate When the time comes, I will draw up a
petition ; and then some one will have to go to Moscow
and make interest with the secretary and chief-secretary,
whom I used to know when they were less exalted persons.
But never you fear, Alexyéi Stepanitch, my dear sir :
our case depends on law, and we can't lose it. The only
thing they can do is to defer the decision "

My father could not at once believe that the judge at
Lukoyanoff would deceive him : he smiled and said :
" Very well, Pantelyéi Grigoiitch ; we shall see what the
decision is in the provincial court." In the sequel, the
prophecy of the blind man of business was fulfilled to the
letter.

The weather grew less severe, and at last Shrove-
tide came round. My sister and I went sleighing ; and for
the first time in our lives we saw the village boys and girls
coasting fearlessly down the slope from the stackyard on
skates and sleds. I felt that I had not sufficient courage
for this diversion ; but the noisy merriment of the children
was cheerful to watch. One would fall headlong, and
another, dashing down upon him, go head over heels in
turn ; and their loud laughter echoed over the snow-covered
fields and hills, which the sun's rays were just beginning
to warm. We had a little toboggan-run of our own in
front of the bedroom windows, made by Theodore and
Yevséitch ; I was not afraid to come down this with my
sister ; but, where there were only two of us, it was not so
amusing as in the noisy crowd of children collected from
the whole village. But we were not allowed to join them.

There was an incident which marks out that Shrove-
tide in my mind. Some guests, who had never been to the
house before, paid us a visit—Pelagéya Ardalionovna
Rozhnoff and her son " Mitinka." * Though not very
old, she was very stout herself, and he was so monstrously
fat, that the pet name by which his mother called him
sounded especially absurd. It was not, however, only
the bulk of these visitors that excited the curiosity of myself
and all the household, but also the cause of their visit.

* A double diminutive of Dmitri . " Mitka " is the usual form

Mme. Rozhnoff wished to marry her son, and they came to inspect a possible bride in my Aunt Tatyana. In view of such an important occasion, my Aunt Alexandra had been specially invited. My mother took a lively interest in the affair, and was very anxious that Tatyana should be married. In former times, no one had wished this more eagerly than grandmother, but now she was breaking fast and incapable of any eager desires.

On the appointed day, all was ready for the reception of the visitors at ten in the morning · the house was scoured and swept, and the furniture arranged with special care ; the serving-men, who generally wore what they pleased, were smartened up and had pomatum on their hair ; and so it was with all the maids. My aunt was dressed in her best clothes ; even poor grandmother was made to wear a silk jacket and skirt, with a silk handkerchief over her cap, instead of the scrap of cloth she used to wear there, which had once been white but had hardly been changed since grandfather's death. In a word, the whole house looked as smart as possible, and ready for some high festival. Only my mother wore her ordinary clothes, and so did we children. At last a cry was raised, " They're coming, they're coming ! " Grandmother, who now walked with difficulty, was led hastily to the drawing-room ; and my father, mother, and aunt repaired to the same place. My sister and I and even the baby, of course with our usual attendants and all the maids, occupied the windows of my aunt's and grandmother's rooms, to watch the guests arriving and getting out of their sledges. And it really was a sight worth seeing ! First a covered leather sledge drove up to the door, and two sturdy footmen pulled their stout mistress out of it with some trouble, and brought her up the steps, where she halted. Next came a low sledge of remarkable size, in the depths of which something was seated that looked like a haystack on a smallish kalmuck cart The two footmen were quite insufficient in this case : they were reinforced by our man Theodore, Nikolai who belonged to my aunt, and two more of our servants. The united efforts of six men proved sufficient to release the love-sick swain from his vehicle and haul him up the

steps. When the visitors entered the hall to take off
their wraps, all the maids rushed headlong to the passage
and the pantry, to watch the suitor and his mother walk
through the parlour into the drawing-room. The door
from grandmother's room into the hall was generally kept
locked ; but Parasha unlocked it and left it ajar, so that
we could see the mother and son, as they freed themselves
of their winter coverings and warm wraps. They really
were an astonishing couple ! Unable to restrain myself,
I said aloud to Yevséitch, " I declare, it's Mavlyootka ! "
Yevséitch, who could hardly help laughing aloud, pressed
his hand over my mouth. At the door of the parlour,
the visitors were met by my father ; after many bows,
fine speeches, and embraces, he conducted them to the
drawing-room. All our group were astonished at the huge
size of the suitor. " There's a fine lump ! " said Yevséitch
as he took us back to our rooms ; " he beats even
Mavlyootka ! "

The words, " bridegroom " and " bride," " courtship "
and " marriage," had long been known to me, and my
mother had explained what I may call their outward
meaning, as far as it was possible and right for me to understand them. Applying my notions to the case in point,
I said to Parasha and Yevséitch : " How can aunt marry
Rozhnoff ? It is a wife's duty to help her husband , but
she is so slight and he so huge, that if he fell down, she
could not lift him." Parasha laughed and answered by
a question, " Why on earth should he fall down ? " But I
was prepared with an undeniable argument : I said that
I had once with my own eyes seen my father fall down,
and my mother lifted him up and helped him to his feet.
Afterwards, when my aunts heard what I had said, they
made me repeat it (but always when my mother was not
present) and laughed so much that I was completely
puzzled.

When we two were summoned to dinner, all the party
were already seated at table. Mercifully, we only bowed
to the visitors ; otherwise, I feared they might smother us
with their embraces. During the whole of dinner I never
took my eyes off the suitor ; it was positively awful to

watch him eating ; I noticed that no one could help watching his plate. His mamma was no mean performer with the knife and fork, but she found time to speak in praise of her son. According to her, he was the quietest and kindest of men, who would not hurt a fly ; at the same time he had a thorough knowledge of agriculture, went himself to the fields, understood everything and looked after everything ; his one amusement was coursing. Her only complaint was on the score of his weak health ; she took such care of him, that she made him sleep in her own room. Then, with a sort of wink, she added : " Mitinka will have quite good health, when he marries ; and, if God grants him good fortune, his better half will be a lucky woman." While saying the last words, she looked meaningly at my Aunt Tatyana, who blushed, bowed down, and looked at her plate. The suitor must have eaten too much ; for immediately after dinner he began to doze. His mother said in excuse that he was accustomed to lie down after dinner ; but, seeing that in another moment he would roll over and begin to snore, she ordered her horses to be put in ; and then with a shower of excuses, allusions, and compliments, she carried off her poor invalid. When they had gone, there was much jesting and laughter ; and my aunt declared that nothing in the world would induce her to marry such a man, so fat and so lazy. I was glad to hear it. The suitor was given to understand that the lady was unfavourably impressed ; and the formal courtship went no further.

CHAPTER XVII

MY FIRST SPRING IN THE COUNTRY

In the middle of Lent a rapid thaw set in. The snow began to melt quickly, and water appeared everywhere The approach of spring in the country had a remarkable effect on me : I was conscious of a new and peculiar excitement. This was due a good deal to what I heard from my father and Yevséitch. Both rejoiced in the spring, partly as sportsmen, partly as men who had grown up in the country and felt a " passionate love of nature," though they were not quite conscious of it, had never defined it to themselves, and never in their lives used the words which I have just applied to them. Finding in me an eager sympathiser, they could not resist the pleasure of describing to me the joys of spring. First the snow on the hills would melt and pour down their sides in torrents ; the sluices of the dam would be raised, and the water spread everywhere Fish would be swimming over the fields and get caught in traps and weels. The migratory birds would return, the larks begin to sing, the marmots to wake from their sleep and whistle, sitting erect on their burrows. The fields would grow green, the trees and bushes would clothe themselves, and the song of the nightingale would fill them with melody. Their simple but enthusiastic descriptions went deep into my heart, striking some unawakened chords and exciting in me unfamiliar feelings, troubling and yet sweet. We three were unlike the rest of the household : to us it was not sad or wearisome to watch the darkening roofs and walls of the buildings, the bare branches of the trees, the soaking wet ground, the dirty heaps of snow, the grey sky, the fog and damp in the air, and the rain and snow which fell together or alternately

from the low dark clouds. Though confined to the house
—for in wet weather I was not allowed even to stand on
the steps—I followed none the less closely each stage of
advancing spring. From every room, almost from every
window, I had noted certain places or objects, by means
of which I carried on my observations. From the new
room, *i.e.* from our bedroom, I could see on one side the
Chelyayeff hill, whose steep round top gradually grew
bare of snow, and on the other side a part of the river, which
had melted long before, with the further bank. From the
drawing-room dark bare patches could be seen on the
Kudrinsky hill, especially by a round pond fed by springs,
which was used as a flax-dam. From the parlour window,
a pool which flooded the " Jackdaw Wood," shone like a
mirror. From grandmother's room, I could see the stackyard at the top of the hill, and along the slope a quantity
of marmots' burrows which rose higher every day above the
snow. The patches of bare earth grew broader and longer ;
the pool in the wood spread further ; the water came
through the fence and was visible between the cabbage-
beds in the kitchen-garden By me every change was
noted exactly, and each step of spring was hailed as a
victory. From morning till night, I ran from room to
room and posted myself at my points of observation. All
my occupations were forgotten—reading, writing, games
with my sister, even conversations with my mother. Of
what I could not see for myself, I received regular reports
from my father and Yevséitch, from the men and the
maids :—

" The surface of the pond is blue and swollen ; it is
dangerous to drive over it. and a man with a sledge fell in "
—" the water has risen to the level of the machinery in
the mill ; grinding is impossible, and it is time to raise
the sluices "—" Antony's dyke came down in flood last
night, and the Mordoff dyke is dark and swollen ; it will
soon be impossible for sledges to pass anywhere "—" the
paths are getting washed away ; we can't get to the
kitchen ; Mazan fell down with a basin of soup and spilt
the soup ; the gangway is covered, and the servants' bath-
house flooded.''

Such were the reports I was constantly hearing, and I heard them all with delight. For some time the jackdaws had been walking about in the courtyard, and they were now beginning to build in their own wood. The starlings and larks arrived; and then the wild birds, called "game" by sportsmen, began to appear. My father told me, with delight, that he had seen swans flying so high that they were scarcely visible, and long skeins of wild geese. Yevséitch had seen divers and mallards alighting on the pond, rock-pigeons about the stackyard, thrushes and lapwings round the springs. How many sensations for me! how I shouted for joy! The floods rose and rose, and no time was lost in raising the sluices. And I was not there! The weather was too bad, and I did not venture even to ask leave to go; but my father's description did something to satisfy my curiosity. Every day, my reports became more frequent, more important, and more tantalising. At last Yevséitch in wild excitement declared, that birds of every kind were there in such multitudes that they were jostling each other; and the limits of my endurance had been reached. It was no longer possible for me to hear all this and not see it; and backed by my father's approval and my own tears and eager entreaties, I wrung from my mother permission to go out, on condition that I was well wrapped up, for the wind blew damp and piercing I was allowed to sit on the little veranda, just opposite the river and looking out on the garden. The inner door was still blocked up; and Yevséitch carried me round the house, as there was water and mud everywhere. And indeed, one who has never seen it can form no idea of what I then saw going on in the sky, on the earth, and on the water; nor can it be seen now in the same place, because the number of migratory birds is less nowadays.

The river had left its banks, and covered the trees and bushes on both sides; next it had spread over half the garden and united with the lake in the "Jackdaw Wood." The edges of the water were crowded with wild birds of every kind; a multitude of ducks were swimming on the water, between the drowned tops of the bushes; and, all the time, large and small flocks of different birds were on the move—some flying high and steadily, others low and often alighting, and others moving from one point to another. The air was full of their calls, cries, and whistles. I did not know what bird was flying or walking there before me, or how important it was, nor could I distinguish their calls; I was awestruck and stunned by the spectacle. My father and Yevséitch, who were standing beside me, were much excited themselves Each kept pointing out birds to the other, and named them, often deciding by the note, for only the nearer birds could be distinguished by their plumage. " Pintails! pintails! " cried Yevséitch in a flurry, " flocks and flocks! And mallards too, I declare, beyond counting! " And then my father struck in : " Can't you hear the snipe, how they're drumming ? But they're terribly high up And look at the rollers playing over the wheat-field, a perfect cloud of them! What a host of ruffs too! I never in my life saw such flocks! " Though I could not then understand the scene before me, and only looked and listened, while my pulse seemed now to stop and now to beat like a hammer, yet it all came before me later, as it does now, clear and distinct ; and it gave me then, as it gives me now, unutterable delight. And to think that the sportsman alone is capable of understanding this fully! I, while yet a child, was a sportsman at heart : so my feelings on my return to the house may be guessed. I seemed, and could not but seem, a crazy, half-witted creature : my eyes were wild, I could see nothing and heard not a word of what was said to me. Clasping my father's hand, I kept my eyes fixed on his face, I could not bear to speak to any one else, or on any other subject than what we had just seen. My mother was angry and threatened that she would not let me go out, unless I became sensible and cleared my head at once of ducks and snipe. Good heavens, how utterly impossible! Suddenly there was a report close to the house : I rushed to the window, and saw a little cloud of smoke clearing away, and the old falconer Philip standing there with his gun, while the poodle Triton—generally known as Trenton —stepped out of the water holding a bird in his mouth by the wing Philip soon came in with his spoil, it was a mallard, I was told; and the plumage was so lovely that I long lingered over it, admiring the velvety green head, the purplish throat, and the curve of the dark green tail-feathers.

By degrees I became accustomed to the approach of spring and its various sights and sounds, always new, startling, and delightful; I say "accustomed," meaning that I ceased to be stupefied by them. The weather became warm; and my mother made no objection to my going to the veranda; I was even allowed to run about where the ground was dry, and my sister with me. Every day some one of the men shot a duck or snipe; Mazan even killed a wild goose and brought it to my father in triumph; he described minutely how he crawled through the reeds up to his neck in water, till he got close to a pair of geese swimming on the pond, and how he aimed at one of them; and he ended his story with the words, "As soon as I hit him, he turned right over that very minute." Old Miséitch, a man who could read and write, brought in large fish of different kinds every day—pike, tench, and perch. I was fonder then of fish than birds, because I knew and loved angling; I imagined each big fish at the end of my line, and pictured to myself how he would have struggled and flapped, and how joyfully I would have hauled him out on the bank.

In spite of all precautions, I somehow caught a chill, which led to a cold and cough, so that I was forced to stay shut up in the house, which to me seemed as tedious a prison as any I had read of in my books. Further, as I was much excited by Yevséitch's tales, he was forbidden to report to me the perpetual changes which spring was bringing with it. My mother hardly stirred from my side; she was not quite well herself. On the first day, disappointment aggravated my feverish state; but I soon grew more resigned and played all day long with my sister, or read a book, constantly running, if only for a minute, to the windows, from which I could see the whole extent of the floods in the kitchen-garden and half the flower-garden. It was possible to see birds too from there, but I was not allowed to stand long at the window. My recovery was delayed by an unaccountable attack of sleeplessness; and this put my mother off her sleep, as she slept best in the early part of the night. To send us to sleep, we took the advice of my aunt and summoned to our aid Pelagéya, the housekeeper ; she was a capital hand at telling fairy-stories, and even my late grandfather had been fond of listening to her. My mother had known of this before ; but she had no love for fairy-tales or the people who told them, and she consented with reluctance on this occasion.

Pelagéya was stout and no longer young, but her complexion was still red and white. She came into the room, said a prayer, and kissed our hands ; then she heaved several sighs—a regular custom with her—repeating after each sigh, " Lord, have mercy on us sinners ! " Next she sat down by the stove, rested her head on one hand, and began in a rather sing-song voice, " In a certain country, in a certain kingdom. . . ." The story she told us was called " The Scarlet Flower." * I need hardly say that I stayed awake till the story was ended, so that I slept even less than usual. The story proved so attractive and so exciting to my imagination that it might have cured me of sleeping too much, if that had been my ailment. It sent my mother to sleep at once ; but, when she awoke some hours later and found that I had never been asleep, and was discussing the story with Pelagéya, she sent her off ; and it was very long before fairy-tales were again used in the house to send people to sleep. This prohibition might have been a great grief to me, had not my mother allowed Pelagéya to tell me fairy-stories occasionally in the day-time. The very next day, I heard " The Scarlet

---

* This tale, which I heard at least a score of times in the course of a few years because I liked it so much, I afterwards learnt by heart and used to tell it myself, with all the interjections, grimaces, sighings, and groanings of Pelagéya. I imitated her so well that every one in the house laughed to hear me   Then I forgot it, naturally , but lately, when reviving my memory of the past, I came unexpectedly upon a number of fragments of the story ; many words and expressions started into life again, and I tried to recall it. The strange combination, oriental fancy and construction and many phrases obviously translated, with the manners and language of Russian peasants, and the traces of successive narrators—all this seemed to me remarkable   To keep the continuity of the narrative, the tale is given in an Appendix   (*Author's Note*)

Flower " a second time   From that time till I was quite
well again, *i.e.* till the middle of Passion-week, Pelagéya
told me every day one of her large stock of fairy-tales.
Those I remember best are, " The Maiden Queen," " Ivan
the Fool," " The Bird with Fiery Feathers," " The Dragon
that lived in a Mountain "   I was so much taken up by
the stories that I wearied less for the free air and felt less
longing for reviving nature and flooded fields and the realm
of all the returning birds   On Holy Saturday the courtyard was dry, and my sister and I were walking about in
it.   On that day my father and my aunts Tatyana and
Alexandra—the latter was staying with us for the occasion
—went to Nyeklyoodovo to spend the night and to greet
Easter Day in the house of God there.   The journey was
very difficult ; for the floods, though abating, were still
high.   They crossed over the dam of the mill-pond in
peasants' carts, and drove through the fields for some
distance.   The water came up to the axles ; and I was
told by the men who escorted them on horseback, that my
Aunt Tatyana was frightened and screamed loudly, but her
sister Alexandra only laughed   I heard Parasha whisper
to Yevséitch, " That one fears nothing," and   I was
astonished at my aunt's courage.   On Thursday in Holy
Week the dyeing of Easter eggs began ; red and blue
sandal-wood, broom and the tops of onions were used,
and the eggs came out red or blue or yellow, or pale pink,
or chestnut.   My sister and I watched the process with
great satisfaction.   But my mother had a special art of
dyeing eggs a mottled colour, by means of scraps of cloth
and Armenian silk ; and besides, when the egg was dyed,
she could scratch on it with a common penknife the most
artistic patterns and flowers, with the words, " CHRIST
IS RISEN."   She prepared an egg like this for every one ;
but I alone watched her at her labours.   My egg was the
prettiest of all and bore the inscription, " Christ is risen,
dear little Seryozha."   My mother was very sad not to
hear the service on Easter morning, and was surprised
that grandmother bore this deprivation so coolly ; but
grandmother, who had been very pious, was past nearly
everything by now.

I went to sleep at the usual time, but for some reason woke up suddenly in the night. The room was brightly lighted, the doors of the tabernacle were open, and before each *ikon* burned a wax candle with gilt paper round it. My mother was on her knees, reading in a low voice from the prayer-book and weeping as she prayed. I felt an irresistible desire to pray with her, and asked if I might. She started at my voice and seemed disturbed, but gave me leave to get up. I jumped out of bed, fell on my knees, and began to pray with a peculiar fervour which I had never felt before ; but my mother had risen from her knees and soon said, " That is enough ; go back to bed." I read in her face, and heard in her voice, that I was a hindrance to her prayers. With all my might I tried to go to sleep at once, but my childish excitement and the emotion which I could not explain did not soon calm down. At last my mother, having ended her prayers, put out the candles and lay down on her bed. The bright light was extinguished, and only the lamp burnt dim before the *ikons*. I do not know which of us went to sleep first. To my great annoyance, I overslept myself and woke to find my mother fully dressed. She took me in her arms, wished me a happy Easter, and gave me the egg which she had ready ; then she went to grandmother's room. In came Yevséitch bringing his Easter greeting with a yellow egg. " For shame ! " he said, " you've slept too long   Surely I told you you ought to watch the sun rising on Easter Day and showing his joy in the Resurrection." I was much vexed myself and dressed in haste ; then I looked in on my sister and brother, kissed them, and ran on to my aunt's room, from which the sun was visible ; and, though it was now high in the sky. I looked at it through my fists. The sun seemed to me to move up and down, and I called out loudly, " Yevséitch spoke the truth : the sun is keeping Easter ! " My mother came out of grandmother's room, smiled at my excitement, and took me to wish grandmother a Happy Easter. She was sitting in grandfather's armchair, wearing a silk dress and a silk handkerchief over her head ; in her festival dress she seemed more sunken and older than ever. She did not intend to break her lenten fast till the Easter cakes were brought back blessed from the church ; but my mother, saying that she would have tea with cream * in it, took me away with her.

My father and aunts returned before noon, just after my sister and I had been allowed to go out. The return journey was easier, because the floods had fallen a great deal in the night ; they brought with them Easter cakes, hard-boiled eggs, and salt baked on Holy Thursday ; all these had been blessed in church. The table was laid in the parlour, and we all met there to break the fast. To tell the truth, the fast had not been properly kept, except by my father and his mother and sister : my mother had fasted in Passion-week only—and she had had tea with cream in it that morning—and my sister and I only on the last three days ; yet we were hungrier than the rest, because we did not get the ordinary Lent diet, but fish-soup, bread and tea, and honey. There were special cakes for the servants . from inside and outside, they all gathered in the hall and parlour, and, after the Easter greetings, each received a piece of Easter cake and two dyed eggs. First they crossed themselves and then began to eat. Noticing that our cake was much whiter than what the servants got, I asked out loud, " Why is the cake, which Yevséitch and the rest are eating, less white than ours ? " My Aunt Alexandra replied at once in an angry voice, " That's more of your nonsense ! People get worse cake than that." I tried to ask another question, but my mother said it was no business of mine.

So the fast was broken, and the order was given an hour later to serve dinner. As the day was warm, even hot, my sister and I were allowed to stay in the courtyard and run about. The servants' children, in their best clothes —which meant in some cases a clean shirt—with their faces washed and their hair smoothed, were all running about amusing themselves and beginning to roll their eggs along the ground, when suddenly the attention of all was attracted by two men walking down the Kudrinsky hill on foot. They

* While fasting, orthodox Russians abstain from butter, eggs, and milk as well as from meat

came wading through the water past the submerged bushes, and made straight for the ford. The servants at once collected, and soon recognised them as the old miller, Boltunyonok, and Vassili Petroff, one of the young outdoor servants. Both were returning from the mass at Nye-klyoodovo. Their purpose was clearly to wade through the floods to the summer-kitchen, which was connected by a gangway with the high bank of our courtyard; and the folly of this attempt proved to all that they were not sober. They evidently wished to avoid the long round by the dam. Though the river had fallen so much, that in most places it was not more than knee-deep, yet there were many holes and deep places round the kitchen—in summer these were cleaned out—where the depth of water was considerable. At once it was feared that the pair might stumble into a hole and be drowned; such an accident was quite possible, even for sober men. My father was informed; he came at once and saw the danger. He gave orders to harness a horse instantly and drive to the mill for a boat, in which it would not be difficult to bring the two to the bank. Meantime the miller and red-haired Vaska (as he was commonly called) moved forwards, singing at the top of their voices; sometimes they kept together, and again they separated, when one wished to take to the right, the other to the left; their voices were clearly audible All the servants, joined by a constant stream of boys and girls from the village, were keenly interested, talking loudly, laughing, and disputing. Some said that they would suffer no worse mishap than a cold bath which would sober them effectually; that the water was shallow everywhere except for one hole near the kitchen where it was neck-deep; and that the men were good swimmers. Others declared, that it was all very well to talk like that on dry land; but the river was deep in many places, as much as eight feet in the old channel; even sober men might sink in wet clothes, and drunk men would go to the bottom like a key. The spectators forgot, that, though their voices could be heard, their words could not be distinguished; and they all began to gesticulate violently and call out directions: "More to the left!"—

" More to the right ! "—" This way ! "—" That way ! "
—" Not that way ! "—and so on. The two men, who had
sunk waist-deep in the water more than once and even
deeper occasionally, seemed really to have been sobered :
they stopped singing and calling out, and walked straight
ahead in silence. Suddenly they changed their direction
and took to the left, where there was a submerged ditch,
only distinguishable by the rapidity of the current ; it
was called the new ditch, and was, at that time, deep.
The spectators raised a loud cry which the unfortunate men
must have heard ; but they paid no attention to it, and
perhaps took it for a sign of approval. On getting close
to the ditch, they stopped and said something ; from their
gestures it was clear that Vassili wished to change their
direction. A dead silence followed, as if all were trying to
hear what they were saying. On they came, below the
ditch, fortunately, but along the very edge of it. At this
moment, the young miller, Boltunyonok's son, galloped up
in the cart ; and, when the boat was carried to the bank
and lowered into the water, he pulled with the oars, and
punted himself over the far bank of the river into the old
channel. Just as he got there, his father disappeared
beneath the water. A terrible cry rose beside me and was
hushed at once. It was clear that the miller had stumbled
and fallen into the ditch ; but all expected to see him come
to the surface ; the ditch was narrow, and it was possible
to reach the bank in a moment ; but there was no sign of
him. Horror seized on all : many crossed themselves ;
others said in a low voice, " He is lost, he is drowned " ;
the women began to weep and wail. We were taken off
to the house. I was so frightened and stupefied by what
I had witnessed that I could give no account of it to my
mother and aunts when they asked me what had happened.
Yevséitch and Parasha were not there : as soon as they
had deposited us in the room, they ran back to the river.
There was not one single servant left in the whole house.
My mother and my aunts knew this much, that some
drunken men were walking over the fields to the ford ; so
when I at last got out the words I had heard from others—
" The old miller is lost and drowned," then the full extent of

the calamity became clear to them My aunts went out
themselves, to learn the details and to send some one to
attend to us. Soon Grusha, grandmother's deaf maid,
hurried in with Parasha, and told us that the body could
not be found ; a number of men with poles had managed
to cross the old channel, but, if they found anything now,
it could only be a corpse, as he must be dead long ago.
" It is very sad," Parasha added, " to look at his children
and his ailing wife ; but no man can escape his destiny."

So our bright Easter day was clouded over. All were
depressed ; and as to myself, it is hard to describe my state
of mind. I had often read, and heard still more often,
that people do constantly die ; I knew that death was the
end of all men, and that soldiers fall by thousands in
battles ; I had a lively recollection of grandfather's death,
which had taken place close beside me, in another room of
the same house. Yet, for all this, the death of the miller,
who under my very eyes had walked and sung and talked
and then instantly disappeared for ever, produced on my
mind a different and much more powerful impression ; and
to be drowned in a ditch seemed to me much more terrible
than to perish in a shipwreck—I was familiar with them
from books—and sink in the bottomless depths of a boundless ocean. I was seized with a blind fear that something
similar might happen at any moment to my father or
mother or all of us.

By degrees the servants came back, all bringing the
same report, that the body had not been found. The hour
of dinner, which is usually earlier on the first day after the
fast, had long gone by. At last the table was laid and
dinner served. My father was summoned, and he came in,
much depressed and upset : since his childhood he had
known the old miller and was very fond of him. Our
dinner was a gloomy meal, and my father went out again,
as soon as we rose from table The search for the body
went on till evening. At last, when the searchers were
about to go home, weary, wet through, and hungry—for
they had not had time to break their fast properly—a shout
from the young Boltunyonok made them all turn round.
" Found ! " he cried. The son's pole had caught hold of

his drowned father's coat ; and aided by others, he dragged out the body by a great effort. It appeared that the drowning man, carried down by the swift current, had got under the bare roots of an old alder, which grew, not by the new ditch, but on the bank of the old deep channel, where it curved round the island. As soon as the news of this discovery reached us, the house was again deserted for a time : all the household hastened to view the body, and then returned with such horrid particulars that I hardly slept all that night . as I pictured the old miller to myself, I trembled all over and broke out in a cold sweat. But I had the firmness to overcome my horror, and did not wake my parents. Night with its suffering passed away, dawn appeared, and my morbid fancies sank to rest at sunrise. I went to sleep in peace.

The weather now changed, and the rest of Easter week was wet and cold. So much rain came down, that the floods, when thus reinforced, rose again, and remained at their former level for twenty-four hours, after which they fell rapidly. At the same time, as often happens in April, the summer warmth set in. Within a week of St. Thomas's Day began that marvellous season, not always clement at its opening, at which Nature awakens from sleep and begins to live a full, young, rapid life ; the season of universal movement and excitement, of sound and colour and fragrance. I was too young then to understand it and appreciate it in detail ; but I felt new life in myself and became a part of Nature. Not till I had grown to maturity and recalled this time, did I consciously appreciate all its enchanting spell and poetic beauty. But I then recognised what I had before dimly guessed at, when I greeted spring in our house at Ufa, in our poor little garden, and in the muddy streets. At Sergéyevka, our arrival had been too late : I saw there only the end of spring, when Nature had reached her full development and full splendour, and the constant change and forward movement had stopped.

The sad death of the old miller soon passed from my mind, crushed down and squeezed out by new and powerful impressions. My heart and mind were full ; some mysterious business seemed to weigh on me and make me

anxious; I felt a mysterious desire to go somewhere.
And yet, in reality, I went nowhere and did nothing; I
neither read nor wrote. It was impossible to read and
write, when the fragrant bird-cherries were breaking into
blossom—when the crinkled leaflets, as they opened, threw
a veil of whitish down over the black gooseberry bushes
—when the larks hung all day right over the courtyard,
pouring out a stream of unvarying song till it died away
in the sky, a song which caught at my heart and affected
me to tears—when all the slopes were covered with tulips,
purple and blue and white and yellow, and the funnel-
shaped grass-blades and close-sheathed flower-buds stole
everywhere out of the ground—when ladybirds and
beetles of every kind came out into the kindly light, and
white and yellow butterflies began to flash past, and bees
and bumble-bees to buzz—when there was movement in
the water, noise on the earth, and the very air trembled
—when the sunbeams quivered, as they made their way
through the moist atmosphere filled with the elements
of life. How much business I had, how many anxieties!
Twice every day I had to visit the wood and make sure
that the jackdaws were sitting on their nests; I had to
listen to their incessant cawing; I had to watch the lilac-
leaves opening to let out the plum-coloured clusters of the
coming blossom—the finches and warblers establishing
themselves in the gooseberry bushes and barberries—the
ant-heaps waking to life and movement, where first a
few ants showed themselves and then multitudes poured
forth and began their labours—the swallows flashing past
and diving into their old nests under the eaves—the clucking
hen brooding over her tiny chickens, while the kite made
circles and floated above them. Oh, I had business enough
and cares enough! I ceased to run about the courtyard;
I did not roll eggs on the ground, or swing with my sister,
or play with Soorka. I walked, or more often I stood still;
I seemed depressed and uneasy; I walked and looked and,
for a wonder, was silent. I was tanned like a gypsy by
the sun and wind. My sister laughed at me; Yevséitch
was astonished that I did not play in the proper way or
ask leave to go to the mill, but was always walking and then

standing stock-still : " What can there be you have not
seen there, my little falcon ? "—he used to ask. My
mother, too, did not understand the state I was in, and used
to look at me anxiously. I got more sympathy from my
father : he often went with me to the garden, to look at
the birds in the bushes, and explained to me that they were
beginning to build their nests. Or we went to the Jackdaw
Wood, where he was very angry with the jackdaws for
killing the tops of the birches by breaking off twigs to make
their clumsy nests ; he even threatened to destroy them.
How charmed he was, when he saw the red clover for
the first time ! He showed me how to twitch off the pretty
flowers and suck the sweet white tubes. He was even
more delighted when he heard in the distance, also for
the first time, the song of the mocking-bird. " There,
Seryozha," he said to me ; " all the birds will start singing
now : the mocking-bird is the first to begin. And pre-
sently, when the bushes are in leaf, our nightingales will
begin ; and then life will be still more cheerful at Bagrovo."

That time also came at last : the grass grew green, the
trees and bushes put forth their leaves, and the nightingales began to sing Night and day they sang, never
ceasing. By day their song did not strike me as wonderful :
I even said that the larks sang as well ; but in the late
evening or at night. when silence everywhere began to
reign, under the light of the fading sunset-glow or the glitter
of the stars, the song of the nightingales was an excitement
and joy to me, and for a time prevented me from sleeping
There were a great number of the birds, and they evidently
came close to the house at night. One corner of our bedroom ran out towards the bend of the river, close to the
bushes swarming with nightingales, so that their calls and
rapid cadences came loudly through the shuttered windows
on two sides. My mother used to send out at night to
frighten them away. I had never before believed my aunt,
when she said that her rest was disturbed by the nightingales. I don't know if my father's promise came true,
that life would be more cheerful at Bagrovo ; nor can I
say whether I was at this time in what could be called high
spirits ; but this I know, that the thought of that time

has been, throughout my whole life, a source of quiet happiness in my heart.

At length I became calmer. My eyes were satisfied with seeing, and I became used to the sights, or rather marvels of Nature around me. Nature herself, having attained her full magnificence, seemed to grow calmer. I began to play games or read sometimes, or to sit and talk to my mother : and I was glad to see that this pleased her. " Well, you seem to have regained your senses," she said, kissing and stroking my head ; " but you were quite like a mad creature : you took no interest in anything, and forgot that you had a mother ! " I could see tears in her eyes, and her reproach stabbed me to the heart. I was vaguely conscience-stricken before ; but now scales seemed to fall from my eyes. Though I had not forgotten the existence of my mother, yet I had seldom thought of her, had never asked how she was, though her health was not strong, and had ceased to impart all my thoughts and feelings to her. I was overcome with remorse and peni- tence ; I blamed myself mercilessly, begged forgiveness, and promised it should never happen again. I believed that I should love her henceforward more passionately than ever, that I had never before appreciated her truly, and that I was unworthy of a mother who had more than once saved my life at the risk of her own. I went so far as to believe that I was a bad ungrateful son, who deserved the contempt of all. Unfortunately, my mother sometimes either could not or would not check my tendency to run to extremes : it was a feature of her own character, and, when my feelings ran in the same channel as her own, her enthusiastic temperament did more to increase my excite- ment than to allay it. This was often the case in later years, and it was so especially on the occasion I am describing. Influencing one another, we worked ourselves up to violent expressions of mutual repentance and pas- sionate affection ; all difference of age and relations between us disappeared ; we both wept hysterical tears and sobbed aloud, while I confessed, that I did not love my mother enough, and she, that she had not done justice to so precious a son and had grieved him by her cruel reproaches. Just at this moment. my father came into the room. The first glance made him turn pale : he never flushed but always lost colour, when alarmed or excited. " What is the matter with you ? " he asked, with agitation in his voice. My mother said nothing. but I began at once to explain exactly. He looked at me with astonishment at first, and then with pity. When I stopped, he said, " It is a strange pleasure you two find in tormenting yourselves about trifles and making yourselves ill. You are still a child ; but your mother ought to know better " His words fell on me like a bucket of cold water. But my mother took up the cudgels for our sensibility, and said much that was offensive and unfair to my kind father. How unfair, I did not, alas ! understand till I was much older : at the time I was convinced that my mother was perfectly right, that my father had little feeling and was incapable of such love as she and I felt. In a few days, of course, my excitement had passed away. my conscience was at ease, and I was convinced that I was not a bad boy and a bad son. My heart was again open to the impressions of Nature ; but for a long time I felt some risk in surrendering to them, and my passionate attachment to my mother grew steadily. Though still a child. I became her friend and confidant ; and thus I heard much that I could not understand at all or misunderstood, and much that I ought not to have known.

Meanwhile, as soon as the floods disappeared and the river returned to its summer channel, and even before the water was thoroughly clear, every servant in or about the house began to fish. Every one who could hold a rod, even some of the old women, took to angling ; for the large fish, such as tench, took wonderfully just then, and the spring take lasted from the first flowering of the bird-cherry till the guelder-roses had fallen. You had only to run down for an hour in the early morning, and you would bring back at least two large fish, after losing at least as many more ; and everybody ate fish-soup, or boiled fish, or fish-pies. Yevséitch had been at it a long time ; he told me of his exploits, and usually added : " Ah, it's not fishing for you yet, my little falcon : it is still wet and dirty everywhere. But in a fortnight the sun will warm the ground and dry it; and, with a view to then, I'm getting lines ready for you."

The time came, as Yevséitch had foretold, for me to fish too. Our warm weather, after lasting a few days, changed once more in the week of St. Thomas to damp and cold, though this did not prevent the growth of green leaf and blossom. The warmth set in again and became settled. The sun heated the earth, and dried up the mud and slime. Yevséitch had prepared me three lines of different sizes, but none so large as those used for big fish; nor could I have managed one of that size. My father, who had not fished once, perhaps because my mother disapproved of it, went with me to the mill-pond where the sluices were still up. Any one might angle in any part of the river; but the mill-pond was forbidden ground for the present. I saw the pleasure with which my father made his preparations. On our way to the mill, where he walked so fast that I could hardly keep up, he said to me :

" Well, Seryozha, there's nothing to be done just now on the river. The lower dam has been carried away by the flood, and it will take some time to restore it; nor is there much fish by the garden now ; but in our pond here the fish are all crowding towards the narrow outlet and are bound to take splendidly. Another day, you will throw a line for the first time in the Boogoorooslan. I suspect that after Sergéyevka you will think the fishing worse at Bagrovo."

I declared that everything at Bagrovo was better. In the preceding summer, I never had a rod in my hand ; and, although the presence of spring had affected me so powerfully, with its unfamiliar marvels—the arrival of the birds and the resurrection of all Nature—that I had almost forgotten about angling, yet, now that my emotions were calmed and I was, so to speak, surfeited with excitements, I remembered my old passion for the sport and turned to it with fresh enthusiasm. The nearer we got to the pond, the greater became my impatience. But the appearance of the pond grieved and puzzled me. The wide expanse, ordinarily covered with water, now presented a bare, dirty, uneven bottom, consisting of slime and mud,

which was cracked but not yet dried up by the sun; it
was covered with a litter of stumps and snags; and
posts, stuck in to hold traps the year before, rose up here
and there. Before, all this had been hidden by the bright
smooth mirror of the water, framed in green banks and
edged with green reeds. The young shoots were not yet
noticeable, and the old beards of dried reeds which had not
been cut down in autumn, formed an unpleasing yellow
patch between the green edges where the pond had overflowed, and, as they rattled in the wind, made a kind of
lifeless sound that was still more unpleasing. I must add
that there was a very bad smell, caused by the drying
slime and the dead fish in the reeds But the disappointment was soon forgotten. We chose the driest places
we could find near the mill-race, and began to fish. My
father proved quite right : we kept on catching perch and
large roach and tench. Most of the big ones fell to my
father, and some to Yevséitch, as they were using long
lines with large baits ; with my small line I invariably
caught a roach, if Yevséitch baited my hook with bread,
or a perch, if he used a worm for bait. I never saw my
father so excited ; and it came into my head to wonder
why he did not angle every day. Yevséitch, too, who was
always excited by fishing, said himself that he was more
frantic over it than he had ever been in his life ; and this
frenzy grew even greater, when my father pulled out a
huge perch and a still huger tench, and Yevséitch himself
first lost a big fish of some kind and then had his line broken
by a pike. He looked so absurd, as he slapped his thighs
and bewailed his bad luck, that my father laughed and made
me laugh too ; but soon another pike treated my father
in the same way. I wanted to catch something bigger ;
and, though Yevséitch declared that I could not pull out
a good-sized fish, I begged him to give me a longer line
with a large bait. He did so, but no success followed :
on the contrary, even the small fish ceased to take. I got
tired of it and wanted to go home ; my father and Yevséitch
were not thinking of stopping, and, but for my presence,
would have stayed by the pond till dinner-time. As he
was wrapping up our tackle and preparing to go home,

Yevséitch said : " What would you think of coming here early, Alexyéi Stepanitch ? What grand sport there would be then ! " My father seemed rather vexed, and said that the morning was impossible for him. " And you've never once taken out your gun, you who used to be so fond of it ! " To this my father said nothing. I paid particular attention to what Yevséitch said, and also to the fact that my father was out of spirits during our way home.

The fish we had caught could hardly be got into two buckets. We carried them straight to grandmother and my Aunt Tatyana ; my Aunt Alexandra had gone back to her own estate before this. They took a great interest in our catch : with cries of surprise they examined and praised the fish ; both were fond of fish when cooked, and my aunt was an angler herself. But my mother refused, with an impatient gesture, to look at our booty, and said that it smelt of damp and decay ; she even declared that we two smelt of the slime in the pond, and perhaps this was actually the case.

When alone with my mother, I asked her why my father did not fish, when he was so fond of fishing , and why he never took out a gun, though I knew from himself that he loved shooting. My mother did not like these questions. She replied that nobody prevented him from doing both, if he chose ; but at the same time she spoke with contempt of those sports, especially of fishing, which she called an occupation for idle and empty-headed people who had nothing better to do, and a pastime suitable only for children. I felt a little ashamed of my own passion for it. I was beginning to consider myself as beyond the childish age : my reading, my conversations with my mother on grown-up subjects, the phrases with which she fed my vanity—" you are no longer a child ; you understand every thing ; what is your opinion about this ? "—and similar expressions in which, at moments of expansion, she treated me mistakenly as her equal in age—all this had made me conceited, and I was beginning to look down on others as my inferiors. My shame of my favourite pursuit, however, did not last long. On the third day, my desire

grew so strong that, under the pretext of my youth, which,
in other cases, I refused to acknowledge, I got my mother's
leave to go again to the pond with my father. With
Yevséitch alone, I would not have been allowed to go there.
I had a very strong reason for not putting this off : I knew
from my father that two days later the pond was to be
refilled. Yevséitch and my father took measures to
prevent the pike from biting off the hooks : they used
casts of gut or wire, which the pike, for all their sharp teeth,
could not bite through. The hopes and expectations of
our party were not disappointed. We caught many fish,
including six pike, of which four fell to my father and two
to Yevséitch.

The closing of the dam (or rather, the result of this,
as I was not allowed to see the process itself) was also a
novel and interesting scene for me. As soon as the sluice
was lowered and the current cut off by degrees, the river
became quite shallow below the dam, and, except in the
deep holes, the great Boogoorooslan shrank to a little
rivulet. All along the stream, right down to the lower
dam where the sluice was open, the banks were covered
with people, young and old, armed with wicker hurdles
and snares to put across the water. As soon as the fish
perceived the fall of the water, they began to wriggle down
stream, stopping sometimes in the deepest places, and
naturally fell into the snares spread for them. Yevséitch
and I stood on the high bank which commanded a distant
view up and down, and watched the animated scene, accompanied by the cries of the women and children. Petticoats
knotted at one end, and sieves were used as nets by the
children ; they even caught fish in their hands, sometimes
pulling out fair-sized roach from under a snag or out of a
crab's hole ; eels also were taken, which like a crab's hole
at any time to coil up in. The crabs amused me by the
way they stretched out their claws and crawled about the
shallow bottom ; from time to time they inflicted a sharp
pinch on the bare arm or leg of some wader, and a loud
shriek arose from some boy or girl, usually the latter.

The Boogoorooslan, though not broad, was very rapid
and deep and full of holes. Towards evening the pond was

getting full, and at night the water was running into the mill-race ; early next morning the mill was working, and our river ran once more with its former depth and volume. I was vexed at not seeing the sluices lowered, and my father's description increased my vexation and aggravated my grievance   I did not fail to demand an explanation of my mother, why she had not let me go ; her answer was that I had no business to go among a crowd of *moujiks*, and to hear, for no purpose, their rough talk and coarse jokes and abuse of one another.   In vain my father declared that there had not been, and never was, anything of the kind ; and that there was no rough language, though plenty of fun and noise.   I was bound to believe my mother, though I wished to take my father's account for truth.

As soon as the land was dry, field-labour began with the sowing of the spring wheat, and my father drove every day to the ploughland.   Every day I asked to go too, but only once did I get leave from my mother.   At my urgent entreaty, my father agreed to take his gun with him, as there was plenty of game in the fields ; but, as my mother said she was afraid the gun would go off and kill me, my father left it at home, though he assured her that he would not have loaded it till we got off the car.   I noticed that he wished himself to take the gun ; and I wished it very keenly and therefore went off in a depressed frame of mind. But the sight of the spring landscape soon caught my attention ; joy made an end of my grief and mastered my heart.   Going uphill from the stackyard, I saw that all the hollows were thickly covered with bright green grass ; and the shoots of the almond-trees, which trailed along the slopes of the steep hillocks, were loaded with small pink flowers which sent out a strong sweet smell.   On the hills cherry-trees and wild acacias were in flower.   Above us the larks poured out their song ; from time to time the note of the crane came to us ; the snipe drummed at a distance ; the hoarse cry of hawks was heard ; bustards rose from the road and settled down on it again.   More than once my father said, " A pity we have not the gun with us ! " The fields had a bird-population of their own, quite unlike that which peopled the waters and marshes down below ;

and this seemed to me even more beautiful than that. On
the high ground I felt for the first time the immeasurable
difference of the air on the hills and in the plain, and perceived the justice of my mother's complaints against the
low situation of Bagrovo. There, the smell of stagnant
water and heavy damp was constant; here, the air was
sweet and dry and light. Black strips of ploughed land
soon came in sight; and, when we got near, I saw a
labourer, a man past middle life, walking at a vigorous
and measured pace backwards and forwards over the field,
and scattering seed, which he took from a bast wallet
hanging across his shoulder. Some distance behind him
three labourers were ploughing; the horses which drew
the ploughs, though they looked small and weak, went
steadily on, and, without any violent effort, broke up the
black soil with the coulters and parted the friable earth
to right and left. The land was not virgin soil, but what
we called "pulp," having been ploughed several times
before. Behind the ploughs came three harrows with iron
teeth; the horses which drew them were like those in the
ploughs, and were driven by boys. Though it was still
early and there was a spring freshness in the air, all the
labourers were in their shirt-sleeves. As I watched the
regular and unceasing movements of men and horses,
I forgot the beauty of the spring morning. The important
and even sacred nature of their task, though I was too
young to understand or appreciate it fully, made a strong
impression on my mind. My father walked up to a place
where the land had been ploughed but not yet harrowed,
made some measurement with his stick, and began to
calculate. I looked round and saw the same scene, the
same regular movement of men and horses backward and
forward, going on in other places; and it made me reflect
very deeply, though I did not quite know what was the
subject of my reflexions. My father now came back; and,
finding that I had never stirred, he said, "Well, Seryozha?"
I replied with a volley of questions about the men and boys
at work in the field, and got from him full and satisfactory
answers. His words sank deep into my heart. I compared
myself with these boys, who lived on bread and water, and

R

spent the whole day, from sunrise to sunset, in tramping backwards and forwards over the rough plough as if it were so much sand ; and the comparison made me feel sorry and ashamed, and I resolved to ask my parents to put me to harrowing. Full of these thoughts, I went home and began to impart to my mother my feelings and my wish to work. When she laughed, I grew excited ; at last she said, in a dignified way—

" Put this nonsense out of your head ; ploughing and harrowing are not your business. However, if you wish to try it, I give you leave."

Not long after I was really allowed to try my hand at harrowing. But it turned out that I was no good at it : I could not walk on the ploughed land, nor hold the reins and guide the horse, nor force it to obey ; the village boy who walked by my side laughed at me. I felt shame and vexation, and never spoke of trying farm-work again.

At this precise period of my life at Bagrovo, I spent little of my time with my sister, and kept at a distance, as it were, from her, though this did not in the least mean that I loved her less The temporary separation was due partly to my new amusements, in which she, as a girl, could not share, and partly to my closer relations with my mother. When talking to me as to a friend, my mother always sent my sister out of the room, and forbade me to repeat to her our frank conversations. She loved her daughter less warmly than her son and took less notice of her. I was the favourite—the name was often applied to me—and, consequently, a spoilt child. A spoilt child I long remained ; but that never prevented a warm affection between me and my brothers and sisters. My grandmother and aunt loved my sister and were not very well-disposed towards me ; they were always suggesting to her that she was an unloved daughter ; that my mother, at a look from me, would do anything I wanted ; and that the son was everything and the daughter nothing. But all these harmful insinuations produced no effect on the loving heart of my sister ; and no feeling of envy or discontent ever darkened for a moment the bright goodness of her fine character.

As before, my mother refused to take over the management of the household. Full control remained with my grandmother, or rather my aunt. All my mother would do was to order meals for herself and for us; but nevertheless it was clear that she was the real mistress of the house, and that all was done, or would be done if she chose, according to her will and pleasure. Young as I was, I understood that my mother was not loved by the household, and that all, except Yevséitch and Parasha, feared her, although she never said a rough word to any one. This was a riddle, which I was still too young to answer.

When the roads were dry, all our neighbours, who were mostly relations, came to visit us. The Chichagoffs also came, but did not bring Mme. Myortvavo; of course my mother was very glad to see them and spent much of her time in lively and intimate conversation with Mme. Chichagoff; from their *tête-à-têtes* even I was excluded. Twice I caught a snatch of what she was saying, and made out that she was complaining of her position, and was dissatisfied with her life at Bagrovo; and this thought was a constant cause of wonder and distress to me.

Peter Chichagoff, like my mother, knew nothing and cared nothing about the management of a house and estate. All that, he left to his wife and her mother; his own pursuits were reading, writing, painting, plan-drawing, and shooting. Knowing that we had plenty of game, he brought his gun and a dog, and went shooting every day in our marshes, which contained a great number of woodcocks, snipe of all kinds, marsh partridges, and landrails. My father went with him once, and they brought home full game-bags. M. Chichagoff was always bantering my father.

"Alexyéi Stepanitch," he said, "does not like to waste powder and shot; he likes his bird rather large and rather near; snipe are not much to his taste; a duck is more in his line; there's more meat about it."

My father parried the joke by admitting that, for want of practice, he was not a good shot at small birds; Chichagoff had certainly killed four couple of snipe, but, on the other hand, he had sown the marshes with shot, apparently

hoping for a crop of it next year. Chichagoff laughed
heartily with the ringing laugh peculiar to him, of which
my mother used to say that you could see his intelligence
even in his laughter. Sometimes he gave up a little of his
time to conversation with me. This was generally after
the day's shooting, when he had changed into dry clothes
and was sitting on the drawing-room sofa, smoking his
large meerschaum pipe. "Well, Seryozha," he would
begin, "how are our old friends, Sumarokoff, Cheraskoff,
and especially Lomonossoff? How does Karamzin hit
it off with the brotherhood of modern bards?" By this,
he meant that I was to start reciting such poetry of those
authors as I had by heart. He himself made jokes at the
expense of all of them, even Lomonossoff, for whom he
had much respect all the same. Derzhavin he praised
warmly, and yet made fun of him; Dmitrieff was the only
poet whom he praised without qualification, but without
enthusiasm; unfortunately, I hardly knew anything of
either of these. He was much amused by my style of
reciting, or, as he called it, my declamation. I had never
heard any one recite poetry except my uncles; and my
uncle Alexander had a passion for imitating the tragic
actors of the Moscow theatres, so that I had formed my
own style by trying to reproduce his imitation. It may
easily be believed, that my performance, accompanied as
it was by misplaced emphasis and uncouth gestures, was
really amusing. None the less I recall with sincere satisfaction and gratitude the hours of my childhood which I
passed with Peter Chichagoff. He was a man of exceptional intellectual gifts, and towered above the society
in which he lived. His clever witticisms became fixed
in my mind, young as I was, and probably served to
prepare me for a juster estimate of contemporary writers.

In later years, when I was at college and afterwards in
the public service at Petersburg, whenever I came home for
a holiday, I never failed to see Chichagoff as soon as possible.
I read to him anything new in the way of literature, and I
shared with him my impressions and youthful views and
convictions. His judgment was often sound and always
pointedly expressed. With special clearness I remember,

how, not long before his death and when he was very ill,
I repeated to him some verses on Derzhavin and Karamzin.*
Forgetting his illness and frequent attacks of pain, Chichagoff laughed heartily over the verses and repeated some of
the lines and phrases. "Well, my friend," he said afterwards, and his face looked bright and animated as he
spoke, "you have done me so much good, that I shan't
need my dose of morphia this time." In his fits of pain,
which were beyond mortal powers of endurance, he used to
take small doses of morphia.

Summer heat now set in. The large fish had ceased to
take, and my angling was restricted : using pins for hooks,
I caught gudgeons and small mullets and roach in shallow
safe places, beginning at the house and going up the river
as far as what was known as Antony's Gangway, which he
had built opposite to his own cottage ; the river was deeper
higher up, and we might not go there without my father.
I went every day, either morning or evening, for two hours ;
and Yevséitch went with me. Just beside the house there
was no shade ; and therefore my sister and I used to go to
the Jackdaw Wood or the island, where we played or sat
and read. The island became dearer to me every day, and
it was really a charming place. The banks were planted
with birches which had grown tall and spreading and
afforded a dense shade ; the island was cut in two by a
lime-avenue ; the trees were planted close together, and
it was always dark and cool beneath them. This avenue
served as a refuge for moths in the daytime ; a few years
later it was a great hobby of mine to collect moths. My
aunt Tatyana pretty often came with us to the island ;
sitting in the cool shade, on the bank of the full and rapid
river, and sometimes holding a fishing-rod, she liked to listen
to my reading. Sometimes she brought her " Song-book "
and read it herself or made me read it ; and, however
absurd and shapeless these songs, by Sumarokoff and his
circle, may have been, yet by us they were read and
listened to with sincere sympathy and satisfaction. To
this day I remember by heart a hunting-song by Sumarokoff.

We told my mother how cool and shady it was on the

* These verses, quoted in the original, I have not translated

island on hot afternoons, and sang its praises so loudly, that she decided to go there with us for once. At first she liked it, and ordered a large rug to be brought, for her to sit on, upon the bank : she never sat on long grass without something underneath her, for she said it was damp and harboured quantities of insects which lost no time in crawling upon one's skin. The rug was brought, and leather cushions also ; and we all sat down on them. But, for some reason this precautionary and artificial treatment of nature damped my pleasure, and I was not by any means as lively as when alone with my sister or aunt. My mother looked with indifference at the green limes and birches, and the water flowing round us ; the sound of grinding and the clack of the mill, which sometimes reached our ears and died away as the breeze rose and fell, seemed to her monotonous and tiresome ; the damp smell of the pond, which none of us had ever noticed, she found unpleasant. So, after an hour, she went back to her stifling bedroom, heated like a furnace by the sun's rays. We stayed on by ourselves ; the rug and cushions were removed, and the island recovered its charm for me. My aunt was fond of making inscriptions on the smooth white bark of the birches ; sometimes she carved with a pocket-knife or scratched with a large pin verses from her " Song-book." On this occasion, she carved on a tree, " Sofya Nikolayevna visited the island," and added the date in full.

From time to time, I went with my father to see different kinds of field-labour. One was the watering of the spring-sown crops—oats, spelt, and wheat. Another was weeding : I watched the women and girls constantly stooping as they pulled out the weeds ; when they had gathered a whole bundle on the left arm, they carried it carefully to the side of the field, threw down their load, and went back to their weeding. The work is fairly heavy, and tiresome too, because the good result of the labour is not obvious. At last the season came for haymaking, which began a week before St. Peter's Day. I had not seen this form of field-labour before ; and. when I saw it, I thought it the pleasantest sight of any.

On a fine summer day, long after the sun's rays had dispelled the morning freshness, I drove with my father to what we called "The Sacred * Wood"; it consisted chiefly of young limes, of fair size by this time, and straight as pine trees. It had been formally protected from the axe some years before, and was very strictly guarded against thieves. As we rose from the sunken road to this wood, I began to catch low noises unfamiliar to me—a regular swishing sound repeated at very short intervals, and also a rasping metallic sound. "What is that?" I asked at once. "You will soon see," said my father, smiling. Our view was blocked by a thick undergrowth of young aspen; but, when we turned the corner, a wonderful spectacle lay before me. Forty labourers were mowing, strung out in one long line; the scythes, as they came up, flashed in the sun, and the cut grass lay in thick regular swathes behind them At the end of a long strip, the mowers stopped, and began to sharpen their scythes in some way, bandying jests meantime, as could be guessed from their loud laughter; their words were still undistinguishable. The metallic sound was caused by the sharpening of the scythes against wooden hones, smeared with clay and sand; of this I was told later. When we got close, my father hailed them with the time-honoured phrase, "God speed the work!"—and their loud reply, "Many thanks to you, *batyushka* Alexyéi Stepanitch," filled the field and echoed in the sunken road. Then they set to work again. How easy and graceful were their movements, how broad and free was the sweep of their scythes! About this work there was something so kindly and cheerful, that I found it hard to believe, what I was told, that it was very laborious. The air was light, and a wonderful fragrance came from the wood, and from the grass which had been mown in the early morning; it was full of flowers, which had begun to fade in the sun's fierce heat, and to send forth a peculiar pleasant smell. The uncut grass stood up like a wall, waist high; and the men

---

* To preserve a wood from illicit cutting, the priest and people walk round in solemn procession with banners and *ikons*, and a date is fixed, before which it may not be entered

said, " What a hay crop ! It's a regular bear." *   Crows
and jackdaws, flying across from the wood where they had
their nests, were walking along the high green ridges of
cut grass ; and I was told they were picking up beetles
and caterpillars, which, now that they had lost their thick
cover, could be seen running about on the prostrate stalks
and bare ground.   I went close and convinced myself by
my own eyesight that this was quite true ; and I also
noticed that the birds were pecking berries as well.   There
were wild strawberries in the grass, still green but very
large ; in exposed places they were already ripening.   My
father and I each picked a large handful of the berries,
where the grass was cut ; and some of them were larger
than a hazel nut ; many of them, though not red yet,
were already soft and sweet.

I enjoyed the hayfield so much that I was unwilling
to start off home at my father's summons.   In the wood
there was a dell with a little babbling stream ; and from
there we heard the cooing of wood-pigeons or turtles, and
also the sound of caterwauling, and the melancholy cry
of the oriole ; the sounds were so distinct and so unlike
one another, that I found it hard to believe, that they were
all produced by the same pretty little yellow bird.†   From
time to time the piercing trumpet-like note of the wood-
pecker was heard.   Suddenly a hawk flew out over the
field, soared high into the sky, and circled over our heads,
keeping a watch for the small birds which the mowers
kept startling out of the grass.   When they appeared, he
fell on them, like lightning from the clouds.   Admiration
for his rapid and graceful movements was tempered by
keen sympathy for his victims ; and the labourers greeted
with loud cries both the attacks of the bold robber and the
escape of the small birds, every time they succeeded in
dropping down on the grass or hiding in the wood.
Yevséitch was more excited than any one, and followed
with shouts of applause the marvellous speed of this

* I could never explain to my satisfaction this phrase, which was
applied also to a tall thick crop of uncut corn.   I suppose that by the word
" bear " they meant to denote strength, i e the substance, height, and
goodness generally of the grass or corn.   (Author's Note)

† The oriole

beautiful and fierce bird of prey   For a long time we
watched the hawk, as he dashed at his prey and missed
it ; but at last he struck a bird and carried it off to the
wood in his talons.   " Ah, the poor thing is caught ; he
has struck it and carried it off to his nest, to feed his young
ones · " such were the cries of the mowers, interrupted and
sometimes drowned by the rasping of the scythes against
the hones and the rustle of the grass as it fell in swathes.
My father repeated that it was time for us to go, and we
started.   All the way, the pleasant picture of the hayfield
stuck in my head ; but, when we got home, this time I did
not rush to my mother, to tell her of my new impressions.
Experience had taught me that she did not enjoy descriptions of farm work, of which she knew nothing except by
hearsay ; if she had ever seen it, it was only in passing or
from a distance.   I hastened to describe it all, first to my
sister, next to Parasha, and then to my grandmother and
aunt.   These two had watched haycutting and the hay-
harvest many a time, and, as a matter of course, knew
much more than I did about the whole business ; what
puzzled them was my enthusiasm.   My aunt added, however, " It's all very pleasant to look on at, but mowing
in this heat is terribly heavy work , " and her words made
me thoughtful.

My sister, though she could not take part in some of my
summer amusements, was my faithful companion and helper
in collecting grasses and flowers, in watching the nests
of the small birds which bred freely in the old gooseberry-
bushes and barberries, and in collecting caterpillars, butterflies, and beetles of different kinds.   My inborn taste for
pursuits and observations of this kind, and for natural
history in general, was brought out by the volumes of
Reading for Children.   When we noticed the nest of any
small bird—it was generally a linnet or a redstart—we
came every day to see the hen sitting on her eggs , sometimes, for want of care, we frightened her off the nest ; and
then, carefully parting the prickly branches, we looked at
the pretty little coloured eggs lying in the nest.   It
happened sometimes that the bird resented our curiosity
and deserted her nest.   If we saw that the little bird was

absent from the nest for some days, and did not flutter round us chirping as usual, then we took the eggs, or perhaps the whole nest, and carried them home, considering ourselves the lawful owners of the dwelling deserted by the mother.   But when the bird succeeded, in spite of our interference, in hatching her eggs, and we found unexpectedly in their place the naked little fledglings constantly opening large mouths and cheeping pitifully— when we saw the mother flying to the nest and feeding them with flies and caterpillars—what words can describe our joy ?   We continued to observe the young birds as they grew and got feathers and at last abandoned the nest.

The grasses and flowers which we picked we pressed and dried in books, using by preference Rollin's *Roman History* and Buchan's *Domestic Medicine* ; and, to prevent the pages from being discoloured or injured by damp, we placed each flower between sheets of writing-paper.   The phosphorescent light of glow-worms was a great attraction to us—about phosphorus I knew already out of *Reading for Children*—we caught them and kept them in paper boxes, supplying them with grasses and flowers of different kinds ; and we applied the same treatment to all caterpillars which had sixteen legs.   The glow-worms did not live long, and almost always had lost by the next day their power to display at times their fascinating light, which we liked to watch in a dark room.   The other caterpillars lived a long time, and sometimes, to our great joy, turned into chrysalises   The process took place in the following way. The smooth caterpillars, by means of a sticky substance, hung themselves up, or rather gummed themselves, to the top or side of the box ; and the hairy caterpillars rolled themselves up in leaves and wound round themselves thin white transparent threads, on which they rested as on a bed. After a period which differed much in different cases, the outer skin of the caterpillar peeled off like a shell, and a chrysalis was left, either hanging or lying down.   The former kind had projections and horns, and were grey with patterns on them, or flesh-coloured, or sometimes gold coloured ; the latter were always dark in colour, and looked just like tiny dolls, closely swaddled in cradles.   I knew that the hanging chrysalises ought to turn into butterflies, and the others into moths; but, as I did not know then how to manage them, the development of our chrysalises was arrested; and this was inevitable, because we were constantly looking at them and even feeling them, to see if they were alive. Only one came out, a gold-coloured chrysalis which I had found under some projecting boards; it developed into the commonest sort of butterfly, a cabbage white; but our delight was of no common kind!

The wild strawberries ripened at last, and were brought to the house—no mere cupfuls and basketfuls now, but whole bucketfuls. Grandmother often sat on the veranda to receive the fruit from the pickers; she seldom praised the berries, and generally grumbled and scolded. My mother was very fond of them, and believed them to be good for her: she took them as medicine several times a day and ate little ordinary food at that season; and we children were allowed to eat as many as we liked. Besides all the other ways in which the fruit was used, a drink was made out of it which had an incomparable taste.

On hot summer days, long ropes, propped at intervals on forked poles, were stretched over all the courtyard, from the outdoor storehouses to the underground cellar, and from the stables to the workshop. On these ropes clothes of all kinds were hung out to dry, or to keep them from moth—men's garments and women's garments, fur coats, woollen dresses, warm quilts, and stuffs of all sorts. It was a great amusement to me to examine them. Many of the garments were such as people had ceased to wear, and were made of stuff which it was no longer possible to buy; so I was told. One day I was strolling between these hanging walls or screens, where motley colours and even gold and silver embroidery were swinging in the wind, when I came without thinking to my aunt's storehouse. It stood opposite the windows of her room, and almost in the middle of the court. Her maid, Matrona, a stout girl with a red-and-white complexion, had been stationed at the door as sentry; but she was sound asleep, although the hot sun was shining directly on her face. Hanging on props round her, or lying on the ground by the door, were a great number of pieces of cloth, broad and narrow, and a quantity of table-linen, furs, silk materials, dresses, and so on. I looked attentively at them all, and noticed that some of the linen was yellow with age. Curiosity made me go inside the storehouse. There I saw trunks standing open and empty, and bags hanging from the ceiling; and on two rows of shelves, which ran along the walls, there was a vast store of miscellaneous articles—glass and china ware, tea-pots and tea-cups, milk-jugs, lacquered trays, small boxes and drawers, and even bottles with new corks; in one corner lay an immense feather-bed, or rather a great sack full of down; in another there was a large new tub covered with a white cloth; I was inquisitive enough to raise the cloth and was astonished to find that the tub was nearly full of lump sugar. Just then I heard the voices of Parasha and my sister, who were walking between the hanging garments, looking for me and calling out my name. I hastened to meet them; but, as I ran out, I awakened Matrona. She was horribly frightened, when she saw me running out of the storehouse. "What were you doing in there, sir?" she cried angrily; "that is not your place at all. Now your aunt will be angry with me: she never allows a living soul to enter her storehouse." I said that I did not know that; but I would tell my aunt at once and ask her leave to examine it all thoroughly. But my words increased Matrona's alarm: she rushed forward, kissed my hands, and begged me not to tell my aunt where I had been. Overcome by her appeals and entreaties, I promised to hold my tongue; but suddenly I saw Parasha standing close before me, and holding my sister's hand, with a sly look on her face. She had heard everything, and, when we got a little distance from the storehouse, asked what I had seen there; and I, naturally, told her, very precisely and minutely. She heard me with impatience, and, when I came to the lump sugar, she flared up and began:

"What wonder that we servants hide away an odd piece of stuff at times, or carry off a lump of sugar, when real ladies, with long pedigrees too, act like that? I assure you that she scraped together all that you saw in her storehouse by robbing her father, while her mother winked at it. It's a regular ants' nest, and she's collected it all as a marriage portion for herself. That sugar—for twenty years past she's been stealing and hoarding it! She has whole bags of tea and coffee hanging in there, I would swear!"

But suddenly Parasha recollected herself: exactly as Matrona had done a few minutes before, she began to kiss my face and hands and beg me not repeat to my mother what she had said of my aunt. She reminded me how she had incurred my mother's wrath before for speaking in a similar way about my aunts. She cried and said, "I shall certainly be banished to Old Bagrovo, and, likely enough, be parted from my husband, if Sofya Nikolayevna hears what I said in my folly." "The devil tempted me," she went on, wiping away her tears; "it was too much for me; I was so sorry for you. I had heard long ago of these doings, but I did not believe it; and now you have seen with your own eyes. Oh! I am utterly undone!" she shrieked, bursting out again in floods of tears. I assured her that I would say nothing to my mother; but Parasha could not rest till she had made me swear that I would not speak a word. She kissed my sister and said, "She's my good girl; she won't say a word against her poor old nana;" and my sister kissed her without speaking. I swore, as she wished; it was the first time in my life I had ever used the name of God in that way, though I had often heard others using it freely enough. I wonder now, that Parasha was able to induce me to take an oath, a thing which my mother severely condemned.

My intention not to get Parasha into trouble was carried out. I remembered very well, how the year before I had nearly brought misfortune upon her, and how sorry I had been afterwards; but to keep the whole thing secret was impossible. I told my mother at once, what I had seen in my aunt's storehouse, and how frightened Matrona was, and how she begged me not to tell my aunt. All I kept back was Parasha's outburst. At first my mother smiled, but afterwards she said severely—

"You are to blame, for going where you have no

business to go without permission ; and, as punishment for your fault, you must conceal the truth from your aunt. Otherwise, if she knows that you were in her storehouse, she will beat Matrona."

The word " beat " took me aback . I could not believe that my aunt, who was sorry to crush a midge, was capable of beating Matrona. I would certainly have asked my mother to explain ; but my uneasy conscience told me that I was concealing the truth already, by keeping back from my mother what Parasha had let out to me. I felt rather uncomfortable all day ; I did not even go near my aunt, nor did I spend much time with my mother, but went about with my sister or read a book. But by evening I had invented the following excuse for my conduct : if my mother herself told me that, in order to save Matrona from a beating, I must conceal from my aunt my visit to her storehouse, then I was also bound, in order to save Parasha from banishment to Old Bagrovo, to conceal her outburst from my mother. This reasoning quite consoled me, and I went to bed in good spirits.

The summer was hot and thundery. Rain fell almost daily, accompanied by lightning and peals of thunder which made the whole house shake   At such times grandmother lit candles before the *ikons* and said prayers ; but my aunt, who was frightened of the thunder, buried herself in her large featherbed and down cushions. I was not a little frightened ; for, though I had often read, that one ought not to fear thunder, how could you help being frightened of what might kill you ?   I was constantly hearing rumours of disasters caused by it. The storms soon passed over, and then the air became so fresh and good, and I so light-hearted, that I felt an almost insane happiness and disturbed other people by my noisy mirth ; but, when they asked the reason of my conduct, I could not explain it, because I did not understand it myself.

These constant short showers were followed by an unusually large crop of mushrooms. A report that mushrooms were growing in the Sacred Wood—the ground was paved with them, said our old bee-man who lived in the wood with his bees—excited my aunt and my father, who were very fond of picking mushrooms and especially the kind called *groozdi*. They settled to start for the wood that very day after dinner, accompanied by all the maids and a number of the outdoor women. It vexed me very much that, during the whole of dinner my mother kept scoffing at the pleasure of picking mushrooms, and laughing especially at my father, because, for the sake of this expedition, he had put off till next day some necessary business. I thought that nothing would induce her to let me go; so, only by way of experiment, I said in a hesitating way, " Will you not allow me too, mamma, to go and pick mushrooms ? " To my surprise, she at once agreed, but said to me in a voice full of meaning, " I make one condition, that you keep close to your father in the wood; or else, once they get occupied with their mushrooms, they will lose you." Pleased by this unexpected indulgence, I replied that I would not leave my father for a single minute. My father was rather disconcerted; and I even thought that he blushed. Our preparations were begun in haste, as soon as dinner was over. Two long cars and a cart were already standing at the front steps. All the party provided themselves with baskets of every shape and size, some of bast, others of wicker. As many as could find room, took their places in the vehicles; and some had walked on ahead. My mother and grandmother sat on the veranda to see us off, and we started in complete silence, which continued as long as we were in the court-yard. But the moment we got out of it, lively conversation began in all the vehicles, and was soon succeeded by loud chattering and laughter : and, when we had got a *verst* away from the house, the women and girls began to sing, and my aunt actually joined in ! Everybody was unusually gay and lively, and my own spirits rose high. I had not heard much singing, and the delight it gave me then is fresh in my memory to this day. Red-cheeked Matrona, who had a wonderful voice, led the singing. After the incident in my aunt's storehouse, she had become convinced of my discretion, which she rewarded by showering caresses on me on every suitable occasion, and calling me " clever boy " and " kind young gentleman." When we drove up to the

wood, I ran to Matrona, praised her beautiful voice, and
asked why she never sang in the maids' room at home.
She bent down and whispered in my ear, "Your mother
does not like to hear our country songs"; then she gave
me a kiss and hurried off into the wood; and I was very
sorry to lose her, because the songs and her voice had made
a strong impression on me. Soon the whole party were
scattered through the wood, and lost to view. The wood
seemed to be alive: on all sides rose cheerful cries and
halloos, ringing laughter and snatches of song; Matrona
sang louder and better than any one, and for a long time
I could distinguish her voice, as it got more and more
distant. Yevséitch, my aunt, and my father (from whose
side I never stirred) walked through the young wood,
keeping pretty close together. My aunt was the first to
find a clump of mushrooms. Coming out into a little
clearing, she stopped and said, "There are bound to be
mushrooms here: I positively smell them;" and a moment
later she called out: "I declare, I stepped on them."
My father and I walked towards her, but she would not let
us come near: "They were her mushrooms, and she had
found them, and we might find out another clump for
ourselves." I watched her go down on her knees and feel
the earth under the bracken leaves; then she pulled out
the mushrooms and put them in her basket Before long,
my father and I came upon a nest of them; like my aunt,
we set to work, first feeling for them and then carefully
taking them out from under their wrapping of last year's
leaves, overgrown with grass and woodland flowers. My
father worked away with a sportsman's ardour, and
especially admired the baby mushrooms. "Look,
Seryozha," he said, "how charming the button-mushrooms
are; pick them carefully—they are brittle. Look! they
have a sort of down underneath; and what a scent!"
And I really thought the baby mushrooms very pretty;
and they had a pungent smell. After strolling about the
wood for two hours, we had filled our baskets entirely with
young *groozdi*. We then walked back to the place where
we had left the horses; and Yevséitch gave a loud hail:
"Time to go home! All come back to the horses!" A

few voices answered his hail. It was some time before we
found our vehicles ; and the search would have lasted still
longer, had we not heard from a distance the snorting of the
horses. Tightly tethered to oak saplings, our good horses
were suffering horrid torments from the attacks of blood-
sucking insects ; the worst of all these is the *stroka*, because
it chooses for its bite places on the animal which are not
protected by hair. The poor beasts, bitten till they bled,
were constantly shaking their heads and manes, swishing
their tails, pawing the ground, and twitching their whole
bodies, in the attempt to drive away their tormentors.
The man who drove the cart had been left on purpose to
protect the horses with a long leafy bough which had been
cut for him ; but we found him sleeping peacefully in the
shade of a tree. My father scolded him ; and Yevséitch
threatened he would tell our old coachman, Trophim, who
would not let the offender off in a hurry. Many of the
maids soon joined us, with baskets full of *groozdi*, but some
seemed to have gone far afield ; we started home without
waiting for them   Matrona being one of those who had
returned, I begged that she might come in our car. She
found a place on the back seat with her basket, and sang
some more songs as we drove, to which I listened with great
satisfaction. We got back just in time for tea. Grandmother was sitting on the veranda, and we laid out before
her our own baskets and the big baskets of Yevséitch and
Matrona, full of *groozdi*. She was fond of mushrooms in
general, and especially fond of this kind ; she liked them
fried in sour cream. boiled in brine, and, best of all, preserved with salt. She spent a long time in sorting them,
taking a childish pleasure in dividing them into three
heaps according to their size. Grandmother had strange
tastes : she liked her boiled eggs stale, and her mushrooms
old and maggoty ; and now, finding some yellow and
decayed *groozdi* in Matrona's basket, she sent them at once
to the kitchen to be fried for her.

I ran to my mother's bedroom, where she was sitting
with my sister and little brother, busy in cutting out some
underclothing for us. I told her all about our expedition—
that I had kept close to my father, that I had enjoyed the

s

singing and Matrona's voice, and that all the party had
been merry : but I did not say a word of what Matrona had
whispered to me.   I kept this dark, without any previous
consideration : a voice seemed to whisper to me to hold my
tongue.   But afterwards I pondered long over what I had
done, at first with grief and remorse : but then I became
easier in mind, and even assured myself, that I had acted
as I should have done, and that Matrona's words would
have vexed my mother.   I was quite aware that, even as it
was, my mother was not pleased by my account , and,
strangely enough, some instinct had warned me of this
beforehand.   All that evening and the next day, my mother
was sadder than usual, and I felt myself guilty in some way
which I could not understand.   I was sad and uneasy.
Forgetting, or rather abandoning, my own pursuits and
amusements, I spent more time with her and was more
demonstrative than usual.   She noticed the change, and,
without entering upon any explanations, was gentle and
tender with me beyond her wont.   When I thought that
she was more at ease and more cheerful even, I went
back with eager zest to my fishing-lines, and hawks, and
pigeons.   And so time went on till the very day of our
departure.

I had long known, that in the beginning of August we
were to visit Praskovya Ivanovna at Choorassovo.   She was
determined that my mother should see in its full perfection
the splendid garden of seventeen acres at Choorassovo, which
contained an immense number of apple-trees of the rarest
sorts, cherry-trees, pear-trees, and even bergamots.   My
father did not at all want to leave Bagrovo at the very
busiest season.   It was barely a week after the beginning
of the rye-harvest ; and it was also time to sow the rye,
which was always done at Bagrovo about the 25th of July.
He saw himself that the field labour was not so well done
as in his father's time, and was determined to mend matters
by his personal supervision.   Grandmother too grumbled
at our departure : she said—

"Bother Praskovya Ivanovna ! 'Come and see my
garden,' says she, ' and neglect your own land.' Don't you
rely on me, Alosha ; I am little use now, and I don't

understand things. I would not dare to speak to your new foreman : he is such a talker.''

All this my father understood very well, but it was impossible to neglect Praskovya Ivanovna or break his promise. He tried merely to postpone the visit as long as possible, starting on the 10th of August instead of the 1st ; and he gave as an excuse, that, owing to the wet summer, the apples would not be ripe before the Assumption of the Virgin (August 15th). But one day he got a letter from Mihailushka, the agent and favourite of Praskovya Ivanovna, to say that my father's presence was urgently required at Simbirsk by his lawsuit against the Bogdanoffs ; the letter said, that Praskovya Ivanovna instructed him to go at once and begged Sofya Nikolayevna to lose no time. All farming plans were dropped, and we began hasty preparations for the journey. Grandmother, though she ceased to speak against it, was very reluctant to let us go, and made my father promise that we would return for Intercession Day, October 1st. I too was sorry to part with Bagrovo and all its amusements—the angling, the hawking, for which the season had just begun, and, above all, the pigeons with feathered legs and double tufts, of which two pairs had lately been given to me by Ivan Kuroyédoff. He was a rich neighbour of my aunt Aksinya, and was paying court to her daughter, a very pretty girl, but too young yet to marry. My aunt was much pleased by the prospect of such a son-in-law, but the girl's age— she was just fifteen—made her put off the conclusion of the affair for a year. The young man was a great pigeon-fancier, and, wishing to show attention to my aunt's relations, gave me this precious and unexpected gift. Everybody, including my father and Yevséitch, declared that they had never in their lives seen such splendid pigeons. My father had a pigeon-house made for them, a large cage surrounded by an old net. This cage was attached to the back wall of the stable, at no great distance from the front steps of the house ; and I was constantly running there, to see if my pigeons had food enough and water in their trough, and to look at them and listen to their cooing. One pair were already sitting How much

it cost me to part with all this ! My sister too was not
anxious to go to Choorassovo ; but I saw that my mother
made her preparations in good spirits. To make it less
dull for grandmother in our absence, my aunt Elizabeth
and both her daughters were invited to stay with her ; and
she promised to come and to remain there till our return,
which was a great satisfaction to my father In a few
days our packing was done ; and, on the 2nd of August,
after morning tea, when we had said good-bye to my
grandmother and aunt, and put them in charge of my baby
brother, whom Praskovya Ivanovna had not told us to
bring with us, we started on our journey in that very same
English carriage of which my readers have heard before,
and, of course, took with us our own horses.

CHAPTER XVIII

A SUMMER VISIT TO CHOORASSOVO

THREE years exactly had passed since my last experience of a long journey in summer. At the age of eight, three years mean a great deal; and it might have been expected, that I would now appreciate far more keenly and more consciously the beauties of the picturesque and varied country through which we had to travel. But it did not turn out quite so, in fact. Three years before, on the journey from Ufa to Bagrovo, from the town to the country, I was like an escaped prisoner. At every step, I came face to face with novelties and natural objects which I had never seen before; and Bagrovo itself, to judge by my father's descriptions, seemed to my fancy a region of enchantment, like the fabulous "Islands of the Blest" which Vasco da Gama discovered on his voyage, as I had learnt in *Reading for Children*. But now I was leaving Bagrovo, which I had learnt to love passionately; I was leaving all my favourite pursuits, and was going reluctantly to Choorassovo, to live in the same two rooms which we had occupied before, and to face the same eternal visitors, in a house which, though splendid, was not our own. The garden, with its apples which I was not even allowed to eat, had no attraction for me; no fishing, no hawking, no pigeons, no freedom to go where I pleased and say what I pleased! And, above all, I knew that my mother would pay less attention to me and talk to me less than at Bagrovo. For she was sure to be busy—sitting in the drawing-room or the balcony, or walking in the garden with our hostess and her visitors, or receiving visitors in her own room. The very word " visitors " began to have a hateful sound for me.

With my head full of these thoughts, I sat in sadness beside my sister, squeezed up in one corner of our carriage. My father was sad too : like me, he was sorry to leave Bagrovo, and still more sorry to part from his mother, whom he dearly loved, and who, as all noticed, had declined very much of late. But my mother was glad to leave Bagrovo : she did not like it and always said that all her illnesses were due to its low and damp situation. After a longish silence, my mother turned to me and asked : " Why do you hide in that corner, Seryozha, never speaking, nor looking out of the window ? " I replied, that I was sorry to leave Bagrovo, and gave full expression to my feelings. My mother tried to convince me that Choorassovo was a much nicer place than Bagrovo. The air there was dry and healthy ; instead of a stagnant pond, there were a number of splendid springs, spouting out of a hill and running over pebbles. The garden at Choorassovo was so large, that one could not see it all in three days ; and it contained several thousand apple-trees covered with red ripe apples ; there were hothouses, peaches, and pears, as well as abundance of sweet-smelling flowers. Finally, there were many books there, which I had not yet read. All this she said with eager warmth, and it was all true besides, and I had not a word to say against her glowing description ; but, though my reason was completely conquered, my heart refused to agree ; and, when she said, " Well, is it not true that it will be much nicer at Choorassovo ? "—I answered instantly that I liked Bagrovo better and was happier there. My mother smiled and said, " You are still young and have never seen any place but Bagrovo ; wait till you have seen Choorassovo in summer, and you will tell a different story." I said that I would never change my mind. She was a little vexed, and said, " You have little sense yet." This increased my sadness ; and under the influence of these thoughts and feelings our journey was continued.

Though I had made the journey to Choorassovo once before, yet the district through which we now passed was totally strange to me. The former journey had taken place in winter, when nothing was visible or noticeable

under the snow; and also our summer route was, to some
extent, different, and kept more to the steppes. We spent
the first night near a Tatar village, called Baitoogan, on
the bank of the Sok, a large river and full of fish. As a
matter of course, we had four rods and lines tied under the
carriage; and my father, Yevséitch, and I found time to
fish, and caught a number of fine perch, which did something to relieve all three of us from our depressed state of
mind. On the second or third day—I am not quite sure
which—we came in the morning to a large hamlet where
the land was tilled by discharged soldiers; it was called
" Fair Settlement," and lay on the bank of the Kondoorcha,
a smaller river than the Sok, but just as pretty and deep
and full of fish. We turned off the road, and made a halt
close to a bridge. I have a special recollection of this halt,
because we all, for some reason, found it so pleasant.
My father and I, submitting to our fate, had ceased to
mourn for Bagrovo. My mother, who had undoubtedly
found our long faces rather trying, was much pleased by
the change, and did her best to improve our spirits. She
actually proposed that we should go and fish at the mill,
which was so close that the splash of the water falling from
the mill-wheels, and even the creaking of the stones,
filled our ears and forced us to raise our voices. Before
we had time to unharness the horses, boys from the settlement ran up, bringing us a quantity of large crabs which
bred freely in smallish lakes near the river. My father and
I welcomed the crabs, not only as a dainty dish but for
another reason. we used them for bait, and not in vain.
My father and Yevséitch, using the raw crab-tails for bait,
caught in a very short time a number of large fish, especially
perch, which took without stopping, in a deep hole under
the sluice, near the weir and the mill-race. To my great
grief, I was too young to take part in this: with my small
tackle I pulled out small fish in a safe shallow place,
sitting on the mill-dam. When we went back in good
spirits with our rich spoil, my little sister ran to meet us
with a shout of joy, carrying a basinful of ripe blackberries,
which she (or rather Parasha) had picked on the bushes that
fringed the picturesque course of the stream. My mother

felt well and was in unusually good spirits, even gay.
Our table, consisting of boards propped on two logs was
laid in the shade of the carriage ; seats were brought from
the mill ; and I thought that there could not be in the
whole world a better and more cheerful meal than ours
was that day.   When my mother was well and cheerful,
she had the gift of spreading cheerfulness around her ;
this I had noticed before ; and over this dinner I entirely
forgot the parting from Bagrovo and became reconciled
to the prospect of Choorassovo.   I was convinced that my
father felt as I did ; for his face, as it seemed to me, became
much brighter ; even my sister, who was a little afraid of
my mother, chattered away as playfully for once as she
often did when we were alone.

We arrived at Vishenki early next day.   In winter I
had seen nothing of it ·   but summer now revealed it as a
most dull and tiresome place.   The little stream Berlya
had run dry in many places ; at the village it was dammed
up by an artificial dyke, or there would not have been a
drop of water left in summer   The pond was not at all
pretty : it was covered with a kind of scum, and its banks
had disappeared under mountains of manure, surmounted
by straggling rows of peasants' huts.   The shaft of a well
rose up here and there, but the water in these was cloudy
and tasted of malt, so that drinking-water had to be fetched
from a small spring at some distance   There was not even
a green bush, let alone a tree, for the eye to rest on ;   and
the country was quite flat.   A single pair of large willows
grew in a low cabbage-patch.   Yet the village was thought
to be very prosperous ;   and this was amply proved by the
abundance of old corn in the stackyards, the large herds
and flocks, and equally large droves of excellent horses.
These we saw for ourselves at sunset, when the animals
belonging to the proprietor and those of the peasants were
driven home.   A terrible cloud of dust hung long over the
village, and the evening silence was long broken by the
lowing of cattle and bleating of sheep.   My father told me
that the larger half of the stock were left out in the fields
all night.   He spoke with great enthusiasm of the fertility
of the place : the black mould was in some places seven feet

deep. In the evening, when talking to the village headman, my father said—

"You are well off in other ways, but you've no water.
It was a mistake of my uncle, Mihaila Maximitch, not to
place the village three *versts* lower down; there's plenty of
water in the river there, and you would have had a mill
close to you."

The headman bowed and explained that there had been
no mistake—

"It all came about from our own folly, *batyushka*
Alexyei Stepanitch. Though I was only a little boy, when
we were brought here from our old place, yet I remember
that there was plenty of water, not only in the village, but
five *versts* higher up, where the river begins; and all along
the river there were trees. But our fathers, and we after
them, cut down all the trees; and the cattle trampled
down the springs, and now the water is dried up. Bear
Hollow, for instance—what a wood there was there!
But it's all gone, nothing but young sprouts—not fit even
to make shafts for a cart. We suffer for it now: we heat
the houses with straw, and for torches and farm repairs,
we have to buy wood."

My father was much vexed to hear this: he gave orders
that Bear Hollow should be strictly preserved: he would
inform Praskovya Ivanovna of this at once, and promised
that she should send special orders to this effect.

The rooms, which we occupied here, were all in readiness
for a visit from the agent, just as they had been the year
before. Just as before, the knight frowned under his vizor
in the picture hanging on the wall of our sleeping-room.
The other picture was there too—bunches of purple grapes
in a basket, a slice of red melon with black seeds on a dish,
and juicy apples on a plate. But in myself I noticed a
change: the pictures, which I had liked so much at our
first visit, pleased me less now.

After dinner, my father drove to inspect the crops.
The rye had all been cut here, as the grain ripens a fortnight earlier than at Bagrovo. On the other hand, here
they were only beginning to sow the proprietor's rye,
though at Bagrovo this work was finished. The harvest

of the spring-sown wheat and spelt had been going on here
for a week. The fields were a long way from the village,
and my mother would not let me go : nor, indeed, was my
father willing to take me, as he feared I should be over-
tired.

Next day we made a not very early start and halted
by the ferry over the Cheremshan, a fine but narrowish
stream, at the village of Nikolskoe, which belonged to a
gentleman called Doorassoff. We did not cross the river ;
we pitched our camp on the sandy bank, untied our rods,
procured worms for bait, and were proceeding to fish in a
place where, according to the boys angling near the ferry-
boat, the fish took splendidly and even sterlets were
caught. We had hardly begun, when a very smart footman
appeared, bearing a request from M. Doorassoff that we
would do him the honour to dine with him, and intimating
that a carriage would be sent for us immediately. Doorassoff was a well-known millionaire, who kept a splendid
establishment and prided himself on his hospitality ; he
had made our acquaintance the year before in Praskovya
Ivanovna's house at Choorassovo. My parents thought it
would be rude to refuse, and accepted the invitation. But
to me, this was a terrible blow and altogether unexpected.
I had a faint hope that my sister and I would be left
behind ; but my mother said she was afraid of the river,
so deep and so near . she feared I would run to the bank
and fall into the water. As my sister was not likely to
go to the river, she was left behind ; but I was told to
put on my best clothes and join the party. A smart
carriage with four horses soon drove up, with an outrider
and two footmen. My father and I were not long in
changing our clothes ; my mother made the little hut
where the ferrymen lived into a dressing-room, and took
some time over her toilet ; she came out smarter than I
had seen her for a long time. How pretty she was, and
how everything she wore became her ! I ran over in my
memory all the ladies I knew, and once more decided that
in the whole world there was no one prettier than my
mother.

The village consisted of a large open space, two sides of

which were covered with rows of peasants' houses, while
in the centre there rose a church built of stone in what was
then the latest fashion in architecture. The manor-house,
built of stone and two-storeyed, was connected by open
colonnades with the wings, and formed one side of a square
court with round towers at the corners. The various
offices served as it were as walls to the court ; a spacious old
garden, with ponds and a stream running through it,
bordered it on one side ; and the main front of the house
overlooked the river Cheremshan. Never having seen
anything of this kind, I was much impressed, and at once
applied to the scene before me the descriptions, which I
had read in books and which still lingered in my memory,
of feudal castles or country palaces of English lords. My
curiosity was awakened, my imagination became busy, and
I began to look at everything with an expectation of something out of the common. We drove into a large quad-
rangle, with a marble fountain and a sun-dial in the middle,
and laid out in fine large flower-beds and gravel paths.
A grand portico adorned with lanterns, vases, and statues,
and a still grander staircase, with carpeted steps and hot-
house shrubs and flowers in pots placed at intervals—these
surpassed my expectations ; and my fancy flew from the
palace of an English nobleman to the enchanted castle of
Scheherazade In the morning-room we were met by the
owner of the house, who was no longer young, rather short,
and quite unpretentious to look at. After the usual
greetings, he offered an arm to my mother and led her to the
drawing-room. The mahogany furniture adorned with
bronze and covered with velvet or tapestry—some marvellous clocks on pedestals, one in the body of a lion, another
in the head of a man—the pictures in gilt frames—everything was so expensive and luxurious that the splendour of
Choorassovo might be called poverty when compared with
such a palace as this. In the course of his preliminary
inquiries, our hospitable entertainer discovered that my
sister had been left at our halting-place, and proposed to
send a carriage to fetch her. My mother would not hear
of it at first, but was obliged to yield to his persistent
entreaties. Meantime Doorassoff proposed that we should

look at his garden and hothouses. It was not difficult to discover that our host was fond of showing off his house and garden and whole establishment, and eager to sing their praises; he said plainly, that everything about his place was immeasurably superior to what other people had.

"Yes, and I've pigs too, the like of which have never been seen here; I imported them from England, and they came all the way in a caravan. Now they have a house to themselves. Would you like to see it? It is not far from here. I visit them twice a day."

My parents agreed, and off we went. We actually found a pretty little house at the far end of the garden; in the front room lived a swineherd and his wife, and two other large rooms were inhabited by two monster pigs, each as large as a moderate-sized cow. Our host stroked them and called them by pet-names. He especially directed our attention to their ears, and said · " Do look at their ears; they're just like shutters." When we had admired the pigs, which I thought alarming rather than agreeable, we went through the conservatories and hothouses, which contained a great quantity of rare flowers and plants, grapes and fruit. Our host made haste to tell us that the flowers were only a second display, the first having been removed already. While we were in the houses, Parasha brought in my sister, who saw us at some distance and ran to meet us, while Parasha hastily withdrew. Doorassoff picked fruit and flowers indiscriminately, and handed us so much that we had no place to put it. He made much of my sister, who was surprisingly at her ease and attractive; he called her a beauty and his little wife. This brought back to my mind my quarrel with Volkoff in bygone days, and, though I reflected with some pride, that I, who was a foolish child then, understood now that a girl of seven could not marry a man of forty, yet the word " wife " still sounded unpleasantly in my ears. We had just returned to the drawing-room and sat down to rest after a great deal of walking, when a man came in, richly dressed and looking very like our Governor at Ufa, and announced that dinner was on the table. At once I whispered to my mother, " Who is that ? "—and she

managed to whisper back that he was the groom of the
chambers. This was no answer to my question, as I had
never heard this title before, and was completely puzzled
by it. Doorassoff gave one arm to my mother, while with
the other hand he led my sister. Passing through several
rooms, one richer than another, we entered a dining-room,
very large and splendid, and so high that there was a
second row of windows above the first. The round table
of moderate size was luxuriously decorated : on the centre
stood a beautiful tree, bearing flowers and fruit ; and my
eyes were dazzled by the cut glass and gold and silver plate.
Our host made my sister sit beside him and ordered an
embroidered cushion to be brought for her. He praised
the fish-soup before it appeared, saying that in all Russia
there were no better sterlets than in his river. The soup
had hardly been handed round, when the inner wall of the
room began to move and rose up, and the sound of music
smote on my ears ! I saw before me a raised platform, on
which sat a number of men holding in their hands instruments unknown to me. The only instruments I had ever
heard were the fiddle, on which my uncle used to make
some attempts, the *balalaika** on which the servants played,
and the bagpipe of the Mordvinians. My astonishment was
crushing, overpowering. Holding my spoon in my hand,
I remained petrified, gazing with open mouth and staring
eyes at this group of men, *i.e.* the orchestra, all busily
pulling and pushing at their instruments or blowing into
them, and producing enchanting magical sounds, which
seemed now to die away and now to rise into the howling
of a tempest or even the roar of thunder. Our host was
much amused at the sight of my bewilderment : he laughed
loudly and reminded me that the soup would cool ; but
my thoughts were not of eating. My mother did not
approve of my confusion, or rather stupefaction : she
whispered to me to stop looking at the musicians and go
on eating. But it was hard for me to obey her to the
letter. Dipping my spoon in the soup, I constantly
glanced aside at the orchestra, and each time dropped the

* A popular instrument with two or three strings, played with the
fingers.

soup on my lap. Doorassoff laughed still louder, and my
father smiled ; but my mother reddened and was vexed.
At first my sister was as much surprised as I, but she
recovered at once and went on with her dinner, and laughed
when she looked at me. I ate a little of the wonderful
soup and gave up my plate nearly full. The music stopped,
and all praised the skill of the performers. I was beginning
to set to work in earnest on some dish which I had never
seen before, when two young ladies, in pretty white dresses,
with bare arms and necks and in ringlets. appeared on the
platform. Holding sheets of paper in their hands, they
advanced to the very edge of the platform, made a low
curtsey, and began to sing. I acknowledged their curtsey
by a bow ; but my politeness only made Doorassoff laugh
and my mother blush once more. But I was not carried
away by the singing : the words were unintelligible to me,
and the tunes still more so. I thought of the singing of our
maids, and decided that Matrona sang much better. After
this decision, I gave my attention to eating and got through
dinner without again attracting the attention of my host.
We marched back to the drawing-room, Doorassoff again
giving his arm to my mother. After coffee, Doorassoff
proposed that we should go out in a boat on the river,
taking horns with us, and assured us that his horn-blowers
were incomparable ; but my parents declined this treat,
on the ground that they absolutely must cross the Volga
early next morning. Doorassoff ceased to press them,
took a most affectionate farewell, kissed my sister, and
escorted us to the carriage, which we found loaded with
flowers and fruit and two immense packets of sweets.

On getting back we quickly changed our clothes and
resumed our journey. Nearly all the way to our halt for
the night, I went on asking questions of my parents, and
especially my mother, about all I had seen and heard during
the day. Answers led to fresh questions, explanations
called for fresh explanations, till at last I exhausted my
mother's patience, and she told me to ask her no more
questions about Nikolskoe. I turned to my father and continued the subject in a low voice, taking the opportunity to
communicate to him my own observations and suggestions.

But some of my problems met with no solution at all,
for instance · " Why did the water from the fountain
flow upwards ? "   " How is a sun-dial made, and how does
it show the time ? "   " What is the platform for, on which
the musicians sat ? "   When I asked who the pretty young
ladies were who sang, my father told me that they were
servants and serfs of Doorassoff's, who had been taught
singing at Moscow.   But what they sang and in what
language—that neither my father nor my mother could
tell me.   When our host came under discussion my mother
took part in our conversation.   She said that he was a
kind man, not clever or well-educated, but ambitious, who
had seen the extravagant, luxurious life of millionaires in
Moscow and Petersburg and wished to copy it   Not being
able to organise things himself, he had hired certain skilled
Germans and Frenchmen to help him ; but finding that
this did not answer, he had discovered a gentleman, some
said, a prince, who had run through a fortune, whose
business it was to put the whole establishment on a princely
footing.   Doorassoff was very rich, and grudged no expendi-
ture on his fancies ; several times a year he gave entertainments at which all the county assembled.   My mother
scolded me for behaving so absurdly when I heard the
music : " You were just like a little beggar-boy," she said,
" who has never seen anything beyond the walls of his
own hut, and then is suddenly introduced into a gentleman's
house."   I replied that I was astonished, just because I had
never in my life seen anything of the kind.   " One should
not show one's astonishment," she said.   " Why not ? "
I asked.   " Because it was absurd, and I was ashamed on
your account," she answered.   A new objection in the
shape of a question was in my mind and came to the tip of
my tongue ; but I saw that my mother would be angry,
and suppressed it.   At the same moment we drove up
to our halting-place for the night, the village of Fair Bank,
twelve *versts* from Simbirsk and ten from the ferry over the
Volga.   To have a calm crossing, we were bound to be at
the ferry by sunrise, as the wind blew hard every day as
soon as the sun grew strong.

Awaking early next morning, I saw that the horses

had been taken out of our carriage, which was standing on a
sloping sandy bank. It was very cool, and even inside
the carriage there was that peculiar feeling of fresh dampness which one only finds on the sandy banks of great
rivers—quite unlike the dampness from ponds and marshes,
which always has an unpleasant smell. The Volga lay
before me, and I looked with horror at the rapid current and
the two *versts* of water, across which we had to make our
way. We were dressed warmly and made to sit on a boat
that lay there bottom upwards. The traces of retreating
waves had left a kind of pattern on the banks; and it was
possible to see how high they came when lashed by a storm.
Above the water-mark was a smooth bed of coarse sand and
small pebbles. Flocks of seagulls flew screaming over the
water, sometimes dropping into it and diving in pursuit of
a fish. Simbirsk with its churches and the stone mansion
of the Governor, standing on a high hill thickly covered with
flourishing gardens, afforded a noble view; but I paid small
attention to it. Round us was a scene of great noise and
wild confusion. A crowd of people had spent the night by
the ferry; and already one huge ferry-boat, closely packed
with horses and carts, with front wheels raised and shafts
sticking up, could be seen as a black mass in the middle of
the Volga, while a second was loading in haste, to take
advantage of the favourable hour. A number of ferrymen
came from Chassovnya, a village on the bank, and offered
us their services. They had a kind of headman, who
warned my father not to trust them indiscriminately, as
many of them were not ferrymen at all, but to rely entirely
upon him. The second ferry-boat was now loaded to the
utmost possible limit, and the men cast loose the ropes,
pushed out from the landing-place, and poled their way
slowly up-stream, keeping near the side. A third ferry-
boat was then brought up; and on this, which we were
assured was better and more substantial than the others,
our carriage and covered cart and all our nine horses were
placed. Our good horses, unaccustomed to such crossings,
began to snort and foam; it was impossible to tether them
to the carriage or the railing that lined two sides of the
boat; so our coachman and other servants held the heads

of each pair, leaving only Yevséitch and Parasha with us.
No intruder was allowed on board ; and soon our ferry-boat
got under way and was punted slowly up-stream.   " Push
her higher up, my men," the headman shouted from the
bank ; " then hard and straight across ! "   I surveyed the
scene anxiously : I was alarmed to see that the easterly
breeze, hardly noticeable at first, had risen, and that the
surface of the Volga was continually changing colour, now
light and now dark, and that vast strips of its muddy water
were ruffled into great furrows by the wind.   A large
rowing-boat was quickly brought round, and six men sat
down on the thwarts, while the headman himself stood by
the steering-oar   We were caught up and carried across
to this light craft, and set down on benches in the centre of
it.   We pushed off, and the boat moved quietly over the
water.   We went up-stream at first ; but, when we had
gone about 200 yards, the skipper shouted out : " Hats off !
Pray God to help us."   The boat stopped for a moment ;
all the crew took off their hats and crossed themselves.
" Now, my lads," said the skipper, " row your hardest
across, and God be with you ! "   Then he pressed both
hands and the whole weight of his body on the handle of
the heavy steering-oar, till it came right down in the stern
and brought the blade to the surface, when he shifted the
oar to the other side and turned the nose of the boat across
the stream.   The rowers pulled with a will, and we went
along fast.   Fear had mastered me before this ; yet I
struggled against it and concealed it as far as I could.
But now, when the bank began to recede from my sight,
when we got into the current, and when an appalling volume
of water, eddying and flowing on with irresistible power,
caught hold of us on all sides and carried our boat along
like a shaving—then I could hold out no longer : I screamed
out, began to cry, and hid my face on my mother's breast.
My sister saw me and followed my example.   My father
laughed and called me a little coward ; but my mother,
who had no fear of the water, even in a storm, was angry
and tried to prove to me that there was not the smallest
cause for fear.   When I had lain for some time with closed
eyes, I got ashamed of myself and uncovered my eyes

T

enough to see with joy that Simbirsk on the hill was coming nearer us. My sister had recovered already and was chattering gaily. My fear began to pass off; and when we got near the bank, my spirits rose, as they always did with me after a fright. We disembarked and sat down on some thick logs, of which there were many lying on the steep bank. The ferry-boat with our carriage was still afloat in the middle of the river; the dipping oars looked from a distance like a child's toy, and made no visible progress towards us. The wind rose higher, and the carriage caught the force of it, all declared that the ferry-boat would be carried a long way down. On the bank near us there was a row of little shops, where they sold buns, gingerbread, *kvass*,* and quantities of apples. My mother, who was very fond of apples, went herself to buy some, but finding that those offered her were not quite ripe, said they were all "garbage." She managed, however, to get a dozen that were ripe; and choosing a very sweet one, she cut it in two, removed the core and gave half to me and half to my sister. I had seldom tasted raw fruit, and I found the apple very good. While we were waiting for the ferry-boat, my father, who was very fond of fish, went out in a fishing-boat to the tanks and brought back a bunch of live sterlets tied to a string, out of which he intended to have soup made at Simbirsk. I did not even think of asking leave to go with him: I should not have got it, and I was frightened myself of the little boat. But I looked with great satisfaction at the fish: I had never before been able to see them alive, and I was allowed at last to hold them in my hands. The bells of a church close by now rang out for service, and this sound, which I had not heard for a long time, and took little notice of somehow at Ufa, caught my ear and made a very pleasant impression on my mind. At last the ferry-boat with our carriage and horses came to land, after drifting down some distance; the vehicles were taken off and the horses put in harness; my father paid for the passage, and we started to walk to the hill. The hill of Simbirsk is high and steep, and the ascent was such a tough job in those days that even in dry weather

* A drink made of malt and rye

it was considered still more laborious than the passage of the
Volga; but in muddy weather it offered such obstacles
to a heavy vehicle that immense exertions were required
to overcome it: it was quite an exploit, and by no means
free from danger. Our weather, fortunately, was dry.
We walked up to the first curve of the ascent, where the
carriage overtook us; in order to halt on the slope and let
the horses breathe, it was necessary to put the brake on both
wheels and to place under them stones or logs which we
had with us: otherwise the carriage would have rolled
downhill. Then we all walked on to the next turning,
and again managed to stop the carriage there. My mother
was too tired to walk further; so she got inside with my
sister and me, while the rest of the party walked on. Our
strong powerful horses were all in a lather and panted so
hard that it distressed me to look at them. In this way,
stopping repeatedly at each convenient point, we got safely
to the top of this prodigious ascent. At Simbirsk we
stopped at a house belonging to Praskovya Ivanovna,
which she never used herself. The house was a fine house
according to the ideas of those days, well furnished and
full of pictures, for which her late husband, Mihaila
Maximitch, had evidently a great fancy. Had I not seen
Nikolskoe, this house would have seemed to me rich and
luxurious; but after such a palace this seemed unworthy
of notice. My parents saw no one at Simbirsk: they only
waited to feed the horses and to eat the sterlet soup. I
thought the soup better than Doorassoff's; I hardly ate
any at his house, and did not even notice the taste; I had
other things to think of then! At two o'clock we started
from Simbirsk and reached Choorassovo about noon next
day.

Praskovya Ivanovna had been expecting us for some
time and was overjoyed to see us. She was especially
loving to my mother and said—

"But for you, I know that Alexyéi would never have
stirred from Bagrovo at the busy season; and I warrant
that his mother tried to keep you. Well, now I will
show you my garden in all its beauty. The apples are just
ripe, and some are still ripening. They are a very fine

crop, as if on purpose for you. I shall see now whether you like them "

My mother embraced her kind hostess with sincere pleasure, and said that she would never have left Choorassovo, if it had depended on her. Alexandra Kovrigina welcomed us also and at once sent information of our arrival to the Minitskys. At present there were no visitors, but a number were expected. Then our hostess, giving us no time to rest and recover ourselves after the journey, led us straight to the garden, which was really splendid. There were an immense number of apple-trees laden with apples of every possible sort, both ripe and ripening; the colours of the fruit were brilliant, and the trees bent under their weight. Many branches were propped, and some were fastened to the trunk of the tree; without these precautions the abundance of fruit would have broken them. All along the slope of a hill there were active springs which poured down the steep places in natural waterfalls with bubbles and foam, and then became pretty transparent streamlets, which freshened the air and gave life to the scene. Praskovya Ivanovna was an indefatigable walker: on she went till dinner-time, leading us now to a favourite spring, now to a favourite apple-tree; and she carried a long forked stick, with which she hooked down the best ripe apples for us to eat. My mother was really very fond of apples and ate so many that at last our hostess ceased to press more upon her. "Well," she said, " I suppose you would spoil your dinner." Twice over, the old butler, Ivanushka, came to report that dinner would get cold. We had to go back to the house, before we had seen half the garden. We went straight to the dining-room and took our places. This was the first time that my sister and I were allowed to sit at table with the grown-up people at Choorassovo. Henceforward this was the regular custom, to the great satisfaction of my mother. Praskovya Ivanovna was so cheerful and talkative, so simple and direct in her speech, her smile was so good-natured and her glance at us so kindly, that I liked her at once much better than before. She seemed to me quite a different woman, as if I saw her for the first time. As

before, we occupied the sitting-room and the nursery which
had once been a bedroom ; but now we were not confined
constantly to our own rooms, but could at times walk and
run all over the house , this freedom was probably due to
the absence of visitors, but it went on even in their presence.
The Minitskys, whom no one counted as visitors, came
from their estate of Podlyessnaya, and greeted my parents
with sincere affection.   The day was spent like the
previous day : till dinner-time, we all examined the remaining half of the garden, and also the hothouses and conservatories ; but for these Praskovya Ivanovna had no
great fancy.   She liked everything that grew naturally
in the open air, and cared much less for what was artificial
and required a great deal of trouble.   The hothouses
she only put up with, and she would not have done that if
she had not found them there already   To me the chief
attraction about the garden was the springs, in which I
found, among other pebbles, a number of what are called
" Devil's Fingers " of unusual size.   I made such a collection of them that it took more than one window-sill to
display them.   Soon, however, I grew weary of this amusement, and even more weary of the orchard.   I began to
think with sorrow of Bagrovo, where the perch would be
taking splendidly and the falconers bringing back every day
a fine bag of quails.   I found most satisfaction in the books,
which I was allowed to read with greater freedom than
before.   At this time I read several novels, for instance,
*The Vicar of Wakefield,** and *Herbert; or "Riches, Farewell ! "*   The mystery of *The Iron Mask* pleased me most
of all, and the interest was increased by the author's statement that his story was not an invention but the account
of a real incident.

My father paid a visit to Old Bagrovo, and also travelled
to Simbirsk and Lukoyanoff, to attend to his law business.
He remained there much longer than he intended, and much
vexed my mother by doing so.

Meanwhile, visitors began again to come to Choorassovo,
and the routine of the year before was resumed.   This

* Goldsmith's novel was published in 1766 . the boy, of course, read it
in Russian, the only language he knew.

time I had more opportunities of watching it at close
quarters : my sister and I now dined regularly with the
visitors and were present much oftener in the drawing-room
and lounge. Card-playing was generally going on in the
drawing-room, and the players were elderly people who were
taken up by their game and did not talk much. But
the lounge was the regular haunt of the young people who
did not play cards ; there was always more noise and gaiety
in this room, and sometimes there was singing Some of
the songs were Russian ; and I still remember some stanzas
of a song by Prince Khovansky, which Praskovya Ivanovna
was fond of singing herself ; each stanza ended with the
refrain—

" All thy friends are far away ! "

The verses—printed, I think, in *The Muses*—were very
poor ; and yet not only as sung, when the tune and voice
of the singer cover the deficiency of the words, but as
read, they produced on me a strong and affecting impression. I learnt them by heart and used to repeat them with
much fervour on my part and applause from my hearers.
Praskovya Ivanovna, when my mother told her of this,
was delighted by my fancy for her favourite song and made
me repeat it in the presence of visitors in the lounge. She
praised my performance warmly ; and from that time I
began to enjoy her special favour.

The men and maidservants at Choorassovo aroused
my mother's fears as much as ever or even more, and from
the first she took measures to preserve me from harm. I
was strictly forbidden to speak to any of them, or to listen
to their talk, or to watch their free and easy behaviour to
one another ; and Yevséitch and Parasha had orders to
keep us at a distance from the servants. But the fulfilment
of such orders is not easy, and it is never possible to rely
upon it. One cannot keep ears and eyes closed ; and,
when one has heard or seen something new and exciting,
one wants to hear or see the continuation of it. The strict
prohibition was itself a spur to curiosity ; and uninten-
tionally I noticed much that I had no business to hear or
see. Fearing that some unpleasantness might follow, as

it had before in the case of Parasha, and fearing still more
a scolding from my mother, I did not tell her everything,
excusing myself on the ground that she herself had encouraged me not to tell my aunt Tatyana of my visit to her
private storehouse. Children have surprising memories,
and it often happens that a careless word, spoken in their
presence, encourages them to do things which they would
never have done without it.

I had always preferred the company of grown-up
people to that of other children ; but, for some reason, this
did not content me at Choorassovo. As I sat in the lounge
and listened attentively to what people said and what
excited their loud laughter, it puzzled me that they should
find it amusing to talk of such trifles. No one had power to
arouse my sympathy ; and all the anecdotes about the
neighbours, which must have been very laughable because
every one laughed at them, seemed to me neither interesting
nor amusing. I even tried sitting in the drawing-room
beside the card-players, but I soon wearied of this too ; for
I did not understand the game or the terms used or the
disputes between the players, which were sometimes lively
enough. Two of Praskovya Ivanovna's favourite visitors
were Alexander Karamzin, and his brother-in-law, Nikita
Philosoffoff. Karamzin was commonly called a Hercules ;
and, in fact, it is seldom possible to meet a man of such
powerful and athletic build. He was tall, with uncommonly
broad shoulders. rather stout and at the same time very
well made ; his chest stuck out in front of him " like a
wheel," to use the Russian phrase. He was excitable and
gay : he would sometimes exhibit his herculean strength,
by playing with weights of eighty pounds, as if they were
light balls. Once in an excess of high spirits he caught
hold of Darya Vassilyevna, who was tall and stout, and
went through the military exercise, using her as a rifle.
The despairing shriek of the old woman. whose kerchief
and cap tumbled off while her grey hair fell in disorder over
her shoulders, made all the card-players jump up, and a
general shout of laughter rang through the house ; but I
was sorry for poor Darya Vassilyevna, though at the same
time I could not help thinking what a splendid knight

Karamzin would have made, with a barred helmet on his head and armed with spear and shield. Philosoffoff was a short man, but very lively and active. They used to say of him that his tongue was a razor ; he never stopped joking, and I often heard the phrase applied to him that he would make a dead man laugh. But I repeat that I found little interest in all this ; and I sought more and more the company of my little sister which I had rather avoided at first. That time passed pleasantly with her, because the two Minitsky girls, who were great friends of hers, were constant visitors at Choorassovo. The elder of the two was just my age and quite as fond of reading as I was. She brought with her a manuscript book of poems by Prince Ivan Dolgoruky. She much admired his poetry and preferred it to all the verses which she heard from me. I took up the cudgels for my poets, whom I was familiar with and knew almost by heart, and we had some very warm debates. She would not take my view, and I, in order to punish her for insulting my favourite writers, took to abusing Prince Dolgoruky, although, to tell the truth, I admired his poetry very much : indeed, without her knowledge, I learnt his best poems by heart. We sometimes went so far as to quarrel, but not for long ; by way of making it up, we used to repeat together a piece by the same author called " The Contention." The subject was a comparison between the sun and moon. I poured forth an enthusiastic panegyric on the sun, while she repeated one line again and again, which came as a refrain at the end of nearly every stanza—

"Quite true, but I prefer the Moon "

The last four lines of the poem were a sufficient proof of the amiability of the author, and they were recited by me—

"Contend no more ? Be wise in time,
    And learn, O foolish man,
That words, which flow from lips we love,
    Prove more than logic can."

The result of our recitation was the following scene. My unwearied efforts to propagate my literary creed at last

induced my fair antagonist to make some concessions ;
and she used Dolgoruky's own line in his defence, declaim-
ing in her clear voice with total indifference to the metre—

"Quite true, but Dolgoruky I prefer "

The long absence of my father, which my mother so
much resented, caused Praskovya Ivanovna to send to his
assistance her head agent, Mihailushka, who was considered at that time the most skilful manager of a law-suit
in the Government of Simbirsk ; he was the best pupil of
our blind friend, Pantelyéi Grigoritch. Without saying a
word to my mother, Praskovya Ivanovna wrote to my
father, bidding him return at once. He complied with her
instructions, and came back at once to Choorassovo,
leaving Mihailushka to take his place. My mother rejoiced,
but her joy was diminished, when she learnt that he had
returned in obedience to his aunt ; and I heard some
rather heated discussion between them on this point. A
few days later my father said to Praskovya Ivanovna in
my presence : " Well, aunt, I have done what you wished ;
but, if I am not present to watch over my case, I lose it ;
that's all." But she replied that he was talking nonsense,
and that Mihailushka was much more competent in the
matter. So he stayed, but very reluctantly. His prophecy
was fulfilled : a fortnight later Mihailushka came home and
reported that the decision was given in favour of the
Bogdanoffs. My father was in despair. Mihailushka
assured him that it was of no importance, that the final
decision must rest with the Senate—this was what Pantelyéi
Grigoritch also had said—and that to spend money in the
inferior courts would have been useless expense ; for, if
we had won, the other side would have appealed and
carried the case to the Senate, as we must do now. All
this had no effect on my father ; but he was obliged to
hold his tongue, because both my mother and Praskovya
Ivanovna took Mihailushka's view of the case. It was
settled that Pantelyéi Grigoritch at Bagrovo should draw
up a petition to the Senate ; and for this purpose, Mihailushka was to take steps to procure as soon as possible a
copy of the judge's decision.

The end of September was now near, and my father informed Praskovya Ivanovna that it was time for us to be off : he had promised to return home by Intercession Day ; and his mother was always ailing and now very feeble. But our hostess would not hear of our departure. " All nonsense ! " she said ; " your mother is not feeble at all ; she is quite happy with her daughters, and you left the little grandson, too, to cheer her up. I will let you go in time for Apparition Day." My father pointed out that it was more than two months to Apparition Day, the 27th of November, and that by mid-November the roads would be impassable for the carriage in which we had come. Admitting the justice of this objection, she said, " Very well ; so be it. I will let you go on St. Michael's Day, the 8th of November." However anxious my father was to keep the promise made to his mother, and to return to his own house and estate at Bagrovo, and to take up his regular life in the country with its occupations and amusements, yet the thought of disobeying Praskovya Ivanovna never entered his head : as always, he gave way. I was just as much vexed as he was by this decision. Every day I grew more weary of this town life in the country ; even my mother wished to hasten her return to Bagrovo which she did not love, because my little brother, who was now three years old, had been left behind there. My father was very much depressed and sometimes even shed tears. Alexandra Kovrigina and Mimitsky, as the two chief intimates of Praskovya Ivanovna, made an attempt to induce her to release my father at least, if not all of us. But she resented their intercession. " Suppose," she said, " I were to let Alexyéi go, that would vex his wife ; but I love her so well, that I don't want to vex her and don't want to part with her in a hurry." It could not be helped : we had to submit and give up all thoughts of immediate departure ; and the gay life at Choorassovo went on as before. At last Intercession Day came. Waking rather early, I saw my father sitting on his bed and heard him groan. When I asked him the reason, he got up quietly, not to disturb my mother, came over to me, and sat down on the sofa on which I generally

slept. Then he said in a low voice : " I have been awake
a long time. I have had a bad dream, Seryozha, and I
am sure my mother is very ill." I saw the tears in his
eyes, and felt so sorry for my poor father that I put my arms
round him and was ready to cry myself. Just then my
mother woke and was much surprised when she saw me in
my father's arms. She thought I must be ill, but he told
her what it was and also described his dream, but spoke
so low that I could not catch a single word. She tried to
cheer him, declaring that his bad dream was not one that
meant anything ; and she quoted the proverb, " What
you dream on the eve of a saint's-day, comes true before
dinner-time." These words sank into my mind ; and I
said to myself : " Why, mamma always used to say that
it was foolish to believe in dreams, and that all interpretations of them were utter nonsense ; but she said herself
just now that my father's bad dream meant nothing. Do
some dreams then mean something ? And do dreams come
true on saints' days ? To-day is a great festival : well,
we shall see what will happen before dinner-time." My
mother appeared to succeed in comforting him ; for
they soon began to talk cheerfully. Soon we all got up
and dressed and went to church. Praskovya Ivanovna
was there already, and by degrees all the visitors and
members of the household assembled. The service began ;
the priest and deacon were wearing new chasubles embroidered with gold ; our hostess stood in the choir among
her own private singers and took part in the service.
When mass was over, every one wished her happiness on
the day and then went back in good spirits to the house,
some on foot, some in carriages, as a light rain was falling.
Tea and coffee awaited us in the drawing-room Suddenly
a servant came in and handed my father a letter, which
had been brought by special messenger from Bagrovo.
My father turned pale, and his hand shook ; he unsealed
the envelope with difficulty and read the first lines ; then
with a sob he dropped the letter on his knee, and said :
" My mother is desperately ill." This caused a general
sensation, but my mother and I were especially struck,
because we remembered the dream. Without finishing

the letter, my father turned to Praskovya Ivanovna and said resolutely : " As you please, aunt, but we go this very day. If you keep my wife, I will go alone, by cart, and trust to getting relays of horses." Praskovya Ivanovna was much moved : she said, " Do go at once, all of you ! I won't keep you." My father went out instantly, to give orders for our immediate departure. Then the letter was read through, and it was thus that my aunt Tatyana had written :

" MY DEAR BROTHER,

" Come back at once. Mother is desperately ill. For three days she has been in a high fever and delirious. We have sent for the priest. I send this by special messenger, my servant Nikolai. I have ordered him to travel day and night   When mother is conscious for a moment, she always asks for you."

There was a postscript to say that the priest had come, had given her absolution without her being able to confess, and had administered the Sacraments ; the priest said there was little hope. It was obvious that Praskovya Ivanovna was much moved and distressed by this news. She felt great remorse for having kept my father without any substantial reason, when he wished to return to Bagrovo for Intercession Day. Her brows were knit, and her face was sad and stern. She said nothing for a long time, and there was a general silence. She broke it by saying, " If he does not find his mother living, then may God preserve and have mercy on us ! " Then she got up and went to her own room   Fear and pity contended in my heart : I was sorry for her and still more sorry for my father ; but superstitious fear soon got the mastery and swayed all my feelings   My father had promised to return for Intercession Day ; on that very day he had dreamed of misfortune, and within a few hours, before dinner-time on the same day, the dream had come true. " What is the meaning of that ? " I asked myself. " How is it possible after that to disbelieve in dreams ? Does not God send dreams ? " And I did believe in them for a long time, though, to confess the truth, my own dreams never came true.

My mother went off to pack up, and by dinner-time all was ready. Before dinner was served, Praskovya Ivanovna came to our room; she was calm by this time and spoke with a steady voice as she urged my father not to torment himself before he knew the truth, but to rely entirely on the goodness of God.

" I hope," she said for one thing, " that God will not punish me, a sinner, so grievously for a fault which I committed in ignorance. I hope that you will find your mother still living, and that on this day, which is the day of the Intercession of Our Lady, she will feel relief from her sickness." My father seemed cheered to some extent by her words. She then took the hands of both my parents, and led them to the parlour, where a number of guests invited for the festival were waiting for us. She made us sit near her and paid special attention to us. The carriage came round to the front, while we were at dinner. When we had finished dinner and drunk our coffee, which our hostess would not let us omit, she got up first, said a prayer, and spoke thus :

" Good-bye, dear friends I thank Alexyéi Stepanitch for his obedience and compliance with all my wishes, and you, Sofya Nikolayevna, for your love and friendship ; I think you and I will never cease to be friends. Send me a special messenger with news of your mother."

A few minutes later, we were driving slowly along the muddy road. The wind was blowing ; a thin autumn rain stabbed at the window-pane near which I was sitting ; and constant streams of water, chasing and overtaking one another, covered the whole pane from top to bottom. I watched them mechanically, and had hardly time to realise where I was, before darkness came on, and, much sooner, it seemed to me, than usual, surrounded our carriage. There was just a faint red glimmer of sunset in the west. We were all absolutely silent · nobody spoke a single word.

CHAPTER XIX

A JOURNEY IN AUTUMN TO BAGROVO

AT ten o'clock next morning we drove into Simbirsk. The weather was as unpleasant as possible . a thin autumn rain fell from time to time, and a terrible wind never ceased blowing. We stopped at the same house as before, fed the horses, and started at once for the ferry. The descent of the hill of Simbirsk was now infinitely more difficult than the ascent had been : the hill had become a slough, the brakes would not act, and the carriage slipped down sideways at the steep turns. To remain inside was dangerous, and we were all obliged to walk down, in spite of the mud and rain But the Volga—it is terrible even to think what the Volga was like ! The whole of it had turned into hills of water which moved backwards and forwards, yellow and brown over the sandy shallows and black in the centre of the stream. The water was in constant turmoil and commotion, and actually moaned ; the waves continually lashed the bank and ran up many feet over it. Over all the expanse of water, and especially in the centre of the river, " white horses " were running : the crests of the waves, having risen to their full height, suddenly collapsed and were dispersed in broken water and white foam. Unspeakable horror came over me ; the mere thought of that terrible passage froze my blood and nearly deprived me of my senses. On the bank we were told that we could not cross at present, and that all the ferrymen had gone off, some to the public-house, some to take a meal But my father was determined to start at once, and sent to hunt up the men. Several of them soon turned up and said we must wait an hour or so ; the wind would abate before sunset, and it would then be possible to land us safely

on the other side. In the meantime, while waiting for the
propitious time, they began to put the cargo on board.
Once again they selected a new ferry-boat, the best they
had, and loaded it with our carriage and cart and all the
horses. The wind seemed really to be falling. A ferry-
boat was seen to put out from the other side, and our own
was quickly unmoored and poled up-stream along the
bank, with the object of starting as high up as possible.
Parasha and Yevséitch stayed behind with us. Next a
large row-boat was got ready for us. Our old acquaintance,
the headman or skipper, as he was called, of the ferrymen,
made his appearance ; he intended to steer with the stern
oar himself, and picked out six men to row us ; but he
suggested a delay of half an hour or so. Thank God he
did ; for the wind, which had sunk for a few minutes,
now began to rage, and the river to seethe, more fiercely
than before ; and even the ferrymen said : " We can put
you across, no doubt ; but it would be a trifle awkward ;
the boat would dance a bit, and the gentry might be
frightened." At this point I seemed to recover from a kind
of stupefaction : with tears, I begged and prayed that
the crossing might be put off till next day. I saw my
father angry with me for the first time : he said I was a
worthless little coward : " Just look at your sister, and be
ashamed ! She is only a girl, but she does not cry and ask
us to stop ! " It was true that my sister was not crying ;
but, when asked if she felt courage to go, she said that she
did not. My mother, seeing that I was shaking all over
with terror, began to press my father to wait till the
morning ; but he would not give way. For some time the
ferrymen looked at us without speaking ; at last the
skipper said—

"Well, sir, is it to be for to-morrow ? The wind is
bound to fall at dawn, and we will put you across in no
time. Just now it's bad enough, and your ferry-boat
will drift down a terrible long way She's not begun to
cross, and you see she's below her starting-point already.
She'll drift two *versts* down. They'll have to lie to for the
night in the cove below, and I doubt if they reach the
landing-point to-morrow before you do."

This settled the question. But now another difficulty
arose : we had neither shelter nor bedding nor food. Our
clothes, pillows, beds, and provisions had all been started
on their way to the other side ; and twelve hours must
pass before dawn The skipper rescued us from our difficulty : he offered us the lodgings on the water-side occupied
by himself and his men, and promised to procure us something to eat from the tavern We gratefully availed ourselves of his offer ; the rain had wet us thoroughly, and
we were glad to enter the warm cabin, the whole of which
was made over to us. Tea could not be got at the tavern ;
but here again the skipper came to our aid. A merchant
whom he knew lived not far away at the foot of the hill ;
thither went Yevséitch and the skipper, and an hour later,
we were sitting at a meal of tea and rolls, which was
pleasant and did us good. None of us was inclined for
supper, and we went very early to bed, making the best of
dry hay spread over the wooden settles

Dawn was hardly breaking when we were called ; it
was dark even to put on our clothes How unwilling my
sister and I were to get up ! To leave our warm little nest
for the damp and cold autumn air, just at dawn when sleep
is sweetest, and with the immediate prospect of the boat
before us ! But my father never ceased to hurry us, and
when dressed we almost ran down to the starting-place ;
a red dawn burned through a grey cloud, a sure sign of
high wind There was no rain falling, but one could not
call it still : a cutting breeze was already blowing steadily
and ruffling the surface of the water. The rowers were
seated on the thwarts, oar in hand. The skipper led us
quickly along boards into the boat and made us sit down on
benches in the centre. Fear clutched at my heart, and I
sat there more dead than alive. We first went up a little
way and then turned to cross. The oarsmen pulled lustily
and the boat flew along ; but, as soon as we had reached
mid-stream and lost the shelter of the hill, a strong wind
blew, we encountered awful waves, and the bow of the boat
began to rise and the stern to sink. I screamed out, threw
myself on my mother, and squeezed tight against her with
my eyes shut I kept them shut, till I heard that the

bank was not far off. And we were really near the bank,
but there was some confusion going on in the boat, which
I had not noticed before with my eyes shut ; and the
skipper looked very anxious and even frightened. Only
four men were rowing, and the other two were baling out
the boat, one with a long pannikin, the other with his hat.
Water was coming through the boards and wetting our feet,
and there was a good depth of it at the stern. I did not
fully understand how serious this was, and was much
surprised when my father, having seen us all safe ashore,
turned in a rage to the skipper.

"You scoundrel," he cried, " how dared you give us a
leaking boat ? You very nearly drowned us. I tell you
this, that I shall send you off at once to the police-officer
at Simbirsk."

Our poor skipper, standing bare-headed and bowing
respectfully, replied thus :

"Can Your Honour think that I am glad at what has
happened, or that I am tired of my own life ? I should
surely have gone down with you. It is a punishment for
my sins. I wished to serve you well I gave you my best
boat, my new one ; I never give her except to the quality.
She has not been used over a dozen times. We have not
set a finger on her since Assumption Day. There was not
a drop of water in her, when we started. I cannot understand how such a misfortune came about. The blame
falls on me, but I am innocent. Be merciful and forgive,
and cause me to pray all my life to God for you."

And down he fell at my father's feet. He was told to
get up at once, and assured that his fault was forgiven
and no complaint would be made against him.

The ferry-boat with our carriage had not yet arrived
at the landing-place. the prophecy of our skipper was
fulfilled to the letter. She was poling slowly up-stream,
and the ferrymen said that she was still not less than a
verst from where we stood. As my father was anxious to
discover the cause of the leak in our boat, she was hauled
ashore and turned upside down, when it was discovered
that she had been bored through close to the stern with
some sharp-pointed instrument ; the hole was two fingers

U

wide. How this had happened, no one was able to explain. The men discussed it for a long time, and decided that some malicious person had used a tool for the purpose. The hole was some distance above the water-line, and in calm weather there would have been no danger ; but the crests of the high waves had found their way in. Had the men not noticed it and begun in good time to bale out the water, the boat would have filled and settled down, and then disaster was inevitable. At last I began to understand the danger to which we had been exposed ; and from that time, an aversion to crossing great rivers became firmly fixed in my mind. At last our ferry-boat came to land ; she had lain to for the night in the shallow water of the cove further down, made fast to poles stuck in the sand. Our servants reported, that they had never in all their lives had such a fright, and that they were up all night struggling with the starving horses, which refused to stand still and several times nearly upset the boat. There followed further delay and further loss of time : we had to drive to Chassovyna, the village on the river, to feed the horses which had had nothing to eat for nearly twenty-four hours. My father was changed beyond recognition : usually quiet and composed, he was furious at the loss of so much time, and constantly lost his temper. My mother was obliged to reason with him and pacify him, and thus reversed their usual parts—a reversal which I watched with much interest. She spoke for a long time, and better than a printed book. For one thing, she said, that it was unreasonable to be angry with the Volga and the storm, that such hindrances do not depend on human agency, and that it was sinful to murmur at what was sent by God ; we ought, on the contrary, to thank Him for the preservation of our lives. But it is impossible for me to repeat what she said without spoiling it. At last, he grew by degrees more composed, though he was still very sad. When the horses were fed, we resumed our journey. We did not spare our good horses, driving nearly ninety *versts* in two stages ; and we reached Vishenki next day at dinner-time. After a halt of four hours, we started again and spent that night at a village called " Lonely Yard." Fortune

was determined to try my father's patience to the utmost.
When his whole soul was longing for Bagrovo and the
bedside of his dying mother, hindrances sprang up at
every step. Ill luck pursued us through all the fatigue
and grief of our journey. At first, constant rain turned
the black soil of the roads into such an appalling slough,
that we could hardly cover fifty *versts* a day. Then it
suddenly became cold; and, when we rose at dawn, to
make an early start from the filthy village of " Lonely
Yard," we found the mud frozen and a shallow coating
of snow on the ground. At first this caused my father no
anxiety: he said that the frost would make the work
less hard for the horses; and my sister and I were pleased
by the sight of the clean white fields. But the snow came
down heavier every hour, till by evening it was more than
a foot deep. The road became terribly heavy, and we
could scarcely proceed at a foot pace, as the wet snow stuck
to the wheels and even blocked them. Thus, we covered
only thirty *versts* in the whole of the next day. Towards
evening, rain fell and nearly melted the snow; and, though
the mud was worse than ever, this was a relief to the
horses. But here another disaster befell us: my mother
fell ill, so ill that we were obliged to stop after twenty-five
versts and could not proceed for more than twenty-four
hours. How sad my sister and I were! We were lodged
in a dirty Choovash cabin. My mother lay under a canopy,
while my father and Parasha gave her some medicine from
time to time. We two sat in a corner, whispering low to
one another, or praying to God that He would send relief
to our dear mother.

It was only on the seventh day that we reached Nyeklyoodovo rather early in the morning, and drove up to
the steps of the oddly-built house of the Kalpinskys, not
more than twenty *versts* from Bagrovo. My sister and I
had never been there; and my father would not have gone
there now, but for the necessity of feeding our jaded horses.
Mme. Kalpinsky met my mother at the door and took
her into the house, while my father lifted us two out of the
carriage and led us in. In the parlour we were met by
Ivan Kalpinsky; my father exchanged greetings with

him and asked at once, "What news of my mother?"
"Is it possible you have not heard?" asked the master
of the house. "We have had no news for more than a
week," was the answer. "She died on Intercession Day,"
said Kalpinsky very coolly; "she left a message for you,
wishing you long life." The effect on my father was
terrible. He clasped his hands, crying in a low voice,
"On Intercession Day!"—then he turned pale, shook all
over, and would certainly have fallen, had not Kalpinsky
caught him and put him on a chair. My mother, who
had heard meanwhile in the drawing-room of my grandmother's death, now hastened to meet us, and was terribly
alarmed to see my father in such a condition. She rushed
to his aid; cold water was brought, and his face sprinkled
and his head wetted; he regained consciousness, and the
tears flowed fast down his colourless cheeks. He was given
a glass of water to drink and was taken by Kalpinsky to
the study, where he wept like a little child for more than
an hour, saying over and over at intervals: "God will
judge my aunt! The weight of this sin lies on her soul!"

Meanwhile eager and even angry conversation went
on around him, between Mme. Kalpinsky and her sister,
Mme. Lupenevsky, who was staying in the house. In the
minutest detail they described the last sufferings and death
of my poor grandmother—how she called in vain for her
son; how on the very day of the funeral snow fell so heavily
that it was impossible to convey the body to Nyeklyoodovo,
where a grave had been dug; and how they had been obliged
to bury her at Mordovsky Boogoorooslan, seven *versts*
from Bagrovo.

"See how God disposes, when man proposes!" said
Mme. Lupenevsky: "Stepan Mihailovitch, our uncle who
is gone—the kingdom of heaven be his!—never liked
Nyeklyoodovo and would not hear of being buried there;
and yet his bones are lying beside our church. But our
aunt loved us like her own daughters, and wished with all
her heart to be laid at Nyeklyoodovo by her husband's
side, and gave orders that it should be done; but she
is forced to lie near her father Vassili at Mordovsky
Boogoorooslan"

Mme. Kalpinsky then said in a low voice as if to herself :
" They didn't want it themselves, and that was the reason.
It was the General's lady ; it always is. It was quite
possible to bring the body heie : the snow was gone in
twenty-foui houis." But the other replied at once :—
" No, no, sister ! That is a wicked slander against
cousin Elizabeth and them all. It was impossible to get
through either in sledges or on wheels ; we started ourselves for the funeral and had to turn back at Bachmetevka :
the bridge over the Savrusha had disappeared ! Nor was
it possible foi them to wait : the snow might not have
melted. No, sister, do not say such wicked things ! Clearly
it was the will of God. But it makes one's heart ache, that
our cousin did not find his mothei in life."

This was the kind of consolation administered to the
beieaved son by the ladies of the house. They began to
quarrel and spoke louder and louder. My mother begged
them all to leave my father alone ; she cleared the room
even of us and stayed with him herself. She told me afterwards that he wept on for a long time, but at last fell asleep
in her arms. Mme. Kalpinsky had three daughters and
one son, almost a baby. We were complete strangers, and
they were shy of us at first, but soon became very friendly,
and we thought them very good-natured. They tried to
comfort us ; for we were both crying for our grandmother,
and I was crying still more for my father, for whom I felt
moie soirow than I can express. They gave us tea and
food, and wished to give some to my parents ; but, when
I looked in at their door, my mother made a gesture of
refusal ; and I asked that they should not be disturbed.
Two hours later, my mother came out and said : " Glory
to God ! Alexyéi Stepanitch is quieter now ; only he is
anxious to start at once." But, as the horses needed food
and a good rest, we stayed two hours longer and even dined
there ; my father would not come to table and ate nothing.
Immediately after dinner we said good-bye and started off.
During the rest of the journey I never took my eyes off
my father's face It expressed deep and inconsolable grief ;
and I fancied at once that he had loved his mother more than
his father · though he shed tears at grandfather's death,

yet I had never seen him wear such a sad expression. My mother took pains to talk to him and tried to make him answer her questions. She spoke of grandmother with much feeling and tenderness, and said to my father :—

"You may comfort yourself with the thought that you were always a most dutiful son, never causing her anxiety and always scrupulously fulfilling her wishes. She lived long, for a woman,"—she was seventy-four years old —"and after your father's death nothing gave her comfort : she wished herself to die soon."

The violence of his grief had passed, but he still wept as he said :—

"That is all true, and I should not feel it so terribly, if only I had received her last blessing and been present to close her eyes. It is all due to my aunt. Why did she keep me there ? From mere caprice."

But my mother stopped him, begging him not to be angry with Praskovya Ivanovna and blame her : she could not foresee such a misfortune, and was terribly distressed herself, though she made no display of her feelings. "True, true," said my father with a sigh ; and again his tears fell as he embraced my mother. All the time my sister and I were crying quietly, and even Parasha was wiping her eyes. The journey from Nyeklyoodovo to Bagrovo was spent in conversation of this kind, and came to an end sooner than I expected. As the carriage thundered across the bridge over the Boogoorooslan, I realised for the first time that we were so near our dear Bagrovo. The thought dispelled my grief for the moment, and I turned quickly to the window to look out at our large pond. But oh, how gloomy and sad it looked ! A fierce wind was blowing, and the dark waves drifting all over the pond made me think of the Volga ; a lowering sky was reflected in the water ; the reeds were yellow and withered and sent forth a dull melancholy sound, as they were lashed to and fro by the wind and waves. Of the green banks and green trees, there was not a trace. Trees, banks, mill, and peasants' houses—all alike were wet and black and muddy. The joyful bark of Soorka and Tresor (a setter, and another great favourite of mine) welcomed us in the court ; and immediately afterwards I was aware that six persons were standing on the steps, my four aunts and my uncles Yerlykin and Karatayeff. They greeted us with that loud wail of mourning which I had heard before at grandfather's funeral. Our carriage had been sighted some way off, when we began to descend the hill; and therefore not only our relations but all the servants and many of the labourers and their wives were assembled near the front door.

CHAPTER XX

THE reader can imagine the scene at the door—all the kissing and embracing, all the weeping and sobbing and wailing. My mother soon took us children into the house, but it was long before my father joined us : he had to receive and return the sorrowful greeting of each individual. At last we all met in the drawing-room, and our baby brother was brought there also. He was delighted to see my sister and me ; during our short separation he had grown bigger and much prettier, and was beginning to speak plainer Our cousins, the two daughters of Mme. Yerlykin, were there too ; we were glad to see them, but they did not receive us warmly. The whole evening was devoted to mournful accounts of grandmother's illness and death. She had a presentiment that she would never see her son again, and often spoke of it before her illness began ; and, when she became ill, she had no doubt she would soon die and said, " I shall not see Alosha again " It appeared that her illness was not due to any fatal disease but to the rich unwholesome food, of which she was so fond. She had given no special directions before her death ; but she had commissioned my Aunt Aksinya, as her oldest daughter, to beg my father and mother to be kind to Tanyusha ; she also left a message for my mother, asking forgiveness for wrongs which she had done her. And this message Aksinya delivered in public, to the great surprise and annoyance of her sisters. I heard later that they had tried all means—threats as well as entreaties—to stop her from using terms which they thought humiliating to their dead mother ; but she would not listen to them and even repeated the words in their presence. This was my mother's answer :

" I forgive her with my whole heart, if she—the kingdom
of heaven be hers !—ever was in anything unjust to me.
It is a great grief to me that I could not ask her forgiveness ;
for I was not guiltless myself, as regards her ; but I hope
that she forgave me, for she had a kind heart."

Then the conversation ran for a long time on the fatal
date of Intercession Day . by that day, grandmother had
asked us to return, and on that day she died ; again, my
father had been alarmed by a portentous dream and had
received news of his mother's illness on that same day.
To all these topics I listened with special attention.   Calling
to mind our first stay at Bagrovo and some expressions
which had forced their way from my mother's lips and had
been noted by me at the time, I tried to form some clear
and definite idea in my own mind of the wrongs which
my mother and grandmother had been guilty of, in their
conduct to one another.   And my belief in presentiments
and prophetic dreams was much strengthened in consequence of these conversations.

Early next morning, my father went with my Aunt
Tatyana to Mordovsky Boogoorooslan.   Next day was the
ninth since grandmother's death, and all the family were
to meet there, to hear a mass for the repose of her soul ;
but my father was so impatient to see his mother's grave
and to weep over it, that he was determined not to wait
a whole day longer.   Long before dinner-time he came back,
pale and distressed.   My aunt reported that, as soon as
he saw his mother's grave, he ran to it in a sort of frenzy,
threw his arms out on the damp earth, and lay there as if
dead.

" My brother terrified me," she went on ; " I thought
he was dead and began to scream ; Father Vassili and
his wife came running out, and the three of us drew him
away with difficulty and took him half conscious to the
priest's house.   There, glory be to God ! he grew calmer,
and we said the prayers for the dead.   I gave orders for
the requiem mass to-morrow, and they will toll the bell as
soon as we arrive."

Again I thought that my father was much fonder of
grandmother than of grandfather

That same day, a special messenger was sent to Praskovya Ivanovna. My mother wrote her a long letter and read it aloud to my father, who only added a few lines of his own. I thought her letter wonderful at the time ; but I was too young to understand and appreciate it fully ; and, when this letter fell into my hands later, I was amazed by the tact and even artistic skill with which it was written. It contained a perfectly true account of grandmother's death and my father's terrible grief ; yet, at the time, it was expressed in such affectionate and considerate language that it was calculated to allay rather than embitter the sorrow of Praskovya Ivanovna, who was bound to be deeply affected by the news that grandmother had died before our arrival.

On the ninth day, the usual day for a requiem service, the whole family, except us three children and our two cousins, made an early start for Mordovsky Boogoorooslan, taking with them Mme. Kalpinsky and Mme. Lupenevsky, who had come to the house the day before. My mother wished to take me too ; but the weather was cold and damp, and I was not well, suffering from some fever and headache. I had probably caught cold, from running several times to look at my pigeons and hawks in their winter quarters When the house was empty, I looked into grandmother's room : it looked bare and sad, just as I had seen it after grandfather's death. The very same pair, Miséitch and red-haired Vaska, were chanting the Psalms for their mistress. I wished to chant myself, but I could not get through a whole page : every word echoed in my ears and hurt my head. The whole party returned in time for dinner, bringing the priest and his wife with them. A large table was laid in the parlour and covered with a great number of dishes ; at the end of dinner pancakes of different kinds were served, and all the party, except, of course, my father and mother, ate heartily of them, crossing themselves and making mention of the dead, just as they had done after my grandfather's death. I hardly ate anything and was half asleep ; I felt so ill. But I remember that my mother refused to sit at the head of the table, saying that her sister Tatyana, so long as

she remained unmarried, would always be the mistress of
the house. I remember, too, that both my uncles, and
even Mme. Kalpinsky and Mme. Lupenevsky, drank a
great deal of beer and strong waters, and were uncommonly
cheerful before dinner was over.

When we rose from table, I lay down on a sofa and went
to sleep ; I was carried off to bed later, but I remember
nothing of it. For three days and nights, I lay in the
delirium of fever. When I became conscious again, I
thought at first that I had awakened after a long sleep.
My mother was sitting at my bedside ; she looked thin
and pale ; but what joy that face expressed, when she was
convinced that the fever had left me and that my mind
was not wandering ! What tears of happiness flowed
down her cheeks ! What a look there was in her eyes as
she gazed at me ! How she kissed my hands ! I received
her caresses with astonishment, and was still more
astonished when I noticed that my head and hands were
bandaged, and felt pain in my chest and the back of my
head and calves of my legs. I wished to get up but had
not strength to rise. Then my mother explained to me
that I was ill and suffering from fever, that I had poultices
of black bread and vinegar and crushed juniper berries on
my head and hands, Spanish blisters on my neck and chest,
and mustard-plasters on my calves. It may be that all
this was needless ; or it may be that my rapid recovery
from fever was really due to the healing virtue of these
applications. The chief pleasure in the world is recovery
after a bad illness, especially when one sees the joy it gives
to all around one. My father came to my bedside my
sister, and my little brother ; they all kissed me with
smiling faces, but my mother threw herself on her knees
before the shrine of the *ikons*, and wept while she gave
thanks. Remembering at once that my mother never
prayed in the presence of others, I wondered what this
could mean ; but my heart soon told me the reason. When
her prayer was done, she turned her whole attention, her
whole being, to the task of watching over me. Fearing
that the presence and conversation of others might excite
me, she allowed no one to stay with me long. In fact, I

was so weak that I was tired out and soon fell asleep;
and this time it was real sleep, the sleep which restores
strength, so that I woke up in a few hours much stronger
and more cheerful. Then I had more visitors—my aunts
Aksinya and Tatyana, very much pleased to see me better,
and next Yevséiteh, who even cried for joy. From him
I learnt that all the visitors and relations had dispersed,
the day after I was taken ill ; my Aunt Aksinya, my godmother and the kindest of women, alone stayed on at
Baglovo, though her own children at home were far from
well at the time ; but she saw the terrible anxiety and
alarm of my parents, and hoped to have an opportunity
of helping them. My mother warmly appreciated her kind
and loving heart, and did all she could to show her gratitude.
When she saw that I was much better and on the way to
recovery, she urged my Aunt Aksinya to go home at
once.

My convalescence lasted about a week. It was long
enough for me to understand and feel a mother's love in
all its strength. Of course, I had known before, and saw
at every step, that my mother loved me : I had been told,
and I dimly remembered for myself, how she had watched
over me in infancy, when I was so feeble that my death
was expected at any minute ; and I knew that her constant
care had saved my life. But knowledge derived from recollection and the reports of others is not at all the same
thing as a fresh immediate experience of one's own. When
I was well and no danger threatened me, the ordinary course
of life did not call forth or display so vividly the infinite
treasure of a mother's love, hidden in the depths of the
heart. For some time past I had never had an illness ;
and then, suddenly, in the depth of the country where no
medical aid was procurable, my mother saw her first-born
son, the darling of her heart, fevered and delirious. Is it
hard to understand the agony of fear she suffered, or her
passionate joy when the danger had passed away ? I was
older now, and was able to understand that passionate joy
and the strength of a mother's love. That week did much
to open my eyes and develop my mind ; and my attachment to my mother became more conscious and grew to a

pitch seldom reached by a child of that age. From my recovery until we left Bagrovo, I spent all my time with her, and the stormy autumn weather made this more natural. It need hardly be said that half our time was spent in reading aloud, sometimes she read to me, and she read so well that I listened to what I had long known as if it were new—listened with peculiar pleasure, and found in the pages which she read to me, merits which I had never discovered before.

Meanwhile, the special messenger who had carried the letter to Praskovya Ivanovna, returned before I had completely recovered. He brought with him a long letter dictated by Praskovya Ivanovna; she did not write herself, because writing was to her a difficult business. It was long, compared to the ordinary letters dictated by her or written in her name, which were usually comprised in a few lines. She had fully appreciated or, I should rather say, felt my mother's letter to her. Her gratitude for it was strongly and warmly expressed; and she spoke again and again of my mother as her "dear friend." She expressed much sorrow that the death of my grandmother had taken place before our arrival, blamed herself for having kept my father, begged his forgiveness, and urged him not to torment himself but to submit to the will of God.

"If I was not afraid," she wrote, "of causing you trouble, I would come myself, as soon as the snow makes travelling possible, and share this time of sorrow with you. Yours, I am sure, is indeed a house of mourning: with no neighbours and not a soul to speak to, you will only make one another more wretched and depressed. Would it not be a good plan, if all of you, including the children and Tanyusha, would come to Choorassovo and spend the whole winter with me? Do consider this. I should feel less uneasy about you all, and happy in the society of Sofya Nikolayevna"—and more to the same effect.

This invitation, coming in the middle of her letter, was regarded as a passing idea which was not really serious but had chanced to come into her head. My father said, "Another strange fancy of my aunt's! If one spends all one's life travelling and visiting, one might as well have no home at all." My Aunt Tatyana added, that a rich and fashionable house, crammed with visitors from morning till night, was no place for a plain woman like her ; and, besides that, she had no mind for merriment just now. Even my mother said that it was impossible for her to drag about three small children in the depth of winter. A letter was written in accordance with these opinions and sent off by the earliest post to Praskovya Ivanovna. Her kind proposal was passed over in silence.

My father spent whole days at first with his blind agent, Pantelyéi ; then he set to work to write ; next he listened while what had been written by Pantelyéi was read by his pupil, Ivan ; and finally he read to Pantelyéi what he himself had written. They were working together at the framing of a petition to the Senate, with reference to the lawsuit with the Bogdanoffs. Pretty often I heard disputes, and rather warm disputes, between them, in which the blind agent, though the most modest and respectful of men, always came off victorious. It was said that he knew all the laws by heart, and I believed it ; for I often heard him quote an *ukase*, giving the exact date, the different articles and paragraphs, and the precise language, as confidently as if the book were lying open before him and he could see it with his own eyes. His own language was very bookish, and he chose his words with the utmost care when speaking on the commonest topics. Thus he would commonly address my father like this : " Would you have the goodness, my dear Sir, Alexyéi Stepanitch. . . ." He dictated very fast and fiercely, with constant movements of his head and hands. Sometimes I crept into his room so softly that he did not hear me, and stood there for a long time, leaning against the stove : there he sat curled up on a high couch, smoking a short pipe, which he was constantly cleaning out and refilling ; then he struck a light on a piece of tinder and began to smoke again. He spoke in a loud animated voice, and his pupil, a rapid writer who had been with him constantly for years, had hardly time to take it all down and repeat aloud the last few words of what he had written. I looked with respectful awe at this blind man, and marvelled at the intelligence and memory which made up for the loss of his eyes.

I spent nearly all my time in my mother's room and practically lived there : I read and wrote and, as my bed stood there, generally slept in that room. The consequence was that I played less with my sister and saw her less often than before. I have said before that my mother was less tender and loving to her than to me ; and so it was natural and inevitable that my sister should not be tender and loving to her ; she was even rather timid and uneasy in my mother's presence. Though my mother never sent her away from the room, yet my sister felt a kind of oppression there, and slipped off when she had a good opportunity. Then my mother would say : " That child has no affection at all for me ; she's always watching for a chance to leave me and go back to her nurse." I thought so myself then, and I was silent and sad ; for I could not defend my sister and believed that she had little love for her mother. The truth was, that her love for our mother was always much warmer and deeper than my own ; but this did not appear until later.

The conduct of my Aunt Tatyana, or rather her bearing towards others, underwent a sudden change about this time ; she seemed at least quite different. She had been a rather lively and cheerful girl, with a full measure of the freedom and independence natural to a grown-up daughter of the house ; but now she became depressed, quiet, and timid, and so ready to oblige, that my mother, who was the chief object of her attentions, did not like it. Indeed, my mother said one day to my father :

" Alexyéi Stepanitch, I wish you would tell your sister not to run errands for me in that way, just as a maid-servant might I am ashamed to accept services of that kind from her ; and, in general, I object to it."

But my father took a quite different view of the case.

" Come, come, my dear," he said, " I see nothing objectionable in that. My sister is accustomed to show respect and attention to the head of the household—to my father while he lived, and then to my mother ; and now, as you are mistress at Bagrovo, she shows the same attentions to you."

My mother did not discuss it; but I was in the room a few days later, when my aunt ran to place a footstool for her. My mother stopped her at once and said in a very determined voice:

"I beg you, sister, never to do that, unless you wish to make me angry. I have long been intending to speak to you frankly of our present position, and this gives me the chance. Please sit down on the bed beside me, and listen attentively to what I say. Much of it will not please you; but I do it, not to create a quarrel, but to get rid of a possible cause of discomfort between us in future. I want you not to be mistaken about me, not to suppose that I know nothing and understand nothing. That is not so: I know very well that your sisters, except Aksinya, never liked me, carried false tales against me to their father, and wished to do me any harm they could. Your mother believed them implicitly, took their view of everything, and even dared not—their character was stronger than hers—go against them. You did the same; but I do not blame you: it was impossible for the youngest daughter to act in opposition to her elder sisters and her own mother. From your earliest years, you were accustomed to believe them and obey them. Now I have no wish to conceal that I never loved your sisters, and have not forgotten the slights they put on me; but I will never try to punish them. Your case is different: I have long ago forgiven and forgotten all that was unpleasant. They have tried to make you believe that I am your enemy; and you have sometimes believed it though you have a kind heart. The truth is that I am your well-wisher, and I shall prove it by my actions. You know your brother's character, how slow he is to act and how apt to postpone business; it would take him a long time, to get your affairs settled, I mean, to secure you the legal ownership of your serfs and transfer them to your land; and the land, too, though the price has been settled, is not yet paid for. If I say nothing, he will do nothing about it, likely enough, till you come to be married; and, since the unsettled state of your affairs may prevent your marriage and deprive you of a desirable suitor, therefore I give you my word that everything shall be settled in the course of the present year. I shall give Alexyéi Stepanitch no rest till he carries out the wish of his parents and makes good his own promise. You will have then a roof of your own , and, if you prefer to live here, you will do so of your own free will. For my part, I shall be very glad if you will stay with us. The management of a house is not a thing that I am fond of, and I shall be grateful to you if you attend to it as you have done in the past. But I must ask you not to jump about in my presence or run my errands ; I want you to behave to me as my equal, and, in short, to do just as you did in your mother's lifetime. Will you agree ? "

Long before she ended, my Aunt Tatyana had dissolved in tears. She had made several attempts to rush into the arms of her " darling sister," if not to bow down before her ; but each time my mother held out an opposing arm. As may be supposed, she agreed heartily to everything, and could not find words to express her gratitude for my mother's " great favours and benefits." She added that she had collected all the personal belongings of her mother and made an inventory of them ; and they would all be handed over to her sister-in-law. My mother replied with much warmth :

" Do you really think that I mean to claim the clothes and other odds and ends left by my mother-in-law, when her own daughter is still living and unmarried ? Ah, how little you know me ! I won't have any of the things ! I won't even look at them ! They are all yours."

There naturally followed a fresh burst of the warmest gratitude on the part of my aunt.

This scene served to explain to me fully for the first time the position which my mother had held in my father's family. When I recalled what I had heard at different times from Parasha, and also certain words which had burst from my mother's lips in the course of heated discussions with my father, I could form a pretty clear conception of the people with whom she had lived, and of their ways. It is easy to understand what a superior being my mother

x

seemed to me. I began to look on her with veneration, was proud of her, and loved her more dearly every day.

Suddenly and quite unexpectedly a letter came to us by the post from Praskovya Ivanovna; and we were all surprised to find that it was twice as long as the first. One by one, she went through all the reasons which made it undesirable that we should spend the winter at Bagrovo; and this time she positively insisted that we should travel to Choorassovo in six weeks' time and stay with her till Lent. The letter consisted partly of tender entreaties and partly of positive commands; and, without a word said, every one felt that a refusal was out of the question. A special note was enclosed for my Aunt Tatyana, very kind and very urgent. Praskovya Ivanovna wrote that she would prepare for her a pretty room, quite apart from every one else; Darya Vassilyevna had occupied it but was now transferred to one of the wings; Tatyana would live there in peace and undisturbed by any one; just when she felt inclined, she could enjoy our society and that of the mistress of the house. When both letters had been read, nobody spoke for some time, and there was a general air of dissatisfaction. At last my father broke the silence and began : " Well, my dear, what's to be done ? We must comply with my aunt's wishes. We have really no good reason for refusing; and she would be displeased." My mother answered that she, too, did not know how to get out of it ; the move in winter for the children was her only difficulty. " And what do you say, Tanyusha ? " asked my father. My aunt said at once that nothing would induce her to go : she would die of home-sickness at Choorassovo ; and she was unwilling to go so soon to such a distance from her mother's grave. " Where will you live, then ? " my father went on ; " it's impossible for you to stop alone at Bagrovo." My aunt thought for a moment and then said that she would go and stay with her sister Alexandra, and that they would visit the grave together once a month and pray there and have mass said. Thus the talk went on, and the party broke up without having settled anything definitely.

I felt, however, that our going was inevitable, and disliked the prospect more than any one else. I felt it the more, because I had learnt a new amusement and become very fond of it, a few days before we received the letter. Yevséitch had taught me how to set a bow-trap for the small birds that abounded in our garden. There was already a light covering of snow on the ground; and Yevséitch cleared a patch and strewed chaff and dregs of hempseed on it for bait. As it was getting hard for the birds to find food, they welcomed the supply and in a day or two became accustomed to fly to the bait. Then Yevséitch set the trap behind the bare patch, with a net over it, tied a cord to it, and brought the cord through a gooseberry bush, behind which it was easy for one or two people to hide themselves. When the birds got accustomed to the trap, and began to settle near it and pick the seed without fear, Yevséitch took me cautiously to the bush, where we could watch through the leafless branches all that happened on the bare patch.

"Bend down and keep quite still," whispered Yevséitch, crouching down; "better birds will come soon—just now they're all linnets; then you catch hold of the cord and pull! All the birds will be trapped, and you and I will pick out the best and put them in a cage."

I was ready to do as I was told. In a few minutes Yevséitch called out, "Now! pull!" Trembling with excitement and delight, I pulled with all my might, and we jumped up from behind the bush and ran to the trap. It was not quite successful: I had pulled too hard, so that one side of the trap had been raised, leaving part of the patch uncovered; yet some birds were left fluttering under the net, and we caught a pair of goldfinches, a chaffinch, and a linnet. I ran home with our booty; Yevséitch ran too; for it was one of his strong points, that every kind of sport excited him as much as it did me. I soon learnt to use the trap with skill; and, as I was unwilling to let go the birds I caught, when I had filled several cages with them, I put a number of all kinds in a sort of aviary with a net round it, which was not far from the front door, and in which my pigeons lived in summer. It was empty now, because the pigeons were spending the winter under the stoves in peasants' cabins. In the aviary there was a trough with water, in which I put snow when the water froze; and there were two small birch-trees, on which the birds perched and roosted; and I scattered food of all sorts on the ground. It was a real joy to me, to stand by this aviary, and watch the quick lively movements of the pretty little birds, and to observe them while they ate and drank and squabbled with each other. Sometimes I would have stayed there the whole day with my face pressed against the rime-covered net, unconscious of the cold of early November and my insufficient clothing, had not my mother sent for me, or Yevséitch carried me off against my will to the warmth inside the house.

The day after Praskovya Ivanovna's letter was received, my parents, who had probably talked it all over by themselves, announced their intention to start for Choorassovo as soon as ever the snow made travelling possible. That very day, orders were given to all concerned, to be ready for the journey, and make all necessary preparations. The time of our departure depended on the freezing of the Volga; and information of this event was to be sent us at once from Vishenki. My Aunt Tatyana kept to her intention of not going to Choorassovo but living with her sister Alexandra till our return. My mother did not press her to go with us; I heard her say to my father that Tatyana would feel constrained and unhappy at Choorassovo. A letter was written at once to my Aunt Alexandra to inform her of this plan. My Aunt Tatyana had one cause for uneasiness · she was unwilling to part from her store-house, or rather from all its precious contents. She confessed her doubts to my father: she feared that, when Bagrovo was empty, thieves might break into the store-house at night and steal all her property, which she had scraped together, "thanks to the generosity of her father and mother, continued by her brother and sister-in-law." She asked my father to provide her with horses, so that she might transfer some part of it at least to Karatayevka for safety. My father, though he thought this unnecessary, yielded to his sister's persistent entreaties. Later I heard

Yevséitch and Parasha whispering to one another and making fun secretly of my aunt's apprehensions.

Snow went on falling almost every night, and there was a fresh surface of it every morning. My father was fond of taking a gun and tracking hares through the snow; but, sad to say, he would not take me : he said I should be in his way and would get tired out. But, to make up for this, and give me some fun, he told one of the men to get on a horse and mark down a hare ; then he took me with him, intending that I should see the hare caught in a net.

" Look ! there is the hare's form, Seryozha," said my father, pointing to a patch of withered rushes, near some bushes at the foot of a hill. " As the hare will run up hill, the nets are laid on that line. Do you see them, hanging on the bushes ? Now watch how they do it."

We had a score of beaters ; some kept behind, while others walked forwards at the sides ; so the line advanced in a half-circle, while the men shouted and beat the rushes with long sticks. In an instant the hare sprang out and made like an arrow for the hill ; then he struck the net, and carried it along some feet by his impetus, till his head and paws were caught and he was finally entangled and upset. The beaters shouted and ran as fast as they could to the imprisoned hare, and I did the same. What a beauty that grand old hare was ! How I admired the black tips of his ears, his black stump of a tail, his yellow chest and forelegs, and the striped and curling line that ran down his back ! I was half-choked by a passionate joy which I could not explain myself.

And from all this I was doomed to go away, to spend a whole winter at Choorassovo, which I did not love, where many of the perpetual succession of visitors were not to my taste, where I must avoid contact with the objectionable servants of the house, and where I should have to spend most of my time in the rooms which I knew so well and disliked so much. And besides, I should enjoy much less of my mother's society. My sister too was unwilling to go to Choorassovo, though that place offered her the special advantage of my constant society ; and she loved me so tenderly that in my presence she was always quite content and very happy.

When forty days had passed since her death, the time came for the commemoration service for my grandmother. The roads, thinly covered with snow, had turned into heaps of frozen mud, formidable for wheels or sledges; yet all the members of the family met at Bagrovo the day before. Early on the 9th of November the whole party, except us children, were conveyed to Mordovsky Boogoorooslan, where they listened to a requiem service and had prayers offered over the grave. Then they returned to drink tea and coffee, which were soon followed by dinner; and this meal of mourners was an exact repetition of the scene I have described more than once already: the party ate and drank, shed tears and spoke of the departed; and, when all was over, they went away.

And now deeper snow came down, and hard frost set in and made the walls of our house crack. My Aunt Alexandra had come to fetch her sister. At last we got news that the Volga was frozen and trains of waggons were making their way across it. The day of our departure was fixed. A sledge was brought round to the steps, and room in it had to be found for myself, my sister and Parasha, and my little brother with Matrona, who had now exchanged the duties of foster-mother for those of nurse. Another sledge was brought round for my parents. Plenty of food had been cooked for the journey; we packed ourselves into our places; and on the 21st of November the sledge runners began to creak on the snow and we started. My mother could not bear this creaking noise; nor more could I, and I cried, as I took my seat in the sledge. My Aunt Tatyana was to start the same day with her sister for Karatayevka.

Our journey from Bagrovo to Choorassovo was accomplished successfully and quickly. Sledging in Russia at the beginning of winter is magnificent, if the snow has fallen evenly with calm weather, and, while deep enough to cover all the uneven places in the road, is not so deep as to make it impossible to drive three horses harnessed abreast. It was just like that on this journey. We had our own

horses and travelled faster than we had ever done before.
The pace was so great and the snow so powdery that the
creaking of the runners was hardly audible, and both
my mother and I were almost without any feeling of
sickness throughout the journey. At Vishenki we only
stopped to feed the horses. My father, of course, had an
interview with the bailiff, asking him many questions and
noting down the answers to report to Piaskovya Ivanovna.
The winter aspect of the castle or palace of Nikolskoe
reminded me of the noble entertainment provided for us
by Doorassoff; and, though only a few months had passed
since then, the excitement and astonishment which I had
then felt, already seemed to me absurd. Doorassoff was
not at home, and we put up at the house of a well-to-do
peasant. My father always talked to the householder,
whenever we stopped for food or sleep; and I enjoyed
listening to these conversations. My mother, as a rule,
was bored by them; but our host on this occasion was a
remarkably intelligent man, who talked about his master
in a way that much amused my mother and interested us
all. He appeared to praise Doorassoff and yet always
displayed him in a very absurd light. We talked of the
magnificent pair of pigs, one of which had died.

"Yes, yes," said the man, "such a calamity! The
best of the pigs is dead! Our master—God grant him
health and long life, a kind and merciful gentleman, with
a soft heart for all manner of beasts—he went away and
left the place; he wasn't so fond of us, you see. That was
just it : he had plenty of us, but only two pigs, and they
came from over the sea, while we were born on the place.
Oh, a kind gentleman, one can't say how kind ; and so
ingenious too. Just outside the village we had two wells,
with splendid cold spring-water. Well, he made us put up
by each well a wooden woman, dressed in a red *sarafan*,
and gold lace round her middle, but her feet were bare ; she
had one foot on the well and the other lifted up as if she
were going to jump. Well, every one who passes, on horse
or on foot, stops and looks, of course ; but the peasants
have ceased to draw water from the wells ; they say that
it does not look nice."

The man was fond of talking and said much more of
the same kind. Much of it I did not understand, but my
mother said that it was all clever and malicious. What I
did understand, however, was enough for me to draw a
conclusion and make a discovery : the peasant had made
fun of the gentleman, whereas I was accustomed to think
that all peasants looked up with awe to their masters, and
never criticised what was said or done by them. I decided
to pay special attention to all conversations between
Yevséitch and Parasha, to find out whether they too made
fun of us in private, while praising us to our faces and
kissing our hands. When I told my mother of this intention, she laughed and said, " What good will it do you to
know that ? We get good service from Parasha and still
more from Yevséitch ; but their opinion of us is a matter
of indifference to me." But I felt curious on the point,
and did not give up my intention.

Next day we drove over my old enemy, the Volga,
on ice as smooth as a mirror ; but even this aspect of the
great river frightened me. The ice over the Volga was
unusually clean that year. There had been few blizzards
and little snow, so that there were few blocks of ice and
heaps of frozen snow on the surface. Frost alone had
fettered the surface of the river. and one could look through
the transparent ice and see the water running below,
circling and eddying, and white bubbles coursing here and
there. I confess that I could not, without trembling, look
down from the carriage-window upon that awful mass of
moving water, over which our horses were galloping.
Suddenly I noticed on one side, not far from the beaten
track, something that looked like a long opening in the ice,
and smoke rising from it. I was astonished and asked
Parasha to look and explain it to me. She looked and said
laughing—

" Oh, that's a gap in the ice, where the water never
freezes ; it's Volga breathing, that makes the smoke come
out ; and stakes are put along the edge, to prevent any
one from tumbling in at night."

This was new to me and interesting, but my head was
full of one single thought—that we might go through at

any moment and plunge under the ice. Fear mastered me, and I had recourse to my usual expedient in such cases : I shut my eyes tight and never opened them till we reached the other side of the Volga.

At Simbirsk we got news that Praskovya Ivanovna was not quite well and very impatient to see us. Next day, the fifth since we left Bagrovo, just at noon, the four crosses of the two churches and belfries at Choorassovo glittered before our eyes.

It is impossible to describe the joy which Praskovya Ivanovna showed at our arrival. Forgetting her ailment, she ran, rather than walked, out into the hall. Never had I seen her wear such a face of delight. She embraced my father and mother, held them tight in her arms, and would not let them go, especially my mother ; she even kissed us children all round, which she never used to do, only giving us her hand to kiss.

" Oh, so the little Blackamoor has come too," she said laughing ; " he's grown much prettier, but where on earth did he get that nose from ? Hearty greetings, friends from over the Volga ! How are your friends and neighbours, the Choovashes and Mordvinians ? You are welcome, my friends. And Tatyana has not come ? She was frightened, I suppose, and shut herself up. I daresay she went to Karatayevka ? Well, if the gentleman there takes too much to drink and gives her a beating, she will repent then that she didn't come to me. Well, glory be to God, I have got you at last. Let us go straight to the drawing-room."

In the parlour and drawing-room we were met by the inevitable crowd of visitors.

We settled down again in our familiar quarters and began the old life again. There was this difference, that Praskovya Ivanovna was infinitely kinder and more winning, as it seemed to me. It was plain to all that she was warmly attached to my mother and to us all ; nothing was too good for us, and she tried every means to make us happy. But I noticed, in spite of this, that Alexandra Kovrigina and Darya Vassilyevna were not so pleased as on our former visits. As to the servants, men and women, it was still clearer that we were simply unwelcome to them.

When I told my mother what I had noticed, she said it was utter nonsense, and that I had no business to notice such a thing. I was not content, however, with this explanation, and repeated my discovery to Yevséitch in Parasha's presence. "Yes," he said; "it's clear they are tired of us; we *are* coming terribly often"; and Parasha added: "They don't fear the other visitors, but your family is different: they're afraid of your repeating something to Praskovya Ivanovna." I was convinced in my own mind that this was perfectly true, though my mother would not admit it.

The Minitskys soon came to the house, bringing the two eldest of their daughters with them. My sister and I were fond of them and glad to see them; and we began again our former games and our former readings. From morning till night I was inseparable from my sister: all indoor occupations and amusements were shared alike by both of us.

As regards the harmful influence of the men and maids at Choorassovo, my mother had no need to trouble herself on that score: as if they had passed the word, they all avoided us and never spoke a word in our presence. Even Ivanushka, the butler, when we were there, gave up his old custom of coming in for a chat with Yevséitch; and Yevséitch said to me one day, with a good-natured laugh, "Better as it is! They're actually fighting shy of us!"

Praskovya Ivanovna soon recovered entirely from her slight cold. Christmas Day was the festival on which the new church, erected by herself, had been consecrated, and she kept the anniversary with all the pomp and display that was possible in a country place. Such a number of visitors were invited that they overflowed both wings of the house, and some of the smaller landowners and some bachelor neighbours were put up in peasants' houses. I was told that no such gathering had ever been seen there; I cannot confirm that statement, but this I know, that the visitors were a greater nuisance to me than ever. I hardly saw my parents at all; and nothing but the friendship between my sister and me, which grew stronger daily and even hourly, beguiled for me the dullness and weariness of life at Choorassovo. My sister had now become a real friend, with whom I could share all my childish feelings and thoughts.

So December passed away and a new year began, and I met it with a vague belief that something was going to happen. On the 2nd of January, my mother surprised me by saying: " Seryozha, would you like to go with me to Kazan? Your father and I are going there for a fortnight."

I was delighted to leave Choorassovo and answered that I should like very much to go. " Very well, then, get ready," said she ; and I promised to be ready in half an hour. Then I suddenly thought of my sister, and asked whether she would go with us. When my mother said that she would stay behind at Choorassovo, I was vexed. On my speaking to my sister of my departure, she wept bitterly. Though I was passionately devoted to my mother and quite unaccustomed to be parted from her, yet my sister's grief made such an impression on me, that I ran back at once, without thinking, to my mother and begged her to leave me behind. She was much surprised ; when she discovered my motive, she kissed me fondly but said, that she would not leave me on any account, that we should be back in a fortnight, and that my sister would soon stop crying. I went sadly back to the nursery, where I found my poor sister in floods of tears She soon had another sorrow to bear : my mother took Parasha with her, and Praskovya Ivanovna moved my sister to her own room for the time, and put her in the charge of her own favourite maid, Akulina, a very discreet and careful woman.

This unexpected visit to Kazan was arranged by Praskovya Ivanovna herself. My mother had said more than once that she would like to visit Kazan, in order to pray at the shrines of the local saints, and adore the relics which she had never seen ; she wished also to be present at the mass celebrated by the Bishop. But Praskovya Ivanovna appeared to take no notice of her words. When Epiphany, which was also my mother's birthday, came near, my mother happened to say to Alexandra, in the presence of Praskovya Ivanovna who was playing piquet with my father, that she would like very much to go away somewhere for the 6th, perhaps to Old Bagrovo

" I detest my birthday," she added ; " you will have a host of visitors, and it will be a real infliction to me to receive congratulations and wishes for all earthly blessings from them all "

Praskovya Ivanovna suddenly turned round and said to my mother—

" Listen, Sofya Nikolayevna, to a plan I have thought of You wanted to pray at the shrines of the saints of Kazan, and you don't like your birthday—nor do I like mine either—well, why don't you and Alexyéi Stepanitch take a run to Kazan ? You will be back in a fortnight ; the distance is only 92 *versts*."

My mother accepted this suggestion very readily, and on the 3rd of January, we were galloping along the road to Kazan in a fine sledge with glass windows, which Praskovya Ivanovna had given us. Though I had got a reprieve from life at Choorassovo, and was going to see for the first time a famous city of which I had heard much, yet I had no feeling of happiness ; my heart was torn with grief. My dear sister, weeping bitterly with her eyes swollen, grieving for her brother and her nurse, but submitting without a word to her fate—such was the picture constantly before me ; and I wept myself for a long time in a corner, paying no attention to what went on around me, and not dreaming, as I generally did, of what lay ahead of me in the future.

What did in fact lie ahead of me was the beginning of a very important episode in my life.*

*   *   *   *   *

Here ends the narrative of his childhood by the young Bagroff. He asserts that his narrative, if continued, will relate, not to his childhood, but to a later stage of his youth.

* The episode was his entrance on school life, which is described in the later part of *A Family History*

APPENDIX

THE SCARLET FLOWER

A FAIRY TALE TOLD BY PELAGÉYA, THE HOUSEKEEPER

IN a certain kingdom, in a certain country, there lived a rich merchant, a man of great name. Much wealth had he of every kind—costly wares from far lands, pearls and precious stones, and gold and silver treasure And this merchant had three daughters, all of them fair to see, but the youngest was the fairest of them all ; and he loved his daughters more than all his riches—his pearls and precious stones and gold and silver treasure—because his wife was dead, and he had no one else to love ; he loved his elder daughters, but he loved his youngest daughter best, because she was the fairest of them all and the most loving to her father. And once on a time this merchant made ready to cross the sea on the business of his merchandise ; he was to cross 27 lands and travel to the 27th kingdom and the 30th country ; * and thus he spoke to his dear daughters—

" O daughters whom I love, daughters dear, daughters fair to see, I am going on my business as a merchant over 27 lands to the 27th kingdom and the 30th country ; and whether I shall be absent a long while or a short while, I know not ; but I bid you to live in honesty and peace when I am far away ; and if, when I am far away, you live in honesty and peace, then I will bring you back gifts, such gifts as you yourselves shall desire. And I give you the space of three days to consider ; and then you shall tell me what gifts you desire."

For three days and three nights they considered ; and then they came to their father, and he asked of them, what

* In Russian fairy-tales these are stock phrases for distant lands.

gifts they desired. The eldest daughter bowed down to her father's feet, and spoke first and said—

"My lord and father that begot me, bring not for me gold or silver brocade, nor fur of the black sable, nor great pearls, but bring me, I pray, a gold crown of precious stones; and let a light come from the stones as from the full moon or the red sun, and let the crown turn dark night into the light of day."

The honest merchant thought a while, and then he said—

"Daughter dear and beloved and fair to see, it is well: I will bring you a crown such as you describe. There is one I know across the sea who will procure it for me. Such a crown there is, and it belongs to a princess beyond the sea, and it is hidden in a treasure-house of stone, and the treasure-house is buried twenty feet deep in a mountain of stone, behind three iron doors and three cunning locks. The labour will not be light; but I have a golden key to open every door."

Then the second daughter bowed down to his feet and said—

"My lord and father that begot me, bring me no gold or silver brocade, nor black furs of the sable of Siberia, nor necklace of great pearls, nor crown of shining gold. But bring me a mirror of crystal of the East, crystal pure and perfect, that, when I look upon it, I may see all the beauty under the sky, and such that, while I look upon it, I may never grow old, but my maiden beauty may increase."

The honest merchant thought again; and when he had thought, a short time or a long time, he spoke thus—

"Daughter dear and beloved and fair to see, it is well: I will bring you a crystal mirror such as you describe. Such a one there is, and it belongs to the daughter of the King of Persia, a young princess, whose beauty no tongue can tell, no pen can write, no heart can imagine; and that mirror is buried in a high tower of stone, and the tower stands on a mountain of rock, and the height of the mountain is two thousand feet; and it is hidden behind seven iron doors and seven cunning locks; and three thousand steps lead up to the tower, and on every step stands a Persian warrior day and night, holding a naked sword of Damascus steel ; and the keys of those iron doors the princess carries at her girdle. There is one I know across the sea who will procure for me this mirror. This task is harder than your sister set me ; but my golden key will open every door."

Then the youngest daughter bowed down to her father's feet and said—

" My lord and father that begot me, bring me no gold or silver brocade, nor black sables of Siberia, nor necklace of great pearls, nor crown of jewels, nor mirror of crystal ; but bring me the Scarlet Flower, the most beautiful thing in all the world."

The honest merchant thought ; harder he thought than before. Whether he thought a long time or a short time, I cannot tell for certain ; but, when he had thought, he kissed and caressed and fondled his dear youngest daughter, and thus he spoke—

" You have set me a harder task than your sisters. When a man knows what to seek, he may surely find it ; but how can he find a thing of which he is ignorant ? A scarlet flower is not hard to find ; but how am I to know that it is the most beautiful thing in the world ? I will do my best ; and be not angry, if I bring not the right gift."

And he sent away his daughters, virtuous and fair, to their maiden bowers. And he began to make ready for his journey and for his travel into far countries across the sea. Whether he took long to prepare, I know not and cannot tell : a story is quickly told, but a deed is not so quickly done. He departed on his journey and his travel ; and lo ! the honest merchant traversed strange countries across the sea and unknown kingdoms. He sold his own wares at a great price and bought foreign wares at a small price ; he bartered merchandise for merchandise, and they gave him silver and gold into the bargain ; and he loaded ships with coin of gold and sent them home. He found the magic gift for his eldest daughter, the crown with precious stones that turned dark night to the brightness of day. And he found the magic gift for his second daughter also, the crystal mirror which reflected all the beauty under the

skies, and which was such that she who looked in it never
grew old, but grew ever more young and beautiful. But
he could not find the magic gift for his youngest dearest
daughter, the Scarlet Flower, which was the most beautiful
thing in the whole world. In the gardens of tsars and kings
and sultans he found many scarlet flowers, whose beauty
no tongue can tell and no pen can write ; but no man could
give him surety that this flower was the fairest thing in the
world, and he himself did not think it was so. And,
as he journeyed on his way with his faithful servants
over shifting sands and through sleeping forests, suddenly
there fell upon him robbers ; infidels were they and foul
pagans, Turks and Indians. And the honest merchant,
when he saw calamity that he could not escape, left his
rich caravans and his faithful servants behind, and fled
into the dark forest. " Better that wild beasts should tear
me asunder, than that I should fall into the hands of
heathen robbers and spend my life as their prisoner and
captive ! "

So he wandered in that sleeping forest, through which
no man passed either walking on foot or carried by horses ;
and, the further he went, the better the road became ; for
the trees seemed to make way for him and the thick bushes
to part before him. He looked back, and could not put
forth his hand ; he looked to the right, and the fallen
trees and stumps were so thick that a hare could not
have doubled between them ; he looked to the left, and
it was worse even than the other side. The honest merchant
was astonished ; he thought and thought but could not
understand the marvel of what befell him ; yet he walked
on and on, and ever under his feet there was a beaten way.
From morning till evening he walked ; and he never heard a
wild beast roar nor a serpent hiss, nor the hoot of an owl,
nor the cry of any bird ; it seemed as if all was dead around
him. And now dark night came on ; it was black as
pitch all round, but under his feet a bright light shone.
On he walked till near midnight, and he began to see a
kind of glow before him ; and he thought : " Surely the
forest is on fire ; why should I go on to meet certain
inevitable death ? " He turned round, but he could not

move ; he turned to the right and to the left, but nowhere
could he advance ; he pushed forwards, and there was the
beaten way under his feet. Then he said : " Let me stand
still a while ; it may be that the glow will shift its place
or recede from me or go out altogether." So he stood
still and waited ; and the glow moved and seemed to
advance towards him, and it grew brighter round about
him. He thought and thought, and determined to go
forward : a man cannot die twice, and to die once is sure
for all : so the merchant crossed himself and went forward.
The further he went, the brighter grew the light till it was
as bright as midday ; yet he heard no noise or crackling of
fire. At last he came out upon a wide clearing in the
forest ; and in the centre of the clearing there stood, not a
house or a mansion, but a palace, the palace of a king or
tsar, all a blaze of gold and silver and precious stones ;
and it all sent forth a burning light, but there was no fire
to be seen ; it was like the red sun, so that it hurt the eyes
to look at it. All the windows of the palace were open ;
and a concord of musical instruments, such as he had never
heard, came from it. He entered a great court-yard and
great doors that were opened wide ; and all the way was
of white marble, and tall fountains of water, great and
small, spouted at the sides of the way. He entered the
palace by a staircase, of which the steps were covered with
scarlet cloth and the banisters shone with gold. He went
into one of the chambers, and there was no one there ; he
went into a second chamber, and a fifth, and a tenth, and
still there was no one ; but the furnishing of all was fit for
an emperor, beyond aught ever seen or heard of—gold and
silver, crystal of the East, ivory of the elephant and the
mammoth.

The honest merchant marvelled at the untold wealth,
and marvelled more that there was no owner to be seen.
The music went on and never ceased. And the merchant
said then to himself : " All this is well, but there is nothing
to eat." And immediately there grew out of the ground
before him a table, a table richly decked ; the vessels were
of gold and silver, and in them were delicious meats and
wines from across the sea and honeyed drinks. Down he

Y

sat at the table, without fear. He had eaten nothing for
twenty-four hours, and he ate and drank till he could eat
no more ; the food was more delicious than words can tell,
tempting enough to make a man swallow his own tongue ;
and the merchant was ravenous with hunger, after long
walking over the sands and through the forest. He rose
from the table ; but there was no man to whom he might
do obeisance and give him thanks for his hospitality.
Hardly had he risen up and looked round, when the table
and all upon it vanished from his sight ; and still the
music went on without ceasing. The honest merchant
marvelled at such wonders and miracles ; and, as he walked
through the lordly chambers and marvelled at them, he
thought to himself : " It would be pleasant now to sleep
and snore." And lo ! there stood before him a bedstead
carved of pure gold, with feet of crystal, and a canopy of
silver, and a fringe and tassels set with pearls ; and a
feather-bed like a hill lay upon it, made of soft swansdown.
The merchant marvelled at this new miracle ; but he lay
down upon the high bedstead, and drew the silver canopy,
and saw that it was fine and soft as silk. It grew dark in
the chamber, like the darkness of twilight ; and the music
seemed to come from a distance ; and he thought, " If I
could see my daughters, even in a dream ! "—and that very
moment he fell asleep.

When the merchant woke, the sun had risen higher
than a tall tree. And when the merchant woke, he could
not remember at once where he was. All night he had
dreamed of his daughters dear and virtuous and beautiful ;
and he saw in his dream, that his two elder daughters,
the oldest daughter and the second, were merry and happy,
and one only was sad, the youngest daughter whom he
loved best ; and he saw that his eldest daughters had rich
suitors and were making ready to be married without
waiting for their father's blessing ; but the youngest
daughter, the fairest and dearest, would not even hear of
suitors until her dear father came home. And there was
both joy and sorrow in his heart. When he rose up from
the high bedstead, raiment was ready prepared for him,
and a fountain of water poured into a crystal basin. He

dressed and washed, and wondered no more at each new
miracle. Tea and coffee and a rich breakfast stood on a
table. So he prayed and ate his breakfast, and began again
to walk through the chambers, to see their beauty in the
light of the red sun ; and all seemed to him even better
than on the day before. He looked through the open
windows and saw that round the palace there were wondrous
gardens full of fruit and flowers, flowers whose beauty no
pen can describe.

He longed to walk in those gardens, and he went down
another staircase made of green marble and malachite
with banisters of gold. He came straight down to the
green gardens ; and there he walked and marvelled. For
the trees were covered with fruit, ripe and red and so
tempting to the taste that his mouth watered as he looked
at it ; and lovely flowers blossomed, double and fragrant
and bright with every colour ; and strange birds flitted
about, like gold and silver displayed on green and crimson
velvet, and made heavenly music ; and fountains of water
spouted so high that a man could not see their full height
without throwing back his head ; and springs ran and
babbled in channels of crystal. The honest merchant
walked and marvelled ; his eyes ran to and fro, to see such
wonders ; and he knew not what to look at or what to
listen to. Whether he walked a long time or a short time,
I know not ; soon is a story told, but not so soon is a deed
done. But suddenly he saw on a green mound a flower
growing, of scarlet hue, and its beauty was beyond the
power of tongue to tell or pen to write ; no man ever saw
or heard of its like. The honest merchant stopped breathing ; he drew near to the flower, and the fragrance of it
like a stream filled all the garden ; and he shook in all his
limbs and cried out joyfully : " This is the Scarlet Flower,
the fairest thing in all the world, which my youngest dearest
daughter begged of me ! " And when he had spoken thus,
he drew near and plucked the Scarlet Flower.

That same moment, with no cloud in the sky, the lightning flashed and the thunder rolled, till the earth shook
beneath his feet. And there grew up before the merchant,
as if out of the ground, a creature neither beast nor man,

but a monster, covered with hair and terrible to behold.
And the Monster roared with a savage voice and said—

" What hast thou done ?   How didst thou venture to
pluck my favourite flower, the sacred flower in my garden ?
I treasured it more than the apple of my eye, and it was my
pleasure every day to behold it ; and thou hast robbed me
of all my pleasure in life.   I am the lord of this palace and
this garden ; I received thee as a guest dear and desired,
and gave thee food and drink and rest ; and for my goodness thus hast thou rewarded me !   Learn therefore thy
bitter doom : for thy fault thou shalt die before thy time."

And an echo came on every side from savage voices
without number, " Thou shalt die before thy time ! "

The honest merchant's teeth chattered for fear.   He
looked round, and he saw, that on every side, from under
every bush and tree, from the water and from the earth,
foul fiends and hideous monsters innumerable were creeping
towards him.   Then he fell on his knees before the chief
Monster that was covered with hair all over, and spoke in a
piteous voice—

" Thou, whoever thou art, honest man, Beast of the
forest, Monster of the deep—how to address thee I know
not, I cannot tell.   Destroy not my life for my innocent
boldness ; bid me not be cut in pieces and slain ; but bid me
speak to thee.   I have three daughters, lovely and virtuous
and fair to see ; and I promised to bring them each a gift—
for the eldest a jewelled crown, for the second a crystal
mirror, and for the youngest the Scarlet Flower, the most
beautiful thing in all the world.   I found the gifts for my
elder daughters ; but the gift for my youngest I could not
find, till I saw it in thy garden, the Scarlet Flower, the
fairest thing in the world.   And I thought that one so
rich and glorious and mighty as thou art would not miss
the Scarlet Flower which my dear youngest daughter had
asked of me.   I repent me of my fault before Thy Majesty.
Forgive me, if I was foolish and unwise ; let me go back
safe to my daughters ; and, as a gift for my youngest
daughter, let me have the Scarlet Flower.   Whatever price
thou desirest, I will pay thee in golden coin."

A laugh like thunder echoed through the forest, and the

Beast of the forest, the Monster of the deep made answer to the merchant.

"What use is thy golden coin to me ? I have no room to store my own. No mercy shalt thou find from me, and my faithful servants shall tear thee into little pieces. There is but one way of escape for thee. I will send thee home scatheless, I will reward thee with uncounted treasure, and I will give thee the Scarlet Flower, if thou wilt give me thy word as an honest merchant and a writing under thy hand, that thou wilt send in thy room one of thy daughters fair and virtuous. I will do her no mischief, and she shall live in honour and freedom with me, as thou thyself didst live in my palace. I am weary of a lonely life, and I desire to get myself a companion."

The merchant fell right down upon the damp earth, and he shed tears of anguish. He looked upon the Beast of the forest, the Monster of the deep, and he thought of his daughters virtuous and fair ; and he cried out still louder with a voice of anguish ; for the Beast of the forest, the Monster of the deep was exceeding terrible to behold. Long did the honest merchant pour forth tears in his anguish ; but at last he said in a pitiful voice—

"Honest Sir, Beast of the forest, Monster of the deep, how shall I do, if my daughters virtuous and fair will not come to thee willingly ? Can I bind them hand and foot and send them to thee by force ? And what way must they take to reach thy house ? Two years, no more, no less, did I travel on my way here ; and I know not the way I came nor the places that I passed."

The Beast of the forest, the Monster of the deep answered the merchant—

"No unwilling maiden will I have : let thy daughter come hither out of love for thee, of her own will and desire ; or, if thy daughters will not come of their own will and desire, then return thyself, and I will bid thee be slain by a cruel death. And for the journey hither—it will cost thee no pains. I will give thee the ring from off my hand ; and, if any man put it on the little finger of his right hand, he will find himself, in the twinkling of an eye, in the place where he wishes to be. And the space I appoint for thy sojourn at thy home is three days and three nights."

The merchant thought; he thought hard; and this was the sum of his thoughts—

" It is better for me to see my daughters again. I will give them a father's blessing ; and, if they are not willing to save me from death, then I shall prepare me for death as a Christian man should, and return to the Beast of the forest, the Monster of the deep."

And then, as there was no deceit in his mind, he told what was in his heart. The Beast of the forest, the Monster of the deep, knew his thoughts before they were spoken, and, knowing his honest heart, took no written warranty of him, but took the gold ring off his finger and gave it to the honest merchant. Hardly had the honest merchant put the ring on the little finger of his right hand, before he found himself at the entrance of his own spacious court-yard ; and at that moment the entrance was filled by his rich caravans and his faithful servants, who had carried home his treasure and his merchandise, thrice as much as he had taken forth with him. A great noise arose in the house, and his daughters sprang up from their em-broidery frames, where they were embroidering widths of silk with silver and gold ; and they began to kiss their father and embrace him and call him by many fond names ; and the two elder sisters feigned greater joy than the youngest sister. They saw that their father was un-happy for some reason, and that there was a secret sorrow in his heart. And his elder daughters began to ask him, whether he had lost his great riches ; but the youngest daughter thought not at all of riches, but said to her father—

" I have no need of your riches—riches are a thing that can be gained ; but reveal to me your heart's sorrow."

And the honest merchant made answer to his daughters virtuous and fair—

" I have not lost my great riches ; the treasure I have gained is three and four times what I had before. I have another trouble, and to-morrow I will tell you of it, but to-day we will make merry."

He ordered his coffers bound with iron, which he took

with him on his travels, to be brought in. He took out
the crown of gold for his eldest daughter—gold of Araby
that fire will not melt nor water rust—set with precious
stones ; he took out the gift for his second daughter, the
mirror of crystal of the East ; and he took out the gift
for his youngest daughter, the Scarlet Flower in a golden
vase. The elder daughters were beside themselves with
joy and carried off their gifts to their lofty bowers, where
they took their fill of delight over them at leisure. But the
youngest dearest daughter, when she saw the Scarlet
Flower, shook all over and began to weep, as if something
had stung her heart. Then her father spoke thus to her—

"Daughter dear, why do you not take your flower
which you desired ? It is the fairest thing in all the world."
The youngest daughter took the Scarlet Flower, as if unwillingly, and kissed her father's hands, but wept tears of
sorrow. Soon the elder daughters hastened back : they
had tried their father's gifts, and they were joyful exceedingly. Then they sat down at tables of oak, covered with
fine napery and laden with choice dishes and delicious
wines ; and they began to eat and to drink, to refresh
themselves and make merry with loving speeches. At
evening guests came ; and the merchant's house was filled
with guests—kinsfolk and friends, and lovers of good cheer.
Till midnight the company sat and talked, and never had
the honest merchant seen such an evening of feasting in
his house ; and he, and they all, marvelled whence all
things came, the gold and silver dishes and the wonderful
meats, such as never had been seen in the house before.

Next day the merchant summoned his eldest daughter
and told her, from first to last, what had befallen him,
and asked her if she was willing to save him from a cruel
death, and to go and live with the Beast of the forest, the
Monster of the deep. The eldest daughter refused utterly
to go, and said—

"The daughter, for whom her father got the Scarlet
Flower—let *her* go and rescue her father."

Then the honest merchant summoned his second
daughter, and told her all that had befallen him, all from
first to last, and asked her if she was willing to save him

from a cruel death, and to go and live with the Beast of the forest, the Monster of the deep. But the second daughter refused utterly to go and said—

"The daughter for whom her father got the Scarlet Flower—let *her* go and rescue her father."

Then the honest merchant summoned his youngest daughter and began to tell her all his tale from first to last ; but, before he had time to finish his tale, the youngest daughter, whom he loved best, fell on her knees before him and said—

"Give me your blessing, O my lord and father ! I will go to the Beast of the forest, the Monster of the deep, and live with him. It was for me you got the Scarlet Flower, and it is my duty to save you."

The honest merchant shed tears, and embraced his youngest dearest daughter, and spoke thus to her—

"O my youngest and dearest daughter, darling of my heart and fair to see, may a father's blessing rest upon you, because you are willing to save your father from a cruel death, and consent of your own free will to go to the Beast of the forest, the Monster of the deep, to live a terrible life with him. You will live in his palace in great wealth and freedom ; but where the palace is, no man knows nor can tell ; nor is there any way to it for man on horse, or man on foot, or bounding wild beast, or flying bird. Never will a word of tidings come from you to us, and much less from us to you. How can I live out my sad life, never seeing your face, never hearing your loving speeches ? I am parting with you for ever and ever, just as if I were burying you alive in the earth."

And the youngest dearest daughter answered her father—

"Weep not ; do not grieve, O my lord and father. I shall live in wealth and freedom ; and I fear not the Beast of the forest, the Monster of the deep ; I will serve him truly and faithfully, and be subject to him and do his bidding ; and it may be that he will have pity on me. Do not mourn me as dead while I yet live ; it may be that God will suffer me to return to you."

The honest merchant could not be comforted by her

words, but wept and sobbed. The elder sisters came in haste and raised the sound of weeping through all the house : right sorry, forsooth, were they for their dear youngest sister. But the youngest sister showed no sign of sorrow : she neither wept nor moaned, but made ready for a far journey to a land unknown ; and she took with her the Scarlet Flower in its golden vase. Three days passed and three nights, and the time came when the honest merchant must part with his youngest daughter, his darling. He kissed her and fondled her ; his sad tears fell upon her ; he made the sign of the Cross on her and gave her a father's blessing. Then he took out from an iron-bound coffer the ring of the Beast of the forest, the Monster of the deep, and he put the ring on the little finger of his dear daughter's right hand—and in the same moment she vanished, herself and all that belonged to her.

She found herself in the palace of the Beast of the forest, the Monster of the deep, in a lofty chamber built of stone. She was lying on a bed of carven gold, with feet of crystal ; beneath her was a mattress of swansdown, and over her a golden coverlet of China silk. It was as if she had never moved, had lived there all her life, had lain down to sleep and awakened. A concord of instruments, such as she had never heard in all her days, began to play. She got up from the bed of down, and saw all her belongings and the Scarlet Flower in its golden vase, there in the room —set out on tables of green malachite. And the chamber was richly furnished with all things : there were chairs to sit on, couches to lie on, garments to wear, and mirrors to look into. The whole of one wall was a mirror, and another was of gold, and a third all of silver, and the fourth wall was made of ivory of elephants and mammoths, adorned with rubies and sapphires. And she said to herself, " This must be my bed-chamber."

Then, desiring to see all the palace, she went forth to behold all the lofty chambers ; and on she went for a long time, marvelling at all the wonders there. Each chamber was fairer than the last, and all were fairer than the honest merchant, her father, had told her. And she took the Scarlet Flower out of its golden vase, and went down into the green gardens, where the birds sang to her their heavenly notes, and the trees and bushes and flowers waved their heads and seemed to bow before her, and the fountains of water shot higher, and the springs babbled louder at her coming. And she found the high place, the grassy hillock, where the honest merchant had plucked the Scarlet Flower, the fairest thing in all the world. She took the Scarlet Flower out of the golden vase, and was about to lay it where it was before ; but it flew out of her hands of its own accord, and grew on to its ancient stem, and blossomed fairer than before. Much she marvelled at such a miracle, and looked with joy at her Scarlet Flower in its beauty. Then she went back to her chambers in the palace, and in one of them there was a table laid. And she said to herself—

" Surely the Beast of the forest, the Monster of the deep, is not wrath with me, but will be to me a kind lord."

Then suddenly on the wall of white marble there appeared words in letters of fire—

" I am not thy lord but thy obedient slave. Thou art the mistress, and all that thy heart can desire, I will gladly fulfil."

She read the words in letters of fire, and they vanished instantly from the wall of white marble, as if they had never been there. Then it came into her mind to write a letter to her father and give him tidings of her. Hardly had she thought of it, when she saw a gold pen and ink and paper lying before her. And she wrote a letter to her dear father and sisters—

" Weep not for me, neither grieve. I live like a princess in the palace of the Beast of the forest, the Monster of the deep. Himself I never see nor hear ; but he writes to me in letters of fire on the white marble wall ; and he knows all my unspoken wishes and fulfils them on the instant ; and he will not be called my lord, but calls me the mistress."

Hardly had she written the letter and sealed it with a seal, when the letter vanished out of her hands and from her sight, as if it had never been there. The music began to play louder ; and dainty meats and delicious wines appeared

upon the table; and all the vessels were of red gold. Though
never in her life had she dined alone, she sat down cheerful
at the table, and ate and drank, and refreshed herself and
took pleasure in the music. After dinner, when she had
eaten, she lay down to rest; and the music played more
softly and further off, that it might not hinder her from
sleeping. When she had slept, she rose with a light heart
and went forth again to walk in the green gardens; for,
before her dinner, she had not had time to go through the
half of them, or see enough of the wonders they contained.
Every tree and bush and flower bent down before her;
and the ripe fruits, pears and peaches and juicy apples,
seemed to desire that she would taste them. For a long
time, almost till the evening, she walked to and fro in the
garden. Then she returned to her lofty chambers, and
there she saw a table laid, with dainty meats and delicious
wines on the table, all most excellent. And after supper she
went back to the chamber of white marble, where she had
read the words in letters of fire; and again she saw on the
wall more letters of fire that said—

"Is my lady content with her gardens and chambers,
with her entertainment and attendants?"

And the merchant's young daughter, the lovely maiden,
made answer with happy voice—

"Call me not lady, but be thou for ever my lord, a lord
kind and merciful. I will never depart from thy control;
and I am grateful to thee for all my entertainment. Nothing
better could be found in all the world than thy lofty
chambers and thy green gardens; why then should I not be
content? Never in my life have I seen such marvels; I
cannot yet get over my wonder. But I fear one thing:
I fear to sleep alone; in all thy lofty chambers there is not
a living soul but me."

Then out flashed the words in letters of fire on the
wall—

"Fear not, my lovely lady. Thou shalt not sleep
alone; for thy own handmaid, faithful and dear, is waiting
for thee. And there are many living creatures in the
palace, though thou canst not see nor hear them; and
they all watch over thee, even as I do, day and night; and

we will not suffer the wind to blow on thee or a grain of dust to settle upon thee."

Then the merchant's young daughter, the lovely maiden, went to her bedchamber to sleep; and there she found her own handmaiden, faithful and dear, standing by the bed. She was half-dead with fear, but rejoiced to see her young mistress, and kissed her lily hands and clasped her nimble feet. Her mistress too rejoiced to see her, and she questioned her of her father and her elder sisters and all those who served her in her maiden home. And then she told of what had befallen herself; so that the pair of them did not sleep before white dawn.

And thus the merchant's young daughter, the lovely maiden, began to spend her life. Every day new rich dresses were ready for her, with priceless adornments which no tongue can tell nor pen describe; every day there were new entertainments and diversions. She drove through the dark woods in chariots that went without horses, to the sound of music; and the trees parted and gave her a wide smooth road to pass over. And she began to occupy herself with the handiwork of young maidens: she embroidered widths of stuff with silver and gold, and made fringes with pearls close-set; and she sent presents to her dear father; and the richest width of all she gave to her kind entertainer, even the Beast of the forest, the Monster of the deep; and every day she went more often to the chamber with white marble walls, that she might speak kind words to her generous entertainer and read on the wall his answers and greetings in letters of fire.

So time passed, whether much or little—soon is a story told, but not so soon is a deed done—and the merchant's young daughter, the fair maiden, became accustomed to her life nothing surprised her or frightened her any more. She was served by invisible attendants, who ministered to her, and carried her in the chariots that went without horses, and made music for her, and performed all her commands. And she grew daily more in love with her kind lord; she saw that he loved her more than himself and had not called her his mistress for nothing; and she longed to hear his voice and speak with him, without

entering the chamber with marble walls or reading the
words in letters of fire. She began to beg and pray for
this , but the Beast of the forest, the Monster of the deep,
would not quickly consent to her entreaties ; for he feared
that his voice would terrify her. But she continued to
beg and beseech her kind entertainer, and he could not
refuse her. So he wrote for the last time in letters of fire
on the marble wall—

" Come to-day into the green garden ; sit down in thy
favourite bower that is hedged about with leaves and
branches and flowers ; and say these words : ' Speak with
me, my faithful slave.' "

The merchant's young daughter, the lovely maiden,
let no time pass : down she ran into the green gardens, and
went into her favourite bower, hedged about with leaves
and branches and flowers ; and she sat down on the bench
covered with brocade. She was panting, and her heart
beat like the heart of a little bird you hold in your hand ;
but she spoke thus—

" Fear not, my kind and gracious lord, to terrify me with
thy voice. After all thy kindnesses, even the roaring of a
wild beast would not terrify me. Speak to me, and fear
not ! "

She heard a sound of some one sighing behind the bower,
and a voice arose, a terrible voice, savage and untuneable,
gruff and hoarse, though it was speaking low as yet. And
the merchant's young daughter, the lovely maiden,
shuddered at first when she heard the voice of the Beast
of the forest, the Monster of the deep ; but she mastered
her fear and showed no sign of it ; and soon she began to
listen to his kindly words and his wise speeches, and her
heart grew light.

After that time there was constant talk between them,
nearly the whole day, as they walked in the green gardens
or drove through the dark woods, and in all the lofty
chambers of the palace. The merchant's young daughter,
the lovely maiden, would call out—

" Art thou here, my dear kind lord ? " And the Beast of
the forest, the Monster of the deep, would answer—

" Here, my fair lady, is thy faithful slave, thy

unchanging friend." She had no fear of his savage and terrible voice, and they talked as friends to each other without end.

And time passed, whether a short time or a long time—soon is a story told, but not so soon is a thing done—and the merchant's young daughter, the lovely maiden, longed to see with her own eyes the Beast of the forest, the Monster of the deep; but for long he would not consent; for he feared to terrify her. And he was indeed terrible to behold, beyond the power of any tongue to tell or pen to write: not men only but wild beasts, whenever they beheld him, were terrified and slunk away to their dens. And the Beast of the forest, the Monster of the deep, spoke thus—

"Beg me not, O lovely lady and delight of my eyes, to show thee my terrible face and my deformed body. To my voice thou art now accustomed; we live in friendship and concord; scarcely do we part one from another; and thou lovest me for my unspeakable love to thee. But when thou seest all my hideous deformity, thou wilt hate unhappy me, and drive me from thy sight; and I shall die of grief, when parted from thee."

But the merchant's young daughter, the lovely maiden, would not hearken to his words. She entreated him more earnestly than before, and she vowed and swore that no extreme of deformity would terrify her, and that she would never cease to love her kind lord; and she spoke to him thus—

"If thou art old, be my grandfather; if thou art of middle age, be my uncle; but, if thou art young, be as my brother to me; and, while I live, be thou the friend of my heart."

Long, long did the Beast of the forest, the Monster of the deep, hold out against her prayer; but he could not withstand the entreaties and tears of his lovely lady, and at last he said—

"I cannot gainsay thee. Because I love thee more than myself, I will grant thy desire, although I know that I shall destroy my happiness and die an untimely death. Go down into the green garden in the grey twilight, when the red sun is setting behind the forest, and say : ' Show thyself to me, faithful friend ! ' and I will show thee my hideous face and my deformed body. And, if it is impossible for thee to stay longer with me, I will put no force on thee, nor would I have thee suffer without end : thou wilt find in thy bedchamber, beneath thy pillow, the gold ring from off my finger. Put it on the little finger of thy right hand, and thou wilt find thyself in thy father's house⁰; and never more shalt thou hear aught of me."

The merchant's young daughter, the lovely maiden, had strong confidence in herself ; she was not alarmed or afraid. At once, without delaying a moment, she went into the green garden to await the appointed hour ; and, when grey twilight came, and the red sun was sinking behind the forest, she said aloud—

" Show thyself to me, my faithful friend."

And the Beast of the forest, the Monster of the deep, appeared to her at a distance ; he only walked across the path and was lost in the thick bushes. But when the merchant's young daughter, the lovely maiden, saw him, she struck her lily hands together, and cried out in a voice of anguish, and fell senseless on the path. For terrible indeed he was, the Beast of the forest, the Monster of the deep. His arms were crooked, and his fingers were like a wild beast's talons ; he had the legs of a horse, and great humps like a camel's before and behind ; he was covered with hair from head to foot ; tusks like a wild boar's stuck out of his mouth ; his nose was curved like an eagle's beak, and he had the eyes of an owl. The merchant's young daughter, the lovely maiden, lay there a long time or a short time ; and when she came to herself, she heard some one near her weeping tears of anguish and crying with a sorrowful voice—

" Thou hast destroyed me, my beautiful darling : no more shall I see thy fair face ; no longer wilt thou be willing even to hear my voice ; and I must die an untimely death."

And she was sorry and ashamed, and she mastered her great fear and timid maiden heart, and spoke with a firm voice—

" Fear nothing, my kind and gentle lord; I will
never again fear thy terrible shape, I will never part with
thee or forget thy kindnesses. Show thyself to me now in
thy former shape; only because it was the first time, I
was afraid."

And the Beast of the forest, the Monster of the deep,
showed himself to her in his terrible shape so hideous and
deformed; but he did not venture to come near her,
however much she called him. And they walked together
till dark night came, and talked as before with love and
wisdom, and the merchant's young daughter, the lovely
maiden, felt no fear. Next day she saw the Beast of the
forest, the Monster of the deep, by the light of the red sun ;
and, though she was frightened at first to look upon him,
she gave no sign of it, and soon her fear passed away
altogether. And now they conversed together more than
ever : they hardly parted the whole day long ; at dinner
and supper they took their fill of dainty meats and refreshed
themselves with delicious wines ; they walked in the green
gardens, and drove through the dark woods in the chariots
that ran without horses. And time not a little passed by :
soon is a story told, but not so quickly does a thing happen.
And one night, in her sleep, the merchant's young daughter,
the fair maiden, dreamed that her father was lying sick ;
and constant grief took hold of her. And the Beast of the
forest, the Monster of the deep, saw her in her grief and
tears, and was sore distressed, and asked her the reason
of her grief and tears. And she told him of her evil dream,
and asked him to suffer her to visit her father and her dear
sisters. And the Beast of the forest, the Monster of the
deep, answered her—

" What need hast thou of my permission ? Thou hast
my gold ring : put it on the little finger of thy right hand,
and thou wilt find thyself in thy father's house. Remain
there till thou art weary, and this only will I say to thee : if
thou dost not return at the end of three days and three
nights, that will end my life, and I shall die in that instant,
because I love thee better than myself and cannot live
without thee."

Then she began to assure him with solemn words and

oaths and vows, that she would return to his high palace one hour exactly before the three days and three nights expired. She said farewell to her gentle and kind entertainer, and put the gold ring on the little finger of her right hand, and found herself standing in the wide courtyard of the honest merchant, her father.

She went up the high steps of his mansion of stone ; and all the attendants and servants of the house hastened towards her with a noise and shouting ; and her dear sisters ran to meet her, and, when they saw her, marvelled at her maiden beauty and her royal apparel. Then they took her by her lily hands, and led her to her father ; and her father was lying sick—sick and sad, as he thought of her day and night and shed tears of anguish. Exceeding glad was he, when he saw his youngest daughter whom he loved best, dear and virtuous and fair to see ; and he marvelled at her maiden beauty and her royal apparel. For long they kissed and caressed one another, and comforted their hearts with loving words. Then she told her father and her sisters of her manner of life with the Beast of the forest, the Monster of the deep ; she told them all from first to last, not hiding a single crumb ; and the honest merchant rejoiced to hear of the splendour in which she lived, like a queen or empress ; and he marvelled that she had become accustomed to the sight of her terrible host, and had no fear of the Beast of the forest, the Monster of the deep ; he himself, at the mere thought of him, trembled and shook. But the elder sisters, when they heard of the boundless wealth of the youngest sister, and of her power over her lord, as if she were a queen and he her slave, became jealous of her.

The day passed like one hour, and the second day passed like one minute ; and on the third day the elder sisters began to persuade the youngest sister not to return to the Beast of the forest, the Monster of the deep : " Even let him die, as he deserves," said they. But their guest, the youngest sister, was angry with the elder sisters and spoke to them thus —

" My lord is kind and gentle ; and if I repay him by a cruel death for all his goodness and his love unspeakable,

z

then I shall not be worthy to look on the light of day, and I should be given to wild beasts to tear."

Her father, the honest merchant, praised her for having spoken well; and it was determined that the youngest dearest daughter, virtuous and fair, should return one hour before the appointed time to the Beast of the forest, the Monster of the deep. But the sisters were angry at it, and they devised a cunning plan, a cunning and a wicked device : they put back by a whole hour all the clocks in the house; and the honest merchant did not see it, nor any of the faithful servants that waited in his house. And when the right hour came, the merchant's young daughter, the lovely maiden, felt pain and trouble, as if something were pulling at her heart, and she looked constantly at the clocks in her father's house, clocks from Germany and clocks from England—and still it was too early to start on her far journey ; and her sisters talked with her of this and that, and detained her. But at last she could bear it no longer : she said farewell to the honest merchant, her father, and received from him a father's blessing ; she said farewell to her dear elder sisters, and to the faithful servants and attendants Then, one minute before the hour appointed, she put the gold ring on the little finger of her right hand, and found herself standing in the palace of white marble, in the lofty palace of the Beast of the forest, the Monster of the deep.

She wondered that he did not come to meet her, and she cried out in a loud voice—

" Where art thou, my kind lord, my faithful friend ? Why dost thou not meet me ? I returned earlier than the appointed time by a whole hour and one minute."

None answered, none hailed her; there was dead silence all around; in the green gardens the heavenly notes of the birds were silent, the fountains had ceased to spout, and the springs made no noise ; and there was no sound of music in the lofty palace. The merchant's daughter, the lovely maiden, felt her heart tremble, and was aware of coming trouble; she ran through the lofty chambers and the green gardens, and called her kind host with a voice of anguish ; but nowhere was there any answer

or greeting or voice of any that replied. Then she ran to
the grassy hillock, where grew in beauty her Scarlet Flower ;
and she saw the Beast of the forest, the Monster of the deep,
lying there on the hillock and clasping the Scarlet Flower
in his paw-like arms. She thought that he had gone to
sleep while waiting for her, and was now sound asleep.
The merchant's daughter, the lovely maid, began to wake
him gently, but he did not answer ; then she began to wake
him more roughly, and caught hold of his shaggy paw ; and
she saw that the Beast of the forest, the Monster of the
deep, was lying a dead corpse on the ground.

Her clear eyes grew dark ; her nimble feet gave way
beneath her ; she put her white arms round the head of her
dear lord, that hideous horrible head, and cried out in a voice
of anguish—

"Arise, awake, O friend of my heart ! I love thee as
the bride loves the bridegroom, dear and desired ! "

Hardly had she spoken these words, when the lightning
flashed from every side, and the earth shook with a great
crash of thunder, and the stone arrow of the thunder struck
the grassy hillock ; and the merchant's young daughter,
the fair maiden, fell senseless on the ground.

Whether she lay senseless a long time or a short time,
I cannot tell. But, when she became conscious, she was
sitting on a golden throne set with precious stones in a
lofty hall of white marble ; and a prince, young and lovely,
held her in his arms ; and he was robed in cloth of gold,
and wore a kingly crown on his head. And before her
stood her father and her sisters ; and round them were
kneeling a throng of courtiers, all apparelled in brocade of
gold and silver. And the lovely young prince with the
royal crown upon his head spoke thus to her—

"My beauty and my darling, thou didst love me in the
form of a hideous monster, for my kind heart and the love
I bore thee. Then love me now when I wear human shape,
and be my bride. A wicked witch was wrath with my
father, who, while he yet lived, was a glorious and mighty
king ; she stole me away while I was still a child, and by her
foul arts and devilish enchantments turned me into a
hideous monster, and laid a spell upon me, that I should

live in that hideous form, a terror to every man and even to the beasts God made, until a fair maiden should be found, whatever were her birth or condition, who would love me in my monstrous shape and desire to be my wedded wife. Then the spell would come to an end, and I should get back my human shape, and be young and fair to see. Full thirty years I lived a monster and a terror; and I enticed to my enchanted palace eleven fair maidens, and thou wert the twelfth. Not one of them loved me in return for my kindness and good treatment of them, or for my kind heart. Thou alone didst love me, a hideous and horrible monster, in return for my kindness and good treatment of thee, and for my kind heart, and for my exceeding love to thee; and therefore thou shalt be the bride of a glorious king, the queen over a mighty kingdom."

Then all were astonished, and the courtiers bowed down to the ground. The honest merchant gave his blessing to his dear youngest daughter and to the young prince. And the envious elder sisters and all the faithful servants, and all the great nobles and brave warriors, wished joy to the bridegroom and the bride And they began at once to make merry; and soon came the wedding; and they lived happily ever afterwards.

I was at the wedding myself, and drank beer and mead; but it all ran down my chin and none went down my throat.*

* This seems to be a stock ending to a Russian fairy-story. I suppose it implies that, as the feast was a Barmecide feast, so all the narrative must be regarded as fictitious.

THE END

PRINTED BY WILLIAM CLOWES AND SONS, LIMITED, LONDON AND BECCLES, ENGLAND

Telegrams "Scholarly, London." 41 and 43 Maddox Street,
Telephone 1883 Mayfair. Bond Street, London, W

Partners · {E. A Arnold
           {A. L Mumm *March*, 1917

Mr. Edward Arnold's

SPRING
ANNOUNCEMENTS, 1917.

FRENCH WINDOWS.

By JOHN AYSCOUGH,
AUTHOR OF "MAROTZ," "SAN CELESTINO," ETC.

Crown 8vo. **5s. net.**

In the literature of the war a large space has already been occupied by reflections on its spiritual influence and effects, but for the most part the subject has been handled in abstract and generalized terms In the present series of sketches John Ayscough has presented the aspect of the war dramatically, and embodied it in a number of individual concrete instances His creed and calling gave him special opportunities for getting into touch with men of all sorts and conditions, but only a man with his rare endowment of sympathy and insight could have turned them to account as he has done. From what has been said it follows naturally that he is not concerned directly with actual war scenes and episodes, though incidentally he gives us some illuminating glimpses of life under war conditions Most of his stories are in form reports of his conversations with French and British soldiers, as a rule originating in trifling accidents, and conducted in every variety of setting But each conversation is, in fact, a portrait and a history. Our author appears to be equally at home with both nationalities The scenes in which our own people figure have a beauty and truth which all of us can recognize and enjoy, while to most English readers the presentment of the soul of the French soldier-peasant will be a revelation.

LONDON . EDWARD ARNOLD, 41 & 43 MADDOX STREET, W.

A DOCTOR'S DIARY IN DAMARALAND.

By Dr H. F. B. WALKER.

With Illustrations. Demy 8vo. **7s. 6d. net.**

Early in 1915 Dr Walker offered his services to General
Botha, and was appointed to one of the Mounted Brigade Field
Ambulances   He sailed from Cape Town on March 11th, and
after a short stay at Walfisch Bay, arrived on the 22nd at
Swakupmund, where he spent five disagreeable but instructive
weeks   He then started inland, and struggled through with his
unit, or so much of it as could be got along, to the old capital,
Otjimbingwe   There for some time he conducted a hospital,
under grave difficulties, complicated by serious apprehension with
regard to the continuance of the food-supply. Finally he was taken
on to Windhuk, and at the close of the war returned by a not
uneventful railway journey to Luderitzbucht.   Dr. Walker is a
practised observer, and possesses in an unusual degree the power of
recording graphically the results of his observations   Wherever he
goes he notes with unflagging attention the character of the fauna
and flora of the country, and its salient geological and physio-
graphical features   The latter, indeed, were forced upon his notice,
especially during the really terrible journey to Otjimbingwe, in an
extremely drastic fashion, and we venture to assert that his
portrayal of the extraordinary and fantastic region then
traversed possesses a vividness which no record of an ordinary
trek in peace time could approach

But this by no means exhausts the range of his interests   Upon
the solid foundations of physical geography he gradually builds
up for the reader a vivid and convincing picture of the German
colonists, their lives, and their relations with the natives, and of
German colonial methods in general.   Further, though it was his
painful rôle to be always toiling a long way in the rear of his brigade
(the Boers' motto was " To h—l with transport and ambulance !
Let's ride "), he managed in one way and another to pick up a
pretty clear idea of the progress of the war.   Here again his
powers of observation stood him in good stead   The character
of the fighting was determined in the main, as it always is, by
geographical conditions, and his firm grasp of these makes his
book a particularly satisfactory introduction to the story of a
campaign which must surely be unique in military annals.

A RUSSIAN GENTLEMAN.

By SERGE AKSAKOFF.

Translated from the Russian by J. D. DUFF,
FELLOW OF TRINITY COLLEGE, CAMBRIDGE.

Demy 8vo.   7s. 6d. net.

Mr. J. D. Duff, whose translation of Aksakoff's "Years of Childhood" was issued last year, has now ready another volume of Aksakoff's Memoirs This book was called by its author "Family History," but the translation will be called "A Russian Gentleman." It contains the history of the author's grandfather, and ends on the day when Aksakoff himself was born Thus the whole narrative is derived, not from personal experience, but from tradition Yet this seems to make little difference to Aksakoff, who describes the courtship and marriage of his parents as minutely as if he had been present This is Aksakoff's most famous book, and the portrait of his grandfather, Stepan Mihailovitch, the most formidable and most lovable of men, is the finest in his whole gallery. The minute account of Russian life in the days of the Empress Catherine is priceless to the historian; and the dramatic skill and human interest of the narrative have fascinated Russian readers for sixty years past.

Aksakoff wrote one other volume of Memoirs—his "Recollections" of school and college This also has been translated; and it is hoped that the translation may be published at no long interval.

BY THE SAME AUTHOR

YEARS OF CHILDHOOD.

By SERGE AKSAKOFF.

Translated from the Russian by J. D. DUFF.

Demy 8vo   10s. 6d. net.

"'Years of Childhood' becomes the more fascinating the more one reads and thinks about it. Aksakoff read a new and ecstatic meaning into things which are banal and tame to most men and women, and the eager eye of his mind scanned deep into the lives and loves of the people round about him."— *Morning Post*

"A charming Russian book At this time when so many translations from the Russian are appearing, well advised and ill advised, it is good to be able to put the hand on one superlatively good book. Here is a refreshment for tired eyes and tired souls It is put into beautiful English."—*Country Life.*

THE ITALIAN ORDERS OF ARCHITECTURE.

A Practical Book for the Use of Architects and Craftsmen.

By CHARLES GOURLAY, B.Sc. (Glasgow Univ.),

PROFESSOR OF ARCHITECTURE AND BUILDING IN THE ROYAL TECHNICAL COLLEGE, GLASGOW.

With 32 plates   Demy 4to   **6s. net.**

While this work appeals to all who desire an aquaintance with the Italian Orders of Architecture exhibited in their most generally usef l form, it has been more directly prepared to aid architectural students who require to know the Orders so thoroughly as to be masters of them both as Orders and in their application, for the decorative part of modern architecture is largely based upon them   The work will also serve as a reference book by architects when designing, by quantity surveyors, furniture designers, and building craftsmen   The plates have been specially designed and drawn in a decided manner to show clearly the detail of all the mouldings and such parts as are generally of an obscure nature   The preparation of this book has extended over many years, and is the outcome of the author's long experience of teaching and of his frequent visits to Italy, France, and Greece.

THE ROYAL MAIL TO IRELAND.

AN ACCOUNT OF THE ORIGIN AND DEVELOPMENT OF THE POST BETWEEN LONDON AND IRELAND THROUGH HOLYHEAD, AND THE USE OF THE LINE OF COMMUNICATION BY TRAVELLERS.

By EDWARD WATSON.

With illustrations.   Demy 8vo.

This book will fill a distinct place in all libraries of the social history of the British Isles, in that for the first time it presents a reliable account, based on State papers and other official documents, of the postal connection with Ireland which has been kept up for the last three hundred and fifty years   Mr Watson having been for a long time past intimately acquainted with all the circumstances relating to the Holyhead mail service, supplements the particulars relating to the more modern part of the book by facts regarding which he has personal knowledge.

Anyone who is in the habit of using this route will be interested to read of the conditions under which passengers formerly travelled, and will no doubt feel grateful to those who have in the past been instrumental in improving the service.

There are some interesting illustrations from old engravings and portraits.

NEW NOVELS

Mr. Edward Arnold intends in future to make Fiction a more prominent feature of his Catalogue, and is arranging to publish some first-rate novels by popular writers. Among those ready for immediate publication are the following

A MARRIAGE HAS BEEN ARRANGED.

By RACHEL SWETE MACNAMARA,

AUTHOR OF "THE FRINGE OF THE DESERT," "DRIFTING WATERS," " THE AWAKENING," ETC.

Crown 8vo. Cloth. **6s.**

In Miss Macnamara's previous novels, "The Fringe of the Desert" and "Drifting Waters," which achieved both distinction and success, the scenes were overlaid with the romantic glamour of Egypt But it is to a *critique* of another of her books, "The Awakening," that the genesis of "A Marriage has been Arranged" is due "Toye Tempest is an admirable creation One really does not know whether she is a wicked little devil or not. There are extraordinary possibilities in her. She excites our unalloyed curiosity" Although in no sense a sequel to "The Awakening," the principal character in Miss Macnamara's new novel is the impish, uncomfortably attractive Toye It sets forth the story of the great adventure of her life—how she won her heart's desire, and the complications that ensued, and how, having won it, her curious character develops in unexpected directions The scene is laid almost entirely in England—the England of yesterday There is a strong love element running through the book, which is stimulating and attractive.

THE WANE OF UXENDEN.

By MARGARET LEGGE,

AUTHOR OF "THE REBELLION OF ESTHER," ETC

Crown 8vo. Cloth. **6s.**

In previous novels by this author, among which perhaps "The Rebellion of Esther" found most admirers, she has attempted to study the many gradual changes and the transitional condition of the life of to-day, and in "The Wane of Uxenden" is delineated the decline from former prosperity of one of those old English county families whose history is so closely interwoven with the history and the character of the English nation.

After a tragic break in the circumstances of her own life, Hermione Cheadle, a twentieth-century woman journalist, goes back to stay at Uxenden with those friends amongst whom she passed the happiest days of her childhood. She finds the lovely old home almost in ruins, the family prosperity gone, but with their prejudices surviving as strongly as ever, and the family are awaiting, without taking any steps to avert, the impending ruin and break-up of the estate with the same quiet, unflinching spirit that has built up their character through many generations A pleasant and life-like picture of family life at Uxenden gives the setting wherein Hermione moves among these kindly and old-fashioned people, where her beauty and charm of character inspire love and disinterested rivalry.

In striking contrast with this restful country conservatism, Hermione, in the course of her activities in London, is brought into contact with a phase of unhealthy spiritualistic charlatanism to which certain of her friends have succumbed, and is successful in rescuing a relative from its enervating seduction, and in exposing the prime mover and his dupes in a striking and realistic manner.

FETTERS ON THE FEET.

By Mrs. FRED REYNOLDS,
Author of "A Quaker's Wooing," etc., etc

Crown 8vo. Cloth. **6s.**

In "A Quaker's Wooing"—probably one of the best-known novels by this author—she drew a picturesque and vivid picture of Quaker life as it was a hundred years ago. In her latest work, "Fetters on the Feet," the frame of the picture is modern, and only occasional glimpses appear in the background

The principal character, Margaret Grenfield, had been brought up by Quaker relatives, and the story opens amid Quaker surroundings and sentiments, but she is not really of them, as her father had been a soldier and had died fighting, and had consequently been disowned by the rest of the family. So long as her home is with her relatives, who are really very fond of her, and kind in their own strict, undemonstrative way, she falls in fairly naturally with the dull, drab household of Chevin Lodge, and the endless round of guilds, societies, lectures, and missions, but to escape from the quaintly declared admiration of her cousin, she finds a thorough change, both mental and atmospheric, as com-

panion to a wealthy middle-aged lady living amid the wind-swept
Yorkshire moors.

The complications that here ensue owing to the charm she
exercises over various people with whom she is thrown, are made
the more interesting from the contrasts offered by the remains of
her Quaker instincts that still linger from her early upbringing,
and the moral reasoning that seems inseparable from these contrasts is touched in with a light and deft hand

JOHN PARAMOR'S PURPOSE.

By ELLEN ADA SMITH.

Crown 8vo. **6s.**

John Paramor, as a small boy of nine or ten, had already
formed very practical views of life, he had already discovered
that money is power, and at that early age he determined to
grasp it His father and mother and sister lived in a suburb,
and John felt that that was no permanent place for him. His
father had a first cousin married to a lady of title, and nourished
a jealous hatred of him, of his charm, of his prosperity, and
of his charming wife, who periodically pays the suburban cousins
formal visits, but formal only by reason of this small-minded
jealousy, which has no place in her own heart.

The development of John Paramor, stiff, unbending,
methodical, unswerving in the pursuit of money to the stifling
of every finer emotion, forms the motive of this story, in contrast
with the open generosity of feeling and kindliness of his
cousins, which in the end opens the door to his better nature
The fine poetic justice by which John Paramor in the complete
fulfilment of his aims which embrace the utter ruin of his
cousins, is by them utterly ruined in his own self-esteem and
his purpose broken down, is told in a manner which interests
and compels thought

THE MASSAREEN AFFAIR.

By R. K. WEEKES.

Crown 8vo. **6s.**

An unhappy marriage for Anthony Massareen ; a cousin,
Claudia, fond of him and his two children, an elopement on the
understanding that they live together as brother and sister—these
are the elements of the Massareen affair , its developments involve
the fortunes of a second group of persons, the family of a country
clergyman The father is a grim figure, orthodox and very

uncompromising, but withal very human himself, and saved from
fanaticism by an intense interest in human nature, however
manifested, provided it is genuine, in other people. A daughter,
as uncompromising in her own way as he, will be regarded by
many readers as the heroine, and the methods by which she won
her airman and stung into life his dormant nobility of soul, as
providing the main interest, of the book

The other characters are alive and entertaining, they are like-
able and by no means "unco' guid," and throughout the story the
aeroplane plays a leading part, and appears as naturally as a train
or motor-car.

THE SPRING SONG.

By FORREST REID,

AUTHOR OF "AT THE DOOR OF THE GATE," "THE GENTLE LOVER," ETC

One Volume.   Crown 8vo.   6s.

" This is really a very unusual story that Mr Forrest Reid has written.
His pen takes a path of its own , the reader regards it doubtfully at the outset,
so different is it from known roads and methods, the recognized conventions
But, the first suspicions being overcome, an interest develops strongly, it
increases, and we move on to a climax that is full of excitement   Nothing
save the book itself can indicate its peculiar atmosphere and its real merit "
—*Daily Telegraph*

" Mr Reid has hitherto written for an audience of quality only, but his new
book, ' The Spring Song,' should bring him something near the popular success of Mr Kenneth Graham   Not since ' The Golden Age' and 'Dream
Days' has any English writer written with such knowledge, insight, and
absence of sentimental delusion of a family of children as Mr Reid displays
in this delightful tale "—*Westminster Gazette*

' Mr Reid has taken a definite step upward in novel-craft with the publication of 'A Spring Song'   Here is certainly a piece of work that should be
noted for it has imagination, originality, humour, and last, but not least,
a very human wistfulness of outlook   ' The Spring Song' will surely lighten
many grey hearts in these troublesome times "—*Daily Chronicle*

" A very exquisite book, written with rare charm and great art."—*Manchester
Guardian*

" That the field of child life, far from being barren, offers a rich harvest to
the true artist is proved by the success of Mr Forrest Reid's latest book.   It
is the freshest and most alluring story he has yet given us, deliciously simple
with the simplicity that springs not from artlessness but from cunning crafts-
manship " -*Northern Whig*

THE MOTOR-CAR : What It Is and How to

Drive It.   By T. O A. LAWTON and Prof HARVEY GIBSON
Limp cloth   **1s. net.**

Written by a novice and an expert, this book is designed for readers who
approach the subject in a state of complete ignorance , accordingly nothing
is taken for granted.

Arnold's Two Shilling Edition of Popular Fiction.

This series has been started with the object of making known to a more extended public some of the most successful novels published in recent years The names of George A. Birmingham, Dorothea Conyers, and Mrs. Alfred Sidgwick, need no introduction to novel readers, and the following examples of their work are now issued in a popular form, with specially designed coloured wrappers.

THE SEETHING POT. By George A. Birmingham, author of "Spanish Gold," etc *Cloth* 2s. net.

"A very brilliant and detached study of Ireland of yesterday and to-day " —*Spectator*
"An absorbingly interesting book "—*Manchester Guardian*
"The novel should be read by everyone who recognizes in politics an affair not merely of statistics, but of passionate preoccupation "—*Morning Post*

THE BOY, SOME HORSES, AND A GIRL. By Dorothea Conyers, author of " Peter's Pedigree," etc *Cloth.* 2s. net.

"This is the best story of Irish Life which we have read since ' The Adventures of an Irish R M ' Indeed, it runs that masterpiece very close, if it does not equal it From first to last the spirit and humour of it never flags If anyone can read it without laughing, we are sorry for them The story is admirably written, and deserves wide popularity "—*Irish Times*
"Full of graphic description, racy dialogue, and the *joie de vivre* "—*Spectator.*
"Full of humour, true, ready, and spontaneous."—*St James's Gazette*

CYNTHIA'S WAY. By Mrs. Alfred Sidgwick, author of "The Beryl Stones," "The Lantern Bearers," etc *Cloth* 2s. net.

"The book is full of humour, and of what, for want of a better word, we must call ' local colour ' Every page is thoroughly enjoyable, and one lays it down with a deep feeling of gratitude to the author."—*Guardian*
"No one who has lived in Germany can afford to miss Mrs Sidgwick's novel ' Cynthia's Way ' Mrs Sidgwick is one of the very few writers of the present day who can look at Continental life with a thoroughly British eye, but, at the same time, with a thoroughly understanding heart "—*The Sketch.*

GHOST STORIES OF AN ANTIQUARY By Dr Montague Rhodes James, Provost of King's College, Cambridge. *Cloth.* 2s. net.

"We do not hesitate to say that these are among the best ghost stories we have ever read, they rank with that greatest of all ghost stories, Lord Lytton's ' The Haunted and the Haunters ' The author has certainly succeeded in making his readers feel ' pleasantly uncomfortable,' if he has not gone beyond it We read the book with pleasure in such daylight as is afforded by a November afternoon in London, but we turned from it with a shiver at 11 p m "—*Guardian*

New and Recent War Books.

NEW AND CHEAPER EDITION.

A SURGEON IN KHAKI.

By the late A. A MARTIN, M D, F.R C S. ENG.

With Illustrations.   Cloth   2s. 6d. net.

Dr Martin was a New Zealander who had served in the South African War, and being in England when the present war broke out he joined the Royal Army Medical Corps, and was with his Field Ambulance at the Battle of the Marne and for some months after both in France and Flanders   This book describes his experiences, and it has been found so much to the taste of the public that it has already been reprinted five times in its more expensive form   Subsequently, after a visit home, Dr Martin returned to the front, and was killed on the Somme while attending to wounded in the front trenches.

" A superlatively interesting book "—*Graphic*
" A book full of life and human feeling. 'A Surgeon in Khaki' will certainly live as a first-class description of a portion of the great war "—*Field.*
" A book of extraordinary interest   There are many stories, grave and gay, in this book, which should be widely read   It is quite a remarkable book and gives a wonderful vision of what war is."—*Birmingham Daily Post*

LIGHT AND SHADE IN WAR.   By CAPTAIN MALCOLM ROSS, Official War Correspondent with the New Zealand Forces, and NOEL ROSS   *With Illustrations.   Third Impression.*   5s. net.

" The 'big push,' Fricourt and La Boiselle, a visit to the battle cruisers of the 'cat squadron,' and several chapters that are delightful fantasies of bubbling humour, all come in this olla-podrida book   It is full of Anzac virility, full of Anzac buoyancy, and surcharged with that devil-may-care humour that has so astounded us jaded peoples of an older world "—*Daily Mail.*

VERDUN TO THE VOSGES.   Impressions of the War on the Fortress Frontier of France   By GERALD CAMPBELL, Special Correspondent of *The Times* in the East of France.   *With Illustrations and Maps.*   10s. 6d. net.   *Second Impression*

" A deeply impressive, well-informed book   Mr Campbell's book will well repay careful and patient study   It penetrates beneath the surface of the fighting "—*Daily Telegraph.*

A FRENCH MOTHER IN WAR TIME.
By MADAME E DRUMONT   Translated by MISS G BEVIR.
3s. 6d. net.

New and Recent War Books—*Continued.*

A SURGEON IN BELGIUM. By H. S. SOUTTAR, F.R C.S, Late Surgeon-in-Chief of the Belgian Field Hospital. *Illustrated* Popular Edition, paper cover. **2s. net;** cloth, **2s. 6d. net.**

EYE-WITNESS'S NARRATIVE OF THE WAR From the Marne to Neuve Chapelle, September, 1914—March, 1915. Paper, **1s. net;** cloth, **2s. net.**

A YEAR AGO. Being the concluding portion of "Eye-Witness's Narrative of the War," from March to July, 1915. By COL E. D SWINTON, R.E , D.S O , and CAPT. THE EARL PERCY. Paper, **2s. net;** cloth, **2s. 6d. net.**

Scientific Works.

AN INTRODUCTION TO SPECIAL SCHOOL WORK.

By MARION F BRIDIE, L L.A.,
ASSISTANT SUPERINTENDENT OF SPECIAL SCHOOLS, BIRMINGHAM

Crown 8vo   Cloth. **3s. 6d. net.**

This is an attempt to provide a simple non-medical book written from a purely educational point of view for those engaged in the teaching of mentally defective children. This is a subject that has hitherto been developed almost entirely by means of conferences and verbal intercourse, and it is anticipated that the information gained by the author from visits to Germany and the United States, as well as to many towns in England and Scotland, has enabled her to write a book that fills a gap and will be of considerable service to teachers.

MALINGERING
AND FEIGNED SICKNESS

By SIR JOHN COLLIE, M.D., J P ,
MEDICAL EXAMINER, LONDON COUNTY COUNCIL , CHIEF MEDICAL OFFICER, METROPOLITAN WATER BOARD , CONSULTING MEDICAL EXAMINER TO THE SHIPPING FEDERATION , MEDICAL EXAMINER TO THE SUN INSURANCE OFFICE, CENTRAL INSURANCE COMPANY, LONDON, LIVERPOOL, AND GLOBE INSURANCE COMPANY, ETC

New Edition, revised and greatly enlarged.

" This is a valuable book It systematically describes how to examine each part of the body, and discusses the chief morbid conditions simulated by malingerers, with the best means of testing the genuineness of the case or detecting fraud "—*The Times*

ARBOREAL MAN.

By F. WOOD JONES, M.B., D.Sc.,

PROFESSOR OF ANATOMY IN THE UNIVERSITY OF LONDON (LONDON SCHOOL OF
MEDICINE FOR WOMEN)

With 81 Illustrations. Demy 8vo.   **8s. 6d. net.**

". . Professor Wood Jones has added much new information as the
result of his own investigations, and has presented the whole argument with
all the lucidity and brilliance of the conspicuously successful teacher he has
proved himself to be "—*Nature*

"'Arboreal Man'" is not only first-hand, it is first-rate. Those who are
familiar with current anatomical literature recognize that Professor Wood
Jones has earned for himself a place in the very front rank of British
anatomists His new book will enhance that reputation and secure for
itself a permanent place on the select bookshelf of all who seek to unravel the
problem of how man has come by his present estate in body and in mind."
—*British Medical Journal*

THE MIGRATIONS OF FISH.

By ALEXANDER MEEK, M.Sc.,

PROFESSOR OF BIOLOGY, ARMSTRONG COLLEGE, IN THE UNIVERSITY OF DURHAM,
AND DIRECTOR OF THE DOVE MARINE LABORATORY, CULLERCOATS

With numerous Illustrations. Demy 8vo.   **16s. net.**

"A scholarly and exhaustive work 'The Migrations of Fish' is a mine
of information, and will be of the greatest use to all who are engaged in
researches into the marine food supply of the nation "—*Times*

" Replete with valuable facts in regard to the natural history of fishes
in the widest sense "—*Morning Post*

"An exceptionally interesting book "—*Field.*

" The best summary of the geographical distribution of the group that has
yet been attempted A book that will be consulted by all workers in economic
marine biology "—*Journal of Zoological Research.*

THE SOUL AND ITS STORY.

By NORMAN PEARSON,

AUTHOR OF "SOME PROBLEMS OF EXISTENCE," ETC

One Volume   Demy 8vo   Cloth   **10s. 6d. net.**

" It is refreshing and comforting to turn from the terrible daily struggle of
life with death, which now obsesses our imaginations, to this calm and lofty
speculation on the nature and prerogatives of the human soul, which will, in
the author's firm conviction, outlast its earthly vestment and live on in higher
and more perfect surroundings "—*Irish Times*

"'The Soul and its Story' is a great subject for a book, and Mr. Norman
Pearson has risen to the greatness of it He has come at the right time Our
old ideas of the psychology of the Bible, and most other psychology as well,
have had to be radically modified or abandoned altogether, and we have been
looking for some authoritative guide to newer and more scientific conceptions "
—*Expository Times*

LONDON· EDWARD ARNOLD, 41 & 43 MADDOX STREET, W.

CPSIA information can be obtained
at www.ICGtesting.com
Printed in the USA
LVOW03*1100101115
461866LV00009B/52/P